Growing Up

Sex in the Sixties

Also by Peter Doggett

Crosby, Stills, Nash & Young:
The Biography

Electric Shock:
From the Gramophone to the iPhone –
125 Years of Pop Music

The Man Who Sold the World:
David Bowie and the 1970s

You Never Give Me Your Money:
The Battle for the Soul of the Beatles

There's a Riot Going on:
Revolutionaries, Rock Stars and the
Rise and Fall of '60s Counter-culture

Growing Up

SEX IN THE SIXTIES

Peter Doggett

THE BODLEY HEAD
LONDON

1 3 5 7 9 10 8 6 4 2

The Bodley Head, an imprint of Vintage,
20 Vauxhall Bridge Road,
London SW1V 2SA

The Bodley Head is part of the Penguin Random House group of companies
whose addresses can be found at global.penguinrandomhouse.com

Penguin
Random House
UK

First published by The Bodley Head in 2021

www.penguin.co.uk/vintage

A CIP catalogue record for this book is available from the British Library

ISBN 9781847924285

Typeset in 11.5/14 pt Dante MT Std
by Integra Software Services Pvt. Ltd, Pondicherry

Printed and bound in Great Britain by Clays Ltd., Elcograf S.p.A.

The authorised representative in the EEA is Penguin Random House Ireland,
Morrison Chambers, 32 Nassau Street, Dublin D02 YH68

Penguin Random House is committed to a sustainable future for
our business, our readers and our planet. This book is made from
Forest Stewardship Council® certified paper.

For Rachel, Catrin and Rebecca

Contents

      Interlude: Oh! Quel cul t'as!   294

12.   Growing Up With Dr Sex   299

      Acknowledgements   323
      Bibliography   325
      Sources for Quotes   339
      Picture Credits   369
      Index   371

Introduction

Newspapers dubbed her a naughty young foal, a colt in pasture, a fabulous little dish, the sauciest mam'selle in all France. Her films were calculated pornography, flagrant, an undressing marathon. 'Sex – and nothing but sex – is rammed down one's throat', complained *The Tatler* as a heavily censored version of her 1956 hit *Et dieu ... créa la femme* was released in Britain. 'What a bore Miss Brigitte Bardot becomes, with her insistence upon being raped.'

Bardot was eighteen when she married her first husband, the film director Roger Vadim, in 1952. He explained her appeal: 'A woman's promise, from the face of a child. An adolescent with a body cast from the same mould as the Venus de Milo.' But Vadim believed that his young wife was more than just a woman: 'she is half-man and half-girl. She has the bottom of a young adolescent. She has something in the way that she talks, and the way in which she is built – apart from the bust – which is very close to man. She is also psychologically very sentimental, the way a woman is sentimental, very vulnerable in the way a woman is vulnerable, yet absolutely masculine in her mental attitude to sex.' It was his contention that the public only chose to be shocked by Bardot's on-screen nudity and unabashed sensuality to protect themselves from an uncomfortable truth. Bardot personified 'without hypocrisy a woman's right to enjoy sex, a right up to that point reserved for men'.

The only way in which society of the late 1950s could tolerate such flagrant desire was to rob its owner of her humanity: to reduce her to the sex kitten, 'so feline with her wide, hazel eyes and sleek, slow movements', wrote the clearly infatuated Donald Zec of the *Daily Mirror*, that 'I didn't know whether to offer her a cigarette or a saucer of milk'. Bardot played along with the charade: 'You know I have a temper just like a cat. Sometimes I purr. Other times I scratch. I also bite.' And sometimes that violence was turned upon herself.

Brigitte Bardot's first twenty-five years had been tempestuous enough. At the age of eleven, she watched her father attempt to commit suicide. By fourteen, she was on the cover of *Elle* magazine, and no longer her own property. She underwent an abortion when she was seventeen and another, which nearly proved fatal, before her twentieth birthday. When her parents refused her permission to marry Vadim, she attempted to gas herself; they saved her, and bowed to her wishes. *Et dieu … créa la femme* (known in English as *And Woman … Was Created* or *And God Created Woman*) established her as a worldwide scandal, who shamelessly paraded her naked flesh. She was denounced by the Pope, hounded by photographers, treated as a body rather than a woman. As the film critic André Bazin suggested, Vadim 'had effectively created a heroine who only made sense by taking off her clothes'.

After she and Vadim divorced in December 1957, when Bardot was twenty-three, she tumbled through affairs with famous French actors, acted in multiple features every year, and still found time to plot her own demise. 'I love living far too much to ever want to stop,' she insisted to reporters in February 1958, shortly after ingesting sleeping pills and once again trying to gas herself. The press was informed that she was merely suffering from the after-effects of eating too many mussels. For recuperation, she fled to Saint-Tropez, establishing the sleepy Côte d'Azur resort as a honey pot for the paparazzi.

1959 brought a new affair, a second marriage, an attempt to induce an abortion by punching herself repeatedly in the stomach, another failed effort to end her life, a physical assault from her new husband (who compensated with his own effort to commit suicide) and a diagnosis that she was suffering a nervous breakdown. Her son Nicolas was born on 11 January 1960; the birth was traumatic enough to trigger a haemorrhage on a subsequent airline flight. Alarmed by her mental state, her husband distanced her from her child. In May 1960, Bardot began work on her darkest film drama to date, *La Verité*, in which her character employed gas to take her own life. While still ostensibly living with her second husband, she began an affair with her young co-star – an entanglement so tempestuous that it led to the pair trading punches in front of reporters. That summer, her trusted secretary Alain Carré betrayed her, selling his account of her self-harm, depression and chaotic romances to the scandal sheet, *France-Dimanche*. His thirty pieces of silver amounted to fifty million francs (approximately £35,000 at that time).

'My life is becoming impossible,' Bardot revealed in 1960. 'My soul is not my own anymore. Stardom to me is a monster.' On her twenty-sixth birthday, 28 September, she retreated to a friend's villa. First she downed a bottle of champagne, then a bottle of sleeping pills, after which she stumbled unseen into a field behind the house and sliced into both wrists with a knife. She was found by the thirteen-year-old grandson of the chambermaid and rushed to hospital in a coma. Her stomach was pumped, her wounds repaired (she had begun to lose consciousness as she cut herself and failed to complete the job) and she was strapped to her hospital bed in case she came round when she was alone and tried again to kill herself. After two days, she regained consciousness, calling for her mother like a scared child, and then cursing the doctors for saving her. 'I don't care what you do to me,' she is said to have told them. 'I don't care about anything.' In a stunningly inappropriate turn of phrase, the director of the clinic explained: 'She is on the razor's edge.'

Members of the public sent letters to her hospital ward, instructing her how to kill herself more efficiently in future. Her second husband refused to visit her. The director of *La Verité* informed the press that 'She is in danger of being killed physically by her own legend.' The official Vatican City newspaper placed the blame securely on the French film industry, which insisted on reifying its human fodder. But other journalists were less sympathetic.

In the *Sunday Pictorial*, British columnist Felicity Green wrote as if she bore Bardot an enduring animus. There was no hint of sympathy for a woman who had been objectified by the media since she was fourteen years old. Instead, Green described her dismissively as 'the Sex Kitten' and ridiculed the triviality of her problems: 'They arise out of the fact that this girl, with more than her share of money, good looks and golden opportunities, seems to be determined to live her life as though it were all taking place in a film. A corny film. A bad film.'

Bardot, in Green's account, was fully the author of her own mis-fortunes: 'Perhaps for the first time she will recognise the possibility that she is a victim of that lethal combination – too much temperament allied to too little talent. What will she decide to do about this? Will she pull in her protruding bottom lip, grow up and be a Real Actress? With clothes on? Or will she prefer to stay a Sex Kitten with all the tiresome trimmings? In this case, I recommend her for a part in the Folies Bergère, where she could strip away to her heart's content.'

Here was one authentic spirit of the decade ahead, the 1960s: the young woman, exploited mercilessly for her sexuality, and mocked when she broke under voyeuristic gaze. Like so many of those who followed her path through stardom and disillusionment, she had been immortalised and frozen in the guise of a child with the erotic magnetism of a grown woman; and paid the price. Brigitte Bardot's name survived the subsequent decade as a totem of feminine allure. In 1968, she could still quicken the heart of John Lennon, who had fantasised about her since his teens, and who was so nervous about meeting her that he sabotaged the encounter by dosing himself with LSD before he arrived at her hotel. That year, her semi-naked image was marketed to teenage pop fans alongside posters of Jimi Hendrix, Jim Morrison, Mick Jagger and an anonymous nude girl on the back of a motorbike. Even when she jettisoned her career on the eve of her fortieth birthday, opting for a life of privacy and animal welfare, Bardot was stalked and wounded like a big cat's prey.

Yet there was another Bardot beyond the infernally sexy victim: the woman who discovered Simone de Beauvoir's proto-feminist text, *Le Deuxième Sexe*, during a 1964 holiday. For the first time she could diagnose what had ailed her since her initial recognition at fourteen. She translated what she had learned into an otherwise typical showbiz encounter with the press. 'I am independent, different,' she insisted. 'I live – and love – by no rules but my own. Why should I marry? I have tried twice and they were disasters. Now I have the pleasure but not the chains of marriage. Maybe people hate me for this. But I am not a hypocrite. I must have love in order to live fully as a woman. I do not need a scrap of paper to tell me what to do. I love freely, I give freely, and I leave freely when love has gone. For me, I must be able to get up and walk away when love is over. After all, I only do openly what many women crave secretly.'

And here was an alternative version of the 1960s: sexual freedom, self-determination, pleasure without guilt, love as an equal exchange, truth and honesty rather than conformity and tradition. Here was the hippie philosophy in miniature: the ethic of the so-called permissive society, from the lips of the woman who, perhaps more than any other, had suffered from the old morality, with its lip-licking lasciviousness and hidebound hypocrisy.

In just five years, Brigitte Bardot had experienced and expressed the full gamut of 1960s sexuality. The decade has passed into history as a halcyon era of permissiveness and indulgence, in which sex was free and its consequences minimised by changing social mores (and, of course, the invention of the pill). There is a splinter of truth in this cliché; but its vision of orgiastic hedonism, ever-changing partners and polymorphous perversity encompassed only a tiny minority of those who existed at the heart of the decade's social blur. The remaining 99.99 per cent of the British population inhabited a world in which they could read about such guilt-free transactions; but they conducted themselves by a moral code that stretched back from the 1950s to the Victorian age and beyond.

Another misconception has dogged this most controversial of decades. It was the former Conservative cabinet minister, Lord Tebbitt, who bemoaned the 'third-rate minds of that third-rate decade, the nineteen-sixties' during one of his regular assaults on the BBC. Politicians and essayists still often pigeonhole the 1960s as the source of Britain's subsequent ethical, economic, psychological, strategic and of course sexual decline. There has long been an unspoken understanding that it was the free thinkers and liberated lovers of that decade who sapped the nation's moral purpose and spiritual identity. The culprits were the hippies, the students, the rock musicians – anyone who experimented with illegal drugs, grew their hair dirty and long, and swapped sexually transmitted diseases without a qualm.

Perhaps Tebbitt and his chums were looking in the wrong place for their villains and missing the real sins. There were undoubtedly crimes and misdemeanours associated with sexual indulgence during this decade. But most of them were not carried out by contemporary youth. No, the real reprobates were the people who perpetuated the stereotypes with which women could be sexually demeaned and abused, and who set in place the mechanisms whereby children and teenagers fell prey to much older and more calculating men.

For the truth about the 1960s was that there were three sexual revolutions taking place at the same time. The first was the one captured in the kind of montage employed as shorthand by documentary-makers – filled with hippies slathered in body paint or Woodstock mud, young women in miniskirts, actors naked on the stage of *Hair*, and rock stars such as Morrison or Hendrix miming the sexual act for rabid fans. The second is the familiar move towards liberalisation that enabled some male homosexuals to make love legally for the first time, some women to obtain abortions without risking a backstreet clinic, many more to avoid pregnancy entirely, and the entire adult population to relish naked bodies on the screen or stage, without having to step inside a seedy Soho strip joint. And the third? This was the hidden revolution that took advantage of the first two and exploited them for profit or pleasure. It objectified the bodies of women and children, established under-age girls (especially) as legitimate subjects of adult desire, and turned the idealism of the other revolutions into tawdry, callous parodies of sexual enlightenment.

At its most utopian, the sexual liberation imagined by the counter-culture could create a paradisiac playground of experimentation and fulfilment, which existed alongside the era's excursions into the outer limits of the body, the mind and the soul. But the people who fashioned this vision of beneficent excess grew up amidst the repression and exploitation of the old world, and inevitably elements of that decaying culture continued to taint the new. One of the saddest discoveries of the 1960s and 1970s was that the counterculture – the heavenly alternative to the conformist world of the establishment – could create as much discrimination and abuse as the society it was meant to replace. The dream which it was very heaven to inhabit could also become a veritable hell.

As a child of the 1960s, old enough to remember it but experience none of its freedoms, I wanted to learn more about the culture from which I came – the preconceptions, restraints and fantasies that formed my own experience of sex and the world. That culture was centred on my homeland of Britain but shaped to varying degrees by influences and imports from the United States and Europe. In particular, I wanted to discover how sex was represented in that culture – and how, in just ten years, the British media could travel from a position of almost total silence about sexual matters to printing pictures of topless young women in daily newspapers, or representing every imaginable form of sexual encounter in the cinema or theatre.

The union of 'sex' and 'the 1960s' instinctively brings to mind a series of events and people so familiar that they have become clichés: the *Lady Chatterley* trial of 1960, the Profumo affair of 1963, the pill, the legislation licensing abortion and homosexuality in 1967, the unclothed revellers at the Isle of Wight festivals. In this book, I have deliberately chosen not to revisit this well-trodden ground. Neither have I attempted to compile a definitive encyclopaedia of vintage sexuality. Instead, I have identified a dozen representative stories ranging across the entire decade and used them to explore the legacy of the 1960s from unfamiliar angles and perspectives. Together, they highlight the forces that formed the sexual culture of the era and explain how they were employed – and to whose benefit.

Some of these thematic chapters are linked on purpose; elsewhere, coincidences and accidents intervene to translate the bit players of one story into the stars of another. But there is a deeper unity to these narratives, which reveals a constant battle between two forces: the urge to free the body from guilt and restraint; and the desire to control, cannibalise or exploit that liberation for ulterior motives. Nothing illustrates that conflict more vividly than the repercussions of Vladimir Nabokov's novel *Lolita*, which is where this book begins. *Lolita* was arguably the most influential cultural artefact of the 1960s, although it was written by a man born at the end of the nineteenth century and first published as early as 1955. Reflections of its transgressive landscape were refracted across the years that followed.

What emerges here, I hope, is not anything as reductive or shallow as an indictment of a decade. This book is intended as a portrait of a bygone age and the echoes of its influence. As it demonstrates, there are aspects of 1960s life – and sexuality – that seem so familiar we recognise them instantly; and others, frequently disturbing, that make this journey into the recent past seem as jolting as a time traveller's arrival in the Middle Ages. Here is history in fast-forward mode: a tumultuous ride across a decade in which change was experienced so quickly that it outstripped anyone's ability to keep it in focus and understand what it meant. Now we can look back with hindsight – sometimes with laughter, too, sometimes with anger – and discover the authentic nature of the decade in which Britain was eternally Growing Up.

A note of caution: any book that is soaked in the culture of a bygone age must necessarily reflect its prejudices and shortcomings. The 1960s was a decade, for example, when sexuality was considered by the British media to be relevant only to white people. It was a time when transgender issues were treated as a sick joke or a horror story; when lesbians were invisible and ignored; when homosexuality required a 'cure' rather than a culture; when women were seen as vessels for male desire, or shameless hussies; and when teenagers were fair game for abuse and exploitation. By the standards of today, these attitudes are clearly unacceptable, while the behaviour and language that accompanied them are equally offensive. The fact that they were not only tolerated but passed as normal in the 1960s should perhaps make us pause and wonder what aspects of our contemporary lives will seem equally outlandish in another sixty years' time.

1 Mad About the Girl

His advertisement appeared in the refined pages of *The Lady*; then, to widen the net, in a Birmingham newspaper. At first glance, it offered charity: 'Titled family shortly motoring to Scotland and seaside would like to take little girl as guest, aged about ten to twelve, as companion for young son for about [a] fortnight. Preference given [to] child who would not otherwise get holiday.'

The benefactor, in this summer of 1961, was Sir Alastair Miller, the 6th Baronet of his line: veteran of the Irish Guards and the Royal Flying Corps in the first great war of the century, then a pioneering racer of motorcycles and cars. He arrived at the house of a Stoke-on-Trent family in a Rolls-Royce – sufficient, when combined with his title, to allay any fears about his motives. The parents allowed the sixty-eight-year-old aristocrat to take away their eleven-year-old daughter, on the understanding that she would be chaperoned at all times, and would also be in the company of his son and grandchildren. Miller laid out an itinerary, which would involve stops in Cheltenham and Cardiff, before the entire party motored to their holiday destination in Scotland.

Instead, Miller arrived without warning at the Cheltenham home of an osteopath friend, and promptly announced himself too unwell to proceed further. The friend felt obliged to provide accommodation for the Baronet and his young companion: 'the daughter of a commoner', as the London papers would deferentially note. The girl was provided with a room of her own, but was visited every night by Miller, clad in his pyjamas. He showed her a series of photographs, each portraying a girl of similar age, naked or nearly so. Miller assured her that it was quite normal for adult men to take pictures of pretty girls like herself, and she reluctantly agreed to pose for his camera.

But her ordeal did not end there: as she was forced to testify in court on her twelfth birthday, Miller subjected her to a series of indecent assaults. Scared, confused and overawed by his age and nobility, and frightened of the consequences if she spoke out, the girl said nothing to Miller's friend, or the housekeeper, whose suspicions had been pricked by Miller's frequent visits to the girl's quarters.

After a week, the girl was returned to her parents, to whom Miller entrusted gifts. He promised that their daughter would become the prime beneficiary of his will and offered the pledge of a second motor trip. Mother and father were overjoyed, until their daughter broke her silence a week or two later. Police raided Miller's home in Worthing, and a search revealed the photographs he had taken in Cheltenham.

The Baronet was charged with several counts of indecent assault against the 'pretty, fair-haired girl', and another of taking her away from her parents by fraud. Beyond the ordeal of testifying in court, and the assaults she had endured, the girl faced the cruel indignity of being named in several press accounts of the case. Perhaps swayed themselves by the social gulf between the accused and his pre-pubescent victim, the members of the jury chose not to believe the girl's testimony that she had been assaulted – despite the clear photographic evidence to support the rest of her story. Miller did not face any charges for taking or keeping the nude photos. But the jury was convinced that, by removing the girl from home on grounds that proved to be entirely fictitious, Miller had committed the crime of 'taking away by fraud'. He was sentenced to twelve months' imprisonment.

Only then was it revealed, to the jury and the public, that Miller was a prolific offender. During the summer of 1958, police stations across England, Wales and Scotland had been investigating the Baronet. He had been arrested and imprisoned on several occasions during the previous twenty years, having committed a variety of financial offences: fraud, obtaining goods on credit without funds, obtaining money by deception, selling motor vehicles to which he had no legal title … the list betrayed a habitual criminal. On several occasions, he had been picked up by police in the company of children with whom he shared no family connection. But it was only in 1958 that regional forces began to combine their evidence, and it became apparent that Sir Alastair Miller was systematically scouring the country for naïve parents and vulnerable young girls.

That summer, it was the *Catholic Herald* that carried his advertisement, but the premise was the same as in 1961: a man of title and probity, a young son seeking company, a secure chaperone, and the allure of a seaside holiday beyond the means of the parents lured by his bait. Miller did not satisfy himself with a single prey: instead, he secured the approval of no fewer than five families, all of whom were prepared to hand over their daughters to a man about whom they knew nothing more than his title. One girl, aged nine, told her parents that she had been assaulted; others stayed silent, perhaps to this day. But Miller's success in procuring child victims lulled him into carelessness. He targeted the thirteen-year-old daughter of old friends and carried her off to a hotel in Essex. The girl was willing at first to travel with the man she knew as 'Uncle George', until – following his unerring pattern – he entered her room at night and assaulted her. Secretly she obtained writing materials and a postage stamp, and sent a desperate letter to her parents. Please bring me home, she pleaded, 'because Uncle interfered with me. I am scared stiff, because I don't know what to do.'

Miller was convicted of indecent assault and jailed for three years; then found guilty again within weeks on charges of motor fraud and given a concurrent three-year sentence. 'He is a sick man, a man to be pitied', his barrister had told the court, and the first half of that statement was supported by Miller's history: a succession of failed marriages, the most recent having ended in 1957; his first bride groomed from the age of twelve and married at sixteen; his second forced to lie to obscure the fact that she was too young to wed without consent. But the law was unable, or unwilling, to confront his perennial predilection for young girls. By early 1961, he was once again a free man, and ready to resume the subterfuge and deceit that would deliver fresh victims. 'Young children have got to be protected', insisted the judge at his 1958 trial, but only Miller's death in 1964 halted his lifelong pursuit.

Another of the era's paedophiles – fictional, this time – drugged a twelve-year-old girl and waited outside her room for the narcotic to take effect. He imagined how he would find her: 'Naked, except for one sock and her charm bracelet … her honey-brown body … presented to me its pale breastbuds; in the rosy lamplight, a little pubic floss glistened on its plump hillock.' But the pill he had fed her was less potent than he had hoped, and the girl stirred fitfully as he watched her in his bed. Then, a miracle, as victim was transformed into reveller: 'By six she was wide awake, and by six fifteen we were technically lovers. I am going to tell you something very strange: it was she who seduced me.'

Countless abusers of children have clutched at similar logic; few have explained their motives and their history, their fantasies and their dull fulfilment, the incursion of reality into a myth of illicit conquest, with such candour and clarity. But then few of those abusers have been able to call upon the services of a novelist with a peerless vocabulary and a cunning (one might almost say uncanny) insight into the psychological landscape of abuse.

As police prepared their case against Sir Alastair Miller in August 1958, the might of the *New York Times* was focused upon Vladimir Nabokov, the author of *Lolita*. 'There are two equally serious reasons why it isn't worth any adult reader's attention,' wrote Orville Prescott of this scandalous novel. 'The first is that it is dull, dull, dull in a pretentious, florid and archly fatuous fashion. The second is that it is repulsive.' *Lolita* was ripe to be denounced: it masqueraded as the 'Confession of a White Widowed Male', awaiting possible execution for murder. But its narrative revealed a more carnal focus for the convict's criminality: several months of sexual engagement with his twelve-year-old stepdaughter.

The victim, though the 'Confession' rarely presents her as such, is Dolores Haze. 'She was Lo, plain Lo, in the morning, standing four feet ten in one sock', the convict reveals as his manuscript opens. 'But in my arms she was always Lolita.' He is the pseudonymous Humbert S. Humbert, and his exotically verbose, hypnotically self-serving memoir – a fictional memoir, don't forget – became a literary *cause célèbre* in the second half of the 1950s. It endures today as one of the most exquisitely written, morally contentious creations of its century: a literary classic, a shameless defence of immorality, a masterclass in linguistic manipulation; ultimately, simply, *Lolita*.

In an early review, Lionel Trilling, one of America's most revered literary critics, who dedicated his life to exploring what he dubbed 'the Liberal Imagination', captured the ethical dilemma posed by *Lolita*. 'In a tone which is calculatedly not serious,' he explained, '[it] makes a prolonged assault on one of our unquestioned and unquestionable sexual prohibitions, the sexual inviolability of girls of a certain age (and compounds the impiousness with what amounts to incest). [...] All very well for us to have long ago got over our first horror at what Freud told us about the sexuality of children ... All very well for the family and society to take approving note of the little girl's developing sexual charms ... But let an adult male seriously think about the girl as a sexual object and all our sensibility is revolted. This response is not reasoned but visceral. Within the range of possible heterosexual contact, this is one of the few prohibitions which still seem to us to be confirmed by nature itself.'

Yet, as Trilling admitted, the uneasy truth about Vladimir Nabokov's text was compounded 'when we realise that, in the course of reading the novel, we have come virtually to condone the violation it presents.' The critic refused to believe that Nabokov was striking a defiant blow on behalf of the paedophile, with the aim of making that 'a rational and respectable form of heterosexuality'. Instead, Nabokov was perhaps conducting a satirical dissection of 'the peculiar sexual hypocrisy of American life': its prurient obsession with erotic appeal, with the commercial potency of youthful flesh. 'To what end,' Trilling asked ironically, 'is a girl-child taught from her earliest years to consider the brightness and fragrance of her hair, and the shape of her body, and her look of readiness for adventure? Why, what other end than that she shall someday be a really capable air-line hostess?' The effect of Nabokov's seduction of even this most stringent of literary judges was unmistakeable, as Trilling declared: 'in recent fiction no lover has thought of his beloved with so much tenderness, no woman has been so charmingly evoked, in such grace and delicacy, as Lolita'.

Trilling's encomium parroted the theme of the fictional doctor invented by Nabokov to 'present' Humbert's narrative. 'How magically his singing violin can conjure up a *tendresse*, a compassion for Lolita that makes us entranced with the book while abhorring its author!', John Ray's foreword proclaimed. But the young girl who is the presumed epitome of 'grace and delicacy' is utterly devoid of both characteristics; is portrayed, instead, as an icon of banality, ruined less by Humbert's lust than by the vapid materialism of American society. Likewise, Humbert Humbert's idyllic fulfilment of a lifetime's erotic promise – his dream girl, conjured into diffident, gum-chewing life – is both mechanical and, to judge from Lolita's almost universal response, meaningless, even ineffectual. (The exception is their first congress, after which she jokes that she has been raped, and then complains that 'I had torn something inside her'.)

One of the strands of irony that webs the novel, and prepares to enfold the reader, is the gap between the reality of sex with your stepdaughter, and Humbert's inspired vision of the Great Unobtainable: the being he names 'the nymphet'. His definition has effectively passed into our collective dictionary: 'Between the age limits of nine and fourteen there occur maidens who, to certain bewitched travellers, twice or many times older than they, reveal their true nature which is not human, but nymphic (that is, demoniac)'. They can be identified by physical traits, he claims: 'the slightly feline outline of a cheekbone, the slenderness of a downy limb, and other indices which despair and shame and tears of tenderness forbid me to tabulate'. But the infallible measure of a nymphet, in Humbert's telling, is the agonised purity of his response: a lust that transcends eroticism to scale the heights of total possession. In other words, capturing a nymphet is more pleasing to the imagination than to the body. Or so Humbert, and Nabokov beyond him, would have us believe.

To explain Humbert's obsession, Nabokov gifts him one of his own formative experiences: an idyllic seaside encounter with his ideal female counterpart, Colette. As Nabokov related his rhapsody, in his book *Speak, Memory*, he and his angel were too young and (of course) angelic to recognise each other with the tools of physical craving. Humbert, by contrast, is a year or three older when he, at thirteen, meets the twelve-year-old Annabel. The most overtly pornographic passages of *Lolita*, mild by comparison with items sold under the counter, are devoted to their thwarted trysts. But these, though technically illegal, do not constitute any form of abuse; they are encounters between equals, in age and desire. The yearnings of Humbert Humbert – and Sir Alastair Miller – betray an almost solipsistic selfishness; a total lack of care (despite Trilling and John Ray's claims of Humbert's tenderness); finally a gesture of possession that reduces its subject to sub-human status. The frustrated intercourse of Humbert and Annabel does not explain, let alone justify, his obsession with Lolita. That adult misdeed is not a Proustian recreation of a golden past, but an act of violence against the female sex.

The most uncritical and assiduous explorer of the universe created by Humbert, and Nabokov behind him, was Alfred Appel Jr, whose scholarly edition of *The Annotated Lolita* uncovers every linguistic pun and literary allusion within the book's dense, sumptuous prose. But Appel is desperate to distance Nabokov, the illusionist who imagined Humbert, from Humbert's own obsessions. It is indeed the laziest form of criticism to seek a direct equivalent for fictional creations in the lives of their authors. Appel is prepared to acknowledge autobiographical themes within *Lolita* and explains that any one of them 'submitted to the imagination thus takes on a new life: frozen in art, halted in space, now timeless, it can be lived with'. At the same time, he is anxious to explain that '*Lolita* is the last book one would offer as "autobiographical"' – which is certainly true to the extent that Humbert Humbert's life bears almost no resemblance to that of Vladimir Nabokov. He doesn't stop there: should anyone be tempted to claim a finder's fee for recognising the parallel between Vladimir and Colette, and Humbert and Annabel, 'then the trap has been sprung'. Nabokov, he insists, has deliberately exposed that parallel to demonstrate that it has no relevance or potency. If the link is obvious, it must be an illusion, because Nabokov enjoys the game of teasing his readers too much to be anything other than opaque.

There are, however, different levels of transparency; and a theme that persists throughout an authorial career is at least an issue of constant concern to the writer, if not necessarily an obsession (let alone one that cannot be controlled). Nabokov himself granted, after the publication of *Lolita*, that journalists and biographers, those excavators of the blood and soul, would feel compelled to search out a biographical equivalent for Humbert's sexual use of his stepdaughter. No such scandals have been unearthed. At worst, one of Nabokov's nineteen-year-old students at Wellesley College admitted that their lecturer was well known for his flirtatious treatment of the young women under his tutelage. 'He did like young girls', she explained. 'Just not *little* girls.' Such tastes hardly marked Nabokov out from a sizeable proportion of male English Literature professors (many of us can cite examples).

Fewer of those who objectify women in their late teens can be shown to have written, while in their mid-twenties, a poem such as the one Nabokov himself translated from Russian under the title

'Lilith'. Its narrator is journeying through the afterlife when he encounters 'a naked little girl', whose nipples bloom 'tenderly'. The child now merges into a slightly older female from his youth, 'the miller's youngest daughter ... with a wet fleece between her legs'. One or other or both now open their 'pretty knees' for the narrator: 'And with a wild lunge of my loins I penetrated into an unforgotten child'. As he is about to climax, she pulls back and 'Writhing with agony I spilled my seed, and knew abruptly that I was in Hell'. Of course, the author insisted that 'Intelligent readers will abstain from examining this impersonal fantasy for any links with my later fiction', thereby demanding exactly such inspection.

Nabokov's literary quest for the nymphet still had far to run. In a short essay entitled 'On a Book Entitled *Lolita*', which most editions of the novel now incorporate as an essential part of the text, the author recalled that 'the first throb of *Lolita* went through me late in 1939 or early in 1940', by which time he was himself forty or forty-one. It was provoked, he insisted, by a newspaper story about an ape in a zoo, who was encouraged by his keepers to draw – and simply sketched the bars of his cage. Immediately he was seeking to distance himself from Humbert as a sexual predator and to reject the nymphet as anything other than a literary obsession.

His published work, and even more the tales he abandoned and suppressed, spoke otherwise. In *The Gift*, a novel published in 1938, a character imagines a scenario that is in essence that of Lolita: 'the temptation, the eternal torment, the itch', on account of 'a daughter, still quite a little girl – you know what I mean – when nothing is formed yet but already she has a way of walking that drives you out of your mind'. In the contemporaneous novel *Invitation to a Beheading*, a condemned prisoner finds solace in the visits of a twelve-year-old (she is always twelve) girl to his cell. But these texts merely hinted at a theme. Nabokov said that his first exposition of the *Lolita* scenario consisted of a 'short story some thirty pages long', which he had subsequently destroyed. This was probably the novella known to Nabokov's friends as *The Magician* and published by his son, after the father's death, as *The Enchanter*. (Evidently it had not been destroyed at all, as Nabokov probably knew very well.) It depicted an adult man, and a girl (twelve, inevitably), whose physical attractions are delineated in almost repulsive detail, from 'the sleek little foxlike hairs running along the forearms' to the 'small cleft' of her buttocks. A familiar word surfaces as Nabokov describes the child's breasts: 'the indistinct tenderness of her still narrow but already not quite flat chest'. Like Humbert, the protagonist exhausts his prey and then strikes, stroking her 'just slightly parted' legs and unveiling 'those strange, sightless little breasts, swollen with what seemed two tender abscesses' (tender, always so tender, just like his desire, of course).

This encounter ends in bathos and disgrace, as the girl wakes and flees 'wild-eyed' from his 'rearing nudity'. Just in time, as the man has been identified as a rapist from the outset: 'What if the way to true bliss is indeed through a still delicate membrane, before it has had time to harden, become overgrown, lose the fragrance and the shimmer through which one penetrates to the throbbing star of that bliss?' If there is a parallel here with the zoo ape, it is that Nabokov's characters were imprisoned by their own inadequate lust, and – like the creature with its pencil – are compelled to recount their obsessions like Coleridge's mariner. For before *The Enchanter* there was a previous incarnation of the criminal obsession, in a story entitled 'The Satyr'. Its major development of Nabokov's compulsive theme was that the erotic quarry was ten years old and not twelve.

It would be too easy, and quite possibly unjust, to delineate these exercises in writerly infatuation, and translate them wholesale into the private life of Vladimir Nabokov. His persistent return to the grasping and deflowering of a pre-teenage girl might represent a pornographic rendering of a lifelong erotic agony; or a purely literary problem, to place alongside Proust's shadowing of the past or Joyce's quest to transfer the visceral experience of human life onto the page. Readers must make their own judgement; and decide also whether the artistic achievement justifies the endless seasoning of an incendiary pot.

The unsullied accomplishment of Nabokov's writing life was his ability – almost unparalleled in literary history – to transfer in mid-career from his native Russian to his adopted English (with an American flavour). In 1947 he told his fellow author, the distinguished critic Edmund Wilson, that he was at work upon 'a short novel about a man who liked little girls'. To aid his composition, Wilson mailed his friend a volume from the collected works of the English sexologist Havelock Ellis (published, to evade the London censors, solely in

French). It was, so Wilson declared, a 'Russian sex masterpiece': the transcription of a memoir by a Ukrainian paedophile who, having been 'seduced' by two child prostitutes in Italy, embarked on a lifelong hunt for equal bliss, which he discovered in the act of exposing himself to teenage girls. Nabokov was delighted with the book and wrote wistfully to his friend: 'As a boy, [the Ukrainian] seems to have been quite extraordinarily lucky in coming across girls with unusually rapid and rich reactions'.

To another contact, Nabokov wrote that his novel in progress involved 'a very moral middle-aged gentleman', thereby not immediately recognisable as Humbert Humbert. (At this stage, the future Lolita is an aging thirteen.) As his book came to fruition, Nabokov grew to realise – in the words of his unfailingly loyal wife, Vera – 'that Vladimir, as a college teacher, cannot very well publish it under his real name'. It was, Vladimir admitted, 'a timebomb'.

A persistent theme in Nabokov's painstakingly retold account of the birth of *Lolita* was his manuscript's almost mythical rescue from the flames. (Perhaps he clung so defiantly to this tale because he felt it revealed him as a moralist at heart.) The circumstances would vary in the repetition, but the core of the incident was that Nabokov determined to burn his manuscript, or the index cards on which he assembled the book, or his research materials, or (in some tellings) the original draft of *The Enchanter*; but was dissuaded from doing so, for the purest and most philanthropic of reasons, by Vera, who valued literary genius high above the threat of scandal or shame. He took pleasure in recalling this decisive moment in his literary career, for it enabled him to herald *Lolita* as a prodigal son (or daughter) of Biblical stock, renewed and reborn for a higher purpose. 'I shudder retrospectively', he told *Playboy* as he remembered the near immolation of his lucrative classic.

Invariably Nabokov was alone with an interviewer when he revived this anecdote. But in 1966, in conversation with the British novelist Penelope Gilliatt for a *Vogue* magazine interview, his recollection came under challenge. 'I was on my way to the incinerator with half the manuscript to burn,' he told Gilliatt, 'and Vera said, "Wait a minute". And I came back meekly', servant to the higher demands of matrimony and art. While Gilliatt listened, however, Nabokov was interrupted by his wife. 'I don't remember that,' Vera said. 'Did I?' It was an innocent intervention, no doubt, which could be dismissed as a lapse of spousal memory on her part. Or, perhaps, Vera did not recall the parable of the nearly burning book because it was one more Nabokovian invention – a reinforcement, for himself as much as his audience, of *Lolita's* unquenchable crusade.

Equally irrepressible was Nabokov's desire to comprehend, and document for posterity, a moment in American history – or, as he might have seen it, its lack of culture. To that end, he became a fastidious chronicler of America's swiftest and least nutritious products: fast food, generic TV fodder, trite advertising slogans, the boosterism and hyperbole that infused every aspect of the nation's landscape. And, of course, he set out quite overtly to become an expert in the American girl, devouring everything from pre-teen comic strips to psychological studies. He gave himself legitimacy to spy on teenage and pre-teenage girls as they played, or chatted, or rode the school bus home, though he admitted there were occasions when his attention to detail was so assiduous that his motives might possibly have been misconstrued by adults in the vicinity.

The text of this book, which would help to shape the cultural landscape of the 1960s, was completed by the early months of 1954. It was submitted to New York's most prestigious publishing houses, and universally rejected: 'They say it will strike readers as pornographic', Nabokov lamented. Publication in Britain was equally impossible, the nation usually lagging culturally behind its transatlantic neighbour by several years. But Nabokov still had a literary agent in Paris, a city with a traditional willingness to publish texts that exceeded the Anglo-American pale, from *Ulysses* and *Lady Chatterley's Lover* to Henry Miller's lubricious *Tropic* novels.

Miller's work was introduced to the world by the Obelisk Press, a small imprint owned by Jack Kahane. After Kahane's death, his son, who went by the name of Maurice Girodias, inherited the torch and tradition of fearless publishing. In 1953 he approached Henry Miller, reminded him of the family connection, and received by return a text (*Plexus*) with which Girodias was able to launch his own firm: the Olympia Press (named for the unashamed courtesan in Manet's painting). Olympia soon assumed its Janus-faced persona, its catalogue divided between controversial works of (at the very least) some literary distinction; and what he and his friends called 'DBs' (or dirty books).

The second would subsidise the first, or so he schemed; but instead both were scarred by Olympia's low-brow reputation.

The two strands of the firm's output were divided, more or less accurately, between the Traveller's Companion series of erotic titles in the plainest of wrappers; and the more respectable volumes published under the Olympia imprint alone. When the Irish novelist J.P. Donleavy sold Girodias the rights to the otherwise unpublishable (in 1955) *The Ginger Man*, he was horrified to discover that his text emerged under the Traveller's Companion brand. There it joined such titles as *Rape* by the pseudonymous Marcus Van Heller; and a clutch of novels consisting of little more than lurid descriptions of whipping, spanking and caning in every possible setting.

The historian of forbidden and/or erotic literature, Patrick J. Kearney, was one of those who recognised the potency of the Olympia Press and Traveller's Companion brands. He regularly visited Brentano's bookstore on Avenue de l'Opéra in Paris, bought as many Olympia titles as he could carry and, he recalled, 'smuggled them back to England and sold them to a bookseller in West London. He, in turn, would rent them out by the week. Sammy, as I shall rename him, specialised in science-fiction magazines and paperbacks, but for every dog-eared copy of *Weird Tales* or *Planet Stories* on top of his counter, there was a "dirty" book underneath. "Got any readers?", his customers would enquire, and if they were known to him or seemed genuine, out would come the cardboard boxes.' Only one thing would frustrate Sammy and his regulars: Girodias's distressing habit of interspersing his unashamed pornography with titles of genuine literary merit.

Nabokov professed to know nothing of Olympia's dubious reputation when he agreed to allow Girodias to publish *Lolita*. The book duly appeared in two volumes in September 1955, whereupon several of the author's acquaintances hurried to inform him of the milieu which *Lolita* now inhabited. 'It depresses me to think,' wrote Nabokov to Edmund Wilson in late 1955, 'that this pure and austere work may be treated by some flippant critics as a pornographic stunt.' If that was the case, it was a fate shared by others of Girodias's titles: the first unexpurgated, English-language editions of the major works of the Marquis de Sade; Pauline Réage's *The Story of O*, which won the Prix des Deux Magots in 1955; and, by 1958, Terry Southern's sexual satire *Candy* – a cartoon refraction of Nabokov's richly textured prose.

The publication of *Lolita* might have passed without note in the English-speaking world had not the novelist Graham Greene laid his eager hands upon a copy. Greene had endured his own trial by public opinion, after an errant review of *Wee Willie Winkie*, a 1937 film starring the eight-year-old Shirley Temple. 'Her admirers, middle-aged men and clergymen,' Greene wrote in *Night and Day* magazine, 'respond to her dubious coquetry, to the sight of her well-shaped and desirable little body, packed with enormous vitality'. This was a personal and, some might say, perverse appraisal of an entirely innocent film, and performance; and faced with a writ of civil libel, Greene fled Britain for Mexico (inspiration for several of his most enduring works). Regardless of his erotic interests, Greene was a stout defender of literary freedom, and in December 1955 he mystified the readers of the London *Sunday Times* by declaring that *Lolita* – a book few if any of them could ever have seen – was one of the year's three best novels.

Like his Temple review, Greene's column had immediate ramifications. Bibliophile tourists from London to Paris endeavoured to apprehend a copy of *Lolita* for themselves; and then, a more arduous challenge, smuggle it past the British customs officials who were accustomed to confiscating French publications of doubtful repute. More notoriously, the *Sunday Express* editor John Gordon went to press in January 1956 with a critical assault that transcended literary assessment to become a moral crusade. He declared that *Lolita* was nothing more than 'sheer unrestrained pornography' and was, furthermore, 'the filthiest book that I have ever read'. No wonder that later that year Nabokov would tell Greene that 'My poor Lolita is having a rough time. The pity is that if I had made her a boy, or a cow, or a bicycle, Philistines might never have flinched.' (Elsewhere Nabokov claimed that one New York editor had said that the book might be salvaged for US publication if he transformed the alluring girl into a little boy – a telling commentary on contemporary morals.) Greene replied encouragingly: 'In England one may go to prison, but there couldn't be a better cause'. Was this cause *Lolita*, or what it represented? Greene left that conundrum unanswered.

Just before Christmas 1956, the French state moved to suppress sales of *Lolita*. The text was not officially banned; but its sale was curtailed, via threats of prosecution or even imprisonment for offending vendors. Yet the book was only available in the English language, so the likelihood that native French speakers would be investigating its subversive wares was slight. The suppression, it was rumoured, had been carried out at the behest of the British government, which had become alarmed by the regularity with which copies of *Lolita* were being intercepted at the border.

Had the text been in French, Maurice Girodias would have found it easier to assemble a galaxy of authors prepared to protest against this attack on free speech. As it was, he was forced to mount his own 'defence of the writer', in an Olympia Press symposium, *L'affaire Lolita*. It included a brief, uncontroversial extract from the novel alongside Nabokov's essay, 'On a Book Entitled *Lolita*'. At the same moment, *Lolita* made a break for freedom in Nabokov's adopted homeland. The American literary journal, *The Anchor Review*, had made an unassuming debut in 1956 with a selection of essays upon contemporary subjects: poetry and philosophy to the forefront. Its editor, Melvin J. Laski, now resolved to end the stalemate whereby a novel by one of the world's leading authors remained unpublished in the US and the UK. The second issue of *The Anchor Review* was dominated by *Lolita*, with a lengthy (but still discreetly abridged) extract from the novel introduced by the critic F.W. Dupee.

With this gesture, *Lolita* entered the national literary conversation, and the same New York publishers who had spurned the manuscript in 1954 now competed for the rights to present it to the American public. The decision of the US Customs not to treat the book as obscene, and to allow travellers to carry the Olympia edition into the country, reassured editors that they could distribute the book without risk of prosecution. By March 1958, Walter Minton of Putnam's had secured the US rights. (He had been tipped off by 'a tall, pretty, ex-Latin Quarter showgirl' named Rosemary Ridgewell, who was doubtless his regular source of literary expertise.) Meanwhile, the ban in France on the Olympia Press edition was lifted. As the *Guardian* pointed out, 'The case has always been anomalous: for although the interdiction was on grounds of obscenity, no French citizen has ever filed a complaint against the book.'

Orville Prescott at the *New York Times* aside, the critical response to *Lolita* in the American press was overwhelmingly positive. One reviewer declared it was 'one of half a dozen original and exciting novels we have dealt with in seven years of reviewing. By comparison, much fiction of the past decade seems dawdling, mediocre stuff.' Another judged accurately that 'The book is far too literary to damage the morals of juvenile delinquents or even of adults who enjoy flashy fiction.' True, Virginia Kirkus suggested that 'Any librarian will surely question this for anything but the closed shelves', and public libraries in Cincinnati were the first to declare a city-wide ban. But the *New Republic* spoke for the academic establishment when it adjudged Lolita 'a major literary event, worth all the attention we can spare'.

For the first time, Vladimir Nabokov found himself on the best-sellers' lists. No other novel since *Gone with the Wind*, the press reported in September 1958, had sold more than 100,000 copies in its first three weeks of publication. Nabokov himself was now a minor celebrity, much in demand by journalists who hoped that he might deliver some suitably scandalous copy. They were bemused to encounter a dry, scholarly, almost sixty-year-old Russian, who preferred to discuss entomology rather than nymphets – though he admitted to 'a pleasant feeling' in knowing that his coinage had now entered the language. He declared that *Lolita* was 'just a story, a fairy tale, as all stories are'; or, perhaps, 'a detached intellectual exercise – no tears to be shed. You're supposed to enjoy it with your spinal emotions', rather than other areas of the body, 'with a little shiver when you end it.' Through every encounter, Nabokov maintained his playful, almost dismissive air – insisting, for example, that he could not be confused with Humbert Humbert, because his fictional creation did not know the difference between a hummingbird and a hawk moth. Meanwhile his wife Vera mounted a more traditional defence, claiming that *Lolita* was a tragedy. But Vladimir cut her off as she began to paint a tear-jerking portrait of a 'poor girl' in the hands of 'a maniac', for that was not how he saw Humbert at all. Lolita was, after all, he insisted, 'a very ordinary girl'.

The media furore had its amusing diversions. In the *Miami News*, a glowing review of *Lolita* was placed alongside a headline that read: 'Gina's Dreams Come True – Pleasant Teen-Girl Reading'. (Gina, it transpired, was the heroine of a novel aimed at pure-hearted school-girls, discussed next to Nabokov's nymphet.) Nabokov himself was delighted to discover a cartoon in *Playboy* magazine, in which a middle-aged man tries to check into a hotel with a young girl. Behind the desk stands the manager, clutching a copy of Nabokov's novel.

'Dammit, what's the matter with you people?', the would-be guest complains. 'She's my *daughter*, I tell you.'

In West Texas, the tiny township of Lolita was said to be filled with embarrassed residents who wanted to avoid any association with Nabokov's scandalous publication. A Baptist deacon named R.T. Walker circulated a petition amongst his neighbours, which declared: 'The people who live in this town are God-fearing, church-going, and we resent the fact our town has been tied in with the title of a dirty, sex-filled book that tells the nasty story of a middle-aged man's love affair with a very young girl.' Picked up by the news agencies, the story of Texan outrage went around the world, until a reporter travelled to the town, and discovered that Walker had been given the petition, and an encouraging ten-dollar bill, by a publicist working for Putnam's. The debunking of the tale attracted less attention than its initial airing, and a decade later, one of Nabokov's explanatory notes for his nymphet-fired novel *Ada, or Ardor*, declared of the town that 'it has been renamed, I believe, after the appearance of the notorious novel'. In fact, Lolita TX survives to this day.

While *Lolita* was banned from publication in Australia, by censors who had never read the book, publishers in Britain began to joust discreetly for the rights to handle this piping-hot pearl. Many sets of lawyers were at work in parallel, seeking to determine whether their masters might be sued or fined if they proceeded to print the book. Eventually Weidenfeld and Nicolson declared its intention to publish, at some distant point in the future, provoking a heated debate in the House of Commons. One Conservative member of parliament, Sir Godfrey Nicholson, protested that *Lolita* was 'thoroughly obscene. It deals with a disgusting, revolting and cruel form of vice and tends to encourage it.' The publisher was fortunate in having one of its partners, Nigel Nicolson MP (another Conservative), in the chamber to defend its decision. He could not deny that Nabokov's book dealt with 'perversion', but argued his case on terms of morality and punishment: 'If this perversion had been described in such a way as to suggest to a middle-aged man or a little girl – could she have understood it – that the practices so described in the book were pleasant ones and could lead to happiness, I would have no hesitation at all in advising my colleagues that we should not publish it. But *Lolita* has a built-in condemnation of what it describes. It leads to utter misery, suicide [though none of its characters suffers this fate], prison, murder and great unhappiness, both for the man and the little girl he seduced.' All of which begged a question: could any form of obscenity or atrocity now be described in words, as long as its exponents suffered a suitably moral fate? The possibility that the mere description of immorality might be sufficient to inspire imitation did not feature in the debate.

The *Guardian* anticipated publication by previewing the book that was still unavailable in British shops. 'Here we have the archetype of any sexual relationship in which no real reciprocity is possible,' the paper declared astutely. 'The result is a bitter comedy in which the nymphet answers [Humbert's] passion by a demand for more iced lollies or fudge sundaes.' Beyond the insight of those who had read the book, however, a more provocative reading of *Lolita* was being entrenched, as her name became a byword for any teenager involved in sexual activity, legal or otherwise. 'There May Be a "Lolita" in Your Street!', exclaimed the *Women's Mirror* magazine, as May Abbott explored the ever earlier maturity of the nation's teenage daughters. 'One solution', according to the head of the Marriage Guidance Council, 'might be to lower the age of consent and encourage earlier marriages.' The Labour MP Jean Mann was appalled by this suggestion: 'Boys and girls today are NOT more mature,' she insisted. 'They just know too much too soon. Sex knowledge, though important at the right time, fills their minds to the exclusion of everything else.' A report on the prevalence of girls below the age of sixteen bearing children assailed the media: 'Sex is put before them all the time, and there is a climate of opinion that casual sex relationships are permissible.' Striking a tone that would never lose its novelty or relevance, a commentator noted: 'We live in a society that is riddled with sex – films, TV and the newspapers are obsessed with it.'

Meanwhile the more sensationalistic Fleet Street newspapers titillated and shocked their readers with tales of (as US columnist Earl Wilson claimed to have seen in London) 'shivering schoolgirls from the country [who] peddle their person and personalities on the street'. Everywhere, it seemed, there were contemporaries of Lolita who were touting their business: 'they decorate our street corners like painted dolls', a disgusted boy of sixteen lamented. A judge in Hampshire castigated a thirteen-year-old girl responsible for 'bringing down' twenty young men. 'These cases show that the standard of

morals among some of the young girls in this county is quite shocking,'
huffed Mr Justice Streatfeild. 'It is a strong indictment of the apparent
lack of parental control over these girls. It is quite dreadful to think
that the girls are making [themselves] up to look older and are responsible for leading older men astray.'

As 1959 played out, it appeared that, *Lolita* or not, Britain was awash
in pre-teen sexual frenzy. It was claimed that eight young schoolgirls,
the smallest of them nine and ten years old, had been engaged in acts
of 'mass indecency' with a number of teenage boys, and a man of
seventy. The judge in Burton-on-Trent declared that there had been
nothing less than 'an orgy' and sent the offending girls to approved
schools. The young men escaped a similar fate, although the pen-
sioner – as the adult in the room – was sentenced to three years in
prison. In the centre of London, so Baroness Wootton alleged, two
girls under the age of fourteen had been soliciting 'acts of gross
indecency' with passing city workers during their lunch hour. They
were sufficiently business-minded to adjust their fee according to the
apparent wealth, or otherwise, of their clients. Their lucrative business
was only quashed when they made the mistake of propositioning an
off-duty police officer. In this climate, it was quite refreshing to discover
a letter in the magazine *Boyfriend* from a fourteen-year-old girl, who
claimed to be in love with her English teacher, and had invited him
home for tea, though the sensible man had politely declined. The girl
was advised sternly: 'In the eyes of your teacher, you're a baby, and
he'd be a bit soft in the head if he saw you in a romantic light.'
Vladimir Nabokov, meanwhile, opened the door to a trick-or-treater
that Halloween, and was greeted by a girl of around eight, made up
with lipstick and powder to resemble an adult. She carried a hand-
written sign that read: 'Lolita'. 'I was shocked,' Nabokov insisted. 'I
am in favour of childhood.'

As Weidenfeld and Nicolson continued to weigh the legal arguments
for and against publication, a thriving black market arose in London –
fuelled, apparently, by visiting American sailors, who were clearly able
to evade British customs officers. Mrs Leila Adams, a British woman
returning by air from Paris to London, was less fortunate. She had
purchased a copy of *Lolita* quite legally on the Left Bank and was
upset to have it confiscated on the grounds of obscenity as she entered
the country in May 1959. 'We have considered this book,' a bureaucrat

announced soberly, 'and it has been ruled obscene. If the lady does not agree with our decision, she is at liberty to appeal against it.' But Mrs Adams did not wish to fund a test case in the British courts, leaving the publisher no wiser about its probable fate.

Obscene it might be, but *Lolita* was commercial dynamite, under her own guise or as a nymphet. The autumn 1959 collections in Paris included fresh creations from the twenty-seven-year-old designer, Michel Goma. One was 'a discreet but grown-up lilac daytime dress with a belt that dropped below the waist at the back, and a skirt gathered in back under a bow to emphasise the hips'. Goma titled it 'Lolita'; and offered a companion piece named 'Nymphet'. As a fashion reporter explained, 'Both were more girlish than the series of sophisticated black dresses that followed.' By that winter, 'nymphet' style had become an *haute couture* cliché. 'Nymphet' was also the name of an American racehorse; while Nabokov's creation had become so entrenched in the US vocabulary by June 1959 that a horoscope in the *Los Angeles Times* offered the following advice to those born under the sign of Gemini: 'This is the day to think about affairs of the heart, and to pursue that nymphet you have been eyeing in the front office.'

Finally, in early October 1959, Weidenfeld and Nicolson convinced themselves that they would not face an injunction or prosecution were they to release *Lolita* to the British public. The book was published on 6 November, and in London's most famous (and eccentric) bookshop, Foyle's, the entire order of 250 copies had disappeared by lunchtime. 'In our 55 years, I don't suppose there has been anything like it,' said a saleswoman. 'I've had every kind of person from two old ladies to students paying out their guineas.' Intrepid reporters accosted those who were buying the book and demanded to know their rationale. Some, naturally enough, were purchasing 'for a friend'; or because they had an amateur interest in psychology; or because they were already admirers of Nabokov's sparkling prose. Only one customer, an anonymous civil servant, admitted to choosing the book on the basis of its notoriety. 'I buy everything in the controversial line,' he confessed. 'I like to be knowledgeable and talk to other knowledgeable people.' Then a flicker of panic crossed his face. 'No names, please,' he begged his inquisitor. 'My department wouldn't like it.' Just as eager were those local dignitaries who foresaw some self-righteous publicity if they led the counterattack. Sedate English towns competed to become the first to ban the book from their libraries. An alderman led the crusade in seaside Eastbourne: 'I may be Victorian in my ideas, but the disgusting thought of the goings-on in bed of a dirty old man with a young girl does not appear to be the sort of thing on which public money should be spent.'

As the novelist Kingsley Amis wrote in the *Spectator*, 'Few books published in this country since the King James Bible can have set up more eager expectations'. But Amis was appalled by the book ('it is thoroughly bad in both senses: bad as a work of art, that is, and morally bad') and by what he saw as Nabokov's indigestibly calorific prose style. *The Sphere* declared the book 'boring rather than shocking'; the *Birmingham Post* praised Nabokov's satirical edge but concluded that Lolita herself was 'probably the nastiest child in fiction'; the *Guardian*, in its second, less adulatory review, lamented that Nabokov's creation 'is through the taste barrier'.

But in Britain as in America, this was a book for which moral outrage and artistic disapproval were irrelevant: whether it was viewed as a scandal or a cause for celebration, it was undoubtedly an event, and events – especially when they were so luridly previewed – always attracted an audience. More than sixty years on, the mere name of *Lolita* is enough to trigger an immediate admonition from Google: 'WARNING', the site states above each page of search results, 'Child Pornography is Illegal'. The assumption is that the readers of a novel entirely devoid of 'dirty' language and much less erotic than its reputation promises must automatically be interested in seeking out images and tales of abuse against other children. It is almost as if Nabokov's creation, far from inciting a brief flurry of disgust, has seeped into the very vitals of our existence; as if *Lolita* began, from the moment of its dissemination, to alter the sexual culture of the Western world. 'Those whom it could influence would be bored by the work,' Nabokov had objected when accused of poisoning social discourse. What he did not imagine was that the fantasy of *Lolita* – her inescapable allure – would overshadow the girl, and the book, he had concocted. One might almost think that civilisation had been waiting for a Nabokov to unleash the genie of an idea that had lain dormant for generations; and that once it had been released, it could never be forgotten or ignored again.

Interlude: Sex by Numbers

Was Lolita, sexually active at twelve, representative of her generation? Certainly not in Britain, where surveys by sociologist Michael Schofield suggested that only 0.1 per cent of schoolgirls under the age of fourteen had experienced intercourse. (The rate for under-fourteen boys was around 0.9 per cent.) If you widened the age limit to seventeen, 11 per cent of boys had had sex, and 6 per cent of girls; by nineteen, it was almost one-third of boys, and one-sixth of girls.

Who were these experienced children of 1965? Among boys, they were mostly students at secondary modern or comprehensive schools; and the same for girls, except that those at private schools were also much more likely to have tasted forbidden fruit than their grammar school counterparts. Not surprisingly, 28 per cent of boys at boarding schools had some homosexual experience; the rate at day schools was just 3 per cent. (Girls were quizzed about their knowledge that such a thing as homosexuality existed but were clearly considered unlikely to have taken part in anything so indecent themselves.)

Another sociologist, Geoffrey Gorer, reckoned in 1971 that, all media hype to the contrary, 'England still seems to be a very chaste society'. He calculated that two-thirds of women but only one-quarter of men were virgins when they married. Only 5 per cent of married women had slept with more than two men, while the rate among men was forty per cent. Approximately one quarter of the English population was repulsed by the very idea of homosexuality: this feeling was especially strong among male virgins in their thirties. Gorer also noted an intriguing corollary between those men who did not believe that women could experience orgasm, and those who were hostile to homosexuals. Rather distressingly, it was women (one in four, roughly) who refused to believe in the existence of the female orgasm, rather than men, who were twice as optimistic (or experienced). But another quarter of women in these orgasm-denying times did manage to climax as they lost their virginity.

Gorer also quizzed his sample about their opinion of promiscuity. Was it OK for men to sleep around? Twenty-nine per cent of men said yes; but only nine per cent of women. And women? Thirteen per cent of men thought promiscuity was reasonable for the opposite sex to indulge in, but only three per cent of women. 'The double standard of sexual morality, by which men are allowed licence which is denied to women, still has fairly wide currency,' Gorer concluded. 'And, it would appear, it is predominantly women who maintain this double standard.'

Michael Schofield's survey uncovered similar figures. Both boys and girls believed, with almost identical percentages, that the cliché was true: boys wanted sex, girls wanted marriage. More girls than boys agreed that 'Pre-marital sex is OK for boys, but not for girls'. When faced with the stark proposal that 'Pre-marital sex is wrong', boys disagreed (by 45 per cent to 35 per cent); while girls split more than two-to-one in the opposite direction (by 62 per cent to 24 per cent).

But in case anyone thought that young men were the sexual progressives of the 1960s, and girls the natural-born conservatives, Schofield asked one further question. He presented both groups with the blanket statement: 'All homosexuals should be severely punished'. Girls disagreed (by 45 per cent to 35 per cent); but boys agreed by an almost identical margin. Boys were the ones who knew about homosexuality, and who were much more likely than girls to participate in homosexual relations; but they also believed that homosexuals deserved to face the full authority of the law (and perhaps the cane, though fortunately Schofield did not ask that question).

Only in one regard did the statistics about young British girls match up to the scenario of *Lolita*. Of those few who did experience sexual intercourse in their teens, two-thirds had connected with an older partner. Humbert Humbert was surely not entirely alone ...

2 The Nymphet Leaves Home

According to the *Daily Mirror* columnist Marjorie Proops, females could enjoy 'seven ages of sex appeal'. Not yet the defender of women's rights that she became as an agony aunt in the 1970s, Proops scattered contradictory opinions across her pages. One moment she was encouraging teenagers to flaunt their sexuality, telling the child actor Hayley Mills: 'You can wear bikinis without bulging, or shifts which make you look provocatively mature. Anything goes when you're sixteen, Hayley. Make the most of it while it lasts.' The next she was scolding the young: 'Pre-marital sex is impracticable and idiotic'.

The apex of her ambiguous relationship towards youthful displays of sexual allure was reached with her delineation of the 'seven ages' in January 1963. Not acknowledging Nabokov's faith in the eternal charisma of the nymphet, she declared: 'Between the ages of nine and fourteen, a girl is at her least sexy. She is forced to work for exams, play unfeminine games like hockey, gets fat and spotty, and loses her early flair for clothes … Suddenly, at fifteen or sixteen, she emerges again as a desirable female. Almost all girls are sexy at sixteen. Even girls who will get plain later on are pretty at sixteen. And men of all ages see them as alluring women. Their bodies have taken shape and they have begun to know how to use them to arouse male interest. They wear long clinging black pants to reveal long smooth legs and big rough sweaters to excite interest in what's underneath. Sixteen is the teasing age. They lead men on and hold them off. Not always, but mostly.'

Though her classification could be challenged on multiple grounds, it did at least suggest a degree of logic. Girls were unattractive until fifteen, when suddenly they blossomed into perfect objects for the sexual delectation of men. But Proops' definition of sex appeal wasn't that straightforward. Without stating her terms, she announced that 'A girl aged eighteen months is a pretty sexy young bird'. And with perhaps a silent nod to Nabokov, she insisted: 'Nine is a very sexy age for a girl to be. Girls of nine flounce around in frilly dresses with lace on their drawers. They even look cute in Brownie uniforms.'

Not that those nine-year-olds needed to be aware of their innate sexuality: heaven forbid they should understand the apparently inescapable effect of their 'frilly dresses' and 'lace' on the male libido. In another column, Proops responded to the suggestion that a mild form of sexual education should be given to eight-year-old children. 'I feel that a child of eight, hardly out of the fairy-tale, nursery rhyme stage, is too young to bother its little head about sex,' she argued. 'I reckon that a little learning CAN be a dangerous thing. Teach kids about sex – and they might be eager to put theory into practice. Too much absorption in sex, too young, could, I reckon, be unhealthy.' Far better, it seemed, to leave these pre-teen girls to reveal their sexual allure without understanding its power or implications.

In a casual way, Proops was illustrating the dichotomy identified by the French theorist Michel Foucault. In the first of his three volumes of *The History of Sexuality*, he highlighted a series of cultural assumptions that, from the eighteenth century onwards, had 'formed specific mechanisms of knowledge and power centring on sex'. Among them was the 'double assertion that practically all children indulge or are prone to indulge in sexual activity; and that, being unwarranted, at the same time "natural" and "contrary to nature", this sexual activity posed physical and moral, individual and collective dangers.'

No single issue emphasised this ambiguity more clearly than the legal age of sexual consent. As the social historian Philip Jenkins noted, 'Perhaps no aspect of childhood is so liable to the impact of changing social and economic patterns as the age of sexual maturity.' He documented the predilection in Victorian England and beyond for the unformed female body: 'Celebrated pornographic works like *My Secret Life* and *The Pearl* often record encounters with girls as young as nine or ten, yet there is little suggestion that these were specifically catering to a distinct child pornography market. Nor were the men portrayed seen as a special category recognisable by a distinctive term such as "paedophile". The younger girl, especially if a virgin, was regarded as a particularly valuable trophy for a roué, whose tastes would also run to girls and women of almost any age.'

For most of the nineteenth century, sexual intercourse with a young girl was only illegal if she was below the age of twelve. It was only in 1885 that it was raised to its current level of sixteen. In the United States, the age of consent varies from state to state: the scandal of the rock'n'roll singer Jerry Lee Lewis was not that he had married his thirteen-year-old cousin, but that he had neglected to divorce his previous wife. (His sister Linda Gail was married three times before her sixteenth birthday.) France allowed sex with eleven-year-old girls until 1863, when the limit was raised to thirteen. Mexico clings to the tradition of legal sex with a twelve-year-old, as did Spain until 1999 and Hungary to this day, if the child's partner is under eighteen; Italy makes it illicit only up to the age of fourteen; while some predominantly Muslim countries on the African continent make the official age of consent as high as twenty. In each case, tradition weighs as much as reason.

The furore aroused by Nabokov's *Lolita* in the late 1950s did not provoke the sexualisation of young girls; it merely legitimised the subject as a source of debate – and commercial exploitation. It also provided a vocabulary: the German film *Nature Girl and the Slaver*, made in 1957, starred teenage actor Marion Michael, allowing its US distributor to promise on a poster in 1959: 'Her Nymphet Beauty, the Flaming Spark that Could Hurl 1,000 Men into a Blazing Desert War'. Michael was just fifteen when she assumed the title role in *Liane – Jungle Goddess*, an earlier film in which she appeared topless for much of the action. She was billed then as 'Germany's answer to Brigitte Bardot'.

Bardot's former husband, Roger Vadim, was on the beach at Saint-Tropez in 1958 when he caught the attention of fourteen-year-old Gillian Hills. 'When he smiled, I decided to send him some photographs,' she said, 'just in case he might like me for one of his pictures.' Born in Egypt, being educated in France, Hills was celebrated as Britain's very own 'sex kitten' when Vadim invited her for a screen test. She turned up in a black leotard, which Vadim proceeded to rip in order to judge her erotic potential. 'She's very nice,' he crowed afterwards, 'very beautiful and has a nice body' – an asset from which he clearly intended to profit. Vadim wished her to play a central role in *Dangerous Liaisons*: 'a girl of fifteen, seduced by three men'. First he had to obtain her mother's permission for her to be seen naked, albeit from the rear. 'Sexy roles are not at all right for Gillian,' Mrs Hills insisted. 'She is only a child.' But the 'budding Brigitte Bardot' (or 'the Bayswater Bardot', as one paper had it) was soon swept up in a maelstrom of publicity, from which it was difficult to escape. Interviewers relished the way this young girl 'smoothed her long blonde hair, pouted her full lips and glanced provocatively out of the corner of her eyes'. Her mother insisted desperately: 'Gilly is all innocence. She doesn't know what such looks mean. She is a child. Don't you dare say anything else.' But meanwhile her daughter was being encouraged to flaunt her sexuality for the cameras – by the English press as much as the vulpine French director.

This inaugural chapter of Gillian Hills' film career ended when her name began to be mentioned alongside the 'Rose Ballet' affair, which involved French politicians and industrialists attending parties at which under-age girls performed striptease. Hills was not connected with the scandal, but Roger Vadim perceived trouble ahead if he pursued his cinematic obsession with Hills' young body. 'I realise now that she is far too young,' he declared with a patina of innocence. 'It would not get past the censor if Cecile was played by a 14-year-old.' Hills burst into tears before reporters and had to settle for a more peripheral role in Vadim's film.

Her father then intervened to break the seven-year contract that Gillian and her mother had signed with the Frenchman. Instead, she returned to Britain, and – still not yet fifteen – won a leading part in a home-grown movie with the working title *Striptease Girl*. 'This could be your teenage daughter', screamed the poster for the film eventually released in 1960 as *Beat Girl* (or, in America, *Wild For Kicks*). Sullen, tousle-haired, invariably pouting, Hills lent herself to the role of art student Jennifer as if she were acting out her own parental battles. The script required her to assume a worldly insouciance about all matters carnal and romantic. 'Love', Jennifer snorts derisively early in the film. 'That's the gimmick that makes sex respectable, isn't it?' Then she begins to take off her clothes in front of her twenty-four-year-old stepmother. 'Embarrassed?', the girl sneers. 'Why? I've got a nice figure.' A later striptease scene at a party gives the French (of course) director, Edmond T. Gréville, the opportunity to exploit Hills' under-age appeal, although her stepmother intervenes to prevent her removing her underwear.

In the convoluted but ridiculous plot, Hills' stepmother Nicole (again French) proves to be a former Paris prostitute, and the girl ends up at a Soho strip joint. After being described as 'a dish' but 'jailbait' by one of the club's staff, Jennifer is preyed upon by the rapacious manager, played by Christopher Lee. He tempts her with a £55-per-week contract: 'There's a thrill in this work. All the girls say so.' In the final scene, Lee's character attempts a forced seduction, baring her shoulder, stroking her hair; before he is conveniently gunned down by another stripper, and Jennifer and her virtue are saved. (European prints of *Beat Girl* featured a professional striptease routine of – for the time – startling frankness, which had to be removed before the film could be exposed to more delicate British or American viewers.)

If Nabokov's *Lolita* was portrayed as being, at the very least, complicit in her fate, Gillian Hills' part in *Beat Girl* established a more cynical role for the under-age female: the pubescent or even pre-pubescent siren who sets out to incite male desire. In February 1959, a posse of London film producers, theatrical entrepreneurs and television executives were invited to attend a one-night-only performance of Roger Garis's play, *The Pony Cart*. The script had already been rejected by many West End theatres for its controversial theme. As the *Daily Herald* explained, 'ten-year-old Janina Faye will play a girl who is enticed to the house of an elderly man who gives her sweets to undress'. The encounter would not be witnessed on stage, but Faye's youth and the sexual connotations of the plot sparked a brief outburst of morality from the London press. Faye's parents were forced to remove her from the cast, though not, it seemed, because they disapproved of the role. (She was replaced by fifteen-year-old Pauline Knight, who read the script and said in a tone of bewilderment: 'I don't think it's really sexy'.)

The showcase presentation clearly worked its magic, as the screen rights were snapped up by Hammer Films, renowned for its garish horror productions. *The Pony Cart* being altogether too oblique, the film adaptation was renamed *Never Take Sweets* [or *Candy*, in North America] *From a Stranger* (1960). Filmed in Britain but set in Canada, the movie involved girls of nine and eleven, who were given candy by veteran actor Felix Aylmer (silent throughout the film) in return for posing and dancing naked in front of him. 'I know somewhere where you can get some candy for nothing', the elder girl tells her friend, although once again the illicit exchange occurs between scenes. The only overtly sexual moment in the film sees the two girls frolicking innocently on a garden swing, while Aylmer watches them through binoculars and shakes with uncontrollable lust. The script veers back and forth between exposing human wickedness and spotlighting the hypocrisy of a small town that refuses to believe one of its own could have committed such a crime. But adult characters keep repeating lines such as 'Do you think he actually made them take their clothes off?', as if to force viewers to confront the reality of the abuse in their imaginations. The younger of the two girls was portrayed by Janina Faye, this time without a hint of scandal clinging to her name.

A slightly later British film, *The Mark* (1961), offered another view of the temptation presented by pre-teenage girls. Its tragic hero is a man who has been convicted of planning to commit sexual abuse, although as evidence of his decency we see him break down in tears after kidnapping the young girl, and turn himself in. In prison, he undergoes a pioneering course of psychotherapy directed by Rod Steiger. Released under an assumed name, Jim Fuller is encouraged by Steiger to confront his fear that he might offend again, by watching schoolgirls at play through a fence. That night he is haunted by the vision of young girls skipping ... but Steiger continues to reinforce his recovery.

Fuller falls in love with a co-worker, who inevitably has a daughter of exactly the same age as his original victim. He is unjustly accused of another assault, then exposed in the press as a sex criminal; but the script unites him with his girlfriend, and her daughter, who conveniently he loves only in the purest fashion. He escapes the 'mark' of the title, and steps into the future apparently free from the slightest pangs of erotic interest in the forbidden.

Jim Fuller seeks redemption, and is rewarded for his virtue and courage. His victims are unwitting and entirely passive. Humbert Humbert, however, seeks only the fulfilment offered by nymphets, and must therefore be punished. Most of the objects of his perverse gaze are unaware that they are engaging his priapic delight. But Lolita? She, the author tells us, is already an experienced sexual being, inducted by a thirteen-year-old male helper at her summer camp. In Nabokov's narrative, she not only allows Humbert to explore his fantasies, but often encourages him. Their interaction, the union of a predatory middle-aged man and a near-pubescent child, is couched in layers of ambiguity, designed both to beguile and puzzle the (male) reader.

As a *cause célèbre*, a *succès d'estime*, a *scandale* worthy of Roger Vadim, *Lolita* was ineluctably drawn towards the big screen. Placed in the hands of a Vadim or another French director of his ilk, Nabokov's disquieting morality tale might have been portrayed as a shameless wallow in teenage sensuality – limbs entwined in soft-focus, the adrenalin rush of lust transcending any ethical qualms. But any film adaptation had to meet the approval of the solicitous author, anxious to guard *Lolita* as if she were one of his own.

Less than a month passed between the publication of the Putnam's edition of *Lolita*, and the sale of the film rights. The enterprising entrepreneurs were director Stanley Kubrick and producer James B. Harris: each American, thirty years old, and anxious to shake up the conventions of Hollywood. They offered Nabokov an advance of $150,000, plus the prospect of 15 per cent of the producer's profits. The film capital's gossip hounds gathered to lambast the project. Nabokov told a friend that 'Hedda Hopper is waging a spirited anti-*Lolita* campaign – on moral grounds, I understand.' Hopper's rival, Louella O. Parsons, publicly begged Harris (who was 'brilliant', she said) not to become involved in a project which 'is unfit for the motion picture screen. I do not often use such strong language, but this book is the most decadent piece of literature (did I say literature?) I have ever read.' But it was Parsons who inadvertently offered a solution to the most pressing obstacle facing Harris and Kubrick: how to shoot a film in which the erotic *femme fatale* was only twelve years old. 'I suppose they could make her older', she wrote. A month later, Harris was telling the press that he had hit upon 'an ingenious decoction' (an almost Nabokovian turn of phrase) with which they could sneak the scandalous tragedy of Lolita and Humbert past Hollywood's censors. The girl, he told the author, could be portrayed as being much older than in the book – eighteen, perhaps, rather than twelve. Further discussion sparked a more subversive idea: Lolita's age should be unstated, leaving the viewer to ponder the issue, and perhaps implicate his own fantasies (or at least his memory of the book) in the process. 'We have an idea,' Kubrick announced, 'but for reasons of exploitation, we aren't saying yet what it is.' He confirmed, however, that any rumours suggesting that the relationship between Lolita and Humbert might be made more equal, in terms of age, were 'nonsense'.

Who, the Hollywood press wondered, could possibly play the perilous title role? 'I wish Elizabeth Taylor were young again,' Kubrick joked, perhaps remembering her twelve-year-old starring role in *National Velvet*. A columnist faithfully reported his remarks and added that Kubrick 'expects to conduct a talent search for a sexy-looking twelve-year-old'. Indeed, the director revealed, they were being inundated by potential candidates. 'We've had fifty or sixty letters already,' he explained, 'from mothers and fathers around the country, offering us their daughters. They send pictures [which] all look like junior high school graduation pictures.' (Perhaps he expected the parents to mail him portraits of their girls in nymphet pose?) Meanwhile, agents for two young Hollywood stars had also been in touch: Tuesday Weld (aged fifteen) and Patty McCormack (thirteen).

Kubrick and Harris also had to fend off an approach from one of the grand names of Hollywood mythology: one-time swashbuckler, full-time debauchee (and debaucher), Errol Flynn. In 1957, the then forty-eight-year-old star, drenched in booze and haunted by the conviction that he was about to die of lung cancer, awoke one morning to discover that he had a new secretary: fifteen-year-old would-be starlet, Beverly Aadland. Her mother Florence had engineered the position, in the hope that Flynn might 'discover' the teenager – as indeed he did, forcing her to have intercourse with him, and then proclaiming their romantic harmony to the world. (Florence managed to sell the literary rights to her part in the saga on two occasions, the contradictory titles of her memoirs telling their own story: *The Big Love*, followed by *The Beautiful Pervert*.)

Flynn had his own history of Humbertian adventures, facing allegations of 'statutory rape' (or sexual involvement with an under-age girl) on several occasions. Having convinced young Beverly that she was in love with him, he procured her a series of uncredited walk-on parts, in movies as prestigious as *South Pacific*. But in his cups, he fantasised a project that would cement their union as one of Hollywood's great romantic pairings. He offered himself and Beverly as a pre-packaged Humbert and Lolita, reinforced by the girl's mother.

James B. Harris recalled: 'A letter came into the office from her mother claiming she could play this part better than anyone, because she's been living the part. It was shameless.' When Kubrick and Harris failed to bite, Errol Flynn secured his girlfriend her only starring role as his onscreen lover in *Cuban Rebel Girls* – filmed on the Caribbean island as Castro's revolution took hold. Then, before the picture was released, and while *Lolita* was still being cast, Flynn died of a heart attack. Without his backing, Aadlund was reduced to being marketed as 'The Nymphet Tarzan'. In 1960 a young man was shot dead during a violent argument in her apartment, and with this scandal any hope of an enduring career vanished.

The race to capitalise on the 'nymphet' tag now threatened to capsize the Kubrick and Harris project. In a letter to the director on New Year's Eve 1959, Vera Nabokov warned him about 'several pictures which are being prepared by various French and Italian producers, ostensibly based on *Lolita*'. Two weeks later she was able to inform him that the Italian impresario Alberto Lattuada intended to title his film *The Little Nymph*, as if to pass it off as an official adaptation of her husband's book. Kubrick and Harris promptly registered titles that they feared their rivals might use, such as *The Nymphet* and *The Twelve-Year-Old Woman*. But that only safeguarded their interests in America. Three months later, Vladimir became aware of a French script entitled *Les Nymphettes*. He sought legal advice and went to court in an effort to copyright the word he had coined – but failed on the grounds that it had already passed into common usage. *Les Nymphettes* was duly released in January 1961, billed during its brief British exposure as portraying 'nymphettes with the faces of angels ... their manners and morals in the world of Paris after dark!'. In Italy, the title was refined into *Le Ninfette* (no translation necessary); in America the more indistinct *First Taste of Love*. Meanwhile Lattuada was persuaded to rename his project *I Dolci Inganni*, or *Sweet Deceptions*. (Its French distributor opted for the more direct *Les Adolescentes*.)

The star of *Sweet Deceptions* was fifteen-year-old Catherine Spaak, portraying a girl two years older who first fantasises about and then enjoys an affair with a family friend more than twice her age. There was a strange, but not perhaps coincidental, parallel between this scenario and its facilitators: Lattuada was a friend of Spaak's family, and had been urging her father for years to let the girl appear in this film. Perhaps parental misgivings were justified: in a lengthy scene, Lattuada's camera lingered voyeuristically over Spaak's body, clad in a baby-doll nightdress, as she writhed in a nightmare and then gently caressed herself to demonstrate her sexual awakening. But unlike Beverly Aadland, Spaak was not defined by this *Lolita*-style role, and subsequently flourished as both an actor and a singer.

As comic relief from this parade of European nymphets, the much-loved St Trinian's series of British films succeeded in parodying two current scandals: Nabokov's creation, and the first paperback edition of D.H. Lawrence's *Lady Chatterley's Lover*. The 1960 film *Pure Hell in St Trinian's* was, as usual, set in the country's least disciplined and most sinful girls' boarding school. On this occasion, the action begins with the immolation of the school buildings, followed by a trial at London's Old Bailey. The girls are called to testify, including one pupil who is too small to be seen over the witness box. Asked to confirm her name, she replies: 'Lolita Chatterley, Peyton Place, Brighton'.

While Europe groomed its own Lolitas, Kubrick and Harris evaluated the young American contenders for the role. Hollywood columnists assumed that Tuesday Weld was the season's nymphet of choice. James Mason, one of several mature stars being considered for the part of Humbert, agreed: 'She's the only 16-year-old around who could play a 12-year-old convincingly. I don't know who else could.'

Weld had endured a traumatic childhood, and knew enough about exploitation, by everyone from her mother to middle-aged Hollywood stars, to imagine herself into Nabokov's scenario. 'I didn't have to play Lolita,' she admitted a decade later. 'I *was* Lolita.' Only then was she able to reveal that – sent out to work as a child model after the death of her father – she had compressed a lifetime's agony into the years before her sixteenth birthday. At nine, she recalled, she had suffered a nervous breakdown. By ten, she was an alcoholic; by eleven, she was dating adult men. At twelve, she attempted suicide, when a gay man on whom she had an intense crush refused to respond to her advances. Through it all, she starred in countless films and TV series. But the Lolita role passed her by – thanks in part to Vladimir Nabokov, who was introduced to Weld by Kubrick. The author was unimpressed: Weld was, he declared, 'a graceful ingénue, but not my idea of Lolita'. Instead she was snapped up by producer Albert Zugsmith, for his picture *Sex Kittens Go to College*. (Zugsmith was one of several impresarios who had been sniffing around a 'nymphet' project, tagging the fifteen-year-old Polynesian girl Janice Tani for the role; but the picture, and Tani's career, disappeared before they began.)

While James Mason lobbied for Tuesday Weld, *Lolita*'s producers focused upon his ten-year-old daughter, child star Portland Mason. 'Portland is no longer Hollywood's most precocious child,' said a Hollywood reporter. 'She has grown up. I saw her the other night tripping into a premiere in high-heel shoes and a gown that once graced Zsa Zsa Gabor. She was clinging to the arm of a man who looked to be 35. Her parents see nothing wrong in it. "One of my sisters was like that at the age of nine – it's our Spanish blood," says her mother [Pamela Mason]. "Portland loves older men. Her trouble is finding boys of her own age who are tall enough to dance with."' The pre-pubescent girl was already burdened with being told she resembled 'a younger version of Marilyn Monroe'; but rather than being granted the role of Lolita, she instead played a fairy princess in the children's TV series *Shirley Temple's Storybook*.

British child actor Hayley Mills was also considered for the role, though her parents (film stars themselves) demurred. So did Walt Disney, whose studio had her under contract. 'I wouldn't even let her *see Lolita*,' he insisted, 'let alone play it.' Confronted with this quote, Stanley Kubrick retorted that 'I wouldn't let my kids see some of Disney's movies – they're too full of violence and brutality. *Lolita*, on the other hand, is a touching love story. Any child too young to see it wouldn't understand it – and any child old enough to understand it is old enough to see it.' Hayley Mills herself, questioned after she had seen the finished picture, shied away from the suggestion that she might portray a nymphet: 'I don't go madly for that sort of thing, that sort of sensationalism. I don't want to do a sensational sex film – enough people are doing them. I'd be terrified and embarrassed getting my clothes wrenched off.' But, nonetheless, she had regrets: 'I wish I had done it'. It would not be until 1966 that Mills 'grew up' on screen, playing a young bride whose husband is unable to consummate their marriage in the touching *The Family Way* (alias *All in Good Time*).

The year-long debate about who might play Lolita, and how, seemed to free the film industry to pursue the same theme by other means, secure that the public's attention was focused entirely on Nabokov's nymphet. 'Like the average age of puberty, which is said to be decreasing by something like four hours every day,' opined Penelope Gilliatt, 'the age of cinematic personae seems to be dropping fast.' In 1960, the Spanish director Luis Buñuel released his second American production, *The Young One* (alias *La Joven*). Filmed in Mexico with a US cast, it starred Key Meersman (then fourteen) in the title role of Evvie, a naïve thirteen-year-old orphan who lives alone on an island off the coast of Carolina. She is first bullied and then groomed by her grandfather's former business partner. By the end of the film, he has forced himself upon her, with the implication that he takes her virginity – rape in all but name. Earlier, we have seen the girl watched by another adult while she takes a shower, hidden from our view; from which she emerges, clad in a towel, which she almost lets slip over her breasts in an act of what appears to be deliberate provocation. One of the copywriter's promotional lines reinforced the theme: 'He said I'm no longer a child, and not to tell anyone'. It might have been written by Humbert Humbert himself.

The ambiguous mystique of teenage sexuality was so prevalent in the Lolita era that it even seeped into the reliable moral universe of *The Loretta Young Show*. Each of these television dramas resolved to the audience's satisfaction within a fable-like, thirty-minute episode. They reflected the aspirations and fears of middle America back to itself: a mirror of wishful thinking. The programme broadcast across the nation on 13 December 1959, entitled 'Alien Love', starred Young as a school headmistress, who becomes embroiled in a potentially embarrassing dispute. It involves the new, kindly but stern physics teacher, Mr Kronstadt, who is a refugee from Hungary; and Laurie Williams, a flirtatious, vampy, disruptive girl of thirteen, who is, for reasons that only the casting director could explain, surrounded by classmates who look anything up to a decade older. Laurie exhibits all the ploys of the mischievous pupil: chewing gum in class, passing notes to her friends, laughing at the teacher and answering him back.

The set-up had been and would be seen in a thousand schoolroom dramas, but the modern twist was pure 1959. The headmistress learns that Mr Kronstadt has 'made an indecent proposal' to Laurie when they were alone. Anxious not to discriminate against Kronstadt on racial grounds, but sensitively aware of her duty to protect the innocent children in her care, Young calls an after-school meeting, at which

Kronstadt is effectively on trial for his career. Laurie appears self-righteous as she challenges him: 'You talked about my underthings. You're always saying creepy things in class, Mr Kronstadt, but this was *private.*'

It looks bleak for the beleaguered Hungarian, who is prepared to walk away from his job. But the ever-perceptive Young still has faith in his integrity. She continues to quiz the increasingly sullen Laurie, who at first refuses to repeat what Kronstadt said, but finally concedes. 'He said that I was flirting and distracting part of his class,' she admits. 'He said that a girl my age shouldn't be so forward. That I shouldn't wear [and here she breaks down in tears] *falsies*. I was never so shocked in my life.' Kronstadt is vindicated – Laurie's chest enhancement clearly falls within his proper educational remit – and everybody apologises to everyone else. Dignity and morality are saved, and Laurie returns to class, presumably without the aids that Kronstadt has so perspicaciously identified.

The episode went out at 9 pm on a Sunday evening, up against *The Jack Benny Show* and a religious talk about a woman who had five husbands. It would have slipped unobtrusively into re-run purgatory had not the audience that evening included Stanley Kubrick. (Or so the legend goes: in fact, casting director Billy Schaeffer may have been the attentive talent scout.) He recognised Laurie as one of the dozens of young girls who had been suggested to them as a potential Lolita, and one of the few whom they had invited to their office for an interview. Her screen credit listed her as Suellyn Lyon, her real name, but she had been introduced to them simply as Sue. 'They just sat there and asked me questions about my life,' she recalled later.

As James B. Harris conceded, 'Sue Lyon got by us. We had interviewed her and kept going. Then one day Stanley came into the office and said, "You know, last night I saw an episode of *The Loretta Young Show*. Remember that girl that was in here? What about *her*?" He said she was a terrific little actress' – and she was, striking exactly the right note of brazen self-confidence followed by gauche teenage embarrassment. Kubrick insisted they should call her back in. Harris continued: 'She was bright, and she had a good sense of humour. And she saw the humour in [*Lolita*].'

Born in Davenport, Iowa, in July 1946, Sue Lyon lost her father when she was only a few months old. A loquacious 'friend' of her mother described her to the local paper: 'She was always a little dickens with a sparkling personality, and she's been a little doll all her life'. Her husband chipped in: 'Suellyn is a natural beauty – the kind you would turn around to look at in the street'. By this time, she was fourteen years old, and fair game to the world.

The Lyon family had migrated to California precisely, it seemed, so that they might be able to capitalise on Sue's good looks. An Iowa paper explained: 'The well-developed girl may be familiar to readers through the courtesy of the J.C. Penney mail-order catalogue, for which she modelled junior dresses and bathing suits.' To steal a phrase from Buñuel, the young girl had already matured into a none too obscure object of desire.

While Lyon was screen-tested alongside James Mason, now installed as Humbert Humbert, her school life continued. In February 1960, aged thirteen and a half, she was chosen as the Princess of Smiles in a County Dental Society oral health competition. She was, the judges adjudicated, 'the girl with the most perfect teeth and the nicest smile'. Film careers have been built on less; but it was Lyon's personality that won Kubrick and Harris over. She was unfazed by the film's scenario; unafraid of Mason, who was gentle and patient with her inexperience; and willing to listen and learn, unlike her TV alter ego Laurie.

There remained the thorny issue of how much Lyon should be told, and needed to know, about Humbert Humbert and his distinctive erotic obsession. When her name was announced to the media, she faithfully parroted the official studio line that she had never read *Lolita*, because her mother said it was not suitable for her. Later she admitted that she had dipped into the book, but found the language too ornamental and abstruse. Much the same reaction was experienced by many readers of the Olympia Press edition, who threw down the book in a fit of disgust when they realised that Nabokov's style was more concerned with linguistic experimentation than groin-tingling sexual description.

With their stars in place, Kubrick and Harris needed to confront the central quandary that would face anyone seeking to depict Nabokov's fiction on the screen. Humbert Humbert did not just fall in lust and eventually love with his stepdaughter. He devoted his entire sexual life to the pursuit of nymphets, or at least adults who might pass as teenagers in his erotic imagination. How could the producers reflect the Humbertian perspective without devoting the entire movie to portraying him as a sex criminal? As James B. Harris revealed several decades later, 'There was a certain amount of craftiness, shrewdness, about survival in our minds.'

They turned initially to Calder Willingham, the American novelist who had scripted their 1957 production, *Paths of Glory*. He appeared to have impeccable credentials for the task: a taste for oddball, ironic, subversive humour, and a penchant for the unashamed portrayal of sexual infatuation. Harris loved the script he delivered, but Kubrick felt that it didn't solve the problem of allowing James Mason to play a character that would be, at least in part, sympathetic to the audience's worldview. Willingham had also retained Nabokov's chronological narrative. But Harris reckoned that they could transform the viewer's attitude to their morally repugnant hero by refashioning the plotline.

As he remembered telling Kubrick, 'We've always said that this is a bizarre love story. And we really want to engage an audience into reversing what they perceived as a dirty old man. By the time the picture ends, they should really feel sorry for him.' Nabokov left his readers with Humbert tracking down Clare Quilty, the fellow pervert who has stolen Lolita away from him, and murdering him in his mansion. Harris suggested that their picture should begin with the murder, as a dramatic episode with no sexual connotation; which would leave them free to end with Humbert declaring his love for the now almost adult, and very definitely pregnant, Lolita – a farewell that might excite the audience's romantic instincts. Then, to soften the portrait of Humbert without obscuring his illegal affair with Lolita, they could omit the wider implications of his hebephilia.

'The craftiness was, what do we have to gain except censorship and defeat if we get into Humbert's predilection for little girls?', Harris recalled. 'Why bring that in at all? Why not make this a love story? When he sees this girl, this is the girl he falls in love with. Why do we have to introduce the idea that he's been chasing little girls his entire life?' As he explained, 'we made sure when we cast [Sue Lyon] that she was a definite sex object – not something that could be interpreted as perverted.' Once again, Humbert seemed to be speaking through a film-maker's mouth.

With this scenario in mind, Harris returned to Vladimir Nabokov, and invited him to craft his own dramatic revision of the novel. The author had already approved the selection of Sue Lyon, whom he adjudged to be a 'demure nymphet'. (Kubrick apparently told him that she 'could easily be made to look younger and grubbier for the part of Lolita', but this may have been a Nabokovian invention.) Ultimately, the authorial draft of the script was too long to be filmed, and too eager to spell out, and then excuse, Humbert's lifelong quest for under-age flesh. Producer and director crafted their own vision of the book, but ensured that Nabokov retained the screen credit, to distract those who might have resented their arrogance in daring to alter the distinguished novelist's tale. 'We feel that we are handling the subject with the greatest dignity,' Kubrick insisted on the eve of shooting, 'but if changes are demanded [by the censor] we will keep an open mind about them.' Harris was more aggressive in his defence of the project: 'This is a highly moral story. The relationship between Humbert and the girl is more psychological than erotic. Tragedy strikes the principals and stays with them right to the end.'

Partly to escape the scrutiny of Hollywood's gossip mongers, partly to suit their British male co-star, Harris and Kubrick resolved to film *Lolita* in England. Sue Lyon was, as Dorothy Manners sniped in her syndicated column, 'being hidden and guarded as if she were a nugget of gold away from Fort Knox'. She was 'barricaded' in a rented house and 'having no girlish fun in London'. (All of this was based on speculation rather than fact.) Harris explained that they were concerned less with protecting Lyon than with maintaining her as a figure of mystery: 'We want audiences to identify her only with the part she plays. She must be presented simply as Lolita and not as a girl with a normal American background.' In the absence of a press call or an exclusive *tête-à-tête*, London's most powerful journalists were forced to confect an emotional response strong enough to fill a page. Donald Zec of the *Daily Mirror* reprised his distaste for 'that grimy bore of a novel' and questioned: 'Whether this is a suitable subject for a night out at the flicks remains to be seen. Personally, the whole idea of filming the antics of this grubby twosome in Vladimir Nabokov's sensational tale pollutes the atmosphere of my sub-conscious.'

His American equivalents tended to rely upon anecdotes rather than ethical speculation – one noting, rather cruelly, that 'Lolita, 14-year-old Sue Lyon, is on a strict diet in London'. Role and actor were already being conflated as if they were one and the same.

Syndicated columnist Hy Gardner was much more astute. He pondered 'how that characterization might affect the teenager in later years. It seems to me that a girl of that age is too sensitive, too impressionable, to risk beclouding her future by even play-acting such a sinful tart. There are plenty of actresses of more mature years, whose appearances belie their age, who could have been given such a role and dismissed its implications a few hours after the last scene was shot.' The following day, as if he'd been up all night grieving for Lyon's psychological health, he returned to the theme: 'There is no question that a young girl, handed overnight fame on a tarnished silver platter of fame in her early teens, risks boredom and frustration by the time she enters maturity. No money in the world is worth such a risk.' And he mused about how deeply her mother had thought through the implications of Lyon's instant notoriety.

The country in which Lyon was accumulating this infamy was struggling to accommodate the sexualisation of young girls. There was an outcry from doctors when an underwear brand introduced a new line for ten-year-old females, a brassiere entitled Teen Form. The manufacturers conceded that few of their potential clients would have a physical need for a bra, but Teen Form was intended to provide them with psychological support, as a signal of their impending maturity. This coincided with a heated and prolonged debate about the precise age at which girls needed to be informed about matters sexual. Few opinion-makers were as insightful as the magistrate who proclaimed that 'Sex isn't a mere matter of sexual intercourse, conception and birth. It is of the emotions. We give children biology lessons in school, but seldom discuss with them their feelings and uncertainties.' She might have added that this instruction in biology often skipped past human coupling and conception, with a sleight of hand worthy of a conjurer. Those who were schooled in the Britain of the 1960s recall biology classes that discussed, in minute anatomical detail, the sex lives of plants, then more obscurely the reproduction cycle in rats, before announcing: 'And that's how babies are born'. There were no textbooks on offer: merely, as a sexual aid, the *Concise Oxford Dictionary*, in which eager or guilty children could find a deathly definition of the word 'masturbation': 'Bodily self-pollution'.

Even experts in the field, such as Dr Eustace Chesser, seemed to exist in a world that denied female sexuality. 'The sex urge in a man is more urgent, more demanding,' he announced. 'But it is equally natural for the girl to refuse it.' He lamented that children saw their parents obtaining goods on hire purchase; and determined that they should experience sex on the same 'want-it-now' basis. The magistrate quoted above imagined a conversation about such matters between mother and innocent thirteen-year-old daughter. What if a boy forces you to kiss him? 'The world won't come to an end if you're kissed when you don't want to be, although it's a horrible feeling ... And don't forget, it may be partly your fault. You may have given him the idea that you would welcome it.' The mother continued: 'Most boys will go as far as they can with a girl, that's their nature. It's up to the girl to see that things don't get out of hand and go further.' Problems arose when girls 'teased a boy and led him on, and just got what they were asking for'. The girl should remember, most of all, that 'Getting him excited and then going cool on him is just about the meanest thing a girl can do'. An anonymous teenage boy wrote to complain about this remark: 'It is often the boy that has to use the restraint with an over-passionate girl'. No wonder that, as enlightened doctor Keith Cammeron pronounced, 'For young people, love is too often a bitter disappointment – from ignorance of themselves and each other.'

The British Medical Association intervened with a timely report, *The Adolescent*. 'Films, posters, plays, advertisements and the open sale of near-dirty books' – *Lolita*, anyone? – 'have all made it virtually impossible to grow up unaware of the lure of sex', the BMA explained. The Church of England joined in, fired by the steep rise in instances of under-age pregnancy. 'These are the children of our society,' the Church's Moral Welfare Committee pronounced, 'moulded by parents, teachers and entertainers, by the Church, and by high-brow triflers with sex as well as by the low-brow and commercial exploiters of it.'

Whether the brows to which they were exposed were low or high, girls were left to make sense of the jumble of sex-related stories that increasingly filled the pages of the popular press. There was the sixteen-year-old girl who had just married the man who had been her guardian since she was eight. It was only when the thirty-three-year-old man saw her dating teenage boys that he realised he was in love with her. Her mysteriously absent parents commended the marriage, on the grounds that she was mature for her age and he immature for his – thereby constituting the perfect match. There were the fashion pages which complained that everything in the latest Paris collections 'seemed to have been designed with the junior miss in mind … Only a teenager could get away with such skimpy day dresses layered round the figure like a bandage.' And there were, always, starlets to follow and imitate: not just Sue Lyon, whose purity was being carefully guarded by her mother and her chaperone during the *Lolita* shoot, but her European counterparts. The London papers loved to dwell on fourteen-year-old Caroline Eliacheff, who was an habituée of the French Riviera, in tandem with her thirty-four-year-old actor fiancé, Robert Hossein. He waited until the day after her fifteenth birthday before taking her as his third wife.

So how was a girl of thirteen supposed to respond to the advances of a mature man: panic, disgust or delight? That was the dilemma facing a Sussex girl, who joined the church guild, and was greeted attentively by the forty-one-year-old rector. He told her that she had 'a nice little figure', and she politely accepted the compliment. A few days later, 'he spoke about posing in the nude, and showed me some photographs of girls in the nude. I agreed to pose for him. He arranged for me to meet him in the parish room on a Saturday. He gave me a list of questions about sex and asked me to write down the answers. He took photographs of me. I was wearing no clothes. Later he told me they had not come out and asked me to pose again. I said yes, so long as it was the last time.' Of course, it wasn't. The rector persuaded her to let him take her for a drive, during which 'he kissed and touched me. I cried and he said he would not do it again.'

Instead, the rector opened a new avenue of attack: psychological manipulation. He told the girl, now fourteen years old, that their relationship meant much more to him than sex. Indeed, he seems to have persuaded her that she had been complicit in introducing an erotic element to their liaisons. The girl wrote to her abuser: 'I cannot help thinking how wicked I was. It was my fault in the first place because if I had not chased after you, we would probably never have got so friendly and you would never have thought of asking me what you did. You must think my morals are very low, but I will try to lead a better life from now on.' In another message, she assured him: 'You certainly did bring me much closer to God – I have found it much easier to pray.'

There was an inevitable dénouement, and a merciful release for the girl. Soon after her sixteenth birthday, the rector invited her to spend a night with him at a hotel in Worthing. Before they ventured inside, he told her to put a ring on her wedding finger, and then donned a similar adornment himself. The manageress was familiar with couples masquerading as wife and husband, but was unusually disturbed by this pairing. The girl, she recalled, looked 'very, very young, and terrified'. The manageress phoned the Worthing police.

Upstairs, the rector worked methodically through his fantasy. 'He got undressed,' the girl said, 'and I took my shoes and stockings off, my skirt, cardigan and petticoat. He came over and took the rest off. He took his pyjamas off. I was on the bed. He kissed me, and caressed me, and said he loved me, and that sort of thing.' She consoled herself with his promise that 'he would never have intercourse with me'.

Fortunately, the rector was interrupted before his self-restraint was put to the test. Two police detectives knocked at the door and asked the rector how old his companion was. 'Old enough', he snapped in return. The girl looked petrified and distraught, and so the detectives arrested the man on suspicion of indecent behaviour. In court, charged with abduction with intent to have intercourse, and indecent assault against the girl when she was still under-age, the rector repeated that he would never have taken her virginity. Then he pleaded guilty to all charges and was sentenced to three years in prison. The prosecuting barrister delivered a volley of moral rhetoric that might have tugged at the conscience of Humbert Humbert: 'I suppose it is possible that, in the early stages [of their acquaintance], she developed a sort of hero-worship. Whether that was so, or whether she loved him, he certainly has played upon her feelings, as part of his technique of seduction. The girl has escaped inviolate. But [the rector] has violated her conscience, her principles and her loyalty.'

The rector's trial in spring 1961 coincided with the release of *The Greengage Summer*, a film in which Susannah York (a twenty-two-year-old playing a girl of sixteen) falls madly in love with forty-six-year-old Kenneth More. He is unmasked as a jewel thief before their affair can take hold, but as the *Women's Mirror* gushed, York's character was transformed by her middle-aged admirer: 'in three short days, something wonderful has happened: she has blossomed from a gawky schoolgirl into a woman'. The following year, *Term of Trial* reversed the *Lolita* scenario, while still retaining the shimmer of the forbidden: Sarah Miles (twenty, playing fifteen) is a schoolgirl who develops a piercing crush for her teacher, Laurence Olivier (fifty-five). When he rebuffs her advances, she accuses him of sexual assault. 'She was hardly more than a child,' the film's poster claimed lasciviously, 'She was bitter-sweet sixteen [not according to the script] with a sudden awareness that she could completely destroy a married man.' If schoolgirls were that dangerous, what hope did a middle-aged man with a penchant for under-age sex have?

Innocence as a lure; innocence as a weapon; innocence disguising rapacious lust: the culture of the early 1960s conjured teasingly with all the baubles on offer from the teenage girl. As if to reinforce the idea that under-age girls were not only responsible for their own exploitation, but positively desired it, the press highlighted any survey that revealed a rise in the instance of venereal disease or pregnancy amongst girls under sixteen. The British Medical Association inadvertently added to the confusion, when one of its senior officers told a conference in July 1961 about an English school in which girls proudly wore a yellow golliwog badge on their uniforms to proclaim that they had lost their virginity. This in turn inspired (if that is the word for such flagrant exploitation) a 1963 film entitled *The Yellow Teddy Bears*; or, in America, the more direct *The Thrill Seekers*, the publicity for which bragged about 'Teenage School Dolls – what they learned isn't on any report card!'. The movie did not deliver the sexual sensationalism promised by the posters; instead, it focused on a teacher who decodes the secret of the teddy bear badges and forces the errant girls to confront the evils of sex before marriage. So moral was the scenario, in fact, that schoolgirls were sent off by the coachload for private screenings, at which the seventeen-year-old 'bad girl' star, Annette Whiteley, made 'the girls aware of the dangers of sexual promiscuity'. (When word got out in the USA that the film was less erotic than some of its audience might have hoped, the producers inserted some continental soft-porn footage of young girls taking a shower and repackaged the flick as *Gutter Girls*.)

The revelation that fourteen-year-old Sue Lyon was to star in *Lolita* had prompted a 'blast' from the editor of the US paper *Motion Picture Herald*, to the effect that 'sick pictures will mean a sick industry'. His definition of 'sick' involved any film that 'deals with unnatural sex in any of its assorted forms, or with morbid suggestiveness and thinly-veiled pornography ... If the current wave of "sick" pictures becomes a flood, prepare to say goodbye to the American film as the leading mass entertainment of the world.' But *The Greengage Summer*, *The Yellow Teddy Bears* and *Term of Trial* were all British productions, while *Lolita* itself was also being filmed in the UK. America also lagged far behind Europe when it came to extending the boundaries of what could be portrayed on screen. The 1963 Greek release, *Young Aphrodites*, hinged around two pairs of lovers: one adult, the other children on the cusp of adolescence. Was the latter's exploration of sex 'unnatural'? Or was it licit because their tryst was set in 200 BC, and the film's direction clearly owed more to the art-house rather than pornographic school? Nikos Koundouros's film picked up awards at several prestigious festivals and was finally cleared for uncut viewing by the British censors in 1967. But the way in which the semi-naked body of Kleopatra Rota (twelve or at best thirteen at the time of shooting) was emblazoned on posters suggested that at least some of the movie's distributors intended to appeal to the hebephiliac tendencies of its potential audience.

Sue Lyon had been protected from such inspection and exposure during the filming of *Lolita*, which ended three months before her fifteenth birthday. Stanley Kubrick and James B. Harris then sat on the finished film for almost a year. There were lengthy negotiations with film censors on both sides of the Atlantic, the British board allotting *Lolita* an 'X' certificate (meaning nobody under sixteen could view the film), its American equivalent insisting that viewers needed to be eighteen to witness Humbert's obsession. Shelley Winters, who played Lolita's mother, dampened fears about the film's content by explaining that Kubrick 'directed the whole thing for laughs instead of sex'. She also gallantly complimented her young co-star: 'Sue Lyon is gorgeous – a sort of young Bardot. I could murder her!'

For reasons of decorum, Kubrick and Harris also wanted to delay the premiere of *Lolita* until Sue Lyon's sixteenth birthday was approaching. But their careful guard of their young ward's decency slipped just once, with consequences that could have been catastrophic, for her and the fate of the film. Towards the end of the production schedule, Lyon was flown to California at the studio's expense, for a publicity shoot with photographer Bert Stern. He was an accomplished commercial lensman, with the knack of putting his female subjects entirely at ease and teasing out their sensuality. 'It's exciting to photograph desire', he once explained, and nothing exemplified his craft better than his memorable swimming-pool session with Marilyn Monroe shortly before her death.

Lyon was an altogether more delicate subject, though equally photogenic. Stern's mission was to validate her as the subject of adult sexual desire, without exploiting her vulnerability. Before he had even met the girl, he purchased a pair of heart-shaped sunglasses – which became the publicity hook for the film (though Lyon never wore them on screen). She donned the bikini she had worn for her first encounter with Humbert and Stern suggested that she should suck a lollipop to accentuate her teenage status. 'I knew all about the birds and bees when I agreed to play Lolita,' Lyon insisted after the premiere, 'so it wasn't difficult to behave like a girl who knows the facts of life.' But it is less certain that she understood the priapic appeal of several of Stern's set-ups, which were much more blatantly sexual than anything seen in the film. When the producers saw the contact sheets of the session, they must have gulped and blanched. The vast majority of Stern's pictures had to be suppressed; had they escaped to the supermarket tabloids in 1962, they might have capsized the film before it was released.

Exploitation was everywhere. 'They lived for violence, sin and sensation', screamed the cover of John Clarke's 35-cent pulp novel, *The Lolita Lovers*, carefully timed to coincide with the premiere. Its cover showed a young couple of indeterminate age, he holding back his arms from her embrace, fists clenched as if to staunch his overwhelming desire, while she stands on tiptoe, pulling him hard against her body. Lyon's name and sunglass-enhanced image were attached to a novelty pop single, 'Lolita Ya Ya', on which she didn't sing. (The flipside, 'Turn Off the Moon', did feature her creditable vocals.) Her mother was inundated with magazine requests to reveal the secrets of her daughter's young life. Star directors and actors, from Federico Fellini to Marlon Brando, were lobbying for the girl's future services, even before they had seen a single frame of her on screen. Manufacturers competed to rush their own heart-shaped shades into the shops; 'Lollipops, too, are back in fashion', it was reported.

No wonder, as the publicity for *Lolita*, unleashed in the American press in early May 1962, zoomed in on Lyon's face, red lollipop sliding into her richly-lipsticked mouth, eyes peeking curiously over Stern's sunglasses. Alongside the image was a simple question: 'How did they ever make a movie of *Lolita*?' In the deliberate absence of quotes from actors or director, it was left to producer James B. Harris to field frantic questions from the press. He repeated his firm belief that *Lolita* was, at heart, 'a moral love story'. But in retrospect, his explanation raised more qualms than it quelled. 'Age is not the important thing when two people are deeply in love,' he insisted. 'Frankly, I see nothing immoral in the affair of a man in his 40s and a girl of twelve.' Or, as the *New York Times* described it on the same day: 'the perverse love of a middle-aged degenerate man for a 12-year-old degenerate girl'.

Kubrick's film was premiered on Broadway in New York City, at Loew's State cinema, on 13 June 1962. The almost sixteen-year-old Sue Lyon braved the ranks of photographers and curious onlookers, some of whom called out 'Lolita!' to attract her attention. She turned demurely towards them, said simply, 'I am not Lolita', and then walked inside. But whereas her co-stars proceeded into the theatre, Lyon was legally too young to see the movie, so she was shepherded into a side-room, and then out of an unattended exit. As she recalled a couple of years later, her cynicism towards her fame already entrenched, 'I was wearing an Oleg Cassini gown and waited for the reviews in a drugstore. A fellow who sat next to me at the counter said, "From now on, any young kid who licks a lollipop will be jailed for immorality". I read the reviews, yelled "Whee!", and spilled a chocolate soda over my gown. What a kick that was.'

The invited audience at Loew's State was prepared for its own kick, especially after Kubrick opened his movie with a brazenly fetishist sequence of Lyon's bare foot being held and caressed by an unmistakeably male hand, which proceeded lingeringly to paint her toenails. But Lolita herself, character rather than body part, was withheld from the viewer a few minutes longer. As in Nabokov's narrative, Humbert Humbert (James Mason) is about to reject Mrs Haze's offer of a rented room, until he spies her daughter in the back garden. Lolita is sporting a skimpy bikini and sunglasses beneath a fluffy-edged sun hat, as she reads sulkily while listening to generic pop music on a transistor radio. As the camera stays on her body, Mrs Haze (Shelley Winters) lists the attractions of her residence. When

Humbert agrees to take the room, Mrs Haze asks him: 'What was the decisive factor? My garden?'

Humbert's insane desire for his 'nymphet' is relayed by Mason's voiceover, as he hymns 'this mixture in my Lolita of tender, dreamy childishness and a kind of eerie vulgarity'. And it's that sense, as the Associated Press reported, of 'just the right combination of gum-chewing adolescent and prematurely smouldering sex goddess that comes off the screen' – misleading several reviewers into believing that Lyon was already eighteen, rather than fourteen, when the film was shot. Indeed, Michael Davie in the *Observer*, who sparked Kubrick's ire by breaking the British embargo on reviewing the film, pointed fun at the disparity between Lolita on the page and in the flesh. 'In life, Lyon is said to be 16,' he wrote. 'In the film, she looks older. Mason, in life, is in his fifties. He, on the other hand, looks younger. At times, they look the same age. At one point, she looks older than him. Thus the novel about Humbert Humbert's corrupt obsession is turned into a film about this poor English guy who is being given the runaround by this sly young broad.'

Davie was exaggerating for effect, but his remarks reflected the shift in emphasis between Humbert's literary vice, and Lolita's cinematic culpability. There is no taboo-shattering sex scene between stepfather and girl to be seen: merely a slapstick fracas of sleeping arrangements. Then, when Humbert suggests breakfast, it is Lolita who says she wants to play a game she has just learned in camp. She whispers her explanation into his ear, he registers his shock ... and then the scene fades, and the couple are on the road again, Lolita downing crisps and Coke like any of her peers. What transpires is part love story (Lolita begs him never to leave her) and part embodiment of the inescapable generation gap, as Humbert turns into the archetypal nagging parent and unwittingly drives his lover into the arms of the equally perverse Quilty (Peter Sellers at his creepiest). There is little sense of sin, and none of despoliation: merely the collision of straitlaced, short-tempered father and annoyingly pesky child. Without Nabokov's sensual prose to convey the transcendent effect of the girl's flesh on his psyche, there is scarcely a recognisable relationship between the pair at all. Indeed, had the movie of *Lolita* been an original script, rather than the adaptation of a notoriously transgressive novel, there might have been no scandal or infamy attached to its name. 'If you are to enjoy the movie,' the female reviewer of the *Oakland Tribune* decreed, 'you have to accept the fact that an otherwise intelligent, somewhat conservative European poet-lecturer in his mid-years could fall for a teenager who lives on Cokes and bubble gum. And that he would in addition suffer the resultant humiliations to prolong his relationship. True, she is well-stacked enough. [*A female reviewer, don't forget.*] But otherwise Lolita is as vapid and uninteresting a female who ever breathed, with no discernible redeeming features.'

That was a verdict on Sue Lyon's fictional character, not her acting performance, which was almost universally praised. 'Sue Lyon makes you believe that she is Lolita!', howled the *New York Daily News* (which was a compliment). Veteran Hollywood watcher Sheilah Graham (once the lover of novelist Scott Fitzgerald) declared that Lyon 'can take up where Marilyn Monroe has left off'. Hedda Hopper lamented that the film 'was just as dirty and degenerate as the book', but that Lyon 'should have an extraordinary future. I've never seen such poise and ability in a child so young except in the one and only Hayley Mills.' Associated Press columnist Bob Thomas also predicted 'a long career' for Lyon, but added (with a hint of poison) 'during which she may live down having been Lolita'.

First she had to luxuriate in the role, and promote the movie. Lyon told Sheilah Graham that 'I believe the public has enough intelligence to know that in real life I'm not a Lolita. It's just a part that comes along once in a century.' But she admitted to another inquisitor: 'Just because I played a nymphet, a lot of people think I'm a bad girl.' Not having read the book, she was left to draw her own conclusions from what she had sought to depict on screen: 'I felt sorry for Lolita. I can understand why she did what she did. She didn't get any love at home. If she had, maybe Lolita would have been a different girl' – and there would have been no film role.

'Believe me, my daughter is nothing like Lolita', Lyon's mother was quick to insist. But that reading did not impress the columnists, who had preconceptions to fulfil. Vernon Scott of UPI found the girl 'sophisticated for her age. And her 34-21-35 measurements are those of a woman, not a little girl.' Interviewers chipped doggedly away at Sue Lyon's privacy, forcing her to admit that she had been dating boys as old as twenty, and that she had once held a crush on her science teacher.

Another star gossipmonger, Dorothy Kilgallen, whose mysterious death three years later would provoke its own tabloid headlines, was the first to pin down an apparent romance. After revealing that 'more than 200 chaps have proposed marriage to Sue Lyon' during a promotional visit to Germany, she delivered the exclusive news that the young star had 'bowled over her producer, James B. Harris ... an old man of 33'. Sheilah Graham countered with the rumour that Lyon was actually dating her screen lover, James Mason. But Kilgallen trumped her with details: Harris, she stated, 'seems to love to buy nice things for child star Sue Lyon. In the glove compartment of that $8,500 jalopy he so conveniently left in her driveway the other day, was a gem-studded gold bracelet inscribed in tender words meant only for her baby blues.' When Lyon crossed paths with Kilgallen a few days later, the actor smiled sweetly and described Harris as 'her beau'. The press feasted on this January-June romance for several months, until Lyon finally admitted that she and Harris were friends, nothing more, and had been feeding the press romantic titbits as a joke. She was quite capable of handling even the most prurient of London reporters, such as the *Daily Mirror*'s star feature writer, Donald Zec. He tried to goad 'the most provocative teenager', 'that lollipop-sucking nymphet', 'the large-eyed, full-lipped schoolgirl', into saying something overtly sexual. Lyon distanced herself with practised ease. 'I'm just an average, normal girl, with average, normal interests', she explained. That kind of insouciance merely appalled Unity Hall of the *Daily Sketch*, who asked: 'If you had a daughter of 16 like this, wouldn't you be terrified? She is the most frighteningly composed, terrifyingly poised and knowing child I have met. The mind boggles at even thinking of her as a child.'

So too did the cameras of John Huston, who cast her as one of the female stars of his 1964 Tennessee Williams adaptation, *Night of the Iguana*. The film's advertising strapline told the story: 'One man, three women, one night'. The man was Richard Burton, who was impatient with Lyon's lack of professional experience and her tendency to behave as if she was (and she was) just seventeen. Burton and Lyon endured a sultry love scene, of the kind to which Kubrick and Harris did not subject her in *Lolita*, and Lyon danced provocatively in a pair of tight hot pants, with the camera unable to drag itself away from her groin and buttocks. 'What's statutory rape?', someone asks Burton during the film. 'When a man is seduced by a girl under twenty', he explains. Inevitably Lyon and Burton were said to have been conducting a sizzling affair off screen, although the ever-present Elizabeth Taylor, Burton's actual lover, was there to ensure no such shenanigans occurred. In any case, Lyon only had eyes for her fiancé, twenty-five-year-old Hampton Fancher III. The former actor turned screenwriter made a nuisance of himself on the set until he was sent home, which ensured that Lyon was now ritually described as a 'brat' by the press rather than a teenage temptress. Lyon was also, for good measure, sleeping with everyone else in town, and had drifted into alcoholism – or so the columnists implied.

She and Fancher were married just before Christmas 1963, and had separated by the following September, shortly after she had delivered a series of interviews about her wedded bliss. A month later, her brother and a male friend were found dead in a stolen station wagon near Tijuana. Mike Lyon was twenty, had narcotics convictions to his name, and left a bride younger than Sue, plus two small children. He was believed to have overdosed on barbiturates, and possibly a little heroin. His final words were scrawled in the dust of the dashboard: 'Sue, I love you'. Sue cast 'a tragic figure at the graveside', the papers said, but continued to plug her movie when the news broke. Many years later, she remembered having to appear on a talk show two days after Mike's death, and being asked: 'Did your brother kill himself because you played Lolita?' 'I got up and walked off', she recalled. 'That's typical of the reason that I can't be a movie star. I never could.' Even before his death, she had begun to show signs of discomfort at the demands of her fame. She appeared as a mystery guest on a July 1964 edition of the popular TV show, *What's My Line*. After being identified, she was asked by the host if she found the movie business exciting. She gulped as if she had been asked to grab a rattlesnake, then looked utterly bereft for a second, before her publicity training kicked in.

Her subsequent life was not always happy. With Kubrick and Harris to guide her career, her choice of roles was suspect, and unrewarding. She was perennially blamed, without any evidence, for breaking up other stars' marriages, as if unable to leave the aura of *Lolita* behind. At nineteen, she was accused of getting 'fatter and fatter and fatter', so she dieted compulsively, and was then scolded that she now looked too young to sustain adult parts. She was set for a starring role in the youthful romantic comedy *You're a Big Boy Now*, until she suffered severe leg injuries in a car crash with her mother on Pacific Coast Highway. Thereafter her roles accentuated her sexuality rather than her acting skills, and her romantic life disintegrated into chaos, as four marriages collapsed – none of them lasting beyond two years. She was pilloried for daring to marry an African-American; then again for wedding an ex-convict with a continuing penchant for robbery (and also a murder under his belt). In later life, she struggled valiantly with mental health issues, and isolated herself from the public gaze. 'She was in a horrible situation,' her first husband said affectionately at the end of the century, 'a kid who was expected to grow up in all kinds of ways she couldn't manage'. At seventeen, she had told a reporter that 'I'd like to be a star and beat the system. Maybe I can. Maybe not. I don't know.' A year later, she was defiant: 'I've seen the hint that playing Lolita distorted my life. It's ridiculous. It was a good break. It gave me the chance to do many things few other people have done at my age. How could that "ruin" me?' It was only a decade after she'd retired from the movies that she was prepared to admit the toll of her premature success, and how it was achieved. 'My destruction as a person dates from that movie,' she announced damningly. '*Lolita* exposed me to temptations no girl of that age should undergo. I defy any pretty girl who is rocketed to stardom at fourteen in a sex nymphet role to stay on a level path thereafter.'

In Nabokov's novel, Lolita's tragedy does not result from her relationships with exploitative adults, such as Humbert and Quilty, but from the perils of childbirth. In the film, she escapes that fate, though Humbert cannot avoid his own demise in jail. Sue Lyon, meanwhile, lived to be seventy-three years old, when her death was commemorated with worldwide headlines that tied her, once again, to the quintessential nymphet. 'You have to learn to avoid what is going to hurt you', she once commented, though she did not know then that what would hurt her most was also what had made her famous. 'Is there something about living in the neurotic age that makes us hungry for the placidity of children?', Penelope Gilliatt asked in a 1963 *Harper's Magazine* article. She was puzzled by the trend of teenage actresses taking the lead in Hollywood films: Sandra Dee, Tuesday Weld and of course Sue Lyon. But the male gaze of the 1960s was not so much hungry for the placidity of these young women as it was greedy for their untarnished beauty. Western society professed to revolve around the protection of its young; but it was willing to sacrifice its emblematic virgins to the predatory needs of the male libido – and nobody seemed to notice.

Interlude: Taking Advantage

Men and women write about sex in different ways, in the 1960s as today.

Sylvia Plath's heroine in *The Bell Jar* (1963) 'thought a spectacular change would come over me the day I crossed the boundary line'. Finally, with Irwin, Esther prepares to surrender the virginity that has 'weighed like a millstone around my neck'. She lies back, 'rapt and naked', and waits for metamorphosis and ecstasy. 'But all I felt is a sharp, startlingly bad pain. "It hurts," I said. "Is it supposed to hurt?" Irwin didn't say anything. Then he said, "Sometimes it hurts".'

Sometimes, as when Dottie first sleeps with the experienced Dick in Mary McCarthy's generational epic, *The Group* (1963), 'it hurt so that she flinched at each stroke and tried to pull back, but this only seemed to make him more determined. Then, while she was still praying for it to be over, surprise of surprises, she started to like it a little' – so much, it transpires, that 'she seemed to explode in a series of long, uncontrollable contractions that embarrassed her'.

Compare that visceral physicality to the florid banality of the men who were fighting for literary glory – for example, John Updike in *Couples* (1968), with its 'velvet' balls and 'phallus sheer silver'; with Piet, the man of the 'ivory rod', recalling his oral seduction of Angela: 'his shaggy head sank toward the ancient alleyway where, foul proud queen, she frothed most'. From the same year, underground writer Paul Ableman's *Vac* tackles the same act of cunnilingus, and discovers that 'Soon her loins were jumping like a rodent ... So I surged up her body and slid my tool deep into her.'

Popular fiction was equally deranged by the female form. Mickey Spillane's hero, Mike Hammer, might stumble across a naked murder victim in *The Body Lovers* (1967) and notice: 'Her breasts were poised in some weird, rigid defiance.' She was clearly related to Ian Fleming's Tilly Soames from *Goldfinger* (1959): 'She held her body proudly – her fine breasts out-thrown and unashamed under the fine silk.'

When it came to being 'unashamed', there was none to rival Leslie Thomas. *The Virgin Soldiers* (1966) was a fictionalised rendering of his National Service during the previous decade. Sgt Driscoll takes it upon himself to relieve the Regimental Sergeant-Major's twenty-year-old daughter, Philippa, of her virginity. She, of course, has been secretly concerned that she is a lesbian. But Driscoll quickly robs her of any such foolish notions ...

Most of the scene is told via Philippa's dialogue, as she confronts the no doubt mighty (and probably silver) phallus of the all-powerful Driscoll. 'Jesus Christ, Sergeant, I'll be too small,' she whimpers as the towering penis looms over her. 'Oh, I knew I'd be too small. I always knew it.' Driscoll eases closer: 'Oh Sergeant, it hurts. Like God it hurts.' He contradicts her. 'But it does. But it does,' she insists. Then, in a moment of high dramatic realism, she begs him: 'Be gentle. I really need a gnome. Oh, how I need a gnome, Sergeant.'

At this point, the reader can be forgiven for hoping that the world's largest gnome will descend rapidly from the heavens, knock out Driscoll, and take Leslie Thomas with it. Instead, Thomas the narrator moves in for the kill: 'Philippa flung her arms around the band of his head and hugged him as though trying to break it. "Now, Sergeant, now. Please now!", she choked.'

It is a moment that calls for great literary sensitivity, and Thomas doesn't let us down. 'Then it was. The pain made her leap, but then suddenly they were over the reef, and then the warm tide flowed and ebbed, and they lay beautifully, moving clean like swimmers side by side. "Oh, Sergeant, you bastard," Philippa said.'

The expectation of such royal treatment was what made Tracy, Ian Fleming's heroine in *On Her Majesty's Secret Service* (1963), plead with James Bond: 'Take off those clothes. Make love to me ... Be rough with me. Treat me like the lowest whore in creation.' (The next morning, Tracy was clearly underwhelmed by Bond's prowess: 'You're a goddamn lousy lover. Get out!')

This was poetry alongside the Number One contender for the literary crown, Norman Mailer. His novel *An American Dream* (1965) was both an existential portrait of contemporary dread and a savage parade of machismo and misogyny. Its hero, Stephen Rojack, celebrates killing his wife by seducing her German maid, Ruta. Conveniently, he finds Ruta masturbating on her bed, and soon he is on her, her fury and his contempt perfectly matched, until 'a thin high constipated smell ... came needling its way out of her. She was hungry, like a lean rat she was hungry ...' and this is his cue to conquer her anus. She tells him, 'No, *verboten*.'

Rojack responds by grabbing her hair so 'I could feel the pain in her scalp move like a crowbar the length of her body to push up the trap. The rest was easy.' For good measure he commemorates his success in words: '"You're a Nazi," I said to her out of I knew not what.' Her response is natural: '*Ja*, don't stop'. For the next few paragraphs he slips easily back and forth between her two entrances, God and the Devil, until, as he comes, 'the Devil reached to me and I went to him ... she let out a cry of rage, for her expectation took a ferocious twist.' She is frustrated and abused, assaulted and anally raped, so of course she congratulates him on his prowess: 'I do not know why you have trouble with your wife. You are absolutely a genius, Mr Rojack.' After which he throws his wife's body down into the street, to convince the cops that she committed suicide, and breaks the news to Ruta.

Within seconds, as she weeps, her breast slips out of her shirt: 'That little tit in my hand was nosing like a puppy for its reward, impertinent with its promise of the sly life it could give to me, and so keen to pull in a life for itself that I was taken with a hopeless lust,' which Rojack satisfies in a thirty-second spasm. That is more than sufficient for Ruta: 'She was beginning as I was done ... she came in ten seconds behind'; a remarkable example of the often-cited German efficiency. Rojack is by any standards a brute. But faced with breasts so versatile – defiant, proud, unashamed, impertinent, finally keen – what else could a man possibly be?

3 The Woman Always Pays

Bill Maitland's female clients come to him because they want a divorce: because – they might be describing the same man – their husbands 'insisted on having intercourse three times or even four times a day'. Males arrive at his office because they have been arrested for sexual offences: indecent exposure, indecent behaviour, indecent assault.

Maitland has a wife, and a lover, and a succession of secretaries, all of whom he propositions. 'When are we going to have an orgy together?', he asks the aptly named Joy. 'You can't have an orgy with two,' she replies coquettishly. 'No, but you can make a start.' As Maitland admits, 'I just talk about it at great boring length mostly to boring, bad-tempered and silly girls', not that this prevents him from sleeping with them, all of them, if he can. No foreplay, though, and certainly no wooing or cajoling: 'Pray God I am never so old, servile or fumbling that I ever have to wriggle through that dingy assault course. Do you like it? Do you want it? – those are the only questions I have ever thought worthwhile going into.'

Of course, he hates himself, and he hates women, and most of all he hates Jane, his teenage daughter, who represents freedom and, to her father, 'the wounds you inflict without even longing to hurt', merely by being young and attractive and beyond his control. 'You've no shame of what you are', he lectures her and her kind, who are 'being allowed to roll about in it and have clothes and money and music and sex, and you can take or leave any of it'. Whereas Maitland can't leave any woman: he must possess them all and hate himself in the process. As recompense, Maitland is abandoned by all those for whom he cares, or ought to care, and reduced to a nullity devoid of purpose or charm.

Bill Maitland, as played by Nicol Williamson at the Royal Court Theatre in 1964, was the playwright John Osborne's typically self-destructive, perennially irascible mouthpiece in *Inadmissible Evidence*, which the *Daily Express* called 'the most important new play in years' and the *Daily Mail* 'a modern *Peer Gynt*'. Osborne was capable of conveying tenderness between man and woman, as in his 1962 piece *Under Plain Cover*, with its mischievous erotic role-playing when Tim and Jenny (husband and wife) enact 'their nursery perversions'. But disgust came more naturally to him, in life and on the page, and Bill Maitland might have been designed to embody a particular kind of 1960s male sexuality – one steeped in contempt and pocked with suppurating emotional sores.

As novelist Penelope Mortimer noted a few months after Osborne's premiere, 'Part of the trouble is that men simply don't see their wives. Englishmen will recognize everything about their women except their identities as people. They really believe that men are people, and women are women.' Or, as her fellow author Edna O'Brien interpreted the position of women, 'The sex war is a ragged term, but it does exist. In the social climate of equality, women are still in the adolescent stage, and of course, adolescents always go through the worst pain.' Indeed, O'Brien seemed to suggest, the pain was part of the pleasure: 'The best relationship between a man and a woman should be based on a kind of sado-masochism. The man should be of the kind who will order a woman, "Get into that room and undress", while the woman, though outwardly protesting, must subconsciously approve of that kind of dominance.'

The notion of equality between men and women was treated not so much as a problem in the Britain of the early 1960s but as an irrelevance. The superiority of the male gender was implicit in every aspect of life – or, at least, every aspect in which they chose to be superior. (Women were encouraged, and expected, to take the lead when it came to household chores and to the hour-by-hour raising of children.) No field of combat accentuated the divide more sharply than sex. There was an assumption, even amongst the most sympathetic of commentators, that desire was felt urgently by men, but had to be coaxed out of women. As the veteran writer on health and relationships, Maxine Davis, advised teenagers in her guide, *Sex and the Adolescent*, it was natural for boys to dream of sexual fulfilment and to become aroused by almost anything. For girls, by contrast, fantasies were dominated by romance and marriage, and issues such as 'the arrangement and equipment of her kitchen' weighed more heavily than the notion of physical excitement. In another book aimed purely at women, Davis reinforced her message. 'As a rule,' she wrote, 'woman does not experience intense sexual desire spontaneously. It is an acquired taste, like caviar or abstract art. She was not born to it as her husband was.' Where she dared to step away from tradition was in suggesting that, with sufficient preparation, mental and physical, women might eventually learn to take pleasure from intercourse. Of course, 'In order to create the soaring harmonies of sexual love, woman must learn her part and perform it with excellence. This is at once her right and her responsibility.' Her 'part' was not to experience her own orgasm, but to display or at least feign sufficient excitement to convince her husband that 'the delight is mutual'. In the distance, like a desert oasis, was the prospect of her own completion, 'the moment when a woman soars along a Milky Way among stars all her own'. Or, to add another ecstatic metaphor, when 'her whole being is a full orchestra playing the fortissimo of a glorious symphony'. But the exact nature of this symphonic form was as mysterious and remote as caviar to the average housewife of 1960.

Maxine Davis was unusual as a female guide to women's sexual matters: most experts were, obviously, men. The more liberal sought to improve the nation's understanding of the mechanics and motives of coupling, at a time when conversation about such topics was considered taboo in polite society. But inevitably their attempts to widen public knowledge merely helped to cement the previous imbalance of power between the sexes.

Dr Keith Cammeron was renowned as 'one of Britain's foremost authorities on Marriage Guidance', according to the cover of *Live with Love Volume 1*, a long-playing record devoted to sexual behaviour. He was also the author of a series of well-intentioned booklets and manuals, which began from the premise that a woman 'is likely to be the victim of bad upbringing. Her parents probably reared her in the belief that sex wasn't "quite nice". From that stage she may have entered married life believing that love-making was a wifely duty to be tolerated for the sake of peace.'

Cammeron might at this point have informed the anxious bride or fiancée that it was possible for her to experience satisfaction from sex: explained the importance of the clitoris, perhaps, or even encouraged her to explore masturbation at her own pace. After all, even the romantic novelist Barbara Cartland, in her own contemporaneous guide to the young, conceded that females could masturbate just as easily as males, and could also achieve climax. Dr Cammeron, by contrast, was less enlightened. He stated frankly: 'Many women rarely, if ever, gain full sexual satisfaction'. There was compensation, fortunately: 'the knowledge that their love has made their partner happy brings its own satisfaction ... Even if you can't enjoy sex, you can still enjoy physical closeness.' And if that failed to materialise, and 'the British woman finds sex difficult, she might well fall back on her capacity for motherhood. She should remember that her husband wants mothering, too.'

Not that motherhood was a failsafe contribution to marital bliss. Cammeron was prepared to admit, in capitals no less, an uncomfortable truth: 'Let's face the concrete fact: THE BRITISH MALE CAN'T MAKE LOVE. He can't make love satisfactorily for both parties, that is.' But rather than aim his advice at men, the doctor continued to hammer away at their female partners, warning that it was their responsibility to make men delay their 'premature climax' by introducing the idea of love into the bestial union of two bodies. This would distract the men from their own frantic rush to orgasm, and possibly even make them donate a moment or two's attention to their partner's enjoyment. Ultimately, though, the blame for poor male performance in bed could be laid only at one door: 'HIS MOTHER. She probably taught him as a child that certain parts of his body were unmentionable.' How could this sorry state of affairs be rectified? Only by women using sex as 'your weapon – or your wealth. If you give your husband as much pleasure as you can on the good days, you can afford to withhold something on the bad ones.' Women could still wield this modicum of sexual power, even if it ensured that their junior status in the erotic relationship would continue unchallenged.

With women being instructed to endure rather than enjoy sex, their role was at least clear. Men, meanwhile, were nagged by the idea that a festival of erotic delight might be available to them, if only they knew how to find it. Many chose to visit prostitutes, whose increasingly visible activities on Britain's city streets in the late 1950s had sparked legislation to sanitise and control their trade. The Labour MP

Lena Jeger viewed them as a necessary evil, an outlet for men who might otherwise commit crimes of violence. She explained that some prostitutes entered their profession because they hated men and wished to force them to pay for something that, by rights, should be theirs for free. Others, she believed, chose to go on the game 'because they are over-sexed – mad about boys'. Not for a moment did she consider that prostitutes might have been coerced or bullied into taking to the streets; or that their earnings might disappear into the pockets of a pimp. In fact, her account of a whore's life portrayed these women as free spirits, utterly in control of their own lives. And the fact that men chose to liaise with them was, ultimately, women's fault. 'I wonder how many wives must take their share of responsibility for the problem of prostitution,' Jeger wrote: if wives were more amenable to male urges, prostitutes would be less in demand.

In what was, for the time, a remarkably daring piece of investigative journalism, Wayland Young took to the streets around London's Paddington Station in early 1959 to interview prostitutes about their trade. With a certain air of cynicism, he titled his report, 'Sitting on a Fortune'. The women he met were as varied as the clients who solicited them, but most exhibited an understandable sense of world-weariness and contempt. One of them stressed the utility of pretending to be violently turned on by their repulsive 'johns'. 'There's some of [the women] lies as still as stones, they think it's more ladylike or something,' she explained. 'But I say they don't know which side their bread's buttered. Listen: if you lie still, the bloke may spend half the night sweating away. But if you bash it about a bit, he'll come all the quicker and get out and away and leave you in peace.' On these occasions, at least, the premature ejaculation was a consummation devoutly to be wished. Given a fair wind and an over-excited gentleman, in fact, 'with a bit of luck, they come before they even get into me'. As ever, these women were widely considered to be authors of whatever misfortune might befall them. When a series of (still unsolved) sex murders occurred in London a few years later, one of the national papers printed a letter to the effect that 'the risk of being murdered is an occupational hazard for prostitutes. This being so, they can avoid this risk by giving up their mode of life. If they choose to continue, they deserve all they get.' That men might refrain from murder was, of course, a sacrifice too far.

This callous disregard for female life, however tarnished by immorality, was echoed in Britain's justice system. There was the case of the Army sergeant, in May 1960, who enticed a thirteen-year-old girl into his house because, by his own admission, he was bored and lonely while his wife was in hospital. They sat on his settee, and as they talked, he placed his hand on her bare leg, above the knee – 'a habit of his when talking to people', he claimed. Awkwardly for the sergeant, the girl started to scream, and so to avoid alarming the neighbours, he put his hands around her neck to quieten her. Then, without warning, 'she suddenly went limp'. Under the circumstances, there was only one course of action available to him, he believed; which was why, two days after she went missing, the girl's body was found stuffed into a manhole near her Wiltshire home. The judge informed the jury of the sergeant's good character, and they responded to this lead by finding him guilty of manslaughter, not murder. He was sentenced to two years in prison, and the judge admitted that he regretted that he was forced to impose any custodial punishment at all.

A few months later, a staff-sergeant from the United States Air Force, based in Essex, shared a 'vodka-and-jazz party' with a 'gay, party-loving' twenty-year-old woman. Also in his house was another young man, an apprentice engineer; and when the staff-sergeant left the room, the woman and the engineer had intercourse twice. 'It may have been', a court was told subsequently, 'that they were seen' by the sergeant, and 'it had the effect of inflaming his sexual desires'. The sergeant produced a pile of bedclothes and a mattress, the woman removed those few items of clothing that had escaped her initial encounter with the engineer, and she settled down to sleep. The engineer then went home, satisfied that his fun was over.

At this point the American's memory became confused. He suggested that the woman was asleep; but also that she was becoming 'amorous'. Then he himself lapsed into unconsciousness, as he recalled. When he awoke, he discovered to his horror that his hands were clasped around the woman's neck (a sergeant's curse, apparently); and she was dead. As in the killing of the thirteen-year-old, the protagonist's military training kicked in, and he did nothing. Rather than call police or an ambulance, or even solicit aid from a superior officer, he moved her body into another room, and left her there for two days. Then he cut off most of her hair – 'I guess I did that so that people would not recognise her' – and finally dumped the body.

His defence, naturally, was that he must have strangled the woman in her sleep – and his. The judge found this excuse laughable. Before the jury retired to consider the charge of murder, his lordship advised them: 'Have you ever heard of a man strangling a woman while he was asleep? We have no evidence that, in all the records of the medical profession, such a thing has ever happened.' But the jury found him not guilty of murder. The relieved American was free to leave the court and begin a period of compassionate leave after his traumatic ordeal. The woman's father expressed a popular view after the trial was over: 'It just seems fantastic to me. This American admits killing my daughter – and now he's off for a holiday.'

And again, in 1962: a man in Liverpool unearthed love letters to his wife from another man. He confronted her; she mocked him and threw her wedding ring in his face; he strangled her. So entrenched was the assumption that such a wicked female deserved her fate, that the entire legal proceedings seemed designed to pardon him, from the decision of the jury to find him innocent of murder (though guilty of manslaughter) to the judge's unambiguously partial comments during sentencing. The convicted man was, according to the bench, 'a thoroughly decent man with a strong sense of the sanctity of marriage'; though not perhaps an equal sense of the sanctity of human life. His wife had mistreated him, by deed and by word, and so he was right to take his revenge. 'I think this is a case', the judge concluded, 'in which I should give you an absolute discharge', thereby determining that male pride counted more heavily with the law than female existence.

This credo reverberated down to the reading matter aimed at teenage and sub-teenage girls, who learned that they wielded a mighty power, and must suffer the consequences. Every week, *Boyfriend* magazine delivered a reliable selection of romantic stories (mostly in strip-cartoon form for the slow reader) and pop star pin-ups. Its philosophy revolved around a series of unshakeable tenets: celebrities were dishy, dreamy and unobtainable; the precious reward of a kiss from the boy next door would come to the nice girl who avoided temptation; and girls who dared to express themselves deserved everything they got. The weekly problem page rotated the same urgent issues: how to deal with an annoying younger brother, how to talk to your mother, and most pressing of all, how to handle boys. The male was driven by primeval urges and had to be suppressed and excused; the female was sneaky, manipulative and determined to lead men astray.

Any teenage girl in 1962 would have ingested these messages as gospel truth. 'Men may have their masculinity,' *Boyfriend* informed them, 'but girls have guile.' (This verdict was underlined, to ensure that it could not be missed.) Not only guile: Rita from Romford admitted that she was 'a very well-developed girl for my age' but complained, 'I find that boys try to take advantage of this'. This made her uncomfortable: 'I don't have much time for all this petting non-sense'. Did *Boyfriend*'s counsellors, the fictitious Talbot Twins, con-gratulate her for her common sense? Not at all. Instead, Rita was accused: 'Are you sure you don't give the boys a "glad eye" a bit too much?' Another girl had been less cautious and had succumbed to pressure from a boy: only to find that he dumped her the next day. 'Things might have been quite different if you had kept this boy at bay', the magazine scolded her. The Talbot Twins checked a third girl in the throes of pubescent passion: 'We think that it is a good thing if girls don't feel too violently attracted to their boyfriend.' The celebrity pages offered an unwitting insight into the opposition. One 1962 profile, chilling in retrospect, encapsulated the tactics of a much-admired disc jockey. 'The rights of man, according to Jimmy Savile, are being able to do what you like when you feel like it, and without offering explanations – if you can get away with it. And Jimmy Savile can!' – and did, for almost another half-century.

As the readers of *Boyfriend* passed the age of consent, another com-plication was added to the conundrum of sexual etiquette: 'You've hooked him, but he wants you to go too far: How to Get a Husband', as the *Sunday Pictorial* summarised the dilemma. To offer a solution, the paper turned to the American writer, C.C. Cabot – author of the newly published *How to Find a Husband After Forty*. In that book, he yielded all the power to women: 'a 300-horsepower Cadillac is easily controlled by a 110-pound matron. It's the control that counts.' And this guidance could easily be transferred, he found, to a much younger audience.

First he set up the scenario. 'You have been dating a single man for some time. Gradually, and in an irresistible, gentlemanly manner, he is taking the initiative.' (And they thought the age of chivalry was dead.) 'Even if you would like the experience yourself, you probably feel deep down inside that intercourse out of wedlock would be wrong. So the questions that dash through your mind are: IS this really necessary to win him? WILL he respect me more afterwards – or less? DOES he really intend to marry me, or is he stringing me along?'

The answer, of course, was control: the man had none, the woman had fists full of reins. 'It's up to her to set the pace and offer resistance, if she has limits,' Cabot wrote. 'But if you are not going to yield to his entreaties to join him in bed, don't just sit there and sulk. Give him a real lecture on your monumental respect for the act as a marital rite. Convince him, if you can, that you have stored up ardour and fire that will create a holocaust once you have a marriage certificate in your hot little hand.'

Cabot was prepared to countenance the idea that the woman might agree to the man's demands for pre-marital sex. But that didn't rob her of potential manoeuvres. 'Don't yield cheaply,' he advised. 'Don't be grudging. Cry a little, but also bite his ear. Tell him that he has made you feel like a real woman for the first time. Tell him that this is just what you were created for, and that you have found the ultimate happiness. He may just have wanted to sample the merchandise on a trial-run basis. But if you are smart, you can create such an emotional climate that he will be begging you to become his wife.'

Everything was manipulation, a tweak or tug on the strings that tied the puppet male to his animal quest for sexual relief. For women who felt outnumbered by their predators, the only solution offered by the agony aunts was to 'endure with quiet dignity' the unwanted advances of workmates and their wandering hands: 'Men are natural hunters. Do not over-dramatize your embarrassment. The one who stands outside the herd is usually made to suffer.' Better to be molested and smile than risk being ostracised.

For the man seeking to comprehend his adversary, the guidance supplied by the pulp magazines on the news-stand was ambiguous at best. One month he might read about a 'Sex Cure for Frigid Wives: a new hope for women without passion'; the next, a lecture on the dangers of 'Over-Passionate Women'. Or he might stumble across a guide for the immature man, such as *Woman Confidential* by the American author Lee Mortimer. His prose reeked of total contempt for the female, however she might present herself. All that she wanted, Mortimer insisted, was a man who knew what it was to be a man: 'Many a career woman would gladly chuck it all for a man with guts enough to lift her over his knee and spank her soundly.' Not that such virile specimens could be found amidst a race as puny as the British, whose men 'are, by and large, sexless. Yet they have a massive need for domination by an all-wise mother.' That was why British women ensured that they should 'appear old and scrawny, and act like a man'. Readers of *Tit-Bits* magazine concurred. In response to an article about husbands inflicting corporal punishment on the wives, women admitted that 'It's better than enduring hours and hours of nagging', or 'It's far better to spend three or four minutes across her husband's knee than endure three or four days of a sulky silence'.

Both sexes were hemmed in by cultural expectations; but, as the *Daily Mirror* conceded in a 1963 editorial arguing against the normalisation of pre-marital sex, 'One of the oldest lessons about love outside marriage and couldn't-care-less morals is that it is the woman who always pays.' She faced unwanted pregnancy; the stigma of being labelled as sexually active or aggressive, and at risk of becoming impossible to marry; even, as Oxbridge students discovered, a double standard for students, whereby male students caught *in flagrante* by college staff might be suspended for a couple of weeks, while their female partners would be expelled. Above all else, she might be held responsible for leading other, more impressionable women astray. A forty-seven-year-old, separated from her husband, wrote an anguished letter to an agony aunt in 1961, recounting that other residents on her 'Street of Shame' were criticising her for entertaining 'a man in a similar situation' overnight. Why was it anyone else's business but hers, she asked? The answer spelled out her obligations as a woman: 'Somewhere along the street where Mrs X lives, someone may be stumbling on the brink of a wrong decision. It might be a married man tempted to desert his wife and family for someone else – just as Mrs X was deserted. It could be a young girl all set to go off with someone she cannot marry ... She is openly breaking the rules of her community. In her place, I should face this fact and refuse to pity herself or expect tolerance from her neighbours.'

If, as counsel in a 1961 court case declared, 'Nice girls in their ordinary social behaviour are kind and good', and men anecdotally wanted to marry a nice girl, why did they lust after women who brazenly exposed and exploited their sexuality, and the pleasure it gave them? It was the chasm at the heart of the marital minefield: the time-honoured categorisation of women into two utterly conflicting modes, as Madonna or whore. And if a man dared to marry the latter ...

The dangers, for a man, of cavorting with girls of easy virtue were exhibited to a voracious global audience by the so-called Profumo scandal of 1963, at the end of which a cabinet minister lost his job, an osteopath took his own life, and two young women, one of them the subject of prolonged sexual abuse as a child, achieved notoriety of the kind that condemned them to lifelong disdain and prurient curiosity. But the attention paid to Christine Keeler and Mandy Rice-Davis, the two 'showgirls' in question, overshadowed a more representative case, which spotlighted the corrosive and ultimately fatal power of female eroticism in the Britain of the early 1960s.

On 2 March 1960, the ITV network screened a thirty-minute documentary about the morals of modern youth, entitled *Living for Kicks*. The presenter, Daniel Farson, visited archetypal teenage hangouts across the country. In a Brighton coffee bar, he encountered self-styled beat poet Royston Ellis. Barely nineteen, rakishly bearded, Ellis presented himself as the grand old man of contemporary ethics, and his outspoken comments seeded much criticism in the next day's papers. He was adamant that contemporary young people would, as a matter of course, experiment sexually before they were married, 'as a natural development of their friendship. And I do believe that no teenager will marry a virgin, for the simple reason that before he marries her, he has sex with her.' Farson's voiceover assured viewers of the prevailing moral climate: 'Doctors say that sex before marriage can be dangerous, because of the guilt complex that can be aroused.' And the teenagers in the Brighton club revealed less sexual experience than Ellis had assumed. One boy who looked, at first glance, like every father's nightmare, assured Farson that he would have far more respect for his future wife if she had indeed managed to safeguard her virginity from the likes of him.

Ellis was asked why some adults wanted to prevent their children from attending coffee bars and clubs. 'Maybe they think their daughters are going to meet up with some nasty character', he mused. Certainly, any girl who ventured into the Whisky-a-Go-Go coffee bar in Brighton, where Ellis had been filmed, would quickly have made the acquaintance of a slightly older man who, like the poet, advertised his bohemian lifestyle with those most suspicious of male affectations: a sculpted black beard and pencil moustache. He resembled a more brooding, even satanic version of the contemporary trad jazz star, Acker Bilk, with the easy familiarity and charm to match.

Harvey Leo Holford, born in 1928 in circumstances that remained a lifelong mystery to him, was the owner of the Whisky-a-Go-Go, and also two adult drinking clubs on the same premises: the Calypso, and the Blue Gardenia. 'I saw myself as the King of Brighton,' he explained in 1963, 'the Errol Flynn of the South Coast, a bearded, swashbuckling Casanova and the fastest gun in Britain.' As one of his former managers recalled, 'Everything he did was big. He liked fast cars, and he even bought a £400 cabin cruiser to get closer to his Errol Flynn dream. He was a member of about forty expensive night clubs in London.' To ensure that he stood out among the gamblers, gangsters, alcoholics, Sussex socialites and glamorous young women who flocked to his clubs, Holford cruised around the streets of Brighton in a £4,000 red Pontiac Parisienne – a Canadian convertible that dwarfed the British models it squeezed off the town's narrow central byways. He was, as the *Daily Mirror* recounted, 'a vain romantic who saw himself as the kind of person who might be the hero of a woman's magazine serial'.

To a teenage girl of seventeen, the child of middle-class parents who imagined a respectable future for their daughter, Holford's flamboyance and trappings of success were instantly attractive. Too young to be drinking legally, Christine Hughes was taken to the Blue Gardenia on 23 December 1959, by her boyfriend – who might have been selected by her parents, as he was the son of a banker. But their fledgling relationship dissolved in the shadow of Holford's glamour and pizzazz. The manager and the errant teenager met only briefly that evening, but each carried away an image that proved irresistibly attractive. Holford heard her refined tones and visualised her by his side, lending authentic breeding to his less salubrious background. Christine saw Holford as her ticket to high society, or at least its local facsimile. These twin fantasies would propel them irrevocably towards disaster.

Christine returned to the Blue Gardenia alone, and magnetised Holford with her adolescent beauty and poise. Surely she could not be as perfect as she seemed? Holford set private detectives on her track to check her lineage and reputation. They put her 'entirely in the clear' and assured Holford that she was free from scandal. The couple began to date regularly, and even travelled to Torquay for a weekend where, Holford remembered, 'We stayed together as man and wife'. Christine invited him to meet her parents, perhaps not aware that his beard alone was enough to damn him. But Holford talked up the prestige and social cachet that surrounded his nightclubs, assuring Mr and Mrs Hughes that they were the haunts of actors and aristocrats down from London, rather than petty criminals and starry-eyed teenage girls. Along the way, he suggested that – although he didn't like to boast about his pedigree – he was actually the son of a Belgian count. Financially secure, apparently blue-blooded, he passed the Hughes' examination, and was permitted to court their daughter.

If Christine Hughes envisaged a future with her much older consort, it revolved around night clubs, socialising, and parading through the city in the passenger seat of a Pontiac, the envy of her friends. For Harvey Holford, by contrast, Christine was a treasure to be protected against marauding pirates such as himself. Deeply insecure beneath his gaudy exhibitionism, he saw every man in the Blue Gardenia and the Calypso as a potential rival and guarded his prize fiercely against them. Christine resented his jealousy and mocked his possessiveness; but each represented so vivid a romantic dream to the other that their relationship endured. Holford's infatuation was both intense and complete, leading him (and his ghost-writer) towards the stuff of cheap romantic fiction when he penned a brief memoir: 'She was like a young faun. She was irresistible. Men fell at her feet. Yet she did not seem to recognise her power.'

Nor, as yet, did she apprehend something that would prove to be crucial in determining the course of her short life: the sexual inadequacy of her lover. Holford was acutely aware of what might delicately be described as his shortcomings. 'A secret fear has followed me throughout my life,' he told his amanuensis in 1963, 'casting a shadow over any happiness I found. It has been my desperate insecurity and inability to relax completely with women. All my adult life I had been unable to satisfy women, and since 1950 I had been consulting doctors and specialists about this. Once I was given a course of hypnosis by a Harley Street man.'

Fortunately – or perhaps not, given what would happen – his young partner lacked the sexual experience, or at least the expertise, to recognise his problem. Whether or not Christine was a virgin when their relationship began, she clearly had few realistic expectations about what was supposed to happen when she was in bed with a man, or how she might hope to feel. Teenagers discussed sex, as they always will, but their conversation revolved around rumour and exaggeration rather than detailed anatomical knowledge. Nor was it a subject taught to young men, or women, in Britain's schools – or if it was, it took such a discreet form that pupils were more bewildered than enlightened by what they heard.

Whatever Christine had expected from their intercourse, or Holford had feared, both parties maintained sufficient faith in their union to embark on the traditional way of proving their romantic bond to the outside world. In early July 1960, Holford appeared at the Hughes residence in Saltdean, and demanded their daughter's hand in marriage. Clearly the lustre of Holford's 'aristocratic' ancestry had lost its allure for her parents, as they refused. The discussion became so acrimonious that Mr Hughes summoned the police, to escort both Holford and Christine off the premises. (Christine subsequently threatened legal action against the detectives and WPC involved in the incident.)

With Mr and Mrs Hughes unwilling to sanction their union, the club-owner and the teenage girl were forced to seek a long-established remedy. They decided to elope, Holford packing no fewer than twenty-four shirts and twelve pairs of shoes for their grand adventure. Since the eighteenth century, many English women and men who were aged between sixteen and twenty had fled north to Scotland, where parental consent was not required for them to marry. Gretna Green, just over the Scottish border, had acquired a reputation as a haven for these marital refugees. But in July 1960, Harvey Holford and Christine Hughes ventured further into Scotland in Holford's Pontiac, with his cabin cruiser trailing behind. They set up camp in Jamestown, County of Dumbarton, where the banns for their wedding were heard.

Word of their escapade reached the British press, several of whose dogged reporters tracked the couple down in a hotel on the banks of Loch Lomond. 'Only one thing spoils our dream now,' Christine told them dramatically, 'our parents'. The journalists concocted an 'emotional plea' to Mr and Mrs Hughes on their daughter's behalf. The eighteen-year-old was supposed to have 'begged' them: 'we both fervently pray you will find it in your hearts to come to us with your blessing'. The parents refused to countenance an epic journey to support a wedding they dreaded.

Meanwhile, Holford did his best to persuade public opinion that, however shady his background, he was now a reformed man – no longer the 'playboy and a bit of a bad lad' that he conceded he had been in the past. He announced that the couple would honeymoon in Miami, and while he was there, he would try to divest himself of his Brighton clubs and their sometimes less than salubrious customers. 'Those days are over,' he announced. 'I'm turning my back on the old times.' He even explained laboriously to the press that when he and Christine had travelled north, he had slept in the car, while she had modestly confined herself to the cabin cruiser. Now they would be legally married, in just three days' time.

The publicity had unforeseen consequences, as it alerted Christine's parents to her whereabouts, and allowed them to mount a legal intervention. On the Tuesday morning, as Christine prepared for the ceremony, Mr and Mrs Hughes obtained an injunction to prevent the marriage and have their vulnerable child made a ward of court. The errant couple were forced to return to Brighton, Holford abandoned his plans to sell his stake in his clubs, and Christine once again slept under her parents' roof. Four months later, her mother and father relented, and Christine became Mrs Harvey Holford at Dorset Gardens Methodist Church in Brighton. Why did the Hugheses change their mind? Because soon after their daughter traipsed home from Scotland, she discovered she was pregnant; and the stigma of illegitimate birth outweighed that of an unsatisfactory marriage.

Christine now joined Holford in his flat above his club empire and awaited the birth of their daughter in spring 1961. Both husband and wife soon became disillusioned by the reality of wedded bliss: the drudgery of housework, for a girl who had imagined a life of glamour and sophistication; her constant criticism, for a man who had idealised her as a picture-perfect adornment to a life of financial success and social esteem. As the *Daily Mirror* characterised their relationship, 'Christine had neither the maturity nor the instincts to understand her husband's needs, while Holford still did not appreciate that his wife was only an inexperienced teenager.'

At the heart of the disagreements was their child: both loved her dearly, but neither wanted to take responsibility for raising her. Usually Holford's mother, Celesta, would take care of the baby, but sometimes Christine simply abandoned her for the evening, while Harvey was schmoozing with customers downstairs. On one occasion, the infant swallowed some sleeping pills that Christine had tossed on the floor, prompting an emergency trip to hospital.

Christine's ventures into Brighton night life inevitably brought her into contact with men whom, for an evening at least, she found more enticing than her husband. Sometimes she would stay out for nights at a time, until Holford was able to bribe her to come home, with jewellery or furs. Unfortunately for him, Christine's more expansive sexual experience led her to reassess Harvey's qualities as a husband. A more skilful and manipulative adulteress might have refrained from criticising her husband's inept technique. Instead, Christine reminded Holford of his failings at every possible opportunity. Harvey sought solace with a female friend: sexually, perhaps, though more likely as a brief haven of emotional support. Christine then accused him of having an affair. Through it all, as one of their close acquaintances saw it, 'They adored each other, but at the same time they couldn't help tormenting each other.' Christine used words; Holford admitted later that he had sometimes 'bashed' her with his fists.

Christine's companion and consolation was a slightly younger girl named Valerie, renowned locally for her platinum blonde hair and bubbly personality. She moved into the couple's apartment and assisted with childcare. Holford declared that she was a bad influence on his wife, because the two young women encouraged each other to take advantage of Brighton's exotic opportunities. One of them, a Swiss barman named Vilasar, worked for her husband downstairs. He and Christine embarked on a sexual relationship in the early summer of 1962, which ended when Vilasar – sensing that Holford suspected him – decided to move to Paris.

Not entirely by coincidence, Christine told Holford that their marriage would be much improved if she and Valerie were able to enjoy a brief holiday away from the baby. Harvey clutched at this frailest of straws and agreed to subsidise a lengthy break in France. He handed his wife £280 in cash and told her to phone or mail him if she needed more. It was an open invitation for hedonism, which Christine seized avidly. Valerie subsequently described their itinerary: 'We first went to Paris, and we met Vilasar there. After that, we went to Cannes, where we stayed at the Hotel Albert. I had a single room, and Christine and Vilasar had a double room. We went from there to San Remo, where Vilasar left us. We stayed there about two weeks. Then I went to Nice, and Christine went to Juan-les-Pins.' But that was merely the sketch of a vividly colourful series of encounters and trysts.

There were letters home from Christine, affectionate enough but focused on money rather than her husband and child. 'Last night we met an American girl and her boyfriend and we went to the Cap Gris Nez night club. It was very expensive ... Our money is not going to last long what with all the travelling expenses and hotels ... I just hate to ask you for money so soon, but I never realised how much things cost ... I am fed up with San Remo and want to move, so please send money by express post.' Occasionally she remembered what she had left behind: 'How is our [girl]? Still very beautiful?' But she was more preoccupied by what she needed from Harvey, while assuring him that she was only enjoying herself under sufferance: 'Val and I are sitting on the beach but it is not very hot ... we don't like Italian people very much. None of them speak English.'

What Christine didn't say was more enlightening. Besides Vilasar, whose liaison with Christine was already obvious to her husband, the young Mrs Holford had slept with a medley of men across France: among them a German drummer named Fritz, and an Italian restaurateur called Franco. As Valerie recalled, 'A woman receptionist said that Christine would have to leave if she brought any more boys into the hotel.'

And then there were the English. On the promenade in Cannes, Christine and Valerie had been approached by a forty-nine-year-old Conservative MP. Richard Reader Harris was also the chairman of Rolls Razor Ltd, a washing machine manufacturer whose fortunes had been transformed by the commercial acumen of its thirty-year-old managing director, John Bloom. Harris lunched with the girls, before inviting them to the Palm Beach Casino, where he introduced them to Bloom. From there it was a short ride to Harris's villa on Cap Ferrat, where more alcohol was consumed, and the girls frolicked in the pool. Christine and Bloom then retired to the businessman's bedroom for the night. The next morning, the millionaire and the twenty-year-old mother relocated to Bloom's own residence in the area.

Bloom was newly married, although his wife remained in England. Within two years, his empire would have collapsed, and his name become synonymous with over-ambition. But in 1962 he was go-ahead, dashingly self-confident, and clearly immensely rich. He was also familiar with Harvey Holford, having occasionally drunk in his bars. Christine was blonde, glamorous, and newly aware of what sexual passion could be. Bloom admitted that he had a young family in Britain, but promised to install Christine in her own Cote D'Azur villa, with the trimmings to match. He reeled off a list of consumer luxuries (stable of cars, private plane, sixty-foot yacht), which set Harvey Holford's Pontiac and cabin cruiser in the shade. If life on the Riviera wasn't enough, Bloom also said he would make a flat in Mayfair available to Christine, whenever she cared to travel to London. Understandably, Christine was smitten: this was the cosmopolitan life she had imagined with her husband, expanded to jet set proportions. She was so entranced by the certainty of her future wealth that she told Valerie she would ask Bloom to buy Harvey the house next door to his Brighton clubs, in recognition of all he had done for her.

Meanwhile, Holford was growing increasingly suspicious: his wife was still in France but had stopped asking him for money. To console her husband, Christine sent a postcard to Brighton, promising that she would be home on 3 August. But she didn't arrive. Meanwhile, Valerie had returned to Sussex: little more than a child herself, she was unable to lie convincingly to Holford about what his wife had been doing. Under prolonged questioning, she admitted that she had seen Christine cavorting with several men, but that these meetings were transitory compared to her new involvement with John Bloom. Holford knew the name instantly, and dragged Valerie to a solicitor, so that she could swear an admission that Christine had committed adultery.

Not that Harvey Holford had given up hope of a reconciliation. On 11 August, he flew to Cannes, determined to sweep his wife off her feet with an extravagant romantic gesture. Christine admitted her affair with Bloom, but – her moods as varied as the company she kept – agreed to Holford's suggestion that the two of them should travel to Majorca and rebuild their marriage. No sooner did they arrive on the island than they began to argue ferociously, and within hours they were on another flight back to London.

In Brighton, it was impossible to conceal the rift in their relationship. 'Christine was playing Mr Holford up,' one of his employees recalled. 'She would be dancing and twisting with all the men in the club bars and talking to them.' Holford would sit sullenly over a drink in the corner of the club, his eyes not leaving Christine for a second.

Back in their flat, they would talk. Valerie recalled that, while they were still in France, Christine was constantly comparing John Bloom's sexual technique with that of her husband. Now she teased Holford about his inadequacies. He responded by maligning her morals: 'I told her she would be nothing but a high-class prostitute. I said, "How can you think about it?" I asked her how she could possibly be happy as a kept woman. I told her that prostitutes were always notoriously unhappy women.' Marilyn Monroe had killed herself, or so it seemed, a few days earlier, and Holford warned Christine she faced the same fate. Another actress, Pat Marlowe, had also taken her life, apparently swayed by Monroe's death. Holford continued: 'I told her that they were two women who had everything in the world, but they were not happy. They had everything that money could buy, but they did not have happiness.' Then his temper flared as he told her: 'You would be like a diseased woman waiting in a room for [Bloom] to use you.' As he recounted later, 'When she came back from France, she could think of nothing else but money. She was a marvellous girl, that wife, until she met Bloom. That is what did it. *He* did it. Bloom.'

On 13 August, Christine wrote a letter to a friend that laid bare her feelings for Bloom – and for Holford. 'I still have not decided what to do,' she began, 'as John is constantly in my mind. I am writing him this evening to see what he says. I have said to Harvey that I will not live in England, and I will wait for him in Cannes, but he won't let me out of his sight for one moment. I have explained about John, not mentioning his name of course, and what I feel for him, and Harvey [is] madly jealous. I just can't believe that anybody should go so mad over me, darling. Harvey said I would be nothing but a high-class "P" and that I would not be able to live with myself. It is very difficult. My feelings for Harvey are nil, gone, finished, kaput at the moment.'

Amidst this turmoil, Christine was forced to concede the toll that her trip to France had taken on her daughter: '[She] does not know me anymore'.

The following evening, after another day of bickering and taunts, Harvey Holford 'hit her', as he admitted. According to his account, Christine respected his anger, and told him: 'I am glad you did that. I wanted you to show me you are a man, not a mouse.' But that didn't chime with the evidence of a local doctor, who had received a call from Holford saying that she must come immediately, because his wife was in trouble. 'For God's sake help her', he said when the doctor arrived. Dr Myers said she 'found her in bed. Her night clothes were blood-stained. She was in a state of terrific hysteria, and her face was swollen beyond recognition.' Her body was also covered in bruises that matched the impact of a clenched fist. Holford was slumped on the floor in front of his wife, begging for her forgiveness. 'We had a bit of a row,' he told the doctor, 'but there will be a reconciliation.' Myers checked Christine over for serious injuries, and left a prescription of sedatives for Holford, who was complaining that he was at his wits' end.

After the doctor left, Christine lapsed into sleep, while Holford watched over her – and brooded. Like a monomaniac, his thoughts returned endlessly to his wife, waiting in Bloom's flat for her lover to return. 'I thought of him coming in and using her,' he remembered. 'Then I thought of what it would do to her when he finally got tired of her and told her to go. I knew what it would do. It would destroy her. She was too good for that. I was desperate. I had to do something.' He searched out a pair of large kitchen scissors, and while Christine lay on the bed, he cut off huge clumps of her hair, so that Bloom would no longer want her. 'I knew I might lose her,' he said later, 'but I thought it would give her time to think and come to her senses.' To his friends, Holford was more candid: he was simply copying what he believed they did in East Germany to a loose woman, which was to make her so unattractive that she would be unable to return to her indecent trade. 'I have probably done the wrong thing,' he told his coffee bar manager, Thomas Williams. 'I have cut all her hair off. But I have to assert a bit of manliness over her and keep her indoors for at least three months.'

The next morning, there was another bout of hysteria when Christine awoke and realised what Holford had done. She shrieked for her parents, and Harvey duly phoned Mr Hughes in Saltdean. 'Christine nearly lost her life,' he told his father-in-law. 'It's not entirely her fault. I have been unfaithful to her. I sent her to France with a girl called Valerie.' Then he mumbled something about a prostitute and a whore, leaving Hughes uncertain exactly what Holford meant. Christine had been estranged from her parents, but Hughes demanded that Harvey should drive her home immediately. 'When Christine arrived,' her father said, 'she ran out of the car. Her hair was slashed, her eyes bruised, her nose damaged, her lips swollen. There were red marks on her neck. I took photographs of her in that condition. She stayed with us that night and the next night. Later, I made a down-payment on a wig for her.' Her father called another doctor, who documented the girl's condition: 'she had both eyes blacked, her face was swollen and bruised, and her hair cut short. Marks on her body suggested that she had been held by the hands around the neck. She was so badly and markedly swollen around the face that I could not see what the matter was with her nose. She later drew my attention to the fact that her nose was no longer straight and asked me if any-thing could be done about this.' Nobody thought to contact the police; it was a husband's right to keep his wife in check.

There followed a mysterious month of mixed signals and mutual fantasy. Christine Holford continued to dream of her new life with John Bloom, but made no attempt to connect with her millionaire lover – apparently deciding to wait until her hair, and her beauty, had been restored. Harvey Holford interpreted this as proof that she had opted for the safety of marriage over the precarious status of being a kept woman. But Christine did not show any signs of remorse: instead, she flaunted herself around Brighton's night spots in her new, auburn wig, and was a familiar sight in the yellow car that Harvey had bought her as an apology. Meanwhile, she taunted her husband, pushing time and again at the same tender spots: Bloom's wealth, her erotic ecstasy with all her French lovers, Harvey's inability to satisfy any woman with his lacklustre equipment. 'Day after day it kept building up inside of me,' Harvey would recall. 'Every bloody day. Every stinking, rotten day, she kept mentioning Bloom, Vilasar and the others. She was back with me, but she might as well have not been there. She had completely changed. She was like a stranger. It was like a Jekyll and Hyde.' Yet her friends would inform the *Daily*

Herald: 'she still saw Holford nearly every day, wining and dining and swimming together.'

One of Holford's club managers remembered that Harvey was so desperate to impress his wife, to shock her into loving him and him only, that he proposed staging a car crash in which he would be seriously injured, so that she could nurse him back to health. Another said he asked Holford what he would do if Christine left him. 'I will probably kill myself,' Harvey replied. 'Or I will sell the club and get out of the town.' On occasions, Holford would mutter that if he could not have Christine, then he would make sure that nobody else would. He talked of launching a court case against Bloom for his interference in their marriage, but was talked out of it by his wife. Meanwhile, he had embarked on renovation work in their apartment, 'building a palace for my princess'.

This was no fairy tale, however. Christine was prepared to let Holford make love to her but, as he recalled, 'She seemed to become cold, frigid. She told me I did not satisfy her anymore. I just felt like something that had crawled from under a rock.' And still the taunts continued. As a contemporary account of their final weeks together concluded, 'Christine's mistake was that she was not old enough or experienced enough to know when to stop. She did not realise that to taunt a man like Holford was to invite violence. Harvey cracked.'

Their long summer of unhappiness climaxed on Friday 14 September 1962. It was, they thought, a day like any other: arguments, accusations, and then a flurry of socialising to demonstrate to the denizens of Brighton's night life that their marriage was perfectly normal. After a month in which she had officially been living with her parents, Christine had apparently agreed to move back into the apartment over Holford's clubs. But Harvey's friend Dennis Slade, who met him for a drink in the Regent Ballroom, a few paces away from the Blue Gardenia, realised that Holford had sunk into an almost catatonic state. 'My words were just going straight through him,' he recalled. 'It was shocking. His eyes were staring. He was miles away.'

Harvey Holford had just read a letter from his wife, which she had written the previous night. 'Dear Harvey,' Christine wrote, 'I am going away from Brighton, and you. Sorry. It is impossible to get on at Queen's Square. Every time I go there, something inside me makes me feel very nasty towards you. I cannot go on.

'It is silly to torture each other like this, so I have made the decision, Harvey. I will always keep in touch with you. I feel so sad and lonely sitting here. I am at the crossroads and don't know where to turn. I cannot talk to my father. But I am frightened that, as the years go on, once a man has hit a woman you can throw everything back in my face and do it again.'

There was a poignant postscript: 'Give all my love to my baby. I never before felt the way I feel tonight. I wanted so much for us in the beginning, and I feel certain we could have had it if it had not been for bad manners on both sides. We could have succeeded.'

Somehow, the couple pulled themselves together the following day, and put on a final show. They donned their finery for a press ball that evening at Hove Town Hall. There they had what Holford called 'a ruck', though it was nothing out of the ordinary. Then they walked down the road to the Hove Club for a quick drink, where Holford briefly made his excuses to Christine. While she demonstrated her charisma on the dance floor, with a willing horde of admirers, he made a discreet phone call to his doctor. 'What were those tablets?', Harvey asked him, referring to the prescription he had been given a month earlier. 'Seconal', the doctor replied. His patient revealed that he had taken two of the pills and was suddenly feeling dizzy. Then he startled the doctor by asking: 'Would six kill me?' The doctor's response was curt and bad-tempered: 'What the hell are you talking about, Harvey? Don't be a damned fool.' Holford apologised and promised that he would not take any more. Then he rejoined his wife and drove her back to the Queen's Square apartment.

They arrived home around 11.30 pm, and about half an hour later, Holford made a brief tour of his various premises. He told the coffee bar manager that he was about to have 'a conference' upstairs and should not be disturbed. The message was relayed to the Holfords' young live-in nanny, Anthea Harris, who had been brought back by her boyfriend at midnight, as promised. Satisfied that her services weren't required that night, Anthea and her partner settled down in one of Holford's clubs for the next couple of hours. It was 2.30 am before she finally climbed the stairs to the apartment, listened carefully at the door to make sure she was not interrupting an important meeting, and stepped inside. The kitchen light was on; on the draining board, she could see Christine's auburn wig – and a trail of what appeared to be blood dripping down into the sink. She admitted later to being scared, and to edging her way towards the Holfords' bedroom; but hearing nothing, she was too frightened to go inside, so instead she returned to her own room, and went to sleep.

Around 3.30 am, Harvey Holford's mother, Celesta, completed her chores in the Blue Gardenia, shepherding the final drinkers outside, and securing the premises against burglars. She left the manager downstairs, where he was checking the takings. Then she too mounted the stairs to the flat and entered the kitchen. There she saw the wig and realised that it was soaked in blood. Less timid than Harris, she knocked several times at the bedroom door, and called out to her son; but there was no reply. She called the manager to help her, and when he too failed to solicit a word from his boss or his wife, he suggested that they should phone the police.

It was PC Terence Sullivan who arrived at the scene, and first stepped into the bedroom. The room was in darkness, and when he shone his torch across the bed, the occupants appeared to be asleep, the woman cradled in the man's right arm. As he moved closer, he saw that her face was distorted and crushed, as if she had been beaten with a heavy object. She was obviously dead, still clad in the silk blouse and black matador pants she had worn to the ball; the man, dressed only in his vest, was breathing, but appeared to be unconscious.

'Gun Riddle Death of "Runaway" Wife: Police vigil at "playboy" husband's bed', announced the first press coverage of the story. Sussex Police revealed that they had discovered a revolver and an empty box of tablets beside the bed, and that Harvey Holford, the 'self-styled playboy', was in a coma, having presumably taken an overdose. Christine had not been bludgeoned but had been shot several times at close range. An autopsy revealed the distribution of wounds: at least two bullets to her back, another into her jaw from the front, and a final, decisive pair, delivered from point-blank range: one to the right temple, the other to the left ear. The firing had been comprehensive, and highly calculated, designed not just to kill but to obliterate her beauty – just as he had attempted before.

Holford's mother was quoted as saying, 'I'll be a mother to [the baby] now', the girl having been found unharmed in another room. Her only comment on her dead daughter-in-law: 'Harvey was madly in love with Christine. She could twist him around her finger.' An anonymous 'friend' rattled the skeleton of the Riviera affair, but concluded: 'I think she was just trying to make him jealous.' The incident was still officially classed as a mystery, pending Harvey Holford's recovering consciousness. The customary 'team of doctors' was said to be fighting to save his life.

With their prime witness unable to testify, detectives sought clues from those on the periphery of the scene, and soon fastened upon Christine's friend Valerie, who was to become a minor celebrity while the case was under discussion. Two British seamen who had been at the Blue Gardenia that night, and then embarked for Rotterdam on the tanker *Vitrine*, were interviewed by Dutch police, but dismissed as suspects. Then, almost exactly three days after his wife had died, Holford emerged from his coma, and began to speak to the Detective Superintendent waiting by his bedside.

Resentfully, his mind wandering as if in the grips of a terrible obsession, Holford rambled through a lengthy monologue that was part self-justification, part self-pity, with a spice of braggadocio to round it off. He grunted his admission that he had murdered his wife, but as yet provided no details. Why had he taken sleeping pills? 'They didn't bloody work, anyway,' Holford snapped. 'I took them, yes.' Why had he killed his wife? 'If you can't guess now, you never will, will you? No particular reason, just a lot of things put together. When a thing goes on and on, you know it goes on and on, doesn't it, it goes on in your mind. Well, have you got it? That build-up, build-up? There comes a time when you just can't take it anymore. It might happen to you. There was nothing on that night. We had an enjoyable time, in fact.'

The detective let him pause, and drift into random phrases that, as yet, made no sense: 'What happens to me? What chance have I got? Do you know what happened over there? You know what happened to Rolls-Royce? [Holford was referring to Bloom's company, Rolls Razor.] What could happen to me? How long for? You cannot get killed [executed] unless it is a robbery. What do you think I might get?' He was officially cautioned, with the customary warning about the evidentiary status of his statements. 'I will make a statement,' Holford resumed bitterly. 'The greatest you have ever heard. This will be the greatest case you have ever heard. Write it down. Good idea.'

Twelve hours later, the Detective Superintendent returned, and advised Holford that he would be charged with murder. 'What can I say?', Holford retorted. 'I shall take my medicine.' Then he dictated a brief account of Christine's infatuation with John Bloom, her compulsive interest in money, and all his attempts to set her straight: 'I tried to show her the error of her ways. I told her that people of that type are only interested in one thing, but it did not make any difference at all. I took her out, night after night, but it didn't make any difference. All she thought about was money.'

At last, he turned to the killing itself, and how it had been triggered when Christine had once again hit upon the points that wounded him most: her passion for Bloom and her other lovers, his pathetic failure as a man. 'When we came home, she mentioned it again.' He omitted any word of her letter, announcing that their relationship was over. 'It was not Vilasar so much as that bastard Bloom and money again. I could not stand it, so I got my revolver from the top cupboard in the kitchen and shot her. It was like a dream. How many times I shot her, I don't know. I have always been a gun fiend. She dropped on the floor, so I carried her up to the bedroom. I laid her on the bed. I wanted to die. I went down to the kitchen and took all the pills in a cabinet. Then I went back to bed and cuddled her.' Finally, there was a note of remorse: 'I now regret I should have done this to the one I love. I will never forget this so long as I live.' And the first hint of a legal defence: 'I was not myself. I was someone else. I had been through hell for two months. I was not myself when I did it.' The Superintendent gave him the statement to check, and as Holford handed it back, he muttered 'And all for a fucking yid' – an anti-Semitic reference to Bloom which was duly added to the record.

Minutes later, he was taken from hospital to the small court in Brighton Town Hall, where proceedings of capital murder – in other words, worthy of the death penalty – were laid against him. Holford was still barely conscious, and there was a heart-breaking scene as his seventy-four-year-old mother sobbed hysterically and grabbed at her son's hands. 'Don't worry, Mum', he whispered as he was dragged away. But asked to plead guilty or not guilty, he remained silent. Then he was taken away, to await trial at Brixton Prison in South London.

A month later, as Holford and his lawyer prepared for the initial magistrates' hearing, to determine whether his case should go to a full trial, the accused man chose to focus instead on his grudge against

Bloom. The particulars were kept secret from the public, but Holford had launched a private case against the millionaire businessman, alleging that Bloom had deliberately enticed his wife away from him. Bloom was cornered by the press at Paddington Station, where his £9,000 Rolls-Royce (registration number JB 111) was waiting to collect him. He refused to discuss Christine or their relationship – his last word on this subject for the next eight years.

Bloom was not among the parade of witnesses who attended the four days of proceedings, at the end of which Holford was told he would be tried at Sussex Assizes in early December. He did not speak or show emotion as the dregs and tatters of his private life were exposed to the outside world; though he wept, finally, when the magistrates were shown the clothes that Christine had been wearing when she was shot.

Two days before his trial, Harvey Holford was once again unconscious in a hospital – this time in Lewes Prison. He had been visited by his solicitor and was being escorted from his jail cell for his afternoon exercise. He managed to pull himself away from the warder, mounted stairs to an upper floor, and threw himself over the balcony, in another apparent suicide attempt – only for his fall to be broken by protective netting, from which he bounced and landed on top of an unfortunate prison officer. The trial was postponed for a further three months – during which time his wife was buried in a private ceremony in Brighton. Holford was barred from attending, but asked for a dozen red roses to be sent to the graveside.

On 21 March 1963, a full six months after the murder, Harvey Holford took his place at the Sussex Assizes. Almost every previous report on his case had referred, usually as a primary description of the accused, to his beard, as if it were a mark of Cain. His solicitor advised him to remove the offending hair before the trial began, so as not to prejudice the jury against him. When he testified, he described for the first time the conversation that had provoked his lethal assault on his wife. He sobbed openly as he recounted the way in which she continually harped on her relationship with Bloom, in a manner that led him to believe that she must have seen her lover since her return to England. 'You can't fight a millionaire and an MP [Reader Harris]', she apparently told him. 'You're getting out of your class, little man.' Holford retorted: 'And so are you. You couldn't have lived that life.

You would have been like an animal. He would soon have got tired of you.' 'I know he would not,' Christine told him. 'He wants me more than ever now. He has told me so. He could buy and sell you a million times over.'

'Then I thought of [our daughter],' he explained to the court. 'She seemed the only hope I had of keeping Christine. I told Christine that even a slut would not leave her baby, and said, "What shall I tell her when she is older, that her mother is a whore?"' Christine spat back at him: 'I am a whore, am I? I will tell you something. I was going to John, if you had not cut my hair. Well, my hair is all right now, and I am going to him.' Holford said that he broke down in tears at this, and Christine mocked him: 'You can stop crying about [the baby], because she is not yours.'

This, he explained, was the moment when his mind split open: 'I felt something go. I snatched a gun out of the cupboard and shot her.' What were you aiming at, he was asked? 'At her. All I could hear was her voice. I just fired at her. I don't know how many times I fired.' Then, as Christine's body lay on the floor, he shook her, to make sure she was dead; before retrieving his sleeping tablets from the bedside table. 'I told her I was coming', he explained, as women in the courtroom wailed and sobbed. 'All I wanted to do then was cuddle her. I wanted to die cuddling her.' But first, he conceded, he had cleaned up some of her blood from the floor, moved her gore-soaked wig to the kitchen sink, and then carried her body into the bed.

It was a clear admission of murder: under duress, of course, and provoked, or so he said, by the jibes (justified or otherwise) about the parentage of his daughter. The prosecution might have chosen to exploit some of the testimony elicited at the first set of hearings: the mysterious phone call to his doctor earlier on the night of the killing, as if he already knew that he would need to take an overdose; the instructions that nobody should enter the flat, because he was 'in conference'. Both could easily have been offered as evidence of pre-meditation. But the entire tenor of the trial was jolted and reoriented by a passage of testimony from another witness: his mother, Celesta Holford. She repeated her account of her movements and actions on the night her daughter-in-law had died, adding nothing to the existing knowledge of the case. But then her son's QC embarked on a line of questioning that shocked everyone in the court.

Having established that his mother had raised Harvey alone, and was unable to state the identity of his father, the defence barrister asked her: 'When he was ten or eleven, there were sexual relations? Intercourse?' Mrs Holford stared at him in horror. 'I wish I had not to ask you this,' he continued, 'but there was such a relationship between you and him, was there not?' 'I don't know what you mean by that,' Mrs Holford replied. The QC repeated the question, and again, and the beleaguered witness tried to pretend that she did not know what he meant by 'sexual intercourse'. Eventually she was forced to concede that she did, after all, understand the question.

The barrister tried again: 'You know, as a matter of truth, that at the age of ten or eleven, this boy had such intercourse?' Her son was openly weeping now, as Mrs Holford replied: 'I cannot remember that.' 'May it have happened?' the QC continued. 'Did it happen with you?' Mrs Holford feigned confusion, twisting her black gloves in her hands like Lady Macbeth rubbing away Duncan's blood: 'Who? My son? I cannot remember that.' Then she thought she glimpsed an escape route: 'He did sleep with me as a boy.'

At this point the exasperated judge felt himself forced to intervene. 'That is a thing you must remember, surely, one way or the other.' He repeated the question slowly and with great emphasis: 'Did you allow him to have intercourse with you?' Mrs Holford was cowed: 'Perhaps he did,' she muttered. 'I don't know.' The judge moved in for the kill: 'You *do* know, don't you? You surely know.' He was met only by silence. With a sigh, the judge signalled Holford's QC to continue. There was one final question: did Mrs Holford remember an occasion when her son was about eleven, and she told him that girls were dirty? More silence.

Over the days that followed, Harvey Holford was dragged painfully through all the sordid details of the case: his jealousy, Christine's provocation, Bloom's promises, his own inadequacy. At every opportunity, his QC intervened to highlight his client's precarious state of mind. Finally, Holford himself had the opportunity to speak on that subject, and recalled a doctor once telling him that he was a psychopath. He also revealed that he had sought medical advice about his sexual difficulties, but the GP had shown no interest in his 'constant complaints'.

There could be no defence against the evidence of the shooting: Holford had admitted the crime, after all. What remained was for his barrister to suggest mitigating circumstances, and he found them in two psychologists who had examined the accused since his imprisonment. One of them recounted that Holford had told him about his incestuous relations with his mother, and about the fact that rooms in their home had been rented to Canadian soldiers, who brought in girls for the night. Holford had claimed that he often took these women their breakfasts, and from the age of thirteen onwards he had sex with some of them.

There were two further medical witnesses. When a psychiatrist took to the witness box, the judge seemed to imagine that he was now acting for the defence. He posed the learned doctor the most slanted of questions: 'Here is a man suffering from certain sexual difficulties, married to a young and attractive girl who goes off to France and, if the evidence is acceptable, runs completely off the rails when she gets there. She taunted him with his lack of sexual powers compared with this man John Bloom. Then she challenges him to show her what a good man he is in that respect – and he failed. So much so, in fact, that he had to go to his doctor. What is the cumulative effect of all these things on his mind?' He was effectively begging the witness to provide an excuse for the shooting. But Dr John Batt refused to be influenced by the judge's rhetoric: 'On almost anybody, it is bound to produce considerable anxiety and a great deal of worry. I do not think it would of necessity produce a pathological process.' The chief medical officer from Brixton Prison was more helpful to the defence, suggesting that Holford's 'prolonged medical stress' and heavy use of alcohol would 'induce an abnormality of mind that would impair his mental responsibility'.

And that now cut to the crux of the case. What was at issue was not death or its cause, but the delicate ego and sexual self-confidence of a man who was being taunted by his wife. Here Holford's QC was in his rhetorical element: 'This man was not an angel. It would be an angel that could repose in the heavens who could continue angelic after intercourse with prostitutes at the age of fourteen or fifteen. Then there entered into this man's life a girl of such astonishing beauty to him that he became clearly affected from that moment onwards. That girl, five foot two and a half, with glorious tresses, most attractive face and figure, became an obsession. This is not a passing desire for a body, but a case of a man who sold himself body and soul to the desires and whims of that girl.' Holford was powerless, the plaything of Christine's vicious sexual appeal and his unstoppable hormonal urges. Then, to make his life unbearable and his actions impossible to control, Christine had strayed from her marital vows, and tossed herself into 'the realms of love, lust and luxury'. Holford had been 'battered by these breakers – Franco, Bloom, Vilasar and Fritz the drummer. What more could he stand?'

Broken, crushed, psychologically destroyed by the torments of this savagely beautiful young woman and her heartless behaviour, Holford had been faced with one last ordeal: the agony of hearing Christine deny that he was the father of their child. She was, the QC suggested, almost asking to be murdered. 'Would something have broken in your brainboxes then, members of the jury? If those words are not provocation, members of the jury, you may say the courts have never heard what provocation is. It is a mystery none of us will ever be able to solve, the innermost feelings of a female in a situation of that sort. We shall never be able to understand the numbness that hits a man who has been exposed to the forces we have touched upon in the course of this trial.'

The judge picked up the theme, reminding the jury that they could find Holford guilty of murder; or of the lesser crime of manslaughter, either on the grounds of diminished responsibility (if he had been mentally disturbed) or provocation (if his wife had driven him to the crime). The law as it stood in 1963 was virtually a licence to commit murder, and plead guilty to manslaughter; and what worse provocation could be imagined than for a man to have his sexual prowess slighted by a beautiful woman with 'glorious tresses'?

It was no surprise that after a brief deliberation, the jury returned to find Holford innocent of murder, despite the evidence that the crime had been planned; and guilty of manslaughter, with every excuse of mitigation available. They also asked the judge to pronounce a lenient sentence. The public gallery was packed with women, who applauded and shouted their approval that the man who had killed his wife would not face the death penalty or life imprisonment.

Once more the judge was in his oratorical element. 'What happens', he asked the court, 'when the wife of his bosom' – the wife he owned, he might as well have said – 'goes out of her way first to mock his sexual capacity and then to tell him the child he believed was his, was not his after all? Do you think there is a reasonable man in the world who would not feel the whole of his life had been knocked out?' He acknowledged that 'there must have been few men indeed who have been subjected to greater provocation than you were', and that Holford had also suffered from knowing that his beloved wife had died by his own hand. Then, just for a moment, he remembered the victim: 'a human life was forfeited, and that human life was taken as a result of the prolonged firing of that gun'. With that brief acknowledgement that a woman had died, the judge passed to his ultimate assessment of how much that life was worth. On 29 March 1963, he gave Harvey Holford a three-year sentence. Ten days before Christmas 1964, the parole board ruled that he had paid the price for his crime, and his time in prison was over.

His notoriety, and the public interest in the crime, ensured that there was a market for his 'memoirs' – two brief articles in the *Daily Mirror*, published the week after his conviction. In these articles, which did not for a second read as if Holford had penned them himself, he acknowledged his crime, but cast himself as a doomed, romantic figure – a pose designed to tug at the emotions of those who had applauded him in court. He recounted his 'indescribable agony' at 'destroying the only thing in life that meant anything to me'. Christine was described as if she had been struck down by a random twist of fate and was now waiting loyally for him in heaven: 'Her poor, sweet body may be dead, but her soul is alive, and I know that I will eventually be with her, when I will see her in all her perfection, as she was.' And he painted their marriage in such rhapsodic terms that a romantic novelist might have been moved to envy: 'We had the most wonderful union that any man and woman can ever have. In the few years we had together, I think we were blessed with a love that only comes to a few people. I have known more love than many people experience in a lifetime.'

After such ecstatic heights, what followed was bathos. Soon after his release from jail, Holford inaugurated the legal process whereby he might change his name, to Robert Keith Beaumont. He remained in the town where he had killed Christine, and in 1974 he quite deliberately brought attention upon himself with a series of very public gestures. 'I cannot hide my past,' he declared, 'and I do not want people to think I am trying to hide anything.' He was appointed secretary of the memorial fund for Maria Colwell, the seven-year-old Brighton girl who was murdered by her stepfather. He also mounted a substantial publicity campaign, demanding that those who killed a child should automatically receive a death sentence. (He remained silent on the subject of those who shot their wives.) At both General Elections in 1974, he stood as a parliamentary candidate: first as an Independent Nationalist, and then as a member of the English Nationalist Party, which would soon be joined by another notorious figure of the time, the disgraced MP John Stonehouse. Holford/Beaumont died of leukaemia in 2006. John Bloom's washing machine business collapsed in spectacular fashion while Holford was in jail; he ran a London restaurant for a while, before emigrating to the USA and then Spain, where he died in 2019. He never publicly acknowledged a sexual relationship with Christine Holford, claiming in his memoirs that he had only met her on two occasions, and had barely spoken to her.

The ruinous affair of Harvey and Christine Holford was emblematic of its time: an era when cocky entrepreneurs could become celebrities, however fleeting; when young girls could fly to the Mediterranean on holiday; when the availability of the pill for married women enabled them to escape the constant threat of becoming pregnant, whether they were sleeping with Franco, Bloom, Vilasar or Fritz; when the national press was prepared to print salacious details of sexual relationships, while retaining a practised attitude of shock and horror; when a young woman could dare to advertise her pleasure in sex, and could be murdered for the crime of being seen to relish it; when a man could kill his wife because she committed adultery, and win applause from the public gallery.

Many of these factors also came into play in the furore surrounding Christine Keeler and Mandy Rice-Davis, John Profumo and Stephen Ward, which supplanted the sorry tale of Christine Holford in London's papers during 1963. But away from these headlines, young women continued to take the blame for the misdeeds and prejudice of others. As a 1965 letter in the *Daily Mirror* complained, 'Some females sicken me. It is because so much of their bodies is exposed that there is so much sex crime today.' (The correspondent was a woman.) Or, as a twenty-four-year-old lamented a few months later: 'Obviously I don't go round telling everyone that I've been raped. A lot of people seem to think it's impossible for a girl to be raped. You know, you often hear people say, particularly women, that a man simply couldn't do it if the women point-blank refused to let him. They always seem to end up saying, "Oh well, she probably asked for it".'

And still the court testimony continued. There was the forty-six-year-old civil servant from Chiswick who installed a peephole and a two-way mirror in the accommodation he rented to young girls, ostensibly so that he could check that they hadn't been overcome by gas fumes in the bath. He was bound over to keep the peace for a year and otherwise not punished. Or the seventeen-year-old girl in Surrey who was 'seduced' by a man and became pregnant: her father was awarded £278 damages for loss of her 'services'. (Quite what those services entailed, one shudders to think.) Or the short-statured man (just 5'2"), who admitted a series of indecent assaults on taller women, 'to prove my virility'. His fate? To be scolded by a judge and told that he should focus his attentions on shorter girls in future. Through it all, one thing was constant: the woman always paid, one way or another.

Interlude: The Sweet Life

Julie Molley was the 'high priestess of the Sweet Life' in the Thames corridor towns of Reading, Taplow and Maidenhead. She was a 'big-time blackmailer' with power over 'a secret circle of sex perverts'. She was a 'drug addict' who specialised in 'some form of sexual irregularity'. She was an 'evil spirit' and a 'wretched strumpet' who 'smelled of vice and misfortune to anyone concerned with her'. And she died of an overdose of drugs in November 1963, which was ruled a suicide by the coroner, but murder by her anonymous friends. In her absence, former lovers, lawyers and reporters were able to call her anything they chose – because, it was assumed, she was a prostitute.

Her calling card was small ads in *Exchange and Mart* or a national newspaper, in which she was apparently offering a smart raincoat for sale. This was code – understood by the cognoscenti – for sexual services. The passing of the Street Offences Act in August 1959 made such subterfuge necessary for any woman who wished, or was compelled, to offer her body to paying customers. Advertisements would be placed in newsagents' windows, offering tuition in various subjects (French lessons were a particular favourite); inviting bids for a 'large chest'; or volunteering to act as a photographic model. Or they might rely on introductions: 'They are distributing their telephone numbers through street touts, unscrupulous hotel doormen, waiters and drinking clubs', one exposé revealed.

In the immediate aftermath of the Act, prospective customers could also view their wares in *The Ladies' Directory*, a small, glossy publication filled with pin-up photographs and classified ads for 'models' and 'call girls'. Occasionally, the women in the pictures were actually available for hire; more often, the publisher simply used photos of unknown actresses. Barbara, as an example, 'offers special services in Correction,

Restriction, Rubberwear, Wigs and Corsets'. (Julie Molley's favourite topics of conversation were said by one client to have been 'sexual deviation, make-up, fashion, the theatre, and mental aberrations in general'. Truly all human life was there.) If Barbara didn't appeal, there were also contact details (addresses and phone numbers) for Miss Fetishe, 43-25-37; Mistress in Satin; Young Coffee Coloured Model; the predictable French Madam; the 'petite' Miss Kane; and the perennial Miss Wyplash, who sold herself as an 'Ex-Governess' (*very* strict, in other words). All were aged between nineteen and twenty-four, or so they claimed.

In November 1959, there was the first of a series of court cases, which would eventually bring *The Ladies Directory* down, and lead to the imprisonment of its publisher, Fred Shaw. Initially, he argued that he was helping to protect the women in his magazine: 'For ten shillings [50p] a week, the girls can advertise in my directory. This means that they can be free of pimps and ponces who batten on them.' Having admitted that the women he publicised were prostitutes, he then tried to deny to the *News of the World* that he had ever imagined anything of the sort. Meanwhile, 'a lovely 23-year-old model and television starlet' (strictly legit) emerged, 'red-eyed with weeping' according to the *Sunday Pictorial*, to complain that Shaw had used her picture without her knowledge. 'This is a diabolical outrage,' she sobbed. 'It could ruin my career.' At his trial on charges of living off immoral earnings, Shaw came partially clean: 'I know it is a legal wrangle, but I advertise the girls as models. What they do in their spare time is no concern of mine.'

Models, call girls, actresses, escorts: every young woman who dabbled in these trades was assumed by the media, and the public in turn, to be involved in one form of prostitution or another. The Profumo scandal of 1963 highlighted the many ways in which richer, older men could collide with enticing female company, a trade-off that was seen as entirely to be expected unless it led to the courts, in which case it was always the sophisticated siren who had led the naïve aristocrat (or minister of the crown) astray. Christine Keeler, the twenty-one-year-old hub of the media frenzy, was forced to testify in her own moral defence: 'I am not a prostitute. I never have been.' Journalists salivated over her 'incredible catalogue of sexual enterprises', and her 'voluptuous lips', 'heavily blackened lashes' and 'faintly arrogant glare', all of which spelled prostitution to their salacious eyes.

If Julie Molley had flourished in Soho rather than Reading, she might have been standing alongside Keeler and Mandy Rice-Davis. Instead, her 'over-sexuality' was catalogued in the coroner's court, and then forgotten. So too were Gwyneth Rees, aged twenty-three; Irene Lockwood, twenty-nine; Hannah Tailford, thirty ... some of the victims of a London sex murderer dubbed by the press (with obvious relish) Jack The Stripper. He was never caught, and although criminologists have continued to unearth possible solutions to the mystery of the so-called 'Hammersmith nude murders', the women were almost irrelevant to their search – because, after all, they were only prostitutes.

4 Mrs Smallgood and Mr Clean

Mrs Anstey was the President and Principal Patron of the Society for the Abolition of Stage Nudity. She was also – pause for a snigger – the owner of a crumpet factory. When an audacious young advertising man dared to sell Mrs Anstey's crumpets via state-of-the-art techniques (i.e. pictures of young women in swimsuits), the rich, eccentric and decidedly fusty old woman was understandably outraged.

Mrs Felicity Smallgood was, according to the BBC, 'determined', 'doctrinaire' and 'completely sincere, but has the disadvantage of possessing a veritable hive of bees in her bonnet'. She was the do-gooder busybody let loose amongst the civic community of Swizzlewick: always willing to locate immorality among those charged with safeguarding the public good. Locked in her sights were those local councillors unable to maintain their marriage vows, and ever ripe for opportunities to profit from corruption and town-hall chicanery.

Both Mrs Anstey and the unsubtly named Mrs Smallgood were entirely fictional characters: Anstey in the humourless 1956 comedy film, *Keep It Clean*; Smallgood among the cast of the BBC's short-lived soap opera, *Swizzlewick*. Combine their characteristics and principles, and you might arrive at an exact caricature of the woman who came to define moral outrage across several decades of post-war British life.

Between 1964, when she first became a household name, and her death in 2001 at the age of ninety-one, Mrs Mary Whitehouse was arguably the most polarising figure in the nation's culture. For those who shared her views, she was a stalwart of traditional British values and Christian teaching. Her opponents, who ranged from luminaries of the theatre to teenagers who wanted to escape from their parents' (or grandparents') stuffy view of the world, saw her as a bastion of suffocating conservatism and outmoded ethics. So expertly did she divide the country that it was almost impossible to remain neutral: you either applauded her as the voice of reason, or lampooned her as a sad relic of Victorian puritanism.

Whitehouse could not avoid the comparison with Mrs Smallgood, for the very simple reason that this 'doctrinaire' character was created in a deliberate attempt to parody (and anger) Mary Whitehouse and her ilk. The inventor and author of *Swizzlewick* was David Turner, a thirty-eight-year-old playwright, two of whose dramas had been screened by the BBC in February 1964. One of them, *Trevor*, aroused some controversy for its frank discussion of marital difficulties. It was, he explained, 'the story of a young married couple discovering that sex was not all-fulfilling. The theme that I use when I talk about love relationships is of people being able to live together and face up to problems together, and I do advocate in very strong terms that they must not rely upon sex. I am a moralist in ultimate terms.'

That is not how either Turner or *Trevor* was depicted at a meeting at Birmingham Town Hall on 5 May 1964. This was the first mass gathering of a pressure group designed to Clean-Up TV. Among the 1,500 people who attended were David Turner; and a group of sixteen-year-old schoolgirls, who complained that his work 'made a mockery of spiritual values and had no tenderness'. He politely asked to be allowed to defend his work, but was refused permission to speak. 'I have never seen so much violence in people who advocate non-violence,' he said afterwards. Thwarted in his initial impulse, he followed Mary Whitehouse's example by taking his cause to the press: 'If you disguise life from youngsters, you don't protect them. No one can hush up truth by concealing it. Sex is not dirty.'

Turner was already preparing a set of scripts for *Swizzlewick*, which was set in a Midlands town hall, with a cast of fictional characters prone to all the usual human vices. Upset by what he saw as the petty morality of those who organised and ran the Birmingham meeting, he added a satirical campaigner and complainer to his soap opera tableau, and Mrs Smallgood was born. Her small-screen fixation was her crusade for 'Freedom from Sex', and her portrayal was anything but even-handed.

Not that this was the aspect of *Swizzlewick* that most disconcerted the stout-hearted conservatives of the English Midlands. The programme was reviewed in the *Birmingham Daily Post* by Norman Tiptaft, a veteran participant in political life who had once stood for parliament as a socialist, but had steadily headed rightwards over the subsequent half-century. A former Lord Mayor of Birmingham, he was in 1964 the chairman of the National Committee of the Anti-Violence League – whose chief policy, ironically, was to call for an extension of the death penalty. He regarded the initial episode of *Swizzlewick*, screened by the BBC on 18 August 1964, as 'unrealistic' and 'unfair'. But his chief complaint was that it 'showed a sexy young female persuading her fiancé to take her to his home while his father – the only other occupant – was out, because the accommodation for fornication outside was not comfortable enough. Father came home unexpectedly, in the middle of their amours. That was supposed to be funny. I did not think so.' As the crusaders for cleaner TV would prove, time and again, any comedy could be robbed of its laughs by being described in such pompous terms. In any case, Tiptaft reckoned that he spoke for the silent masses: 'The vast majority of BBC viewers do not like vulgarity, bad taste and exploitation of sex'. And he vowed to launch his own organisation to rid the country's screens of these corrosive evils.

British life was filled with these well-intentioned, self-appointed moralists. Their activities frequently opened them to ridicule. In 1959, for example, the Entertainments Committee of Hereford Council refused a licence for the Tony Curtis film comedy, *Strictly for Pleasure*, to be screened there, because it was 'not suitable for public showing'. It had already been given an 'A' certificate by the national censorship board, allowing children to see it in adult company. But the same group, on the same day, passed the X-rated *Call Girls* as being fully appropriate for the innocent citizens of Hereford.

In Edinburgh, meanwhile, Lady Hilda Morton told the local branch of the Marriage Guidance Council that any young married couples who preferred a 'good time' to having children were indulging in 'polite prostitution'. 'It simply is immoral,' she added. 'Children are the great stabiliser. They are the natural outcome of love.' In London, a columnist bemoaned the decline of the West End theatre: 'What was once family entertainment has given place to the posturings and crawlings of prostitutes and pimps ... When plays come on in which everyone sleeps in the same bed, and which glorify prostitution, uncontrolled sexual appetites, hopelessness and self-pity, we are urged to see a "new brilliant study of modern times".'

This commentator was far from being a lone voice. A member of the House of Lords decried the decision in 1960 to allow D.H. Lawrence's novel *Lady Chatterley's Lover* to be sold legally as 'the word of Satan'. 'Writings of this nature' should be 'banned for all time', he proclaimed. A similar view fired the campaign to have advertisements for the services of the Family Planning Association banned from the London underground and, to stray further towards the ridiculous, for a dancing trio of policewomen in Middlesbrough to refrain from wearing grass skirts when they performed, because too much of their legs was on display. These constant battles over the territory of sexuality reinforced the belief of the person who wrote to the *Women's Mirror* magazine: 'We've had the Naughty Nineties, the Tuneful Twenties – and now, judging by the present trend in plays and books, we've reached the Sexy Sixties!'.

At their most extreme, these assaults on the prevailing drift towards either a more liberal or a more perverted culture could become self-defeating. It is hard to imagine exactly what impelled a Roman Catholic parish priest in Newport Pagnell to mount a 1963 campaign to prevent girls from the local secondary school from using communal showers – fun for boys, he declared, but 'an assault on Christian morals' for the apparently more innocent sex. 'It is simply that the idea is against the Commandments', he concluded, without explaining which of the Ten the girls were breaking.

The moral well-being of teenage girls was at the heart of many of these campaigns against the modern world, and frequently it was the young women themselves who took the lead. Sixty girls from a Blackburn grammar school formed a Vice Vigilant Committee in 1962, and went so far as to write to the Prime Minister about the film posters to which they were exposed every day – for such dubious fare as *House of Sin*, *Nudes in the Snow* and, more pointedly, *The Young Have No Morals*. Extending this theme, a twenty-three-year-old (male) teacher from Bolton lent his support to what was intended as a country-wide organisation for concerned British teenagers: the National Youth for Decency Committee. In what would become a familiar trope for such campaigners, Bernard Loveland explained that 'A study of sex in all its forms will be needed for us to have clear ideas about the baser aspect of our work'.

So the teenagers who spoke out against *Trevor* at Birmingham Town Hall were not isolated in their distaste for the increased sexualisation of modern culture. As a Senior Mistress at Madeley Secondary Modern School in Shropshire, Mary Whitehouse found herself witnessing all the moral and physical confusion that sex aroused in young people during the early 1960s. The formative experiences of her life as a campaigner were told and retold in countless profiles and autobiographical volumes, varying in tone and detail; but certain incidents were set in her memory. She recalled how the incessant coverage of the Profumo scandal in 1963 had introduced matters of adult sexual etiquette into teenage conversation, and claimed that certain girls at her school had been inspired to 'do things they shouldn't' by the example of Christine Keeler and her friends: 'Well, miss, we watched them talking about them girls on TV and it looked as if it was easy, and see how well they done out of it, miss, so we thought we'd try'. She alleged that a fourteen-year-old girl of her acquaintance had rushed off to have intercourse with a boy after watching a BBC play about sex, and that a boy of the same age had begged her, 'Will you please stop the girls teasing and tantalising us into deep sexual relationships?' In her telling, children were powerless to avoid emulating the behaviour they saw on screen, without for a moment understanding its implications or consequences.

In July 1963, Dr Peter Henderson, Principal Medical Officer at the Department of Education, told a teachers' conference in Cambridge that he could not unconditionally describe pre-marital sex as immoral. Mary Whitehouse was one of those who made her displeasure known in public: by not sacking Henderson, she complained, the Minister of Education had 'undermined everything they [the teachers] had done'. By 29 February the following year, Whitehouse and her like-minded friend, Norah Buckland, had emerged as *de facto* leaders of a pressure group dominated by women, who held a private meeting in Birmingham. She blamed the BBC for screening programmes that 'aggravated the problems with which Government departments were trying to grapple'. A week later, her prejudices were solidified by *What Kind of Loving?*, an early evening show in the *Meeting Point* series of religious broadcasting. Hosted by Joan Bakewell, the episode examined the ways in which girls, and their parents, were dealing with the rapidly changing attitudes in British society to such issues as pre-marital

sex and chastity. To her horror, Whitehouse heard a psychiatrist proclaim: 'it is no longer absolutely necessary for a girl to be a virgin
when she comes to marriage – in fact, some men prefer that she
should not be'. This, she felt, was nothing less than propaganda for
immorality – being delivered by a public service broadcaster with an
ethos of protecting the nation from evil influences.

Her view was supported at another Birmingham meeting of the
Clean-Up TV brigade, at which she declared that 'Young people are
being betrayed and seduced. Their bodies will bear the mark of the
degradation of the BBC.' A local councillor concurred: 'The BBC is
being infiltrated by a small clique of longhairs whose influence is far
out of proportion to its numbers'. It was suggested that the corporation's chairman should be sent a rake and broom, to symbolise the
cleansing that was required of his orgy-ridden Augean stables. All
this disgust was now focused upon the Birmingham Town Hall rally
on 5 May 1964, where the ordinary people of Britain could 'fight for
the right to bring up our children in the truths of our Christian way
of life'.

Three thousand miles away, in Cincinnati, Connecticut, Mary
Whitehouse's closest American equivalent was being profiled sympa-
thetically in *Reader's Digest* magazine. The subject of the article, entitled
'Poison in Print and How to Get Rid of It', was Charles Keating, a
forty-year-old World War Two fighter pilot who was now a corporate
lawyer with offices on the 39th floor of the city's tallest skyscraper.
None of the American TV networks was as daring or as liberal as the
BBC when it came to tackling issues of sexuality in the 1960s. Keating's
eye for offence was turned elsewhere, at the bookstalls and news-stands
that offered 'smut' to the public, regardless of their age.

As *Reader's Digest* explained, 'Keating's concern over the flood of
printed poison was galvanised one day in 1956, when he noticed
youngsters at a news-stand snickering over a display set apart from
the rest of the magazines and paperbacks. Moving over for a look,
Keating was shocked. Besides the "girlie" magazines featuring nudes
in suggestive poses, dozens of publications depicted not only raw sex
but stories of abnormal sex behaviour. By any decent citizen's definition, this was pornography, dirt for dirt's sake.'

Like Whitehouse's account of her baptism in disgust, Keating's
ur-story varied in its location, date and details down the years. But his

abiding sense of alarm was unchanged. He described how he had contacted local police, expecting officers to swoop on the news-stand and close it down, but was told that previous attempts had always been blocked by 'hot-shot big-city lawyers' – though not hot-shot big-city lawyers like him, of course. Unable to persuade the authorities to act, he determined that the solution was to rouse the outrage of the decent citizens of Cincinnati; and his organisation, Citizens for Decent Literature (CDL), was born.

Keating had already aroused controversy in his hometown by intervening in the debate about whether the global population was increasing too quickly to be sustainable. He called for all discussion of the subject to cease, because it inevitably led towards a campaign to make birth control more accessible – which was, he said, against Biblical teaching. (As with Mary Whitehouse, Charles Keating's conviction that he was a flawless reflection of Christian ethics was unshakeable.) But his shift from contraception (against) to obscenity (even more firmly against) propelled him to the national stage.

His tactics were simple, and not dissimilar to those employed by the Clean-Up TV crew in England. Qualified speakers (usually Charles Keating) should address sympathetic audiences and expose the true nature of the smut with which their children were being confronted. Once they had been converted, these 'decent' citizens could be employed to lobby politicians, police chiefs and public prosecutors, in an effort to persuade them to crack down on this pernicious trade. Keating was skilled at inventing statistics to support his case: the traffic in pornography was a billion-dollar-a-year industry, he claimed, or maybe two billion, if his listeners required more ammunition. Three-quarters of this 'filth' inevitably fell into the hands of children; it 'invades schoolyards' and 'breeds involvement of the children themselves in the racket'. His clinching arguments: 'this is volume enough to pervert an entire generation', and 'no child from college age down to the age of five is safe'.

In 1958, he first attended a House of Representatives committee hearing in Washington, flanked by his two blonde daughters to reinforce his family values. By that July, his campaign had become national, and his aim focused upon the 'criminals, Communists and unscrupulous persons' behind the pornography market. These monsters were supplying 'a whole area of literature instructing the young in perversion', he said, explaining that they often won their converts when young people answered apparently innocent advertisements in the back of comics and general-interest magazines. 'So the youngster who sent in for a rocket pistol, for example,' he said, 'soon is getting through the family mail box, lewd solicitations to buy "art photography" or "nudes" – material designed to appeal to the curiosity of adolescents.'

At this point he would generally hold up, for his audience's horror or titillation, examples of the offending literature, which he always insisted he had bought just before the meeting, at an outlet open to the city's impressionable youth. Then he would recite the grim details of rapes, indecent assaults or even murders inspired by a youngster's unwitting immersion in porn. 'The publishers of the material are well aware of what they are doing,' he claimed. 'They know the material will act as a narcotic, and the child will delve deeper and deeper into it until depravity is reached.' Occasionally he was asked whether he was not concerned that he too would be corrupted by his constant exposure to indecent literature. (His hectic schedule of meetings and speeches had, after all, enabled him to amass what must have been a world-beating collection of pornography.) As Keating explained: 'I like to think that, just like a doctor works with the human body, I have a professional interest and have been able to stay somewhat clear of the effects. I do not go into my study with the intention of sucking the prurient interest out of [pornography]. Even so, there are aberrations I'd hate to dwell on.'

What was this depravity that filled Keating's study? In the early 1960s, it was (by later standards) a rather quaint, though undeniably grubby, selection of exploitation and cheap thrills. The 'art photography' and 'nudes' of which he spoke were black-and-white magazines, in which women (usually sporting bikini pants) exposed their breasts to the camera, sometimes in partnership with a naked man (always seen from behind). Or the magazines might – and this was more alarming in 1964 – comprise shots of unfeasibly well-muscled men, either naked (their genitals hidden from view) or clad in wrestlers' briefs. Clearly these were orientated towards a homosexual market that was not only lascivious but (in the view of Keating and his ilk) contravened all the rules of nature.

Equally damaging were what were known as pulps (for the coarse quality of their paper): paperback novels with lurid covers that usually promised more in the vein of erotic or violent satisfaction than they actually offered. These were written to order by hacks who adopted outlandish pseudonyms to disguise their true identities. They bore titles such as *Girls on the Rampage* ('The brutal, shocking truth about girls who go bad', according to the cover), *Sex Field* ('A Doctor's realistic report on the darker side of love and sexual impulses gone wild') or *Isle of Sin* ('Kooks, Beatniks and Babes meet in an orgy of summer lust').

And then there were the men's magazines: not just the likes of *Playboy*, edging its way towards a vestige of respectability with its trademark interviewing of world figures, and stories by luminaries of American fiction, but an even less salubrious brand of periodical, printed on paper that might otherwise have been destined for the pulps. Their covers, in the early 1960s at least, carried gaudy and salacious illustrations, which featured women with unfeasibly exaggerated curves and the most scanty of clothes as either the victims or the protagonists of extreme acts of sexual violence. Titled *Men's Daring*, or *All Man*, or *Man's Age*, they invariably depicted fictional acts of cruelty from World War Two – with Nazi soldiers directing a blowtorch against a young maiden's bare skin, or wielding slavery-era whips to torture the girls' ravaged bodies. Nothing in the magazine lived up to the horror or excitement of these fiendish delights, although strap-lines such as 'A Crypt of Agony for the Screaming Beauties of Belgium' or 'Blood for a Nympho's Flesh' invited the unwary reader into a hothouse of torture and sadism. (In fact, most of the contents merely repeated tales of familiar wartime atrocities and battles, alongside tame exposés of the erotic delights available from big-city back-streets.)

What happened to the young people (usually boys) who were corrupted by this vicious trade? Keating and the CDL answered this question with a series of short propaganda films, which also offered audiences at his lectures a respite from his voice. The earliest of these, *Pages of Death*, was premiered at the 2,500-seater Taft Auditorium in Cincinnati on 27 April 1962. Keating promised that it 'portrays, in a singularly dramatic way, the effects of pornographic literature on the mind of a teenage youth'. *Pages of Death* was not actually made by the CDL; it came from the producers of the Catholic TV series, *Hour of St Francis*. But it served the organisation's purposes perfectly.

Hosted by sportscaster Tom Harmon, the film recounts the fictional tale of the murder and (it's implied) rape of eleven-year-old Karen. She has failed to return home from school, having stopped at a news-agent's store for candy and pencils. There she has provoked the cruel desires of teenage porn addict Paul, who has swept her into his car and then dumped her lifeless, abused body in a ditch. Detectives uncover the magazines and pulps hidden in Paul's den, while his mother declares, 'Paul would never read anything like this!' Eventually the cops break down his guard. 'I didn't mean to do it,' Paul cries out. 'I don't know *why* I did it.' 'I think we do,' mutters the lead detective, as he picks up a fistful of the reading matter that twisted the boy's mind.

Then the cops return to the store where Karen purchased her candy – and Paul became addicted to his literary means of corruption. 'You stand there,' the detective scolds the unrepentant owner, 'while the kids soak up poison that would turn the mind of a grown man … while these kids get the impression that sex is dirt, and lust and love are the same things. That it's OK to try perversion just for kicks!'

Subtle this approach was not. Once their audience had become satiated with *Pages of Death*, Keating and CDL prepared their own efforts in the same unequivocal style. *Perversion for Profit* and *Printed Poison*, both distributed in 1965, adopted mildly different perspectives on the same message. As the narrator of the documentary *Perversion for Profit* claimed, 'A flood tide of filth is engulfing our country in the form of news-stand obscenity, and is threatening to pervert an entire generation of our American children.' *Printed Poison* transferred the theme to the true-crime genre, forcing its audience to witness 'the poison, the rot, the horridly toxic abscess … the soul-searing bacteria of a new disease' at the heart of their society. Both films illustrated this venomous culture with real-life examples of the trade – nudie mag after nudie mag, each picture censored with black or red strips pasted across the breasts, genitals and (strangely) eyes of the unclad models. *Perversion* warned, 'Never in the history of the world have the merchants of obscenity, the teachers of unnatural sex acts, had available to them the modern facility for disseminating this filth.' To emphasise the point, this film offered unaltered portraits of sado-masochistic scenarios, almost as if it was gathering trade for the purveyors of printed poison. Both reels painted the magazine vendors as pimps and killers, the investigators as steely-eyed heroes delving into the sickest avenues of the human heart to protect their kids from its crippling allure.

While Charles Keating (sometimes lampooned as 'Mr Clean') wallowed in filth, seeking to keep his moral compass intact, Mary Whitehouse faced nothing more lubricious than an advance script for an episode of *Swizzlewick*. This was smuggled out of the BBC by a sympathetic technician, before being passed to Whitehouse as an item of *samizdat* literature. Here she found no Nazi torturers, whiplashed bathing beauties or sadistic fiends in female form: merely an errant council member, seen skulking away from the room of a prostitute (Blousie by name) with his clothes dishevelled. It would undoubtedly have outraged Mrs Smallgood, who – as the BBC's magazine *Radio Times* explained – 'dedicates her arid life to putting down Sex whenever it rears its ugly head'. And it prompted Mrs Whitehouse to submit the script as an example of obscenity to the Postmaster-General, who in turn alerted BBC management. The offending scene was cut, and David Turner promptly quit the series after just two weeks. 'My work has been ruined artistically,' he lamented. 'How could a self-respecting writer go on?'

This was a victory of sorts for Whitehouse, as *Swizzlewick* soon ground to a halt without Turner's guiding hand. But her battle against obscenity on television was unrelenting. On the very evening that the soap opera was launched, cabaret star Shirley Bassey was featured on BBC2. She chose to sing an amended nursery rhyme: 'My mother said I never should play with the young men in the wood. / If I do, my ma would say, you'll end up in the family way'. Filth, it seemed, was everywhere.

Whitehouse was now a figure of national renown. In an interview, the *Steptoe and Son* star Harry H. Corbett took the opportunity to lampoon 'the telly protestors' who, he said, 'have something in common with the characters who read a pornographic book from cover to cover before screaming blue murder. One can imagine the moaners, huddled by their sets, one hand on the tuner and the other on the telephone, switching from channel to channel and waiting for the word or phrase or action that will titillate their tiny sense of outrage.' With one minor correction, that was a fairly accurate summary of the methods (if not the attitude) employed by Whitehouse and the stalwarts with whom she founded the National Viewers' and Listeners' Association (NVALA) as a successor to Clean-Up TV. Her organisation systematically chronicled prime-time viewing across all three British television channels for four weeks in the early autumn of 1964, annotating and describing every instance of obscenity, pornography, violence and blasphemy that they could detect. More than 30 per cent of the programmes offered by the BBC offended their sensibilities. No wonder that Whitehouse felt the need to resign her position as a teacher, so that she could concentrate full-time on rallying the forces of decency against the BBC's tide of permissiveness. 'If ever there was a spiritual Dunkirk, it is now', she commented portentously.

This decision had unforeseen consequences. On 6 November 1964, the *Daily Mail* published an entertaining interview with the satirist and TV producer Ned Sherrin, as a preview of his new series, *Not So Much A Programme*. 'I think we've dulled people's capacity for shock and surprise,' he noted drolly, 'but there's always a lunatic fringe. I'm told one woman has already given up her job so that she can monitor the programme and be ready to protest. What puzzles me is what sort of job was she doing that kept her busy at the hours of the night when we're going to be on the air? I suppose she must have been on the streets.' No names were mentioned but, to Whitehouse, the implication was clear. She sued the *Mail*'s publishers for libel, and when the matter reached court in June 1965, they agreed to pay her substantial damages, which were duly funnelled into the NVALA accounts.

Whitehouse's tireless efforts ensured that even if she had missed or been unaware of a potential outrage, she was sure to be contacted by the press for a comment. She also inspired others to raise their own flags against indecency, such as the all-party group of MPs formed in December 1964 to pursue a course almost identical to the NVALA's. Norman Tiptaft, one of her fellow protestors against *Swizzlewick*, was not far behind. Anxious to lead a crusade rather than trail behind someone else's, he founded the Association for Better Entertainment, and mounted his own charge against the BBC. The target of his ire was a two-part radio documentary in January 1965, broadcast at 9.30 pm, on the subject of the *Male Homosexual*. The BBC 'will not leave pornography alone', he alleged after the first episode was aired, and he demanded that the second should be cancelled. But the thoughtful and anything but pornographic programme went ahead as planned, despite the fact that (as one disgusted listener in Birmingham noted) 'it did not deal with the matter as a beastly practice, both wrongful and sinful'.

Tiptaft failed to muster the same force or passion as Whitehouse, and his Association lost ground as its leader became distracted by his all-out war on the modern world. He called for an end to public funding of the arts, a reduction in bank holidays, the dissolution of the Trades Union Congress and, for good measure, an increase in the use of corporal punishment (another striking blow from the chairman of the National Committee of the Anti-Violence League).

In a thoughtful essay in the *Birmingham Daily Post*, triggered by Tiptaft's protests, the writer W.E. Hall regretted the small-mindedness of those who believed that the British people were being forced to wade 'through a morass of filth and obscenity. It isn't true.' He continued: 'The attack of the censors, with its obsession with sex above everything else, actually stands in the way of improvement because it perpetuates the attitudes of a prudish, furtive past and preserves the lines of a battle fought and finished. That battle, for frankness in the discussion of sex and for the toleration of heterodoxy in religious belief (and unbelief) was necessary.' Two groups, however, persisted in behaving as if the battle were still taking place: 'There are those who seem compelled perpetually to demonstrate their emancipation, the avant-garde for ever in a state of delayed adolescence, those whose marriage with freedom has never advanced beyond the sexual excitement of the honeymoon. And there are the Clean-Up TV people, who want to deal with the problems of the newly acquired freedom by doing away with it altogether. The solution is too drastic.'

If there was a single creative force in the Britain of 1965 who would have admitted – nay, relished – the tag of being caught 'in a state of delayed adolescence', it was the maverick, playful and wilfully subversive auteur, Ken Russell. Known for the visual and stylistic invention of his documentary work for the BBC, he had strayed into feature films with the 1964 release of *French Dressing*. Part traditional seaside comedy, part savage satire on the French new wave, it was set in a fading British resort (portrayed perfectly by Herne Bay), briefly enlivened by a film festival visited by a glamorous French star of minimal acting ability (portrayed perfectly by Marisa Mell). 'All I have to do is take off my clothes', she complains to her French producer, and the English expect nothing less from her. In the final scene, civic dignitaries line up with binoculars as the star (or her replacement, as it turns out) prepares to inaugurate the first nudist beach in Britain by walking naked into the sea, while the Kentish rain pours down.

Saucy rather than licentious, *French Dressing* would have been too raw for television viewing in 1964 (although it could now be broadcast on a Sunday afternoon without giving offence). But Russell's work over the next few decades provoked consistent storms of outrage – beginning with one of his most remarkable creations, *The Debussy Film*. Screened on 18 May 1965, this ecstatic blend of fact and fiction seemed as if it had sprung from an unholy coupling of Godard and Fellini, as Russell (in his own words) 'bound the hallucinatory state of [Debussy's] mind to the dream-like quality of his music'.

The BBC's Head of Drama, Sydney Newman, had issued his staff with the Corporation's most recent guidelines about what could be shown on TV: 'Reference to sexual acts, portrayal of near-nudity, the physical handling of someone with sex in mind, couples in bed – all should be considered carefully, from every point of view, before inclusion in a play.' All of these borders were crossed, with fearless *élan*, by Russell's film; but it escaped Newman's censure because it was the product of the Documentary unit, rather than Drama. Russell launched into his action with the mock crucifixion of a young woman in a swimsuit, before arrows were apparently fired into her body to represent the martyrdom of St Sebastian. There followed scenes of striptease, the caressing of a bare female back, and topless swimming – all in the name of art (and if anything qualified for that term, *The Debussy Film* did), soaked in sensuality and sexual liberation. It might have been designed to demonstrate the full extent of television porn-ography, and Mary Whitehouse took the bait – suggesting, amongst her usual accusations of BBC smut, that Russell's work was to blame for a group of boy scouts allegedly assaulting a teenage girl.

Whitehouse and the NVALA met their match in creative figures such as Ken Russell and Dennis Potter, who did not pretend to share her definitions of morality and decency. When she repeated her familiar tale of a fourteen-year-old girl throwing herself at a boy after seeing a BBC play, Potter responded acerbically: 'Mrs Whitehouse may care to know that when I was fourteen, I offered myself to a girl of the same age because of what I had read in a Shakespeare play. Unfortunately the girl was not so literate.'

Further opposition arose when another 'housewife', Avril Fox, formed a rival pressure group: Freedom For TV. The Fox group alleged that, far from wallowing in filth, British viewers were not being given enough sex and violence on television. The two women were pitted against each other by the *Daily Mirror*, with Whitehouse using her superior experience to outwit Fox on points. Her philosophy, after all, was easier to explain: 'The BBC are part of a great moral conspiracy ... They speak of reality when, stuck in their ivory tower, they know nothing of reality.' Fox was provoked by Whitehouse into agreeing that, yes, she would allow her own children to watch scenes of real-life sexual intercourse and murder on TV. 'Heavens above!', Whitehouse replied with an uncharacteristic show of restraint. Her case was not helped, however, by her insistence that the mortal enemies of Dr Who, the Daleks, could provoke a child to kill one of its playmates with their ceaseless cry of 'Exterminate!'

Absurdity was an occupational hazard for the era's moral guardians. Writer and broadcaster Malcolm Muggeridge, who would later join Whitehouse on many platforms under the banner of the Christian group, the Festival of Light, was engaged in conversation by the novelist Len Deighton in the first issue of the men's magazine *King*, in the winter of 1964. It was an unlikely venue for the perpetually pained Muggeridge, who found himself competing for attention with topless photographs of Christine Keeler and extracts from Terry Southern's banned novel, *Candy*.

It was in this context that Muggeridge conjured with the nature of morality, and the social need or otherwise for pornographic literature. 'One feels that in a sane society, pornography wouldn't be necessary,' Muggeridge said. 'This obsession with it must be due to some flagging of normal appetites or an excessive stimulation of them ... My strictest objection to pornography is merely that it succeeds in its purpose. It fills people with sexual desire. I would have thought that for the young it was unnecessary, for the middle-aged it was inconvenient, and for the old it was unseemly.' The discussion turned to the dangers of children being exposed to pornography. 'If you know that a particular book will induce little boys to masturbate excessively,' Muggeridge argued, 'then you can't really say that the book ought to be published.

Can you?' 'Not unless the little boys would otherwise go off and rape little girls,' Deighton replied. Muggeridge's reaction was quick – too quick: 'It might be better for them if they did.'

This pontificating aside, some of the testimony mailed by the British public to Mary Whitehouse could have been extracted from one of Charles Keating's propaganda films. Whitehouse was most affected by a pair of letters she received from a middle-aged couple in March 1967. Their heartfelt confessions were sparked by a BBC Schools television broadcast in the series *Twentieth Century Focus*. It dealt with the timely but surely non-pornographic theme of equality between the sexes in modern Britain. 'Women's legal and social position has changed during this century,' ran the blurb in *Radio Times*. 'But where is there still discrimination against them?' 'In men's magazines' was the obvious answer, and to illustrate the point, the programme briefly displayed a photograph from *Penthouse*, where a young woman in a topless bathing suit was named 'Pet of the Month'.

For Whitehouse's husband-and-wife correspondents, this brief and sensitively handled sequence unlocked memories of the addiction that had blighted their marriage. 'For years I have "enjoyed" these filthy magazines,' Mr N confessed. 'This filth is like a drug. The more you get, the more you want. One moment it seems a desirable private dream. Then later it is empty – and so is life, and you are so awfully alone in your own made private Hell.' His wife's viewpoint was equally poignant: 'I am in the distressing situation of having witnessed my husband in action with so-called "Art Studies" (pornography). It was far worse than just "looking" at pictures. No wife is going to be able to satisfy her husband sexually, once he has indulged in these books or other forms of depravity.' Mr N highlighted the 'terrible seductive forces, television in particular, which have confronted me and others in my position.' And he offered an intriguing legal argument: 'The two offending pictures which were shown on the TV screen, if shown to any person classified by law as a minor by a member of the adult public, would constitute an unlawful and immoral act under the laws of this country, but they can be shown by the BBC to schoolchildren.'

Mr and Mrs N were flapping against the tide. At her most belea-guered, Mary Whitehouse might (as she did in a 1969 interview) hint at a liberal conspiracy, no doubt headed by the BBC, which was designed to sap and pervert the essence of traditional morality: 'People are waking up to a realisation of how the average person has been desperately conned. There has been a massive exercise in persuading the average person that their judgement is not sound, that the intellectuals are the ones who know ... we now have a situation where liberals claim to be creating a free society but are actually creating a society whose resources are being destroyed or undermined.' It was the only way that she, and others who shared her paranoia, could make sense of a nation that was apparently hell-bent on self-destruction. Each manifestation of liberation and licence, especially if conveyed to the masses by the BBC, encouraged her to cry out in horror like an Old Testament prophet, a voice in the wilderness amidst the barbarians of hedonism. But the prevailing drift of culture during the second half of the 1960s was towards liberalisation and freedom, and the ground that Whitehouse was seeking to defend grew thinner and more isolated as each taboo was overturned.

Yet the caricature of Whitehouse and her fellow campaigners as desiccated, pleasureless killjoys, bent on denying the people a chance to emerge from decades of repression and conservatism, was inaccurate, as well as unfair. In her rhetoric, Whitehouse was perhaps prone to making herself ridiculous by overplaying her hand: a Chicken Little in a pleasure garden under a boundless sky. Her sometime confederate, Malcolm Muggeridge, was able to express himself more eloquently, and with more enduring impact. 'The obsession of sex as an end in itself leads to boundless despair,' he predicted. 'Promiscuity and the pursuit of sex end in sterility and self-love. The psychiatric wards are full of people who have followed the path of sexual promiscuity to its destructive conclusions.' And in similar vein, as the legal and medical changes of 1967 took hold: 'You would think that the way to happiness was that everyone should be able to have an abortion, just when she wants it; that marriage should be terminated at will; that contraception should be available to adolescents ... yet if you go to those places where these things are most available, these are the places where the psychiatric wards are fullest, where people are the most miserable, where the art is just a nightmare, and where you have a materialistic society.' He was posing questions that are equally valid today, when the issue of the sexual objectification of young women remains at the heart of feminist rhetoric. But in the culture of Swinging London, he was viewed as being just as outlandish and anachronistic as the visiting American evangelist Billy Graham, with his proclamations against 'long-haired boys and unkempt girls' and their inevitable consequence: 'It is the symptom of something deep down that is happening. London is written up as a swinging city. Then we read that the next thing is the sex act on the stage. It is the symptom of walls being torn down and things beginning to crumble.'

In Graham's homeland, Charles Keating was equally at sea in the permissive society. He devoted exhaustive efforts in 1969 to trying to enforce a nationwide ban on Russ Meyer's risqué but ridiculous movie, *Vixen*. Keating had recently declared: 'There are criminals running amuck in this nation, who are pandering to and titillating the people of this country, particularly our young people, with utterly foul and depraved materials. These unscrupulous merchants have reduced many of the nation's news-racks, motion picture screens and even the mailboxes in our homes, to display unimaginable descriptions, stories and pictures of bestiality, perversion and just plain moral rot.'

It was a familiar theme, but whereas a decade earlier he could have expected all right-minded columnists and reporters to rally to his flag, by 1969 even the most restrained viewers were growing blasé about the threats he envisaged. In Keating's hometown of Cincinnati, journalist George Palmer attended a special screening of *Vixen*, intended to rouse the media to the barricades. Far from being appalled, however, Palmer was simply bored: 'The plot plods. In fact, the plot is bedded down. The acting, for the most part, is atrocious. The general reaction was loud laughter at the amateurish performances. Vixen attacks most of her dialogue, and it lies there, dead.' Even the potentially corrupting nudity was dull: 'It gets a little tiring to see people naked in bed together, naked on the grass together, naked in the river together, naked in the shower together.' And this was the film described by Keating as 'filthy and lascivious' and in danger of 'polluting the minds, hearts and souls of Americans'.

Although he could still find a receptive audience for his lantern lectures, guaranteed to feature genuine pornography, Keating had struggled when he ventured beyond audiences of the converted. In 1964, he was selected for the first time as an expert witness in a trial in Visalia, California, where news-stand operators were being prosecuted for selling 'obscene' literature. The offensive items included paperbacks such as *Orgy House*, *Passion Puppet* (turned that way by 'high

Sue Lyon on display at the Bronx Zoo in June 1962,
publicising the imminent release of Stanley Kubrick's film *Lolita*.

Brigitte Bardot leaving the clinic where she was being treated
after a suicide attempt in September 1960.

Readers searching avidly for pornographic passages in Vladimir Nabokov's *Lolita*
on its UK publication day in November 1959.

A critic claimed there were homosexual overtones in Dirk Bogarde's
portrayal of an outlaw in *The Singer Not the Song* (1960). His next film, *Victim*,
consolidated this association in the public eye.

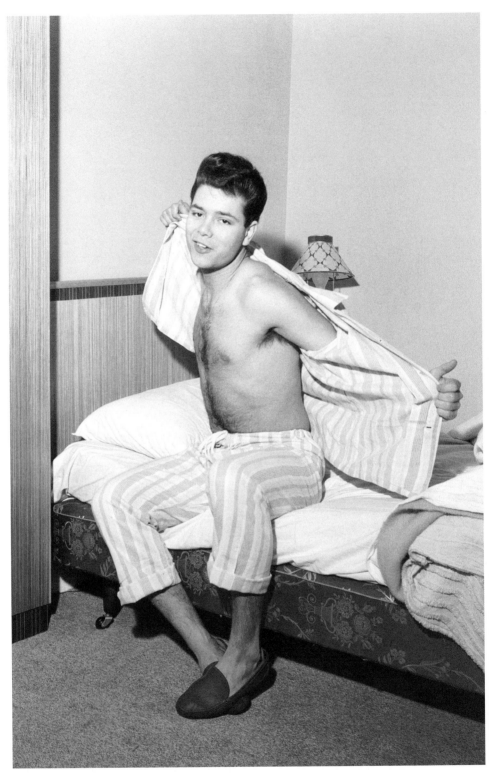

Twenty-year-old Cliff Richard was persuaded to mimic the 'beefcake' poses
of male physique magazines for the delight of his fans in 1960.

The female body and the male gaze, demonstrated in London at the height of the topless dress craze of 1964, and two years later during a publicity stunt at the Lady Jane boutique in Carnaby Street.

Helen Gurley Brown, author of *Sex and the Single Girl* (1964), one of the decade's most successful sex manuals. Her reward was the editorship of the US magazine *Cosmopolitan*.

April Ashley signing the register after her Gibraltar wedding
to Arthur Cameron Corbett in September 1963.

The British obsession with sadism in action: 'Professor' Jimmy Edwards administers corporal punishment to the pupils of the TV comedy *Whacko!* in 1959, while Emma Peel (played by Diana Rigg) undergoes trial by bondage in a 1965 edition of *The Avengers*.

pay and lustful play', according to the cover) and *Lust Circuit* ('her wanton body was bait'). Also seized were copies of *Pix*, the 'Magazine for Men Who Like Action'. A recent issue had featured a lingerie-clad cover model, plus features with titles such as 'Love-Slave to a Sexual Superman' and 'Hideous Whip Vengeance for a Mad Rapist'.

Keating was introduced as 'a person intimately acquainted with community standards of decency', though exactly who had determined the standards of the community was unclear. In the witness box, he defined literature as obscene if it tackled 'illicit sex, stressing deviations from the normal', which again begged to be challenged. The jury had already heard a professor of psychology claim, with more than a hint of hyperbole, that two of the novels in question had 'educational value and social importance', which might have amused their pseudonymous authors. Keating faced the friendly prosecutor without difficulty, but then skipped court, and California, when it was time for his cross-examination. As a critic in the *Los Angeles Times* noted, 'It is easy to dish it out; the question is whether you can take it'.

A few months later, he was standing in front of a House of Representatives committee on matters of education, but his testimony about the vulnerability of children to indecent literature was cut short when the chairman objected to his attempting to read out all the most lurid passages from another cheap paperback, *Love's Lash*. That book, alongside many more of its cousins, was on display in a special 'Publications Room' when Citizens for Decent Literature staged its 1965 conference at the Waldorf-Astoria in New York. Delegates could inspect titles such as *Sexational Stepdaughter*, *Whip and Lash* and *Dominate* – which, an intrepid reporter discovered, 'had a drawing of a curvaceous woman being chain-whipped by her pantherish mistress who, the text explained, had to be addressed as "your lowness"'. As the young man guarding the room said apologetically, 'I'm afraid you'll find it raw'.

In 1967, President Lyndon Johnson commanded the formation of a Commission on Obscenity and Pornography. The National Association of Evangelicals called for Keating to be among its members, but in vain. Instead, the Commission was dominated by more liberal minds, among them representatives of organisations concerned with civil liberties. When President Nixon inherited the Commission in 1969, he found an opportunity to slip Keating aboard.

As the Commission's hearings continued, two matters became very clear. First, the majority of its members were set on taking a sociological or even scientific view of pornography, to Keating's disgust. (He accused them of having already decided what they thought before they saw any evidence – whereas he, of course, approached the issue with an entirely open mind.) Second, Keating himself was more interested in being known as a member of the President's Commission than in attending its meetings. Already convinced that he was in a small minority, he preferred to maintain his ferocious schedule of appearances before more sympathetic audiences.

His new status led him to Britain, where he staged a press conference at the US Embassy in London, at which he attacked pornography, *Playboy* and the Commission in equal measure. He also amused sophisticated Fleet Street commentators by suggesting that, in ten years' time, today's X-certificate films would be shown on television. (He was right, of course.) Then he took the train to Birmingham, where he was a guest speaker at the NVALA's annual conference. After Mary Whitehouse had lacerated the 'trendy, left, atheist, humanity lobby in the BBC', Keating took to the lectern to denounce the journalists from the Corporation whom he had encountered in London. 'They seemed to conform to the definition of nihilists', he pronounced, with their 'long hair, dishevelled clothing and surroundings of general untidiness'. He compared them to 'dogs', in an uncomplimentary sense. Revelling in his starring role at the conference, he also unleashed a rant about the four young people killed by the National Guard at Kent State University in Ohio a few weeks earlier: in fact, he alleged, some of them had been shot by their own side. Then he returned to Cincinnati, to miss more hearings and prophesy about the carnage that the President's Commission would unleash.

As it turned out, President Nixon was no more sympathetic to his Commission than Keating, who insisted that its lengthy report should include a rambling note of dissension from himself and several other delegates. Nixon, meanwhile, chose to ignore all the Commission's recommendations that some restrictions on the sale of indecent literature should be relaxed. Keating warned that the Commission was trying to 'give the smut peddlers of the world freedom to purvey in the United States their scatological, depraved, deviated, sick sex products'.

But just when it seemed that Keating could be dismissed or parodied as a repressive conservative intent on controlling the lives of others, while wallowing with joy in the sheer obscenity of the literature he described with such relish, he offered a piercing insight into the future. 'The exploitation of women as sexual objects,' he declared, 'and play-things for men, as portrayed in some of the mass media, is revolting and harmful to our society.' His stricture might have been pulled from the pages of a feminist journal – in 1970, or indeed today. And his conclusions were echoed by none other than Mary Whitehouse, on a 1971 television programme in which she was accused of being opposed to anything to do with sex. 'Of course I'm not anti-sex', she snorted. 'In my view, the people who are anti-sex are the people who make sex and women properties for advertisement, properties for commercialism, properties for sensationalism.'

Among them she might have included Richard Neville, then twenty-nine, the notoriously free-spirited founder and editor of *Oz* magazine, and one of the defendants in an equally notorious (and ridiculous) 1971 obscenity trial. At issue then was the 'Schoolkids' number of *Oz*, a copy of which Whitehouse tracked down and (according to Neville) displayed to the Pope as an example of contemporary pornography.

The two campaigners, from opposite ends of the moral and spiritual spectrum, had first met the previous year in Copenhagen. Each was accompanied by a television crew, on hand to chronicle their divergent attitudes to the city's legalisation of porn. 'Our encounter was civil, even warm,' Neville reflected in his memoir. 'The single-mindedness of Mrs Whitehouse was impressive, as was her willingness to flout the turning tide, but her agenda was mad and ridiculous.' One's heart yearns to agree, but there is a caveat.

Just before his trip to Copenhagen, Neville's first book, *Play Power*, was published. It was a heady, kaleidoscopic portrait of his adventures in the underground, which doubled as a manifesto for the anarchic counterculture. In it, he defines what he called 'underground sexual morality' in a simple sentence: 'If a couple like each other, they make love.'

He illustrates this credo with an anecdote. He meets a 'moderately attractive, intelligent, cherubic fourteen-year-old girl' on her way home from school. They share two joints, a 'hurricane fuck' and then she 'rushes off to finish her homework' with 'no feigned love or hollow promises'. Utopian vision of a sin-free paradise? Or casual exploitation of an under-age girl? Even though the hedonistic impulses of one's imagination might prefer Neville's Edenic playground to the staid, censorious landscape of Mary Whitehouse, one can't help wondering whether the veteran schoolteacher, who never forgot her anxious sex-ed pupils, might have been a more reliable moral guide for this particular teenager than the prophet of sexual freedom.

Interlude: The Martyr of Soho Square

One day in the 1950s the photographer Jean Straker met a Scotsman, who told him a sad story. 'He had collected pictures of nudes and pin-ups from magazines throughout his youth,' Straker recalled. 'When he married and saw that his wife had pubic hair, he had a fit – he thought she was a monster. His wife said, "Well, if you don't like the pubic hair, dear, I'll shave it off". He told me he has never been able to get over the psychological distress of his first experience with his wife.'

It had long been rumoured that the same distaste prevented the nineteenth-century art critic John Ruskin from consummating his marriage to Effie Gray. But Straker's anecdote dated from almost one hundred years later, when nude photography was available at every newsagent in the country. Yet without fail, every naked woman pictured in the pin-up magazines was mysteriously lacking not only in pubic hair, but in any form of genitalia. So offensive was the female body, it seemed, that it was illegal to depict it *au naturel*.

Straker dated the unwritten rule back to 1929, when an exhibition of drawings by the author D.H. Lawrence was impounded, and the owner of the Warren Gallery in London prosecuted for obscenity. 'The prosecuting sergeant established in the Recorder's court a principle of English law', Straker explained, 'that a picture which shows pubic hair is automatically obscene.'

During World War Two, when Straker registered as a conscientious objector, he worked part-time for the Ministry of Information, taking surgical photographs. He continued this trade for various hospitals and medical institutions after the war, alongside his preferred career as a photographic artist. In 1958, his first portfolio of female nudes was published. 'It had to have pictures carefully selected,' he recalled, 'to ensure that no pubic hair would be shown. We did actually publish a few pictures of which it could be argued that it wasn't pubic hair – it was just a shadow, or paint, or something. This was the silly nonsense that one had to indulge in, to avoid going to prison.'

That year a photograph in an exhibition caught the attention of the police. The controversial picture, entitled 'Sun Worship', showed the model Pinky Russell. It was, Straker said, 'a simple shot of a girl leaning against a wall, with the shape of her absent bikini patterned white on her tanned body, her pubic hair where it ought to be, applying skin oil. I was told by detectives that it was an offence to show private parts, and that I had better stick to bottoms.'

From 1959 onwards, the legislation governing Obscene Publications in the UK was updated to widen its scope, and protect the innocent British public from indecent literature and pictures of all kinds. Not only was it against the law to exhibit photographs such as 'Sun Worship', but it was illegal to keep the negatives, even if they were never displayed to the public. The inevitable consequence was a series of police raids on Straker's studios at 12 Soho Square in Central London, where he also ran the Academy of Visual Arts, which allowed other photographers to make use of his regular nude models. The Met seized almost 1,500 negatives, and several hundred photos – all of which Straker was ordered by magistrates to forfeit. 'I know you are a brilliant photographer,' Mr Leo Gladwell told him during his first obscenity trial, in 1962. 'But I considered [your pictures] with regard to the standards, including modern and ancient, in various European art galleries. I came to the conclusion that these photographs went beyond these standards, and stressed a certain aspect which would tend to deprave and corrupt.' The 'certain aspect', of course, was the offensive female pubic hair. In vain did Straker argue that he was a published author, a contributor to BBC radio and a valued aide to many London teaching hospitals. The prosecution was also unable to answer his questions: 'In what way do my pictures corrupt anybody, and what do they corrupt them to be?'

'Does it make sense to you,' Straker asked a student audience in 1967, 'that for most of my lifetime it's been an offence at common law to publish an honest, natural photograph of a human being? The nature of my crime is quite simply this: that I refuse to falsify my photographs. If I show a photograph of a woman, that photograph must show pubic hair, the vulva and whatever other anatomical details she possesses. I refuse to retouch my pictures. I regard retouching as fraudulent. I say, "What is a photograph worth if it is not honest?" And I contend that the type of blank space which appears in place of pubic hair on the nudes that proliferate in popular magazines is propagating half a truth.'

Although he continued to work as a photographer until the early 1970s, Straker's energy was now targeted at his campaigns against the censorship of the naked human body. Public speaking took precedence over tuition in photography; he published broadsides and pamphlets, rather than portfolios of nudes. Eventually, in 1970, hints of pubic hair began to be visible in the pages of such magazines as *Penthouse* and *Mayfair*. It was a sign that society was now prepared to accept material that ostensibly exceeded the bounds of the law. But was Straker jubilant? Not at all: he was resolutely an artist, who was 'not in tune at all with that type of teasing exploitation of woman, making her a kind of commercial plaything'. The divide between art and pornography would continue to be tested in the years ahead, long after Straker's once daring photographs came to seem restrained and tame.

5 A Fashion for Exposure

To judge from the advertisements in 1964 issues of *Boyfriend* magazine, Britain's teenage girls were anxious about the size of their breasts. Never mind that a large percentage of the readership were still undergoing puberty: the pages were full of encouragement that a fuller bust could be available within weeks, if only you applied this cream or followed that exercise regime. But the magazine's editorial columns sold an entirely different story. 'Busty girls have been in fashion for a long time,' *Boyfriend* advised that July, 'but now the bosom is waning and the flat look is in.'

Never adventurous or trendsetting, *Boyfriend* was doggedly following the soothsayers of adult fashion. Marjorie Proops, employed by the *Daily Mirror* to chronicle the concerns that would shape the lives of the paper's female readers, had already profiled – with some distaste – the girls 'to whom it's all happening. Nearly all of them have flat chests, pale unmade-up faces, and long untidy hair. Their clothes are an odd assortment of unmatched and haphazardly bought jackets and sweaters and skirts and skinny dresses which skim their entirely non-sensual bodies.' Proops considered these 'strange girls' to be 'non-sensual', of course, because they chose not to emphasise women's traditional methods of catching the male attention. 'They despise the sex-symbols their fathers and elder brothers lusted after,' Proops noted with an air of bafflement, 'the bosom-flaunting, deep-cleavage girls who managed to achieve their ambitions by using sexual attraction as useful currency.' And she quoted nineteen-year-old novelist, Shena Mackay, to prove the point: 'Girls who flaunt their bosoms are as disgusting as the ones who pretend to be coy in order to get what they want out of men.'

London journalists had traditionally become confused when young women chose to spurn traditional notions of glamour. A few years earlier, girls had been pigeonholed as 'weirdies' when they dressed down, rather than up: the combination of black woollen stockings, short skirt and sheepskin jacket, worn by some students on the capital's streets, was as damning as brown shoes on a besuited office executive. The philosopher Michel Foucault might have recognised this disaffection with female choices as a reaction against the 'hysterization of women's bodies', whereby the female form was seen as being 'saturated with sexuality'. The 'strange girls', like the 'weirdies' before them, were stepping outside of their allotted roles: neither sex object nor, it appeared, conforming to traditional notions of motherhood.

On 9 July 1964, the same day that *Boyfriend*'s tip about the flat bosom was published, the documentary film *London in the Raw* was premiered in Piccadilly. Its poster promised that it was 'Red Hot! Red-Eyed & Raw!' and would expose 'The World's Greatest City Laid Bare!'. Photographs outside the cinema highlighted the bare-breasted girls to be seen within, their nipples discreetly covered by stars or pasties. Any lustful cinemagoer seeking solitary release would have been disappointed by the movie, as he had to sit through featurettes about a variety of unerotic London pursuits before finally reaching a short sequence about topless dancers: a rice pudding after ten unappetising courses of traditional British stodge, perhaps.

The real action took place outside the cinema, although most of those who attended the premiere would have been unaware of the scandal until they opened the morning papers. As a publicity stunt, the executive producer hired a pair of sisters, both of whom had cabaret ambitions. As they stepped out of their limousine, they threw off their fur wraps, to reveal that they were wearing dresses that entirely exposed their breasts. The pack of photographers clicked their shutters avidly, although their pictures could not have appeared in any respectable publication. Then the girls covered themselves up and sped away in a taxi. Bare breasts, regardless of their size, were still capable of driving male onlookers into a frenzy of derangement – and commanding column inches in the national press. (As an aside, this applied only to Caucasian breasts. The 1960 movie *Climb Up the Wall* was deemed suitable for child viewers, despite including a nude tableau from Soho's Windmill Theatre. It featured three white women, whose breasts were obscured on screen with asterisks; and one black model, whose presumably unerotic bosoms were allowed to be viewed uncensored.)

The two young women in Piccadilly took care to make themselves known to the papers, and to the police; an arrest for indecent exposure was bound to garner publicity. They were revealed as Valerie (twenty-one) and Marion (twenty-three) Mitchell, occupation 'harmony singers'. To prove the point, they were awarded a run at the New Bagatelle club in London's West End, billed as 'The Mitchell Sisters (The Topless Girls)'. In cabaret, they were able to retain their clothes, despite showing sufficient cleavage to 'show why they took the topless plunge'. They were vivacious, it seems, had 'pleasant voices', and had already amassed a set of 'special material'. The solitary reviewer of their debut described one of their numbers, 'Have Yourself a Sadistic Weekend', as 'the most distasteful number I can recall hearing in cabaret', but otherwise appeared to have enjoyed himself immensely.

Meanwhile, the sisters milked their moment of notoriety, almost goading the police into charging them. The officers on duty complained that the exposure had been so brief as to be almost invisible, but their superiors felt that such tawdry behaviour should not be allowed to go unpunished. Marion, the more outspoken of the pair, kept her side of the bargain: 'It's up to women to decide on fashion, not the police', she told one of the hacks who faithfully pursued the story from July into August. Valerie was upset that she might have to cancel her holiday and uttered the perfectly prepared line: 'I think it's all a storm in a B-cup!' Eventually the women were found guilty of indecency but given a conditional discharge. Marion Mitchell would soon become better known under her alter ego of Janie Jones, notorious for her sex parties, and her glorification on the first album by The Clash.

The fleeting exposure of the Mitchell Sisters was merely one bizarre episode in a saga that seized the attention of the world's media during the summer of 1964. The unwitting and (by his account) unwilling protagonist was the gay fashion designer Rudi Gernreich. In 1962, he surveyed the current trends on the catwalks, and told *Women's Wear Daily*, 'Bosoms will be uncovered in five years'. As Gernreich recalled, 'My heavens, the reaction!' Other designers – Emilio Pucci, Ruben

Torres – made similar predictions, though their estimates of when this shocking development might transpire were more conservative. But the germ of the idea had been planted, after which the transition from concept to reality was an inevitability. As Gernreich reflected once the storm had broken, 'Fashion is moving so fast today that by the time you predict something for the future, it's already here'.

Torres was the first to announce that he would be showing a topless collection. He stoked an inferno of anticipation in Paris, and then opted for discretion in the form of sequins that would conceal the nipples from view. Rudi Gernreich feared that Pucci might be planning a similar outrage and was determined not to be overtaken. 'It was *my* prediction', he said defiantly. But his original remark envisaged a world in which young women would simply shed the top halves of their bikinis. Now his rivals were imagining a swimsuit that would amount to something more than merely a pair of briefs. 'Just a bikini bottom would be the *end* of design', Gernreich said contemptuously.

His annual collections had edged ever closer to revelation since the start of the decade. His one-piece suits had shed their inner brassiere, and then lost their lining, so that the silk jersey would cling provocatively to the woman's body when wet. The Gernreich bikinis sliced away at the fabric until a field of flesh was exposed between the tubular brassiere and skimpy briefs. In 1963, he returned to the one-piece, cutting away the flanks until the sides of the breasts were unveiled. Another design covered the arms, but offered a neckline that plunged almost to the navel. (Until the late 1960s, the female navel was deemed to be too indecent to be exposed to the American public. This forced many screen actresses to shoot beach scenes twice: in a skimpy bikini for the rest of the world, and in enormous, navel-concealing briefs for the USA.)

The ultimate challenge was to reveal the breasts while still encasing the body in a suit, rather than just briefs. After several misfires, Gernreich conjured up a prototype that was effectively a traditional one-piece from the crotch to within an inch or two of the breasts. But there the material ended, except for thin halter straps attached to the front of the costume, which travelled up the crevasse between the breasts and wound around the neck. The breasts were left entirely naked, sparking the inevitable question: why would anyone wear this suit rather than the bottom of a bikini?

Gernreich shared the bemusement: 'It's an illogical thing,' he admitted. 'I just don't believe in it.'

At this point, in the late spring of 1964, Gernreich regarded his topless one-piece – which he dubbed the 'monokini' – as the demonstration of a theory, rather than a commercial proposition. He persuaded his favourite model, Peggy Moffitt, to don the suit, to which she agreed on the condition that her husband, William Claxton, took the photographs. *Women's Wear Daily* duly printed a shot of Moffitt hiding her nipples behind her arms, her hands reaching towards her face as if she had been caught in the moment of undressing. Gernreich stated that Peggy was the only woman for the job, as she had the ideal bust: 'young, firm, small, adolescent'.

There the monokini might have rested, its brief moment of notoriety forgotten. Not that Gernreich had suddenly become a prude: his summer collection for 1964 included a transparent shirt, inside which the woman's body could be glimpsed dimly, as if through the muddy light of dusk. But the mere announcement that there was a topless swimsuit provoked a furious demand from retailers and distributors around the world. 'Society is ready for this', said the apparently reluctant designer. 'It is showing off the beauty of womanhood. Puritanism and the hidden body are fast disappearing.'

An official launch was planned, at the Rainbow Room on the 65th floor of the RCA Building in Manhattan. Attendees were promised 'The first public showing of new topless swimsuits for women, worn by living, breathing, gorgeous models'. In fact, the only woman prepared to don the suit was Peggy Moffitt – and she backed out when she heard the clamour of photographers, reporters and voyeurs at the door. The organiser blamed the throng for the cancellation: 'We did not want to turn the thing into a peep show. This is a serious fashion trend.' As the event's publicist sighed, 'a lot of people are just going to have to go home and have a cold shower.'

The non-appearance of the swimsuit did nothing to stem the public hysteria. Stores such as Neiman Marcus and Hess Brothers competed for supplies, and there was sufficient alarm in Philadelphia for female protestors to picket a store that stocked the monokini, clutching placards reading, 'Let's Keep it Clean'. (This was probably another PR stunt.) If they were actually appalled, they weren't alone: the reliable Marjorie Proops, while insisting 'I am no prude', said that the innovation left her 'stone cold'. She added: 'This bare-bosomed swimsuit is one of the most erotic garments to be produced in an era when erotic stimulation has already reached a dangerous level.'

The furore was unbearably tempting for anyone who was eager to arouse a scandal. Like the Mitchell Sisters in London, a cinema usherette in Chicago, Toni Lee Shelly, recognised her cue. She alerted the local press, and then strode into Lake Michigan on 20 June 1964, wearing one of Gernreich's creations. She was promptly arrested. Shelly demanded that she be tried by an all-male jury, perhaps strategising that she might sway them by demonstrating her garment in the courtroom.

When the case was heard a month later, the would-be starlet – she claimed to be a budding film actress – found herself competing for attention with both her attorney and her prosecutor. Her lawyer seized the moment with an impassioned speech worthy of Spencer Tracy in *Inherit the Wind*: 'We are arguing that the human breast is not decent,' he complained. 'But it is God-given. And it is a part of every female that walks the face of the earth. Is the leg a dirty thing? Is the thigh a dirty thing? Is any part of the body a dirty thing?' Shelly's defence was more mundane: she swore that she had worn the suit for reasons of comfort, and had 'no intention of arousing sexual excitement among people on the beach'. To which the prosecutor replied that, in his opinion, she was 'one of the most calculating individuals you have ever seen', who was effectively 'throwing dirt in the faces of the police officers and of the public'. Then he struck his own note of melodrama: 'This is not a joke. We don't want a bunch of degenerates on our beaches.'

Shelly was eventually convicted of indecent exposure, and fined $100. By way of recompense, she said she had been inundated with offers of modelling work, while a quick-witted producer was said to have assembled a movie entitled *The Girl in the Topless Swimsuit* as her debut. Sadly for Shelly, the film never materialised, and her cinematic career ran no further than the role of a mermaid in the 1966 comic debacle, *The Fat Spy*. Meanwhile, her stunt was imitated by a twenty-five-year-old New York dancer who called herself Hope Diamond, and was arrested by the vice squad in Farmington, Connecticut. She didn't even get to play a mermaid.

Similar stories of daring and disgust began to flood in from around the world, as other designers concocted their own variations upon

Gernreich's prototype. A dummy was adorned with a topless swimsuit in the Italian city of Turin, and placed in the window of a dress shop, before police intervened and demanded that strips of paper be placed across the dummy's plastic breasts. A Greek striptease artist was imprisoned for three months for having 'offended public morals' by wearing a topless suit on a beach near Athens. A Peruvian teenager attempted suicide after a furious row with her boyfriend, who was outraged that she had posed for cameramen in one of the revealing suits. 'Since I wore the one-piece bikini,' she is supposed to have said, 'life has become impossible.' In Britain, a sixteen-year-old entrant in a beauty contest in (appropriately enough) Bristol announced her intention to appear topless, but was barred from entering. The organiser of a similar event in Scotland declared that bare-breasted girls would be welcome at his competition, but was forced to admit that he was joking.

Rudi Gernreich was starting to take on the mantle of the Frankenstein of fashion, disturbed and embarrassed by the unwitting consequences of what he had created. 'I never meant for it to be worn in public,' he said of his monokini. 'I meant it for private parties and yachts and private swimming pools.' As one columnist noted, 'A look of real pain crosses his face when he tries to imagine the beaches filled with the wrong women wearing his creation.' He would probably have been relieved to hear that socialite Christina Paolozzi was staging a topless party for her fellow jet-setters at Long Beach; but so many bystanders congregated outside her property that no swimsuits were shed or breasts bared.

In the same month that Gernreich's swimsuit went on sale, London fashion firm Carnegie Models Ltd opened a new front, so to speak, in the toplessness war. Inevitably, it was Marjorie Proops to whom they turned for publicity. She performed her role to perfection, announcing the arrival of 'a bare-topped party dress. It is a black crepe sheath with the bodice scraped out below the bust, designed, they say, to reveal entirely bare breasts. The dress has already been ordered by two well-known London fashion stores.' One of them, Fifth Avenue on Regent Street, confirmed: 'Now that someone has been bold enough to make it, our customers will expect us to stock it.'

Britain was still three weeks away from the Mitchell Sisters' sensational exposure of Carnegie's design at the premiere of *London in the*

Raw. Well before then, the company had backed down: 'We made the original dresses for a joke, not thinking anyone would take them seriously. We want to stop while it is still a joke.' They were too late; and they had also inspired their peers to emulate them. The designer Mary Quant, known for the playfulness of her creations, announced that there would be three topless designs in her next collection. But she had a warning: 'I think that the trouble with the topless dresses is that the women with the wrong shape may try to wear them. They could look very nice – so long as they are worn by very slim girls with boyish figures. It would be awful to see a fat woman in one.'

Less adventurous souls were more alarmed by the moral implications. Ballroom maestro Victor Silvester declared, apparently with a straight face, that it would be 'barefaced effrontery' if 'semi-nude women were parading about the dance floor'. The official newspaper of the Vatican announced that the topless dress 'links certain manu-facturers' unsatiated lust for money with a sub-feminine lack of purity'. The mouthpiece of the Soviet Communist Party concurred: an edi-torial said the trend was a move 'Back to Barbarism'. The Archbishop of Canterbury was typically modest in his approach: 'The worst thing possible for church people is to adopt an attitude of being shocked. We must just accept that young people express themselves in new methods of dress that may seem queer to the older of us. We must get alongside them and understand them.' That was several steps too far for a mother in Chelmsford, who let off steam to the *Daily Herald*: 'As the mother of a teenage family, I am utterly disgusted. Breasts were intended to feed babies, not to be goggled at and made fun of. How dare dress designers pervert our girls!' In similar vein, a reader of the slightly saucy magazine *Tit-Bits* called the trend 'Disgusting! I wouldn't show my figure to anyone – not even my husband.' Another *Herald* correspondent breathed deeply and took a longer view: 'The current eroticism will not last long. After this period of loose morals – this happens every so often throughout history – there will probably be a period of intense puritanism.'

It was time for another blast from Marjorie Proops, who was now denouncing the blaze that she had helped to ignite. She took a decidedly Old Testament view towards young women who went topless: 'If a woman is so provocative in her appearance as practically to invite sexual assault, would a judge be justified in being lenient to a man thus provoked? There could hardly be anything more provoking to a man than a woman in a topless dress. Any topless girl who pleaded before a judge that all she was doing was following current fashion wouldn't, I imagine, get much sympathy from His Lordship. The sympathy would be with the man. It seems to me that girls who go topless are definitely asking for the kind of trouble I wouldn't be surprised if they get. I wouldn't blame a man inflamed to the point of rape by a girl flaunting her breasts.'

Fortunately, there were no recorded incidents in the summer of 1964 that required men to adopt the Proops defence. Rather than being inflamed, most men who were in the vicinity of a topless woman were embarrassed (ostensibly, at least). Such was the case, it seemed, when the bare-breasted dress was introduced to Australia on a ferry-boat in Sydney by a teenage showgirl. The following day, she was said to have contracted 'a severe cold in the chest'. When a young topless woman entered a bar in South London, hardened male drinkers complained that she was putting them off their beer. A London conductor threw a topless teenager off his bus; a mother-of-two (such details were apparently essential) aged twenty-seven was arrested on Westminster Bridge; an eighteen-year-old girl wore a home-made topless creation as she sang 'Jailhouse Rock' at a church dance in Exeter, before being escorted off stage for 'wriggling' too much; a seventeen-year-old blues singer, the daughter of a local Tory dignitary, appeared topless at a gig in Southall, mortifying her father and his friends.

So ridiculous had the entire farrago become that a clothes store in Toronto was mobbed by women, after it advertised free topless and bottomless bathing suits. Those shoppers who eventually fought their way to the till were rewarded with a cardboard box – with nothing in it. And then, as glorious summer in the Northern Hemisphere faded into mellow autumn, the topless craze vanished, never to return. Instead, the moral terrain moved to the issue of French women wearing only bikini briefs on the beach. There was a test case in Cannes, where a wily deckchair attendant paid a twenty-one-year-old gym teacher from Paris to play table-tennis on the beach, wearing only a monokini. The attendant was rewarded with a promenade-long queue of customers, plus a visit from the gendarmerie, who took both him and the playful Claudine into custody. Her lawyer argued that breasts were not sexual, but designed for feeding babies, and that her display was less erotic than the dancers at the Folies Bergère. Both were convicted, but their sentences were overturned on appeal. The final verdict in early 1965 effectively legalised topless bathing on French beaches: 'Inasmuch as the spectacle of the nudity of the human body has nothing intrinsic in it that would outrage normal, even delicate decency, and since Claudine D concealed her sexual parts with a sufficiently opaque monokini, we acquit her.'

The topless swimsuit and the topless dress proved to be a one-season sensation. Short of absolute nudity, there were no taboos left to be shattered, and nowhere for designers to go but in search of intriguing ways of covering up what they had just unveiled. 'I have a marvellous new idea for autumn,' announced Rudi Gernreich at the end of that tempestuous summer. 'It's the trouser suit with the transparent top. It's black satin with a sheer chiffon top – and of course you could wear it with a bra. But it should look erotic and sensuous. It's for married women to wear at home – for their husbands or other lovers.'

By 1965, it was as if breasts had never been exposed. But throughout the 1960s, fashion remained a battleground, between those who saw indecency in every hint of exposure and those who opted for the feeling of freedom, while manufacturers sought to lend even the least erotic of garments the hint of sensuality and beyond.

The champions of morality included some unlikely bedfellows. In late 1959, Soviet leader Nikita Khrushchev visited the set of the movie *Can-Can* in Hollywood, and mocked the civilisation that had produced such 'freedom for the girls to show their backsides. To us, it's pornography. It's capitalism that makes the girls that way.' Heavyweight boxing champion Muhammad Ali filed for divorce from his wife Sonji in 1966, on the grounds that what she wore was unbecoming for a Muslim woman. Already irate that she sported false eyelashes and lipstick in public, Ali was driven beyond endurance when he came home from a training session to find her in 'tight pants'. 'It's too tight,' he explained to the judge. 'Her knees are showing, her limbs are showing. It's lust to the eye, and embarrassing to me.' Once his marriage had ended, Ali laid down his philosophy of fashion: 'These days, you can't tell a housewife from a prostitute. They dress alike. Western women's clothes are lustful. Western women display themselves to taunt and tease and cause trouble – just like a prostitute.'

Designers were relieved to discover that this was not a majority view. Regardless of who or why they were trying to impress, women of all ages were assumed to desire clothes that would make them feel, and therefore look, more attractive. The wording of adverts for women's undergarments was undoubtedly aimed at those who were going to wear the clothes, but it employed the same techniques of tantalising and teasing the consumer as softcore pornography. As an example: in 1960, the Silkskin Locket brassiere assured purchasers of 'a glamorous new you', thanks to its 'cute American uplift, new intriguing separation and lovely deep plunge line'. Buyers of Dorothy Perkins' Indiscreet range were promised that they would 'feel exciting'. The following year, a pundit assured women that 'romance' would be the dominant fashion theme of the year: 'filmy and fragile, as opposed to the smart, hard look'. Both sides of the market were covered by Dreamform underwear, from the 'heavenly brassiere' with its 'wonderful allure' to the 'Risqué Bloomer', 'an exciting novelty for the young at heart'. (A similar illusion of decadent eroticism was being employed with men, via items such as 'Scandal' bathing briefs, and the 'Stag' range of male cosmetics.)

At night, the desirable ladies of 1961 were being encouraged to explore the new 'zizzy' items flown in from Italy and France, 'where the girls know that sleepwear should be a mixture of high-fashion and real sex appeal'. During the day, they could experiment with a flame-red foundation garment entitled Birthday Suit, lighter and more flexible than anything manufactured in the past. For the new season after Christmas, Paris gave birth to the Nude Look – plunging cleavage, skirts sliced open high on the thigh, and peepholes cut into the back of dresses to encourage voyeurs to pay attention. Similar designs were being offered as brand new in 1965, as a substitute for the topless vogue; and again at the end of the decade, allowing respectable young women to masquerade as hippies. By the summer of 1963, as commentator Felicity Green noted, 'In any one shop, on any one rail, a canny customer can find backless dresses, well-nigh frontless dresses, dresses slit to the thigh, dresses with peekaboo cut-outs scattered around like holes in a [Emmenthal] cheese... It seems inevitable, the way things are going at the moment, that clothes will soon be at such a minimum level that the lowest necklines will meet the highest hemlines at half-way mark, and we'll all be back to fig leaves'.

Even amidst the topless months of 1964, it was still possible for holidaymakers on the Mediterranean to fall foul of local law enforcement with clothes that would not have raised an eyebrow in Cannes or Clacton. The island of Malta was particularly squeamish on this account: the wife of a Royal Marine was arrested that June for exposing her bare shoulders by wearing a strapless dress; another young British visitor upset local police by sunbathing in a bikini. She was only cleared when a magistrate ruled that her brassiere had covered sufficient of her 'unbecoming parts' to avoid gross indecency. Women in Sicily were less fortunate: the merest appearance of a bikini on the beach in 1964 was sufficient to merit a visit from a posse of eagle-eyed policemen.

Designers in Paris, London, New York and other chic fashion centres were not concerned about what might make the Maltese cross. Their preoccupation was to negotiate the restrictive and frankly sexless array of underwear that even the most modish females were forced to adopt. At issue was the dilemma of how a woman might, for example, wear skin-tight clothes without disclosing, as Felicity Green put it, 'the edge of her girdle, the outline of her panties, the bumps on her suspenders and the fastening at the back of her bra'. The answer, she revealed, was the body stocking, which 'clings as closely as if it were sprayed on and weighs under half an ounce [14g]'. If you boasted the correct balance of curves to ensure aesthetic appeal, its only drawback was its lack of suspenders. Green advised that stockings could instead be held up by Ultra Hold, the 'garter in a bottle'. This adhesive substance could be brushed onto the thigh in the appropriate position, and the stocking top would cling to it – though removing the stockings might also peel off several layers of skin.

Another vision of the future was provided at Christmas 1964 by children's dolls. A disgusted columnist reported that these innocent toys now sported 'flimsy, see-through negligées, plunging bras and G-string panties', all more suitable for the Folies Bergère than daily wear. Meanwhile, those children's mothers were being enticed by advertisements for what resembled a pair of long-johns, but were actually Vedonis Plus-Twos, 'made in stretchy, clingy twist nylon that's as warm as the way you feel about him, sleek as the way he likes you'. So, one way or another, the entire family was obviously happy that Christmas.

In the post-topless world, designers tried to convey the impression of nudity without revealing the flesh. Besides the body stocking, smart young women were encouraged to buy the 'no-bra bra', with a transparent look in sheer fabric. Variations removed the visible support from the front, back or sides, relying instead on the holding power of nylon tricot. As the director of the US lingerie firm Exquisite Form explained, 'Previously foundation garments were designed to give a good line to a dress. These give a girl a real sexy look when she takes the dress off.' An alternative was mesh, or fishnet, for everything from bikinis to catsuits. In May 1965, French model Chantal donned a mesh siren suit in Cannes, and predictably 'caused a sensation', because 'she wore it over nothing more than a pair of briefs and a suntan'.

If these designs required a combination of Mediterranean weather and sheer nerve to carry off, the British everywoman was being greeted by window displays of undergarments that justified the fashion mag boast, 'Sexy Lingerie is Here to Stay'. 'Why, suddenly, in 1965 do we all want more sexy undies than we did in 1964?', asked Felicity Green. Her answer was that outer garments that autumn were becoming more 'aggressively plain and geometric', and lingerie with a hint of eroticism made the wearer feel more self-confident. 'We may be wearing boots and a Courrèges shift on top,' Green wrote knowledgeably, 'but it's comforting to know our bra may be covered in forget-me-nots, or there's a pink lace insertion on our black lace mini-slip.' To blur the distinction between the housewife and the glamour model, Kayser marketed their lingerie with a picture of a young woman wearing only a pink negligée under the enticing headline: 'Kayser is marvellous in bed'. Convinced that he had a unique insight into the psychological thinking of the modern woman, marriage guidance counsellor Dr William Swartley pursued a similar theme, designing a range of gowns that were guaranteed to revive the spark in a stagnant marriage – among them Peek-a-Boo, Gift Rapt and Pussycat. And all the time hemlines were rising, in preparation for the scandalous trend of 1966.

The great moral debate about the miniskirt began softly in April 1966, when a seventeen-year-old factory worker was scolded for wearing a tight sweater and a skirt that soared a full four inches above the knee. Production on the male-dominated factory line declined noticeably, because the poor men found it so hard to concentrate on their work. 'My skirt isn't indecent,' young Kathleen protested. 'Anyway, the men shouldn't be staring at the girls.' A similar incident saw a young woman in Amersham being asked to leave a café because her skirt offended the female manager. An Oxford college banned female students from wearing short skirts in examinations, because they might distract male students and embarrass the invigilators. The actor Sharon Tate experienced an even more extreme set of reactions: 'It was the miniskirt I'd just bought in London, only a few inches above the knee. The Italian policeman was purple as he handed me a ticket for indecent exposure. And in Munich, angry women kept pulling at it.' By 1967, police in Paris and London were warning that the miniskirt was effectively an invitation to rape: even without revealing their breasts or genitals, women were clearly posing intolerable strain upon the male of the species.

As skirts inched higher, encouraged by the summer collections, the manufacturers of more traditional undergarments struggled to keep pace. The girdle made an uncomfortable, not to mention impractical, partner to the miniskirt, but one firm did their best to sell its restriction as a brand of liberation. The Free'n'Easy Girdle was marketed as being 'dedicated to the freedom of women', 'the greatest boon since women got the vote' and 'the revolutionary girdle dedicated to setting us beautifully, femininely free'. This approach paled, however, alongside that adopted by Mary Quant, in selling her underwear range for summer 1966. 'Mary Quant gives you the bare essentials', her advert promised, and for the first time a lingerie promotion featured an entirely nude woman, seated side on, with her nipple just obscured behind a discreetly raised knee.

The future, Quant foretold, would see young women casting off their brassieres and letting their breasts roam at will, beneath tight-fitting garments. Catwalk models led the way, and by the end of 1966, their American counterparts supposedly gave this trend a name: Swinging Free. One designer was said to be trialling a spray-on bra, while 'a compromise group use strips of transparent adhesive tape to give themselves a little unobtrusive uplift'.

The link between exotic fashion and the promise of erotic delight had never been so blatant. In the first days of 1967, the journalist Paul Francis explored London tube trains, noting the iconography on platforms and carriages: '"Lie back and enjoy it", invites one flimsily clad girl, while another, for no apparent reason, declares that after her bath, all she needs is me. The latest swimsuits for 1967, although not especially daring in their design, are filled with rampant beauties obviously in the last stage of orgasm: there they stand, legs apart, *mons veneri* thrust forward, their mouths open, gazing off-camera feigning shock, or delight, no doubt at some male splendour hidden from the public view.'

Felicity Green informed the readers of the *Daily Mirror* that, 'in the opinion of Miss Jocelyn Richards, a film fashion designer, no one who is young and lovely in London is wearing lingerie anymore'. She checked amongst her suitably qualified friends, and found a noted absence of girdles, with suspender belts unnecessary because girls were now wearing tights. Also missing from the modern miss was that staple of female daywear, the slip. As the see-through blouse, dress or even T-shirt became a standard fashion accessory in 1968, the position of the brassiere came into question: to wear, or to bare? One suggestion was the Blenette, consisting of two stick-on circles that (unlike the traditional pastie) were applied to the front of the blouse, rather than the breast. Another was the paint-on bra, marketed by Lady Jayne boutique in Carnaby Street.

After which there was only one more hurdle to cross: the total removal of underwear. Once again, Felicity Green was the intrepid reporter: 'Some say they've given up wearing undies altogether ... Tights have, to a large extent, now taken the place of three separate garments – a girdle, a pair of panties and a pair of stockings.' She found an obliging actress to support her case. Twenty-two-year-old Connie Kreski, a *Playboy* Playmate, commented in 1969: 'I reckon that none of my generation really wear much underwear, but I think the kids today won't even start.'

By then, the very nature of female underwear had already become an overtly political issue, thanks to the demonstration by supporters of women's liberation at the Miss America Pageant in Atlantic City, on 7 September 1968. The event sparked a surge of enthusiasm for the feminist cause; it also provoked a myth that rapidly turned into a stereotype. Before the event, Robin Morgan, a member of the New York Radical Women group, issued a press release that demanded, 'No More Miss America'. Cub reporter Lindsy Van Gelder was sent to interview her by the *New York Post*, and during their conversation,

Morgan dreamed up the idea of a Freedom Bonfire, in which women could burn all the symbols of their oppression – from make-up and constricting underwear to copies of men's magazines. Van Gelder souped up the story by slipping the idea into her first paragraph: 'Lighting a match to a draft card has become a standard gambit of protest groups in recent years, but something new is due to go up in flames this Saturday. Would you believe a bra burning?' A male sub-editor concocted a headline which read: 'Bra Burners & Miss America'. As another protestor, Peggy Dobbins, explained, a bra-burning would be a metaphorical destruction of female restraint: 'We are put in a position of feeling that we should try to be this kind of ideal, sub-missive community – a combination of sex object and earth mother.'

Not a single brassiere, or any other item for that matter, was burned on the boardwalk at Atlantic City, although various items of underwear joined high-heel shoes in a Freedom Trash Can. One hundred dem-onstrators marched up and down the street outside the arena, while just as many men, and a smattering of unimpressed women jeered and mocked them. As Leah Fritz recounted, the opposition effectively proved the feminist case by catcalling the protestors in entirely sexual terms: 'They were alternating, "Hey, good lookin' – whatcha doing tonight?" with "Boy, get a load of that one – what a dog!" The men acted as if we were conducting a beauty contest. I'd never felt such humiliation.'

In that climate, women were left to consider exactly who was driving the fashion industry's rush towards the exposure of young female flesh: was it led by demand from women, sick of being strapped into girdles that were little more than straitjackets, or men, eager to reduce the female form to a playground for male desire? For all the cries of freedom from women in their teens and twenties, who felt liberated by the creation of the miniskirt or the see-through blouse, there were tales that exposed the all-too-naked arm of male manipu-lation behind the siren call of freedom.

Take, for example, Sue – 'a little blonde in a see-through blouse and a miniskirt'. She was recruited in May 1968 to work on the fore-court of a petrol station in Pulloxhill, Bedfordshire. Her task was to encourage drivers to sample the garage's new brand of fuel, which originated in Russia. And she was duly nicknamed 'The Russian Bare'. Decades of petrol advertising ahead would feature scantily dressed women holding and caressing a fuel hose as if they were cradling a particularly floppy penis. What differentiated Sue was that her naked body, visible beneath her blouse, was being exploited *in situ*, rather than on a poster.

The Sunday newspaper, *The People*, cheerfully pictured Sue in action, beaming coyly at the camera as she clasped the nozzle. 'There's nothing like a dame to put across your sales message', the paper proclaimed. There was even a joke: readers were warned not to drive across the country in the hope of seeing Sue's body: 'After a couple of days in her see-through blouse, the poor girl caught flu'.

It was several weeks before another side to the story emerged. Young Sue was now plying her wares in a North London garage, and was spotted by police, who warned her that they would report her for indecent behaviour. Her boss was told he was aiding and abetting the offence. Sue carried on regardless, so police arrested her. Only then was it revealed that Sue was just fifteen years old. She explained that she had been told to wear a top that 'showed everything underneath', and had agreed, because her ambition was to become a model. Far from fearing for their child's safety, her parents had encouraged her to take the job. As the *Daily Mirror* concluded its account, 'The girl was found to be in need of care and protection, and placed under the supervision of a probation officer'. Was she exploiting her own sexual appeal, or being used by her employers and the male community at large?

As the 1960s came to a close, there was virtually no gap between the sexy underwear on sale in the high street, and the fetishist clothes available as erotic aids from small ads in specialist magazines – the peephole-themed, open-tipped bra, perhaps, or the open-front tights, freshly imported from more permissive continental climes. Those who required pictorial evidence of what lay beneath a woman's blouse need no longer purchase pornography: bare-breasted women were to be seen in the pages of the vanguard fashion magazine, *Vogue*. And in November 1969, when Rupert Murdoch purchased and remodelled *The Sun* newspaper, breasts and nipples became its common commercial currency. Topless young women may not have appeared on Page 3 for another year, but one of the first issues of the new regime featured a centre-spread photo of Uschi Obermaier, the twenty-three-year-old model who lived in a left-wing Berlin commune, exposing her breasts for titillation, rather than under the guise of fashion.

Two years earlier, as the media phenomenon known as Swinging London faded into twilight, Mary Quant was asked to predict the future of fashion, fifty years ahead. The key question, of course, was: 'Will we go totally nude? No, I don't think so. Maybe women will bare their breasts, but not go absolutely naked. There has to be some last unveiling, some remaining bit of mystery.' In subsequent decades, the tides of fashion have ebbed and flowed between concealment and exposure. But anyone impatient with mystery can click their mouse and uncover a universe of titillation, without the barest hint of mystique.

Interlude: Normals and Cannibals

The publication in 1955 of *Homosexuality*, a Pelican paperback by D.J. West that was intended for mass-market distribution, forced a crack in the British wall of ignorance around the subject. Yet, as Bryan Magee (author in 1966 of the altogether more liberal *One in Twenty*) pointed out, there were substantial flaws in West's account. His book 'assumes that its readers know already what male homosexuals do, so it does not tell them', Magee noted. More significantly still, West's book dealt only with men: of lesbians, there was not a word.

An apocryphal tale has passed into social history that Queen Victoria refused to believe that such a thing as female homosexuality was possible, which is why any reference to these acts was omitted from legislation during her reign. Many decades later, lesbians enjoyed – or suffered – the same invisibility, often discreetly avoiding the persecution and discrimination that hounded their male counterparts. Where they were noticed, they were rarely understood. As the American historian Lillian Faderman recounted, 'Some researchers of the early 1950s, who must have believed that the one sexual act of cunnilingus was synonymous with the entire lesbian experience, and who misunderstood even that act, suggested that homosexuality was really a manifestation of cannibalistic fantasies.'

In his appallingly bigoted book, *Variations in Sexual Behaviour* (1957, revised in 1966), the hypnotherapist Frank S. Caprio repeated the standard lines about homosexuality being a sign of immaturity and moral weakness. But he was particularly brutal about lesbians, most of whom, he alleged, 'are emotionally unstable and neurotic', 'essentially sick individuals'. They represented 'a problem of universal

significance'. The negative judgements kept on coming: 'Female homosexuality at best is a form of co-operative, or mutual, masturbation –
a symptomatic expression of a neurotic personality ... a regression
to narcissism, a manifestation of an emotional maladjustment usually
influenced by such factors as a girl identifying herself with her father
or brother.'

A similar sense of disgust was apparent whenever 'unnatural friend-
ships' were discovered among Army servicewomen. Lesbians were
said to be preying upon innocent recruits, such as the eighteen-year-old
who revealed in 1963: 'I used to go out with boyfriends. I had perfectly
normal sex instincts. But in the first two months at the Kingston camp,
I was approached by many other women who wanted me to have
love affairs with them. After two months of loneliness, without any
male company, I became involved with one of the girls. Now, unfortunately, I have no interest in men.' As such activities were not illegal,
those involved in 'abhorrent Lesbian behaviour' could only be dismissed from the Women's Royal Army Corps on grounds of unsuit-
ability.

In 1963, the Minorities Research Group was formed as an offshoot
of the Homosexual Law Reform Society. Its aim was to offer much-
needed 'enlightenment about what has been called the misty, unmapped
world of feminine homosexuality'. The following year, the MRG
launched a newsletter, *Arena Three*, which offered a rare opportunity
for lesbians to feel a sense of cultural belonging. But its membership
and circulation was restricted to a few hundred. The vast majority of
lesbians never stumbled across the organisation or its magazine. They
were left to map their own path across a desert that offered them
little hint of relief or recognition.

On the rare occasions that lesbians did stray into popular culture,
they were either stereotyped in pulp fiction, or else presented as
doomed, tragic figures, as in Lillian Hellman's 1934 play, *The Children's
Hour* (filmed delicately in 1961). Worse than that, they might be portrayed as objects for male conquest, like Miss Pussy Galore in Ian
Fleming's *Goldfinger* (1959): 'Bond liked the look of her. He felt the
sexual challenge all beautiful Lesbians have for men.' When she is
inevitably seduced by James Bond, Pussy talks 'not in a gangster's
voice, or a Lesbian's, but in a girl's voice'. Lesbians were also reported
to be prevalent in prison, divided into sets of 'butches' and 'femmes'

(or 'fems') according to a 1964 report in *Tit-Bits* magazine. Their expert passed judgement: 'In all lesbian relationships, no matter how innocent, danger and corruption lurk. Jealousies lead to fights and worse.' From there it was a short step to violence, as a report in the underground newspaper *International Times* explained in 1966: 'Girls are occasionally mental sadists, but those who are erotically interested in physical sadism are usually lesbians.'

Not until the 1967 adaptation of D.H. Lawrence's short story, 'The Fox', and the 1968 version of *The Killing of Sister George* was a lesbian relationship allowed to dominate a mainstream US/UK movie without being presented as a worrying social issue. Even then, *Daily Mirror* columnist Marje Proops was uneasy: 'I, like most other heterosexual women, prefer not to think about lesbianism', she began. She eventually convinced herself that most lesbians were harmless and didn't prey upon children, but still felt forced to conclude: 'The only general danger would be if lesbianism became a vicious cult.'

Elsewhere in Europe, in the sexually explicit fiction and memoirs of the French author Violette Leduc, for example, lesbianism could be presented as a natural consequence of two women falling in love or lust. In British fiction, almost the only place where a lesbian community was visible during the 1960s was in the work of Maureen Duffy. Her 1966 novel, *The Microcosm*, was a cavalcade of modernist fictional techniques – shifting narrative forms and personae, characters whose names did not necessarily match their gender – all focused upon the House of Shades, alias Chelsea's legendary Gateway Club. Open only to private members, the Gateway attracted lesbians from across London and adjoining counties. (Duffy also discovered another tolerant watering-hole: the Cricketers pub in Battersea.)

For Duffy and her friends, the Gateway was not just a refuge but (as its name suggested) the door to an alternative vision of the world. As Bryan Magee noticed during an exploratory visit, it encouraged a rare sense of freedom. Its members 'clung to each other, kissed each other, fondled each other, stroked each other as they danced. Others throbbed erotically in twists and shakes.' But an evening at the Gateway could not erase the harsher climate outside. Duffy's novel did not disguise the alienation that was felt by many gay women in 1960s Britain. One of her characters presented a stark contrast to the tired tropes of the lesbian as deviant, or as martyr, or even as cannibal, as she watched the 'normal' girls around her, pursuing the fantasy of the 'normal' family. She didn't want to be like them, not for an instant, but gazed clear and cold at her own life: 'Trapped by your own body. All you'd always wanted to do shoved back in a corner, made dream stuff in an instant. Trapped in a role that's alien to you. Condemned for life in the bars of your own flesh.' In the 1960s, recognising your own milieu was not enough to make you feel safe, or established, or anything other than an outsider in an antagonistic world.

6 The Cure With No Disease

It was a day for giving offence. In the *Sunday Mirror* of 28 April 1963, a Church of England vicar was calling the TV personality Bernard Levin 'a thick-lipped Jew boy' and cabaret singer Millicent Martin 'repulsive'. Elsewhere in the paper, the former Hollywood correspondent Lionel Crane responded with some bemusement to the publication of a report into the scandal of a civil servant in the Admiralty who had been unmasked as a Russian spy. The offending bureaucrat, John Vassall, had been revealed to be a homosexual – or, as Crane put it, 'a homo'. His feature hinged around the fact that nobody in the Admiralty had recognised Vassall's sexual proclivities, which in the etiquette of the time suggested a vulnerability to blackmail. 'One or two people Vassall worked with thought he was a bit effeminate,' Crane summarised. 'Some even nicknamed him "Vera". But neither his bosses nor the officials marked to vet him ever appeared to mark him down as a homo, and a dangerous one at that.'

To prevent similar mistakes being made in the future, Crane offered 'a short course on how to pick a pervert'. His article was entitled 'How to Spot a Possible Homo', and was illustrated with a photograph of Vassall wearing nothing but a large pair of boxer shorts. 'Vassall, a spy and homo', read the caption – 'a gilt-edged specimen of his type'. Crane explained that 'homos' could be divided into two categories: 'Obvious' and 'Concealed'. While those who wore eyeliner and adopted 'a gay little wiggle' could be recognised instantly, the undercover 'queers' presented more of a challenge – or threat.

With the help of an anonymous and possibly imaginary psychiatrist, Crane isolated eight stereotypes which, he admitted, were not definitive, but offered a reliable guide to identifying these tiresome and potentially dangerous creatures. 'Most of us have an in-built instinct about possible, or probable, or latent homosexuals,' he argued. 'The object of this lesson is to help sharpen this instinct.' He concluded, 'I wouldn't tell them *my* secrets' – a line that begged to be delivered by one of radio's more overtly camp comedians, such as Kenneth Williams.

His line-up of potential suspects included the unmarried middle-aged man who loves his mother; the man keen to work with young men or boys; the ever-so-humble crawler; the natty dresser who can't stop admiring himself in the mirror; the man who prides himself on cleanliness, and has the fresh-scrubbed cheeks to match; the man loved by older women; the man who drinks alone in a bar; and the touchy-feely man who can't keep his fingers off other men's shoulders or backs. (The magazine *Private Eye* reprinted the bulk of the article, neatly satirising its contents with a pop-art collage to illustrate these types in action.) As the convenient psychiatrist noted, 'Anyone with a grain of sense can *smell* the homos among these men'.

A week later, the paper printed a response from a concerned woman from Bournemouth: Crane's exposé was 'long overdue. As a mother, I believe the public should know the facts.' To balance this view, a London man wrote: 'Surely these unfortunate people are hounded enough'. Or, as a sympathetic friend said to Boy Barrett in the 1961 film, *Victim*: 'It used to be witches. At least they don't burn you.'

Victim, as the *Daily Worker* put it, was 'a sobering picture of the way homosexual inclinations make a permanent nightmare of private lives'. It starred Dirk Bogarde as Melville Farr, a barrister with designs on becoming a QC. He is married to Sylvia Sims, who on their wedding day, when she was nineteen, was informed by her husband of his unconsummated homosexual leanings. 'I was young and conceited,' she tells him. 'I thought marriage would make you content.' As she learns, however, there is contentment, and there is lust. Farr has secretly been giving lifts home to a young wages clerk, Jack 'Boy' Barrett. When Boy is arrested, he kills himself in a police cell. Challenged by his wife as to the nature of their relationship, Farr admits fiercely: 'I stopped seeing him because I wanted him. Do you understand? *Because I wanted him.*'

The exquisitely constructed plot, manoeuvred elegantly on screen by director Basil Dearden, involves blackmail by an almost archetypal couple: a repressed spinster, and Sandy Youth, a provocative young biker. There is the odd expression of homophobia, but most of the characters – even the police inspector investigating the blackmail scheme – are impeccably if modestly liberal. It is this hint of tolerance, plus Farr's refusal to apologise for his inclinations, that makes the film so striking, although its force is compromised by the main character's insistence that he has never actively *been* homosexual, merely felt that way. Even this admission was only made at the insistence of Bogarde, who recounted in his 1988 memoir, *Snakes and Ladders*: 'It is extraordinary, in this over-permissive age, to believe that this modest film could have been considered courageous, daring or dangerous to make.' But it undoubtedly was: in 1962, Bogarde admitted, 'I took a chance playing the part, and according to some people in the know, this piece of casting has ruined my chance of a knighthood'. (In fact, Bogarde was invested as a Knight Bachelor in 1992.) He was also concerned how his loyal fans might react, but recounted that their 'only complaint was that I had grey sideburns! My mail was mostly from young women, married to homosexuals, who had thought that they were the only people who had to go through it.'

Bogarde had become established as a heterosexual sex symbol via his romantic leads in a series of light 1950s movies, but his somewhat diffident style on screen hinted that his feelings might have lain elsewhere. Although he never revealed his sexual preferences in public, and briefly claimed to be engaged to the sultry French film star Capucine, Bogarde was assumed by his friends to be a homosexual. (He explicitly denied it in a 1988 interview, but added: 'If that's what people want to think, they'll think it.') As he wrote to a friend several years later, 'You MUST realise that I have two kinds of life, one public and one private'. He remembered his early fame, and the way it was manifested among his audience, as being 'humiliating'. He endured 'hysterical women hiding in my wardrobes in theatres, [and] one who wandered mournfully about the gardens at night wailing my name, and who was in constant danger of being found floating face downwards in the lily pools ... I had my flies ripped so often that eventually, in public, I had to have a side zip.' When he was forced to play out a romantic scene with a woman, 'of course, the Manhood question did become frightful', he admitted. 'My eyes, my ears and my lips often revolted.'

Bogarde succeeded in protecting his private life throughout his lifetime, even though perceptive critics noticed a sexual ambivalence in his performances even before *Victim*. Reviewing his previous film, *The Singer Not the Song* (1960), Penelope Gilliatt in the *Observer* highlighted what she saw as homosexual overtones between his leather-clad outlaw and a priest.

Victim was much more explicit, even if director, writer and star failed to persuade like-minded souls to join them in the production. 'We couldn't get any of the actors we thought were queer to play in it,' Bogarde chuckled in 1970. 'They all refused. There was a marvellous band of heterosexuals.' Men of all classes and dispositions are exposed as homosexual during the film: some of them adhering to Lionel Crane's crude classifications, but most identifiable only by their anguish at being blackmailed. 'Nature played me a dirty trick', hairdresser Henry tells Farr. 'You ought to be able to state our case – tell them there's no magic cure for how we are, certainly not behind prison bars!' For all its liberal hesitation, *Victim* undoubtedly helped a little to inch public opinion away from the opinions expressed in this 1962 newspaper editorial: 'A subtle attempt to corrupt the nation is being made by certain so-called intellectuals in high places. The campaign to condone and even glorify homosexual practices is typical of what is occurring.'

One of the most famous legal developments of the 1960s was the semi-legalisation of homosexual acts, so long as they were committed by consenting adults over the age of twenty-one, in private, with no witnesses – although not if either party was a member of the armed services or the merchant marines. Female homosexuality never before having been recognised by English law, the passing of the Sexual Offences Act in July 1967 actually restricted rather than liberalised the law for lesbians between the ages of sixteen and twenty, who were no longer legally allowed to have intercourse. The bill was still seen as a victory for liberalism and progress, however. Lord Arran, who helped to steer the legislation through the House of Lords, told Dirk Bogarde that *Victim* 'had done a great deal to strengthen his fight to get his bill through both Houses ... and had certainly helped to sway things in his favour'. Bogarde was delighted by this compliment, telling a friend: 'That is why I did the thing in the first place.'

Scriptwriter Janet Green agreed: 'I have mixed freely with male homosexuals. And when I read of them getting longer prison sentences than the beasts who assault little children, it makes my blood boil.

Many important police officers agree with me that ninety per cent of the blackmail money in Brighton is paid by frightened homosexuals, and that a change in the law would stamp out most of it.' But even after this partial act of liberalisation, the police continued to prey upon men who solicited sexual acts in public places; indeed, the rate of convictions increased sharply in the first few years after the legislation was passed.

Before and after the 1967 Act, doctors, therapists and psychologists of many stripes and schools claimed to have perfected exactly what poor Henry knew was a fantasy: a 'magic cure' for homosexuality. One of the more modest exponents of this trade began to offer her services at the same time as the *Sunday Mirror* was encouraging its readers to spot 'homos'. Doris Munday had an established service as a hypnotherapist in Hammersmith, West London. Her advertisements were discreet, promising 'Rapid results with migraine, peptic ulcers, stammering, inferiority feelings, emotional difficulties, obesity, heavy smoking' – and, as she revealed in the summer of 1963, homosexuality. Those anxious to be rid of their natural leanings did not even have to attend her consulting room. She claimed to be able to treat homosexuals over the phone, and rid them of their desires and urges with a few minutes of mellifluous incantation – plus, it should be assumed, an unhealthy degree of wishful thinking on the part of her 'patient'.

Even opponents of gay life as strident as the newspaper editor quoted above were at pains to differentiate between those who suffered from homosexuality as 'a disease', and those who practised the vice as a result of 'an evil development of character'. The latter deserved the worst punishment that the law provided; the former could be granted a modicum of sympathy. (The editor did not explain how to divide homosexuals between these two strands: presumably the 'diseased' faction comprised those who wanted to be 'cured'.) But even this begrudging acceptance for some unfortunate homosexuals was beyond the editor of the *Gloucester Journal*, who marked the passing of the Act by declaring in print: 'This is perhaps the most revolting human perversion ever known ... a horrible sin ... a disease more dangerous than diphtheria.' A similar view had been expressed in the House of Lords the previous year by the Earl of Dudley, who avoided conjecture by explaining, 'I cannot stand homosexuals'. They were, he added, 'the most disgusting people in the world'.

For the previous century, homosexuality had been widely regarded as a moral rather than a physical illness: a weakness of the soul which inevitably stemmed from the practice of masturbation in young men. Given that the soul was difficult to treat, however, except by Christian prayer or (it seemed) imprisonment, attempts at alleviating this 'disease' concentrated on physical methods: either total abstinence, reinforced by entreaties to the All-Mighty; or, *in extremis*, castration – an all-purpose cure for homosexuals and other sex criminals, from exhibitionists and sadists to child molesters.

For several decades before Doris Munday took to the field, mavericks in the wider American medical community had proposed outlandish treatments for the homosexual. Their approaches varied as greatly as their explanations for why people were, or became, or chose to be (depending on the medical verdict), gay. The Californian doctor Clifford Wright, for example, explained in 1935 that homosexuality emerged as the result of an imbalance of sex hormones. He insisted that 'arrest and incarceration of these abnormal individuals is of no relief for their condition'. Instead, they should be given 'hormones taken from the pituitary and adrenal gland', which would restore a stable hormonal balance. A contemporary therapist in Switzerland went so far as to create artificial male hormones, which would not only produce 'normal' (i.e. heterosexual) desires, but also stave off old age. As a variation, an Atlanta psychiatrist recommended 'injecting a camphor solution into the muscles' to induce convulsive seizures, although he was at a loss to explain exactly *how* this would steer the patient away from homosexual inclinations.

By the late 1930s, the sexual teachings of Sigmund Freud, and his emphasis on the power of the unconscious, had begun to infiltrate not only medicine but also the attitude towards sexual abnormalities, among which homosexuality was thought to be the most prevalent (and treatable). The psychologist George W. Crane operated a syndicated 'Worry Clinic' across hundreds of newspapers in mid-century America. Every few months, he would offer minor variations on the same standard theme: homosexual feelings were perfectly normal during adolescence, but aroused concern thereafter. 'Love is a matter of habits', he pronounced in a typical 1938 column. 'We must teach young men to be heterosexual rather than homosexual.'

After World War Two, the same assumption of congruence between Communism, homosexuality and treason that would condemn spies such as Vassall haunted the era of the McCarthyite witch-hunts. There was a widespread assumption that all homosexuals were open to blackmail and might therefore fall prey to pressure from Russian agents. Numerous psychiatrists and psychologists operated along the lines of Andrew Salter, whose 1949 book *Conditioned Reflex Therapy* said that the key to dealing with any dysfunction of the mind – such as homosexuality – was breaking habits. Bad practices could be discouraged, good ones substituted in their place, all via a system of punishment and reward (or, as the experts preferred it, disinclination and excitation).

What nobody could agree upon in the 1950s was the cause of homosexuality – although there was virtual unanimity that, as being gay was a disorder, it must have a cause, or a variety of them. The defect might be hormonal, and therefore physical in nature; or relate to a childhood trauma, in which case only psychological treatment would be appropriate. And there were some therapists who, tentatively at first, began to argue that people might be born homosexual, in which case a medical cure, physical or mental, might not be possible.

Among those who followed the psychological route, many centred their explanations on the role of the mother: if she were the dominant parent, and the father weak by comparison, boys might subconsciously wish to emulate her, rather than him. But this was merely one of a hundred available theories. An opinion piece illustrated the desperate search for an explanation: a homosexual man might, it suggested, have been made that way by 'an over-pampering mother, or lack of a mother, absence of boy playmates, or a servant or roomer who might want to corrupt the child. Parents who wanted to have a girl and then produced a boy might accomplish harm by over-emphasizing feminine values in the household. Sometimes if a boy is born into a large family of girls, he may get the idea that girls get more out of life ...' and so the guessing game continued, until no variety of parent or family was free from blame.

One thing was certain, proclaimed Dr Clifford Allan: 'All the blame must not be attached to the mother. With a son, often the father is too busy, or too interested in golf, to show much affection to the child. Instead of taking it for a walk, showing it the latest railway engines, talking to it, really giving it a chance to know him so that it can form his character on him, he leaves its education to others with inferior personalities, or of the wrong sex.' So perhaps it was the mother's fault after all ...

Others focused on the next female generation, rather than the last. By 1950, Dr Crane had derived a simple regimen of romantic etiquette, which if followed precisely would banish the problem absolutely. The homosexual, he insisted, 'must now resolutely date a desirable member of the opposite sex and go through the proper motions of dates, picnics, dances, as well as petting, until these proper motions ultimately produce the corresponding erotic emotions'. For anyone who had experienced homosexual pleasure of any kind, he had this reassurance: 'A member of the opposite sex can actually give more erotic delight than a member of the same sex, if properly educated in marital matters.' But it was important, he wrote the following year, for young women to look like young women, if they wished to protect their boyfriends: 'Girls are probably driving boys into homosexuality by their boyish haircuts, cigarettes and liquor, vulgar language and slacks. Don't adopt ultra-short haircuts, for those make you look like anaemic boys, and no real male gets a thrill out of kissing or fondling a "half-man".'

Another syndicated columnist, Mary Haworth, drew on psychological advice in 1955. Apparently, feeling and acting like a homosexual did not mean than a man was a homosexual, the doctor assured her. If a child was robbed of 'healthy satisfaction of the normal hunger to love and be loved, in a maturing pattern of heterosexual attraction' – was not raised in a loving mother-and-father family, in other words – then he would be led inevitably towards 'auto-erotic solace', or masturbation. And that opened the door, just as inexorably, towards homosexual experiences – although why it shouldn't just as easily trigger an interest in being heterosexual was left unresolved.

While the theorists adopted a pose of slightly disapproving compassion, the majority voice, in America and Britain, was much less sympathetic. It was expressed perfectly by the US columnist George E. Sokolsky. As far as he was concerned, modern society (*c.* 1950) was far too soft on homosexuals: 'It used to be that, if one met one of these creatures, he beat him up and drove him outside the pale. But now we say that they suffer from a "neurosis".' In fact, Sokolsky believed, homosexuals were nothing more than sex criminals. 'Most of them are made that way by corrupting influences, by bad companionship, and by lack of moral training. They are products of a soft and corrupted era.' That final sentence might have been uttered by a dozen different conservative commentators during the decades after the 1960s, the era that has often been accused of responsibility for all of society's subsequent ills. But Sokolsky placed the blame on an earlier generation: the hedonists of the so-called Jazz Age of the 1920s.

The Sokolsky strain of homosexual vilification ran through the years ahead. In 1956, Dr Roy E. Hoke, a psychologist in the American South, proclaimed: 'Homosexuality is an abnormality, a perversion, a monstrous craving for the unnatural by phantasy-led, mostly frantically unhappy men and women, with minds run riot.' In 1960, the American evangelist Billy Graham received a letter from a woman who had discovered that her husband was gay. Empathy was smothered by Christian judgement in Graham's reply: the husband was a sinner, and any attempt to provide a psychological or medical excuse was a sin as well. Only faith in Christ could free a man from this 'vicious habit'. Graham concluded: 'Your husband has no excuse'. Fortunately, there was a more liberal attitude on offer from elements of the Church of England, whose Moral Welfare Committee issued a pamphlet in 1956 suggesting that, as there appeared to be no reliable cure for homosexuality, it could not morally be treated as a criminal act, and so legislation forbidding it should be stricken from the statute books.

That was precisely the line taken by the Wolfenden Committee on Homosexual Offences and Prostitution in Great Britain, when its report was published in 1957. Set up by the government in 1954, its conclusions about how to tackle the social problem of prostitution were quickly adopted into law. But its liberal view of homosexuality proved to be exactly a decade premature. The intervening years were devoted to a series of hard-fought parliamentary battles, which only bore fruit with the Sexual Offences Act of 1967.

Despite the support of some prominent clergymen, the liberals in favour of decriminalisation had to contend with the opposition of the British Medical Association, speaking on behalf of the nation's doctors and nurses. Their contribution to the Wolfenden Report insisted that 'Homosexuals congregating blatantly in public houses, streets and restaurants are an outrage to public decency.' For good measure, they added: 'Effeminate men wearing make-up and using scent are objectionable to everybody.' As so often before 1967, lesbians appeared to be invisible to the medical establishment – presumably because they did not offer an obvious threat to traditional masculinity.

The learned explanation of the BMA for men indulging in homosexual acts was that it allowed them the pleasure of sexual fulfilment without the risk of contracting venereal disease, or of getting their partner pregnant. Some men also preferred casual gay sex because it protected them from the emotional bind of getting involved with a woman. The idea that women might be able to experience intercourse without needing to be whisked to the altar the next morning was clearly beyond medical imagination.

The BMA also wanted to warn Britain about a secret cabal of homosexuals at the heart of the establishment, who automatically gave preferential treatment to those of the same persuasion. The organisation explained that this was why gay men tended to congregate in particular areas of life: 'The existence of practising homosexuals in the Church, Parliament, Civil Service, Armed Forces, Press, radio, stage and other institutions constitutes a special problem.' The showbiz columnist Lee Mortimer gave this manifesto a crude American twist: 'the homosexual underground has been organized into an international conspiracy by the Commies'. Their 'warped nature and evil mentalities' had seduced thousands of young soldiers into 'this nefarious and disgusting business'. Predators, it seemed, were everywhere.

This was the climate in which a new generation of therapists and academics searched for a cure for the 'disgusting business' of homosexuality at the dawn of the 1960s. In America, the Austrian-born psychoanalyst Edmund Bergler devoted a series of books to chronicling his treatment of gay men – who could only be cured if they *wanted* to be cured, he stated. In his view homosexuality was simply a form of neurosis, and the desire to maintain it as a way of life was evidence of a tendency towards masochism. Simultaneously in Britain, the Havelock Clinic in London was established as 'an experimental treatment centre' for homosexuals, which would employ 'a warm, friendly atmosphere'. Its methods would range from solitary and group psychotherapy to the use of hormones and tranquillisers. Its aim was to transform the public notion of homosexuality from 'sin to sickness'. The problem, as the *Sunday*

Pictorial explained in 1961, was that 'There are some who could be cured and do not want a cure. They are happily in love.' This struck a new note in public discussion: the idea that there might be a form of contentment in a condition previously described as a corrosive illness or mortal sin.

Across Britain, the 1960s were a decade of sharply contrasting 'breakthroughs' in the search for a cure. Doctors in Surrey ventured to combine two schools of potential therapy: electro-shock, and aversion technique. Their trick was to encourage their homosexual patients to experience the supposed pleasures of their affliction – by looking at pictures of naked men, for example – and then to send electricity jolting through their bare feet. Gradually they would come to associate the pain with their desire for men, and the inclination would be banished. (Or, perhaps, they might develop a taste for homosexuality with a lashing of masochism.)

A more sophisticated version of the same technique was employed in a Bristol hospital. By March 1962, medics at the Glenside Hospital were prepared to reveal that, over the course of five months, they had succeeded in banishing the homosexual desires of a man of forty, who had been exclusively gay since the age of eighteen. 'Though he was highly intelligent and well educated,' staff explained, 'his life had collapsed mainly because he had run into debts in order to attract partners. He came under the care of a doctor after a suicide attempt.'

The patient was placed in a darkened room and injected with apomorphine – a drug that had previously been reserved for treating alcoholics. He was then given a glass of brandy, which combined with the drug to induce nausea and vomiting. Once he began to feel unwell, he was shown pictures of attractive nude men, while doctors played him taped lectures from a therapist, explaining that his homosexuality was a psychological malfunction, which could be cured. His subsequent treatment was similar to that experienced by the brainwashed victim of the contemporary film, *The Manchurian Candidate*. The process was repeated twenty-four hours later, and that night the patient was woken up every two hours and forced to listen to more tapes, which congratulated him on the progress he had made. Finally, pictures of attractive young women were left in his room, and he was given gramophone records to play, featuring a 'sexy' female performer – Eartha Kitt, perhaps, or Shirley Bassey.

As the doctors explained, 'Since his treatment, [the patient] is a new man. He is no longer attracted to his own sex. He has a regular girlfriend and his relations with her are entirely pleasurable.' A year later, at which point he was fully discharged, his 'cure' was still apparently intact.

Doctors in Manchester pursued the electro-shock version of these techniques in 1964, claiming that twenty sessions of twenty minutes apiece would ensure a positive result. 'A photograph of a male attractive to the patient is projected onto a screen in a darkened room,' the team reported. 'The patient is provided with a switch which he presses to remove the photo. If he has not done so in eight seconds, he gets an unpleasant electric shock – and keeps on being shocked until he does remove the picture.' (Once again, the risk of coaching the patient into a life of masochism did not seem to have been considered.) 'Sooner or later,' the report continued, 'he learns to avoid the shock by pressing the switch before the eight seconds are up.' And as before, erotic pictures of women were substituted with no incidence of pain, 'hence associating a female image with relief of anxiety'.

These instances of 'conversion therapy' would come to be viewed as barbaric in subsequent decades. But there was one form of therapeutic intervention that aroused almost immediate controversy – to the extent that it contributed to a legal ban on the offending substance. The psychedelic drug LSD had been used as a method of mind control by the Central Intelligence Agency since the 1950s. Prolonged experiments (there is no other word) were carried out on hapless medical patients, servicemen, prisoners and randomly chosen members of the public, exposing the participants to an acid trip without warning or explanation. The results were studied to discover whether LSD could be employed as a weapon of psychological warfare against America's enemies.

By the 1960s, LSD was being utilised by doctors throughout the Western world as a tool of psychiatric intervention – this time with the full co-operation of the patients. The precise handling of the drug varied. Some clinics employed the familiar pattern of using images of men and women, as appropriate, to switch their subjects' object of desire towards the opposite sex. Others utilised LSD purely as a psychoanalytic aid, conducting sessions while the patient was undergoing a trip. Whatever the approach, the design was the same: to destroy the psychological inhibitions that prevented subjects from experiencing 'natural' heterosexual desires. 'With the drug,' a doctor promised, 'cures can be effected in twenty or thirty sessions. LSD breaks down the barriers people erect against bad memories and allows them to relive the events which made them homosexuals.' There were two drawbacks to this therapy, however. The first was that all use of the drug, therapeutic or social, was banned in Britain in 1966, and in America a year later. The second was that the rate of 'total' cure from LSD therapy was as low as 3 per cent – far below the 25 per cent claimed by members of the American Medical Association in 1965. (A decade earlier, a New York doctor had claimed that 30 per cent of his homosexual patients could 'be returned to society as useful citizens' after drug treatment. That word 'useful' exposed an encyclopaedia-full of prejudices and presumptions.)

If psychedelic therapy was one archetypal 1960s method of dealing with homosexuality, the apparent cure promised by the American poet and philosopher Eli Siegel was equally representative of the era. Siegel, who was slightly younger than the century, won a national poetry prize in his early twenties, and was treated by some critics as the only rival to William Carlos Williams when it came to mid-century American verse. He then aroused a new cult following for his philosophical school of Aesthetic Realism, which provoked one of his adherents to claim him as 'the most important thinker in the history of the world'.

His theories were a fog of vagueness, falling somewhere along the crossed axes of Hegel's dialectic and Norman Vincent Peale's power of positive thinking. Siegel's own explanations were less than helpful: 'Aesthetic Realism says that the purpose of life is to see the world in the best way', he said as if in a Hollywood dream sequence. But when it came to homosexuality, his theories made perfect sense if you accepted his premise: 'All homosexuality arises from contempt of the world, not liking it sufficiently'. Once this was conceded, it was easy to conclude that homosexuality was a way 'a person has of not liking himself'. But nowhere in his work did Siegel attempt to explain *why* homosexuality reflected a sense of contempt or arose 'out of a disproportionate way of seeing the world'.

His patients, who in time became his disciples, publishing transcripts of his therapy sessions alongside their own starry-eyed reminiscences, were adamant that they came to him as homosexuals, and left as perfectly well-adapted heterosexuals. Their wives and girlfriends added their testimony to reinforce the point. As one of Siegel's clients tried to explain: homosexuality was 'an ethic matter ... It belonged to aesthetics ... bad aesthetics'. The confusion between ethics and aesthetics reflected the vagueness of Siegel's philosophy.

The transcripts of Siegel's therapy were refreshingly non-didactic, once he was allowed his assumption that the mother/child relationship was at the core of the problem. (He was scarcely alone in that view, of course.) Another client, Sheldon Kranz, was delighted that Siegel had pointed out that his homosexuality was riddled with contempt and arrogance. Kranz was sneering at the rest of the world, Siegel explained. 'Get rid of your contempt,' he told Kranz, 'and you will get rid of one of the chief ingredients in homosexuality.' 'I can only say I think he was proven right', Kranz concluded.

Aesthetic Realism survived Siegel's death in 1978, but in the following decade, its proud belief in gay conversion therapy came under prolonged criticism – to the point that it was abandoned around 1990. By that point, the psychiatric profession was finally prepared to concede that homosexuality was not necessarily a disorder, or even an issue that required therapeutic intervention. Change had been lamentably slow. In 1952, the American Psychiatric Association published its first detailed classification of mental disorders (DSM-I), which was adopted as an international set of standards. In its pages, being gay was classed as evidence of a sociopathic personality. In DSM-II, released in 1968, it had shifted into the category of 'other non-psychotic mental disorders', where it sat alongside the likes of sado-masochism and paedophilia – something to be tackled and cured, rather than tolerated or celebrated.

By then, generations of gay women and men had struggled to keep their inclinations secret, as Dirk Bogarde was widely assumed to have done; to deny them entirely, as his fellow thespian Wilfrid Brambell did in 1962, when he was arrested for smiling suggestively at men in a public lavatory; or to endure therapy that in some instances amounted to physical or psychological torture, or at the very least brainwashing. It took the passionate and courageous lobbying of a handful of prominent individuals in British life, such as John Robinson, the Bishop of Woolwich, to prepare first parliament, and then the nation as a whole,

to adopt a more liberal view. 'I believe that – as with capital punishment – one more determined push will see reform of something
that is a particularly odious piece of English hypocrisy', he said in
1962. Legalisation, in the limited form allowed by the Sexual Offences
Act of 1967, did not banish prejudice, but it profoundly altered the
culture of Britain, and left the search for a cure looking barbaric and
outmoded, as it remains today.

Interlude: The Adventures of Jeremy and TIMM

A young man could enter a large London newsagent's shop in 1967 and be faced with magazines and newspapers tailored towards every passion. Railway modelling or cricket, electrical engineering or sports cars, and every possible variety of alluring young women; the publishers had them all covered. All, that was, except one: there was nowhere, beyond the most euphemistic of small ads, for the male homosexual to feel that he wasn't alone.

Quite the opposite, in fact. In 1967, the year of partial legalisation, a best-selling weekly paper such as *Tit-Bits* could quote an anonymous doctor on the dangers of actors appearing, and disrobing, in drag: 'Striptease by a man can encourage a youth who is on the verge of homosexuality – or even a middle-aged man who has tendencies that way, but has always fought them – to start indulging in homosexual practices.' A psychologist from Harley Street, no less, rammed the message home: 'Striptease by a man is perverted and stimulating to perverted types.'

The actors' newspaper, *The Stage*, had recently chosen to stop taking adverts from part-time drag artists, because all too often 'These people were touting for homosexuality'. But underground papers such as *International Times (IT)* had few such qualms. 'Active male, highly-sexed, requires passive young men for mutual pleasure', ran a 1969 advert, shortly before the magazine was busted for the sin of encouraging men to solicit sex within its pages. The editors explained that the 'Male' column was being dropped from their small ads because 'they were getting both *IT* and advertisers into squalid scenes'.

By then, another journal aimed specifically at the gay market had discreetly edged its way onto the scene, and then disappeared for good, leaving just over a dozen slightly enigmatic issues behind. *TIMM* (which stood for The International Male Magazine) first surfaced in 1967. It introduced itself carefully: 'The magazine has been designed specifically for male interest. We will present in each issue a selection of the best in Fashion and Physique Photographers.' They also proudly announced the foundation of The International Male Travel Club. Within its tiny but expensively priced pages were advertisements for tailoring and shoes, and some oblique appeals for friendship from other readers. But the bulk of the editorial content was pictorial: pop pin-ups of the kind found in girls' magazines such as *Fabulous* and *Boyfriend*; and faintly erotic photographs of men posing in loincloths, cuddling a suggestive pole, or else without clothes entirely – although no genitals were in sight.

After a second issue in which the ratio of nudes increased, and *TIMM* introduced a film column, there was an abrupt reversal in issue #3: all its photographs of naked men were censored in black ink, to make it seem as if the models were wearing pouches. Readers complained, forcing the editor to explain: 'My view is that [the retouching of pictures] is totally unnecessary, but regrettably there are severe restrictions on the publication of nude photographs in the UK.' Men could be naked if they were naturists, it seemed, but only if they were accompanied by women.

That level of wise timidity was maintained in subsequent issues, even as the models grew recognisably younger, and the illustrations (among them American-styled sketches of leather boys) slightly more erotic. But the restraints imposed on *TIMM* by the law were demonstrated when the only entirely naked men to be seen in its pages were the statues in Rome's Olympic Stadium.

After *TIMM* disappeared, abdicating its crown as 'Europe's Leading Male Magazine', *Jeremy* stepped up to take its place. Initially it advertised itself as 'the best gay mag in the world!', but by July 1969, when its first glossy issue appeared, its front cover suggested a more cosmopolitan approach. True, there was a naked young man in the photo, facing coyly away from the camera; but draped across his shoulder, knee raised to hide her genitals, was an equally nude young woman, one breast visible to the world. This was 'the magazine for people who don't care about sex', according to an ad in *Time Out*, though that made it sound as if it was aimed solely at those who were either asexual or celibate. *Jeremy* itself was slightly more explicit: 'You only have to find one of these two people beautiful'.

The editors had already prepared a dummy issue in April 1969, with more overtly sexual content. There were even pictures of clearly under-age naked boys by the paedophile photographer Ortil. But nothing that obvious (or illegal) was to be found in the commercial edition of *Jeremy*. Indeed, if a naïve reader was not familiar with the modern definition of the word 'gay', they might not even have realised that this over-priced lifestyle magazine was aimed at a homosexual audience. There was only one clue, one feature that focused on someone who was already a gay icon: an obituary of Judy Garland.

7 Pop Go the Virgins

In December 1969, John Lennon was one of three men proposed as 'Man of the Decade' in a BBC-TV documentary. (Women were apparently not considered.) In January 1970, an exhibition of fourteen Lennon lithographs opened in a London gallery. Within three days, the Metropolitan Police closed the gallery down, and confiscated eight of the artworks as 'offensive material'. In April 1970, the legal case against the gallery – that it had staged an indecent exhibition – was dismissed.

The entire episode outraged a primary school headmaster from Lancashire, who had been invited to speak at the annual conference of Mary Whitehouse's NVALA in May. It epitomised everything he despised about the 'permissive society', which made him 'sick'. The head had not actually seen Lennon's illustrations, but the mere knowledge that they existed, with the apparent sanction of British law, left him once more feeling 'sick'.

The pictures, so the headmaster had been told, 'show [Lennon] and his wife – clad, of course, in the regulation permissive uniform of nothing at all – actually copulating in some quite ingenious ways'. The very thought of this impelled the teacher on a collision course with his favourite adjective: 'I am utterly sick of Mr Lennon's private parts, and of the divine mission he appears to believe he has, to display them to the teeming millions of the world. I'm sick of him and of all the other seedy, unwashed apostles of the new morality, whose gospel appears to be that in order to achieve salvation, we must all fling off our clothes and copulate feverishly with everyone in sight.' To his credit, the headmaster conceded that 'if Mr Lennon and others of his kind choose to indulge in practices which I find nauseating, they are, as far as I am concerned, welcome to do so. To put it shortly, they are quite at liberty to go to hell in their own way, provided only that they don't interfere with me, or with anyone else.' His disgust voiced, the speaker then returned to the supposed theme of his talk: the perils of educating children about sex.

A generation of young people had already been educated about sex in ways beyond the control of this teacher, or any other. Their instructors had been the pop group with whom John Lennon rose to prominence in 1963: the Beatles. They were not the first stage idols whose appearance triggered screams of ecstasy and anguish from a young female audience, neither of those emotional extremes entirely understood by those who experienced them. The same response had greeted Rudolph Valentino and Rudy Vallee, Frank Sinatra and Johnnie Ray, Elvis Presley and Cliff Richard. But the Beatles were the first catalysts of such devotion to emerge in an era when sociologists were focusing, almost as a novelty, on the impact and meaning of popular culture. Previous excursions into this virgin territory had inspired more contempt than understanding, from onlookers such as the academic who detected 'a mob mind' amongst the frenzied crowd at a 1938 concert by Benny Goodman's swing band: 'Note how they're all writhing in unison. Their screams are like the noise of excited goats. Most of the audiences are young, and are maturing sexually with no outlet for their emotional urges.'

True, some theorists struck the same note when they heard the Beatles. Dr David Holbrook, writing in the *New Statesman* as an educationalist, regretted that it was 'painfully clear that the Beatles are a masturbation fantasy, such as a girl presumably has during the onanistic act – the genial smiling young male images, the music like a buzzing of the blood in the head, the rhythm, the cries, the shouted names, the climaxes'. (A secondary school teacher wrote to the same magazine to blame the Beatles for inciting some of his boy students to walk hand in hand through the woods, or thrust their hips forward in unison as a group of them crouched around a transistor radio.)

The link between young people's enjoyment of music and sex – often mediated by the allure of dancing, and shadowed by prejudice about race – can be traced back to the birth of recorded music in the late nineteenth century. The same clichés about outrage and corruption recurred, without fail, in adult discussion of every rhythmic fad that followed: ragtime, jazz, the foxtrot, swing, rhythm & blues and rock'n'roll. That the performers understood their sexual potency was beyond doubt. Elvis Presley might have been a mother-loving evangelical Christian, but he moved in ways that stripped his motives bare of disguise. As a Minneapolis paper reported in 1956, 'Elvis Presley, young bump and grind artist, turned a rainy Sunday afternoon into an orgy of squealing in St. Paul auditorium. He vibrated his hips so much, and the 3,000 customers squealed so insistently at the vibrations, it was impossible to hear him sing. None of the smitten seemed to care.'

Of all the musical genres that had appalled parents and exhilarated their children, rock'n'roll left itself most open to moral condemnation. 'Rock Around the Clock' star Bill Haley might have insisted that he owed his fame to 'eight hours sleep each night and good food and a clean life', but his peers in the late 1950s enjoyed a very different diet. Chuck Berry was constantly the target of police investigation because of his penchant for romancing (to use a euphemism) very young women, such as the 'unidentified white teenage girl' whom he propositioned incautiously at her school fraternity dance, until she summoned help from the police. (Race was often an aggravating factor in tales of his misconduct, it should be noted.) His friend and/or rival, Jerry Lee Lewis, was defined for years afterwards by a notorious 1958 scandal involving his third wife. He was twenty-two, she was only thirteen. 'She'll be fourteen in July,' he boasted when the news broke, 'but she's ALL woman.'

Some performers in the pop world were refreshingly candid about their appeal. 'The guitar is the sex symbol of the 1950s,' singer Anthony Newley explained in 1959. 'When you're on stage, knocking your knees together and making your noise, it's the first emotional thrill those little girls have ever had.' 'Sex is screamed at you', lamented fading crooner Tony Martin as he watched the young rockers supplant him. When film star Laurence Harvey appeared alongside the nineteen-year-old Cliff Richard in the satirical 1959 comedy, *Expresso Bongo*, he proclaimed: 'That boy – he's got more sex than age'. But Cliff quickly learned that if he desired career longevity in the early 1960s, he should sacrifice pelvic gyrations and a snarling lip for gentle swaying and an ingratiating smile. By 1962, a magazine column under his name sang the praises of other male stars in a style that could just as easily have been turned upon him: Shane Fenton, he supposedly wrote, was a 'dreamy, near six-footer with luscious blue eyes and fair hair'; Bobby Vee a 'dreamboat'; Bob Conrad 'a luscious hunk'. Luscious dreamboats were the stuff of romantic daydreams, not erotic fantasies, although the fertile young imagination could slide easily enough between the two terrains.

The emergence of British beat and R&B groups in 1963 and 1964 marked a reversion in sound and sexual intensity to the chaotic exuberance of the rock'n'roll era. As the US record producer Phil Spector noted, 'These group boys have a sexual, animal-type appeal for the girls'. But one psychologist didn't agree. Dr Frederick Casson insisted in *Family Doctor* magazine that the Beatles evoked feelings of maternal care among their fans, a large proportion of whom were physically too young to become mothers. 'There is nothing hard or aggressively masculine about them,' he judged. 'Nothing to suggest sex. They look young and unspoilt. Their hair and clothes are appealingly neat and clean. Their hairstyle and their extremely youthful appearance creates an impression of sexual ambiguity. They seem essentially nice boys – the kind a young girl can safely dote on. Their extreme youth appeals very much to young girls, even nine-year-olds. Their informal, boy-next-door manner makes it very easy for the girl to identify with the Beatles.' But he warned that because their charm was so sexless, they would soon lose their novelty appeal with young girls, and be replaced by fresh idols for fans to cherish and adore.

The reality was somewhat different, as those girls who pierced the Beatles' security cordon could confirm. The four young musicians – aged between nineteen and twenty-two when they achieved their first hit record – had shared the adolescent longings and pre-pubescent curiosity of boys the world over, and in some cases were daring enough to bring them to life.

John Lennon was the most outspoken about his earliest sexual experiences, recalling how – at the age of around six – he and some friends had pulled down the knickers of a younger girl, to see what they concealed. 'Some guy came along,' he recalled, 'and she ran off with her knickers down and we all ran away. All the other guys got caught but me.' A few years later, he was introduced to the art of masturbation by stumbling across a gang of other boys in mid-session. He remembered going to the cinema when he was about twelve, and being accosted by 'the man in the pictures with his mac. I'd learned from my cousin that you stick pins in him ... but I didn't have a pin, so I pinched him. But I was undecided – I was quite excited. I was half-and-half. I was petrified as well. I kept telling my mates next to me, "Hey, this guy's got his hand up" – I still had short trousers – and they would say, "Ah, it's just you blabbing your mouth off again!".' Meanwhile he had ill-defined but compulsive desires for something more: 'I was probably making efforts at about eleven, but the girls I was messing with were a lot older'. His first experience of intercourse, 'made proper' as he put it, came when he was about fourteen, again with a slightly older girl. His bandmate Paul McCartney admitted that 'I got it for the first time at fifteen'.

The Beatles' initial sexual experiments came to seem innocent alongside what awaited them when they were transplanted to Hamburg's red-light district in 1960, and fell into a milieu of prostitutes, strippers, transvestites, homosexuals and – most influential and enticing of all – art students. There is a lurid tale of George Harrison, the youngest of the group at seventeen, losing his virginity on that trip, egged on in their cramped sleeping quarters by Lennon and McCartney. By the time they became stars, they had long since shed any sense of embarrassment in each other's company. They were perfectly prepared for the onslaught of young women who thronged outside their hotels or tricked their way into the group's dressing-room, and were seized upon like raw bait by the semi-crazed pop idols.

The Beatles were scarcely alone in taking advantage of what was on offer. In the wake of the revelations about Jimmy Savile's abuse of children and teenagers over several decades, pop stars of the 1960s have become understandably reluctant to discuss their bygone sexual escapades in any detail. Paul McCartney has insisted that the Beatles always chose girls over the age of consent, of whom there were so many available that they didn't need to meddle with anyone younger. There was a strong element of exchange in these contacts: both the musicians and the young women were getting what they thought they wanted, even if (on either side) the liaisons might not have yielded exactly what they were expecting. Moral judgement only surfaced with distant hindsight: the stars were living in the moment, and by the time that there were any repercussions – from an angry parent to an unforeseen pregnancy – they had already left in a van or a train for another flurry of brief encounters elsewhere.

Sometimes the aftershocks were inescapable. Venereal disease was a constant danger for the travelling pop star, who was unlikely to have bothered with any kind of contraceptive protection. Teenage girls around the world were undoubtedly impregnated by performers they had met for a few hours or even minutes, although more often than not their parents would not have believed that it was the singer they'd seen on TV that night who had 'got their daughter into trouble'. On occasion, though, a musician might be confronted by the spawn of his uncontrollable lust. Brian Jones of the Rolling Stones was one of the more careless seducers of his generation, scattering his unplanned offspring around Britain (and probably elsewhere). There have always been rumours about other performers, including the Beatles; Paul McCartney became the target of a sustained campaign by one father, determined to force him to acknowledge his parentage of a new-born child in Liverpool. Press agents became skilled at undermining such talk, and managers at making such embarrassments disappear with offers of money in return for strict secrecy. Every so often, a tale of backstage misdeeds would escape into the wider world, such as the claims in 1964 by the parents of a fourteen-year-old girl in Las Vegas, who said that their child had been 'molested and exposed to ridicule' at the hands of John Lennon. But, as the group's PR manager Derek Taylor said on this occasion, 'We have handed the letter to our lawyer and we do not expect to hear anything more about the matter' – and indeed they didn't.

Even the most scurrilous of 1960s newshounds observed a form of *omertà* around celebrities: they would tacitly agree not to reveal the stars' misdeeds, in return for privileged access. In his interview with *Rolling Stone* magazine in 1970, in which he ritually burned any last vestiges of Beatles mythology, John Lennon suggested that journalists participated in their nightly orgies, giving them an additional reason not to shatter the ring of silence. But some aspects of pop stardom existed outside this mutually convenient safety zone. Involvement in a divorce case – such as when the teenage singer Sandie Shaw was cited as the 'third party' in court proceedings – would invariably attract press attention. And it was Shaw who was one of the first to expose what happened when young stars met equally young (or even younger) fans. Did pop musicians really sleep with their fans, she was asked by *Rave* magazine? 'The groups are only young boys who suddenly find themselves attracting girls,' she said with the wisdom of a world-weary eighteen-year-old. 'I don't blame them, if the girls are silly enough to do it.' Many of them were, and some of them paid a heavy price.

Lyrical content often came under strict media scrutiny. For most of the 1960s – until a tidal wave of unfeigned sexuality overwhelmed the censors' genteel sensibilities – any suggestion in a popular song that a man and a woman might engage in erotic activity, especially outside marriage, was severely frowned upon. So it was that in 1965, that smoothest of crooners, the avuncular Vince Hill, fell foul of the judges of morality. He had been hired to perform a melodramatic tale of romantic betrayal, 'Unexpectedly', for an ITV show entitled *British Song Festival*. But during the rehearsals, the producers realised that the words of Hill's lament involved a hint of bedroom adultery: 'I put on the light, walked up the stairs, there was somebody there holding you tight'. The 'stairs' were the offending item: had his wife remained downstairs, she and her secret love might have been entwined in a chaste embrace. Upstairs equalled bedrooms, and bedrooms connoted sex, so the lines were hurriedly changed. A few years later, a BBC official admitted that they had received far more complaints about airing Frank Sinatra's chart-topping 'Strangers in the Night', which openly announced its gently erotic intentions, than the Rolling Stones' '(I Can't Get No) Satisfaction' – despite the fact that the latter provided pop's first hint of the existence of menstruation, plus a running complaint of sexual frustration.

In Britain, the BBC was always concerned about rude humour, along the lines of the saucy postcards sold openly in every seaside resort in the land. The Corporation had done its best to suppress the more obvious phallic imagery in George Formby's comic songs during World War Two, so it was not perhaps surprising that as late as 1963, they refused to countenance giving airtime to Joe Brown's revival of 'With My Little Ukulele in My Hand'. 'I'm about as sexy as a peanut', Brown said in his defence.

The first major hit by the Beatles, 'Please Please Me', might easily have attracted similar displeasure, from record company, broadcasters or indeed parents. From this distance, its narrative of reciprocal sexual favours seems clear; likewise the singer's frustration at being left short of the resolution to which he had already assisted her. But in the

1960s, it was assumed that any reference to 'love' in a pop song aimed at teenagers symbolised romance, not sex. The next few Beatles hits reinforced that view – after all, what could be less carnal than 'I Want to Hold Your Hand'? It was only in 1965 that John Lennon began to express a few of his own psychosexual dramas in song. Happily married, as far as the fans were concerned, and with any liaisons on tour a closely guarded secret, Lennon's private life seemed uncomplicated. In reality, he was enjoying a series of brief affairs with complex and talented women whose worldliness and intelligence were unlike anything he had encountered before. Echoes of those relationships, and the confusion into which they threw him, were scattered across the Beatles' album *Rubber Soul*, in songs such as 'Norwegian Wood' and 'Girl'. At the end of 1965, another Lennon lyric smuggled the phrase 'prick teaser' into a No. 1 Beatles hit, 'Day Tripper' (the official transcript read 'big teaser').

Letters to America's pop magazines in the mid 1960s exposed a longing for innocence and a reliance on conservative moral values that were sharply at odds with the lifestyles and opinions of the performers. A fifteen-year-old girl told *Teen Magazine* in 1964 that she had been on the verge of convincing her parents that the Beatles weren't so outrageous after all, when the non-married members of the group revealed that they had taken their girlfriends away with them on holiday. 'I feel I've been betrayed,' she wrote. 'After all, how can you be loyal to boys who do things like that, even if they are the Beatles?' Appearance could be just as troubling. 'I almost had my Mom and Dad thinking rock performers weren't so bad when Cilla Black appeared on Johnny Carson's show,' a youthful reader of *Tiger Beat* complained in 1966. 'I must say that even I was shocked at her appearance. Her skirt was so short that really she didn't even need to have one on! It was really embarrassing.' Another British entertainer, Shirley Bassey, was barred from wearing a sequinned dress on two prime-time US shows, because it had triangular cutaways that exposed a little of her stomach. It was 'too sexy for family viewing', the network said. She reserved her gown for a British TV show at the London Palladium, and was rewarded with outraged letters to the popular press, calling her 'disgusting'. One viewer was so upset by the revelation of a few square inches of Bassey's flesh that she had to leave the room.

The American singer P.J. Proby took the notion of self-exposure further. On a British tour in the early weeks of 1965, he wore trousers which split along the seams during every performance – leaving some onlookers to wonder whether he might have planned the whole thing. At first, merely his knees were unveiled; then his trousers began to disintegrate at the crotch; and ultimately they fell to the floor in mid-performance, revealing white tights that offered his unworldly female fans an all too graphic guide to the male anatomy. 'Nothing obscene or indecent happened', Proby insisted, but he was thrown off the tour, nonetheless. By the end of the 1960s, pop singers were blatantly admitting that they stuffed rolled-up socks down their trousers before they went on stage, to suggest their genitals were abnormally large – a confession that drew a predictable howl of outrage from Mary Whitehouse. So too did the Beatles' 1967 television film *Magical Mystery Tour*, which not only featured a (censored) routine by a stripper, but also included John Lennon singing the inflammatory word 'knickers'. There was only one more taboo left to break: Jim Morrison of the Doors may (or may not) have exposed his penis during a concert in Miami. Meanwhile Jimi Hendrix manipulated his guitar like a phallus, cheapening his music but consolidating his reputation as the most sexually charged performer in rock.

Moral campaigners such as Whitehouse must have felt as if they were trying to halt a tidal wave with a spoon. Every month from 1965 onwards, pop radio resounded with songs that sizzled with carnal desire. 'We were playing in Stevenage,' recalled Reg Presley of the Troggs, 'and there was this girl in red hipster pants', and that inspired 'I Can't Control Myself', which reached Number 2 in the British chart despite being banned from daytime airplay by the BBC. 'Your slacks are low and your hips are showing', Presley sang, eschewing the slightest attempt to disguise his intentions. Even more candid, though it was performed like a playground dance routine, was 'Bend It', by Dave Dee and company. Here in three-minute cartoon form was seduction ('please don't tease me, try to please me') and union ('we're made to fit together just like pieces of a jigsaw puzzle'). No wonder Mary Whitehouse was upset: 'Why must our children be exposed to rubbish like this? They are being ruthlessly exploited by adults. Teenagers must have a hero, and they are liable to idolise these long-haired singers with their immoral and often dangerous songs.' From there it was a short step to the Rolling Stones and 'Let's Spend the Night Together' (though the group submitted to US network pressure to censor their lyrics in order to secure a commercially lucrative television plug).

The musicians who would soon become the Status Quo were still masquerading as The Traffic Jam in 1967 when they recorded 'Almost But Not Quite There', in which the singer regretted his inability to bring his girlfriend to orgasm. The song was paired with 'Wait Just a Minute' ('that's all you ever say'). The Who sang the praises of ancient glamour photos in 'Pictures of Lily', hinting but never quite saying that they were a masturbatory aid that cured a teenage boy's sleep dysfunction. John's Children (led by the barely post-teen Marc Bolan) instructed 'Desdemona' to 'lift up your skirt and fly'. And that barely skimmed the surface of late 1960s rock, where one might find such delights as the Velvet Underground reliving the decadent sensuality of Leopold von Sacher-Masoch's novella, *Venus in Furs*; or the Doors' Jim Morrison acting out an Oedipal fantasy in song ('The End').

While the critics of pop culture imagined that school-age listeners were being brainwashed into immorality by what they heard, teenagers themselves insisted that they were quite capable of enjoying a record without adopting it as a philosophy of life. 'When will the older generation stop ramming sex down teenagers' throats?', a seventeen-year-old girl asked slightly awkwardly. 'First it was our clothes, particularly miniskirts, that were disgusting. Now it's our pop songs. I don't run out for a couple of pep pills or dive into bed with anybody just because a song mentions this. Half the time I don't even hear the words of a song, let alone worry about how immoral they are.' To which adults might reply that these lyrics were helping to mould a culture that took pre-marital or casual sex for granted. Or, as one anguished mother put it: 'Our teenagers should be allowed to grow up decently and help to make Britain a great nation again.'

The prevalence of drug-taking amongst musicians from 1965 onwards helped to cloak much of the era's music in a haze of nuance, metaphor and confusion, through which it was possible for adults to make fools of themselves by insinuating malign content when none existed. (A prime example was the conviction of some American radio directors that the gentle folk song 'Puff the Magic Dragon' was actually an incitement for kids to sample heroin. Something similar happened in Britain with Manfred Mann's hit, 'Pretty Flamingo', which was alleged – on zero evidence – to be about a prostitute.) The Mothers of Invention parodied these attitudes in their late 1966 recording, 'Brown Shoes Don't Make It', in which lyricist Frank Zappa stepped inside the 'City Hall mind' to find 'the dream of a girl of about thirteen' with 'a dirty young mind, corrupted, corroded'. The pay-off was that the disgusted male wanted nothing more than to make 'off with her clothes and into a bed, where she tickles his fancy all night long'.

Zappa was a clear-eyed, almost savage observer of the absurdity of the modern world, subjecting his own stardom to the same ruthless analysis as the closed-circuit minds of his elders. He also had an inherently callous view of women, who were subjected in his songs to equal measures of derision and adolescent drooling. All of which made him an ideal chronicler of the 'groupie' phenomenon, in which the hapless young girls who had once thrown themselves at pop stars were transformed into a virtual subculture, with its own language, ethics and even superstars. Zappa aided the process by producing an album by the GTOs (or Girls Together Outrageously), a bunch of groupie luminaries who became the focus of lengthy celebration (or exploitation) in an issue of *Rolling Stone* magazine. 'These chicks are ready for anything,' Zappa told the paper. 'They'll give head without thinking about it, any place: backstage in the dressing room, out in the street, any place, any time. I think pop music has done more for oral intercourse than anything else that has ever happened.' He extended his paean into a vision of the groupie as a boon for wider American culture: 'Eventually most of them are going to get married to regular workers – office workers, factory workers, just regular guys. These guys are lucky to be getting girls like these, girls who have attained some level of sexual adventurousness. It's good for the whole country. These guys will be happier, they'll do their jobs better, and the economy will reflect it.'

If groupie stardom was essentially an American phenomenon, it was a young British woman, Jenny Fabian, who (with the aid of Johnny Byrne) wrote the definitive book about their depressingly barren life-style – *Groupie* (1969). This was a mirror reflection of Thom Keyes' 1966 novel, *All Night Stand*, which comprises the intimate memoirs of the four members of a fictional pop group, The Rack. The singer sets the scene, when he encounters Angela, who claims to be just fourteen: 'I knew I had the girl with the lank blonde hair and tiny breasts. I smiled at her. Yes, it was on. So now I ignore her.' Angela is actually on the verge of her sixteenth birthday, not that the singer knows that when they first have sex. 'Christ, fourteen, it really worried me', he confesses. 'Not the under-age part of it, but that these little girls lapped up the bumps and grinds in such a hard-bitten way. To be out at that age, weeping and having orgasms in front of every singer that twitched in front of a mike ... well, I didn't care. When they got older they got too smart. The blonde was young enough to pretend to think that she was not getting it.' But she does, of course, and so do all the others.

Fast forward three years to *Groupie*, a *roman-à-clef* with Pink Floyd disguised as Satin Odyssey and Syd Barrett as Ben. The narrator gives Ben an epic blow job: 'Then it happened and I thought his body would crack under the strain, the way it buckled. He tasted sweet and when it finished I found there were tears in my eyes.' The same relentless tone prevails throughout, as encounter follows encounter, the groupie as bored with the soft-core porn antics as the stars whose bodies she craves. The novelist (and alleged rapist) Arthur Koestler selected *Groupie* as one of his books of the year. But underground journalist Neil Lyndon dismissed the novel as 'a sordid and commercial cliché ... an assiduous arrangement of all the commonplaces we know and love from hundreds of dirty books. Thus it is a cert for lonely adolescent masturbation.' It took the American sex newspaper *Screw* to rob groupies of any vestige of glamour. 'Just like a man will want to ball everything, so will a groupie', pronounced Ten Years After keyboardist Chick Churchill. The band's drummer, Ric Lee, chipped in: 'I don't mind turning them on and then when they're turned on, telling them to get lost.'

The frozen cynicism that distinguished the groupie phenomenon was equally apparent in the world of mid-1960s pornographic film. Both were milieux from which no participant or spectator could emerge untarnished. In the final weeks of 1965, a typically tawdry production seeped onto the nationwide American circuit for these low-budget movies: *Satan's Bed*. 'At last!', the adverts declared, 'A film that dares to trespass into the shocking world of twisted passions and unsatisfied hungers of the unmentionables.' Or, as the trailer promised, here was 'a film about the depravity of our society – three youths on a wild sex spree, and the girls that they desire'. Among those 'girls' was a thirty-two-year-old Japanese mother (though she looked about fourteen on screen), described by one of the male characters as 'an Eastern delicacy'. As the trailer explained, 'They robbed her of everything she had – including her innocence. Escape was impossible from a prison they made for her.'

The film proved to be particularly popular in Philadelphia during 1966, publicised with increasingly extravagant descriptions: it was, one advert boasted, 'the picture you've been reading about in all the popular daring magazines', whatever those might be. Porn being timeless, it was sold in 1967 as 'the one you've been waiting for', though by 1968 it had been relegated to a supporting feature. Five years later, it could still be seen occasionally in adult cinemas.

What's remarkable is that even when she became a figure of international notoriety via her relationship with John Lennon, nobody in the media seems to have recognised the 'Eastern delicacy' as none other than Yoko Ono. But news of her performance had obviously reached the other Beatles by January 1969, when Ringo Starr and some of the group's aides laughingly described Ono as 'a famous Japanese actress' (though only when she and Lennon were out of earshot).

Her career in pornography was entirely accidental. *Satan's Bed* was concocted out of clips from two separate projects. Ono's scenes were intended for an uncompleted film entitled *Judas City*, which recounted how an innocent Japanese girl arrived in America and was controlled by a lascivious, slimy gentleman as a virtual toy. There was no nudity in this footage: merely emotional, psychological and physical abuse. The filmmaker then sold the material to an exploitation director, who interspersed more overtly sexual footage of young women being stripped and assaulted – standard fetish fare for those who preferred their objects of desire to be in peril or pain. The result was a typically incoherent piece of mid-1960s pornography, with Ono credited as its unwitting star.

As an artist accustomed to working in a variety of media, from music to sculpture, Ono was already familiar with the world of film – even if the *Six Film Scripts* she had published in Tokyo in 1964 bore no relation to *Satan's Bed* (or indeed any genre of mainstream moviemaking). She was a member of the Fluxus Group of artists, whose work was both playful and deliberately single-minded – each piece focusing upon an individual concept, idea or moment. Her initial ventures into film yielded *One* (a slow-motion depiction of a match being struck) and *Eye Blink* (another slow-motion piece). And then there was *Four*, a six-minute silent film in which the screen was entirely filled by a succession of naked buttocks walking on a treadmill. There was no sexuality here, just the bareness of flesh, repeated to the point that the bodies lost their humanity and became as abstract as leaves in the breeze. Participants included Ono herself, her then husband Anthony Cox, and their young daughter, Kyoko.

When Ono and her family came to London in 1966, she extended the Fluxus vision of *Four* into a full-length commercial feature. Her intention was to parade a succession of 365 pairs of buttocks on screen, but that proved too ambitious (not least because the film would have lasted approximately five hours). Borrowing a friend's apartment, she invited friends and acquaintances from the London underground to lend their buttocks to a project that was premiered the following year as *Film No. 4 (Bottoms)*. She left Cox to operate the camera: 'I was so embarrassed', she admitted later, 'that I was never in the same room as the filming'. To attract a wide audience, her buttocks required a soundtrack, and so she abandoned Fluxus simplicity by interviewing the participants about the experience of baring their behinds. The finished movie, now eighty minutes long, was richly comic, and completely lacking in erotic appeal to anyone who didn't have an anal fetish. As Cox explained, 'She settled upon the bottom, out of the range of [body] parts available, because its expression was not controllable, and it was therefore often naïve and beautiful.'

The British Board of Film Censors did not share that view. The Censors watched a few minutes of the pulsating backsides and concluded: 'We did not feel the film was suitable for public exhibition'. Yoko Ono objected: the film could not possibly be described as 'kinky', she said, reflecting the verdict of one of the Board. 'It's an objective study. There's nothing sordid about bottoms. It is an outrageous decision not to give the film a certificate.' Granada Television obviously agreed, screening a brief extract from *Bottoms* to a national audience without adverse repercussions – whereupon the British Board backed down, and awarded Ono's movie an X-certificate. Nudity equalling sex in the popular British imagination, Yoko Ono was now indelibly linked with erotic perversion.

The very fact that Ono was an experimental artist also conveyed sexuality to John Lennon, who met her in October 1966. That impression was reinforced when he was first exposed to 'Cut Piece', which she had debuted in Japan in 1962. As her instructions detailed, 'It is usually performed by Yoko Ono coming on the stage and in a sitting position, placing a pair of scissors in front of her and asking the audience to come up on the stage, one by one, and cut a portion of her clothing (anywhere they like) and take it. The performer, however, does not have to be a woman.' But when it was a woman – as, for example, in the Ono performance captured on film by the Maysles brothers in 1965 – an element of sexual menace was introduced. That day in New York, one of the audience members (a man, inevitably) overstepped the bounds of the implicit understanding between artist and audience, leaving Ono to fear for her safety. 'It was a frightening experience,' she would recall, 'and a bit embarrassing. It was a kind of Zen practice that I insisted on: to dare to do the thing that is most embarrassing for you, and see how you come out of it.'

Despite the popular assumption that any woman who made a film about naked bottoms must be a nymphomaniac, Ono did her best to undermine male expectations. After *Bottoms* was released, she explained, 'some Hollywood producer came and said he wanted to buy it and take it to the United States. Also, he wanted me to make a film of 365 breasts. I said, if we're going to do breasts, then I will fill the screen with a single breast, over and over. But I don't think that was erotic enough for him. He was thinking [in terms of] eroticism; I was thinking about the visual, graphic concepts – a totally different thing. I was too proud to make [a film with] two breasts!' Another exercise in frustrating the assumptions of an audience was her unproduced script from 1968, *A Contemporary Sexual Manual: 366 Positions*. One could already imagine lines around the block when the movie opened. But, as Ono explained, 'The film is of a family scene of a quiet couple and a four-year-old daughter lying on the bed for the whole night': herself, Cox and Kyoko, in other words. 'All they do is just sleep, and the 366 sexual positions are all in the mind of the audience', as the 'performers' moved in their sleep, and their unconscious bodies created 'a slow erotic dance movement'. On the soundtrack would be the voices of the couple in the film, arguing their way towards a separation.

By spring that year, Ono and Cox had formally parted, and by summer, she and Lennon had begun their affair. The new couple decided that they were Adam and Eve – two virgins, discovering sex for the first time. Ono conceptualised that idea into a Fluxus-style film, 'an abstract notion with our first screen kiss', to which she gave the working title, *Two Virgins: Before and After*. 'There wasn't any point in just making love secretly,' she explained. 'We had to make a film which had the same vibrations as making love.' A film crew shot identical head-and-shoulders footage of Lennon and Ono, which was layered over scenes of clouds to create a portrait of togetherness. When the faces were finally separated, the camera panned back to find the couple locked in a tender embrace. It was idyllic, romantic and defiantly non-sexual.

It was also, as far as Lennon was concerned, not enough. When he first heard Ono's music, he wanted to release it on the Beatles' record label, inside a sleeve that would display her naked body. Ono was dubious about the idea, and only agreed when Lennon said he would stand naked alongside her. 'The idea came from John,' Ono insisted. 'I know some people may think, "Ah, that *Bottoms* girl Yoko has persuaded John into this", but that wasn't how it was.' No outside photographer was involved: Lennon set up a timer, and the lens clicked – first capturing them from behind, looking coyly over their shoulders at the camera, and then full-frontal before its unforgiving eye. The resulting picture was both tender and confrontational: it hid nothing, but the very notion of its existence challenged the aura of stardom. The couple looked strangely normal. There was nothing superhuman, after all, about the genitalia of an internationally famous rock star, while Ono resembled not a porn star but a slim woman in her mid-thirties who had once given birth. 'When we got the pictures back, I admit I was a bit shocked,' Lennon reflected. But nonetheless he decided to use them, uncensored and unretouched, as the packaging for an experimental sound collage, also titled *Two Virgins*. And, purely by association, the other Beatles became unwitting participants in the drama.

It was Paul McCartney who surfaced when the news broke, to defend Lennon's nudity in public. 'He really is completely naked,' he explained. 'We took legal advice as to whether we could issue it. There is nothing obscene about the photograph. Until you are five, nudity is something we all accept. After that it becomes something dirty. I don't see why. Underneath we are all naked – and everyone knows that.' As Beatles press officer Derek Taylor added, 'Has anyone ever taken offence at Adam and Eve?' It was Taylor who conceived an advertising campaign that would reveal no nudity, but merely claim: 'It isn't a trend or a trick – it's just two of God's children singing and looking much as they were when they were born – only a little older.' But the British press refused to print the advertisement; announcing the existence of nudity was clearly just as pernicious as exposing it to the world.

EMI Records, who distributed Apple's product in Britain, quickly distanced themselves from *Two Virgins* and all it represented. One national newspaper was prepared to print the full-frontal photograph on its front page; but only with a banner reading 'Censored' slanted across the genitals, and Ono's nipples blacked out. Public opinion – or, at least, that portion of it represented in the letters columns – was overwhelmingly disgusted. Lennon and Ono were 'the lowest form of animal life', one reader declared; another long-time Beatles fan was so upset by the photograph that 'my skin began to crawl'. Another suggested that 'somebody should tell them to keep their clothes on'. 'I've never seen two people so ugly', was a typical response. As Yoko Ono admitted with five years' hindsight, 'We tried to show we were very beautiful. But the people said we were very ugly. We were very surprised.'

It wasn't just 'the people', in their anonymous masses, but the artist John Bratby ('definitely going a bit too far … just not on'), the politician Gerald Nabarro ('revolting and immoral') and the Methodist minister Lord Soper ('a most disagreeable and squalid exploitation of sex for its own sake'). The equation of nudity and sex in this context existed entirely in the mind of His Lordship. Yoko Ono could only reply meekly: 'I'm very shy. John is very shy too. We'd be the first to be embarrassed if anyone was to invite us to a nude party.'

Yet a nude party was exactly what the Beatles and their friends appeared to be staging in the final weeks of 1968. The group's new double-album, issued in November, included a giant poster collage, designed by Paul McCartney and pop artist Richard Hamilton. Here it was possible to see Lennon seated naked on a bed, his genitals safely concealed behind his hands; and (with the aid of a magnifying glass) McCartney nude in a hotel bathroom, penis positioned carefully behind a pole. Vying for sales that Christmas was the equally expansive *Electric Ladyland* album by Jimi Hendrix. British copies were clad in a sleeve depicting a collection of jaded and bored young women, all of whom had shed their clothes. (Hendrix had no part in designing this cover, and regretted its use.) These records took their place in what Donald Zec of the *Daily Mirror* declared was 'an unexpurgated edition of the world', filled with unchallenged sex scenes in the cinema, unashamed nudity on stage, unconfined eroticism in literature, 'the lewd, the salacious or the blatantly pornographic'.

In that context, it was easy for people to believe that, as a garish poster on sale in France seemed to confirm, all four Beatles had posed together naked for the edification of their fans. A quick comparison of Lennon's uncircumcised penis on *Two Virgins* and his rather larger but undeniably cut phallus on the Paris poster proved that one of those images was a fake. In fact, close analysis made it plain that the Beatles' heads had been pasted onto four pictures of the same (circumcised) model, and the images combined to make it seem that the group found nothing more natural than to pose together as four virgins. So unpredictable was their collective image at this point that one of their aides had to consult the group in person, to make sure that the Beatles had not decided to stage a nude photo session after all.

One naked Beatle was brewing enough trouble on his own (or, to be accurate, with his adulterous partner). With Lennon's name attached, *Two Virgins* had commercial potential, even without its notorious cover, but its musical content was only of limited appeal. In retrospect, it would have been a more interesting experiment had Lennon elected to fill his naked album with highly commercial pop songs: the record companies might then have found their moral qualms easier to bear. As it was, EMI and its American counterpart, Capitol Records, judged that the potential legal ramifications of issuing *Two Virgins* outweighed their possible earnings. Other labels picked up the burden, Roy Silver of the US company Tetragrammaton commenting that 'I can't believe anybody can seriously hold the view that the naked human body is, in itself, obscene'.

But that was exactly what was being suggested, and the issue would soon be tested in court. To avoid record shops having to display the offending photographs, Apple coated the *Two Virgins* cover in a brown paper bag, which bore a quote from the book of Genesis to the effect that the husband and wife were unashamed of their nakedness. ('But you're not married!', howled the press in response.) Plans were laid to distribute the record by post, though British record dealers were warned that any legal consequences would rest entirely on them if they were caught with the album in stock, and that it was illegal to send 'indecent material' via the Royal Mail. The United States Post Office came to exactly the same conclusion.

'If we can make society accept these things without offence, without sniggering, then we shall be achieving our purpose', John Lennon said as the furore continued. But even his cartoon caricature of the cover, sketched in a matter of seconds and as obscene as an infant child's aimless scribble, proved too controversial to be shown in public. 'There's such a lot of fighting and hassling trying to stop it,' Lennon conceded in early December, as the album had still not reached the public. 'EMI is putting it round the world – "Don't touch it" – to all their companies. And they're meant to be helping us.' The next day, a head shop in Chicago was raided by the police, because their window display contained a small representation of the *Two Virgins* cover. Their reward was a small fine, and a congratulatory telegram from Lennon and Ono.

It was the first of many legal skirmishes, which involved local prosecutions across America and Canada. A Conservative MP in the Ottawa parliament waved the album cover over his head while denouncing the record as 'foreign-made pornographic material' and 'anti-Christian'. *Rolling Stone* magazine succeeded in publishing the contentious images without facing legal sanction, but smaller publications were silenced when they tried to repeat the trick. 'I expected some noise about it,' Lennon said, 'but not as much as we got. It really blew their minds. It cleared the air a bit. People always try to kill anything that's honest.' His war cry was countered by the California police sergeant who busted a store for placing *Two Virgins* in its window: 'Who in the hell would want a picture like that, with this Lennon standing there showing his private organ? That Japanese girl – she's nothing to look at. Lennon must be soft in the head.'

Attitudes such as this prompted the seizure, at Newark Airport in New York, of 30,000 copies of *Two Virgins*, on their way to a distributor in New Jersey. It was claimed that a carton had 'fallen open' while being moved by baggage handlers, who had then noticed what they took to be pornography. Several months later, Tetragrammaton failed in their bid to reclaim their records, and the covers were 'processed into wallboard'.

There was a similar raid at the New Jersey warehouse, from which another 23,400 of the naked sleeves were removed. A court hearing followed in Newark, spanning several days. The record companies recruited a psychiatrist to testify to the absence of obscenity in the naked photograph, which instead depicted 'a certain primitiveness and friendship'. This was not, he insisted, 'a look that would appeal to prurient interests'. Literature professor Albert Goldman (who would write an excoriating biography of Lennon two decades later) gave evidence that the cover supported the record in illustrating 'a theme of innocence'. Rock critic Ellen Willis (who, as the press gleefully noted, wore a miniskirt in the witness box) explained painstakingly that the naked picture was intended to reflect Lennon shedding his existing public image. But none of this convinced Judge Nelson Mintz, who decreed that the cover was obscene and should not be circulated to the public. The picture, he noted, was irrelevant to the record, but existed 'solely to promote the sale of the record to teenagers'. He added that 'the contact of the bodies' (Lennon and Ono were holding hands) and the 'prominence of the genitalia' (which had clearly caught Mintz's eye) 'are suggestive of sexuality'. That being the case, *Two Virgins* was 'offensive to the community standards at large, and the offensiveness is aggravated when known celebrities like Lennon and Miss Ono engage in this suggestive naked spectacle'. Once again, the fact that they were naked sufficed to demonstrate that the couple's intention was purely sexual.

In the aftermath of the media outrage and legal pressure, however, John Lennon seemed less concerned about artistic freedom or personal courage than about money – and how much he had lost. 'If they'd released *Two Virgins* when we made it,' he said in October 1969, 'it would have been a big seller, because we were Big News. It was the early stages of everyone going nude. But everyone was frightened of it, and the loss of revenue was insane.' Maybe Judge Mintz's jibe about the financial motive of the album cover wasn't so wild after all.

There was fevered anticipation in the spring of 1969, when Lennon and Ono announced their intention to throw their honeymoon at the Hilton Hotel in Amsterdam open to the world's press. Someone risibly described as a 'close friend' of the couple warned that spectators should prepare themselves for nothing less than an orgy: 'They are not ashamed of their love for each other, so why hide it? They only hope that those who come to see them make love will attune themselves to the atmosphere. This must be the century's most uncensored love-in.'

Even hardened Fleet Street hacks blanched at the prospect of having to report on the Lennons' marital intercourse at close quarters. Some were no doubt relieved to arrive at the hotel suite, and discover the couple clad respectably in pyjamas, the only topic on their minds world peace, rather than erotic exhibitionism. 'I hope it's not a let-down', Lennon said. 'We wouldn't make love in public – that's an emotionally personal thing.' Ono added that the couple hoped to conceive a baby, but not while an audience was present. Then she turned philosophical: 'When soldiers are at war, they should let their pants down. They would not feel like making war then – they would feel ridiculous.'

Throughout 1969, the Lennons transformed themselves into apostles of peace – or, in most eyes, international figures of fun. Between their antics and campaigning, and the painful collapse of the Beatles, they also found time to sustain their career as filmmakers. Ono's focus was *Rape*, a seventy-seven-minute exercise in *cinema verité*, which animated one of her *Thirteen Film Scores* from 1968. Despite the title, there was no sexuality in this film: instead, the unwitting star, a young Austrian actress, was subject to what Ono called 'Rape by camera'.

Lennon, meanwhile, had acquired a taste for self-exposure. On the same night that *Rape* was premiered in Britain, at the Institute for Contemporary Arts in The Mall, the small, invited audience was shown *Self-Portrait*. A reviewer in the *Guardian* explained that the film showed 'what I take to be Mr Lennon's own erect penis for half an hour, while Yoko explains on the soundtrack that this is their protest against violence, their prayer for peace.' He added dryly: 'Technically, Mr Lennon gives a remarkable performance.' (This line was misinterpreted in the American press as being praise for Lennon's acting skills, rather than his power of phallic endurance.) 'It wasn't an erection', Ono said, and in a sense she was accurate: what another reviewer called 'the undulations of his appendage' provided the film's only action. Lennon maintained that '*Self-Portrait* has vibrations of love, and it has an immediate message of humanity'. But as a press report noted, 'after the initial shock, it grew amazingly boring and inconsequential'. *Self-Portrait* was screened on a handful of occasions in London, and briefly in a couple of American cities, but has not been glimpsed in public since 1969.

To complete a trilogy, Lennon followed *Two Virgins* and *Self-Portrait* with *Bag One* – a folio of fourteen lithographs to celebrate the couple's marriage. 'They're erotic', he explained as he signed the original run of prints. Lennon had revealed a minor talent for savage cartoon caricatures in his early books of writings and drawings, but the *Bag One* lithographs were more obviously figurative, without suggesting that pen and paper comprised his most comfortable medium. The art world reacted with the innate snobbery of any field invaded by an outsider, though the *Observer* conceded that his illustrations were 'lively anyway from the graphic point of view, or at least some of them are – free, fast scribbles conveying a puckish humour.' They were also candid in their depiction of sexual congress between man and wife. One drawing depicted a double image of husband licking and sucking his wife's naked body, the first Lennon at her breast, the second down between her legs. Other lithographs captured each of the couple in the act of masturbation. 'John is very serious about them,' commented the London Arts Gallery, where the entire set went on display in January 1970. 'He really is so much in love with Yoko.'

The official rationale for the show was that 'Lennon's sex life in the medium of lithography is a poignant comment on modern society'. But predictably the press preferred to be outraged. 'Just what kind of kook is John Lennon, anyway?', asked the *Sunday Mirror*. 'Not content with having a public honeymoon and making a film of his sexual organ, he now insults the world with an exhibition of lithographs ... most of which are unfit for the walls of a public lavatory.' The gallery conceded: 'If these drawings were on sale in Soho they would be pornographic. But this is serious.' So was the money attached to the exhibition (complete *Bag One* sets were on sale for £600, the equivalent of around £10,000 today); and the attention paid by the Metropolitan Police.

During the second morning on which the public were able to view Lennon's work, six plain-clothes CID detectives entered the gallery, spent a few minutes examining the lithographs, and belatedly announced themselves to the staff. The gallery was closed, and the police officers took the names of everyone in the building, workers and visitors alike. Then they removed eight of the lithographs from the wall – though staff refused their request to be told who had already purchased copies of the limited-edition prints. 'I think it is a piece of humbug,' Apple's Derek Taylor commented, 'since Soho persists undisturbed. Neither the press, nor the public, nor the police, were forced to visit the gallery.' Bystanders shouted insults at the officers as they left the premises. But one onlooker was prepared to denounce the exhibition and its 'poignant comment on modern society': 'They should have sent a whole army in to get rid of this kind of trash. If they let these people get away with this kind of thing now, in five years we'll have people fornicating in the streets.'

This anonymous critic might have been reading from the manifesto of the White Panther Party, a radical youth organisation led in Detroit by John Sinclair (about whom Lennon would write a song the following year). Their credo called for a programme of 'Total assault on the culture by any means necessary, including rock'n'roll, dope and fucking in the streets'. They even had a rock band, the MC5, to provide the soundtrack for their revolution. Britain was more concerned about the fucking and other sexual activities that were littering the pop charts in the weeks preceding Lennon's art show. If the Top 30 had become accustomed to innuendo and suggestion, now it was confronted with flagrant celebrations of sexuality. First there was 'Wet Dream' by Max Romeo, a gentle reggae tune about night-time emissions with its repeated instruction: 'Lie down girl, let me push it up'. The father of a fourteen-year-old girl who had purchased the single complained to the national papers: 'How low can the pop business sink? If this is not fanning immorality, I don't know what is.' To which the record company responded: 'Teenagers want to know what they want to know'.

Max Romeo made a feeble attempt to explain away his hit by suggesting that it described the experience of a man lying in his bed and discovering that rain was dripping through the ceiling. But Serge Gainsbourg, mastermind of his chart-topping duet with his partner Jane Birkin, 'Je T'aime (Moi Non Plus)', never hinted at apology or subterfuge. Over a melody so memorable that an instrumental version was also a hit, Gainsbourg and Birkin played out a rather languid sexual encounter – he whispered inanities, she expressed her erotic excitement by veering from ecstatic warbling to a series of plaintive moans, before she climaxed with what sounded like a hearty sigh of relief. Real-life sex might have been more like the hilarious parody recorded by June Whitfield and Frankie Howerd, 'Up Je T'aime', but Gainsbourg and Birkin's simulation of intercourse was authentic enough to satisfy the furtive teenagers who smuggled the record into their bedrooms.

The novelty and notoriety of these singles passed soon enough, but Lennon remained, his irritant factor to British society boosted when he married a woman from one of the nation's wartime enemies, and then returned his MBE medal to the Queen. The Metropolitan Police must have felt that they were acting on behalf of the public, shutting down a menace to 'community standards', as the Americans would have said. Even the newspaper of the liberal elite, the *Guardian*, failed to respond with the expected outrage. True, their editorial declared that Lennon's artworks 'ought not to have been prey to blue lamp tomfoolery'. But they too had grown tired of his provocations: 'One should, in short, feel furious; one does, in truth, feel only mildly peeved and largely indifferent. From the moment these lithographs went on show ... it was obvious that Scotland Yard could well be a part of the Total Publicity Experience.' Indeed, orders for the *Bag One* prints arrived at the gallery from all over the world.

Their duplicated nature meant that the lithographs could inhabit multiple realities at the same time. While they languished at Scotland Yard, Lennon's prints also went on display in a series of American cities, before venturing across Europe. Police in Chicago took away 'the worst of the bunch', but elsewhere the prints were allowed to stay on the wall – although their San Francisco host safeguarded them, and himself, by placing the four most lubricious pieces in a separate room from the rest, to which only 'recognized collectors' were allowed entry.

Back in London, the Met's Obscene Publications Squad prepared a dossier for the Director of Public Prosecutions, and the London Arts Gallery received a summons on the charge of staging an indecent exhibition. Before the court hearing, the ICA hung a collection of erotic lithographs by Pablo Picasso for public display. *347 Gravures*, created by the artist with frantic energy during 1968, was intended to portray every possible aspect of erotic delight. Detective Inspector Frederick Luff, who led the Lennon raid, was asked whether he thought Picasso's equally explicit work was obscene and was forced to agree it was not. Pressed on whether he had noticed members of the public becoming offended by Lennon's work, he said he had witnessed one angry spectator: 'The gentleman said, "Shocking, isn't it?", and then I think he turned and walked straight out of the gallery.' The defence barrister emphasised the comparison with Picasso, whose exhibition had opened without police interference. Four weeks later, the magistrate reopened proceedings to deliver his verdict: not guilty. His decision, he explained, was not a definitive ruling on the obscenity or otherwise of Lennon's marital portraits, but instead hinged around a technicality about the legal meaning of an exhibition.

'I think John Lennon is a very important symbol of the love generation's morality,' commented American publisher Ralph Ginzburg, who had defiantly published the entire *Bag One* collection in his magazine *Avant Garde*. (Police in Australia seized copies of that issue, but once again a court ruled that Lennon's work was not obscene.) 'John and Yoko see the world as an Eden', Ginzburg concluded. But the Lennons' moment of Edenic tranquillity had passed. After a turbulent winter of heroin addiction for John, abuse from the press and public, a terminal falling-out with the Beatles and (most upsetting of all) failed pregnancies for Yoko, the couple retreated into a summer of Primal Scream therapy. Yoko Ono continued to pursue the human body as a landscape for artistic exploration in her 1971 film *Fly*.

The Beatles inadvertently inspired one last piece of sexual iconography with the publication in 1970 of a novel, *Insex Mania*. Ostensibly penned by one Charles T. Kingsley (the initial separating the writer from the nineteenth-century author of *The Water Babies*), it was published in Denmark – although the dollar price on the cover proved that its intended market was always the United States. Today, *Insex*

Mania would be classed as a piece of fan fiction, as it placed the loosely disguised Fab Four in a classic pornographic scenario that climaxed in an orgy, involving group and fans, at the Roundhouse in London. The Beatles might already have split up, but their image retained an erotic power that transcended music and placed them deep within the collective subconscious.

Interlude: A Game of Consequences

Like the Beatles, Michael Caine was celebrated as 'a new kind of below-stairs hero' in the 1960s. It gave him instant access to the women of so-called Swinging London, as he explained in January 1966: 'Girls think you regard them as a pushover, and sort of dawdle in front of you, waiting for you to shove 'em into the bedroom. Cockneys don't behave like that. We're real gents where I come from.'

Not that this etiquette was evident from the film he had just completed. In *Alfie* (1966), Caine plays the title role as a cynical manipulator of women, for whom sexual conquest is not so much a quest as a Pavlovian reaction to the female scent. 'I've a hell of a part to play,' he warned *Petticoat* magazine. 'I have to be a swine, and yet the audience have to like me. Not easy. But I'm told women like men to treat them badly. Maybe it's true.' To heighten the rapport between character and audience, the director, Lewis Gilbert, allowed Caine to break the fourth wall, and deliver a running commentary on his seductions and betrayals. 'Make a married woman laugh, and you're halfway there with her,' he quips as his married lover Millicent Martin trills with post-coital satisfaction. 'Ere, just listen to it. It was dead glum when I met it tonight.'

Alfie wasn't the first contemptuous young man to describe his belles as 'it'. All the blokes in the office where June Ritchie (Ingrid in *A Kind of Loving*, 1962) works denigrate her the same way, though any of them would bed her given a moment's encouragement. Instead she falls for Alan Bates (as draughtsman Vic Brown), and the two walk out on chilly winter dates that end on park benches and bus shelters, where Vic invariably tries to go too far. After a canal-bank embrace, enlivened by Vic's wandering hands, Ingrid reflects: 'I thought at first just now that you wanted to … y'know, do everything.' 'Yes, I might have,' Vic lies, as he has been thinking of nothing else since they first met. To prepare for the golden day, he stops into a chemist's to buy some condoms – but is too shy to explain his needs to a female assistant.

One Sunday, drenched from a typically desultory walk around the town, Ingrid and Vic dry off at her house. She discovers a soft porn mag in his pocket, glances at the black-and-white snaps of topless models, and can't restrain her reaction: 'Oh, you mucky devil. Carrying a book like this. I don't know how they can do it, posing like this.' 'It's just a job,' Vic says defensively, and so is his pattern of attempted seduction, shared by all the working-class heroes of his day. The magazine models inspire a suggestive line: 'I think you've got lovely breasts. I've always thought so.' Within a few minutes, he has handed Ingrid an ultimatum: it's sex now, or their love affair is over. 'I love you, Ingrid,' he assures her as she waits nervously for him to begin. 'We better not go too far', Ingrid insists when she discovers he is not carrying any contraceptives. But inevitably they do, and inevitably she falls pregnant, and inevitably in this age of conformity with no easy access to abortion, they marry. 'I've always wanted you,' she says to assuage his obvious reluctance. '*Now* you've got me', he replies sharply, and the trap is sealed – for in the 1960s, despite its reputation as an era of casual hedonism, sex was always followed by consequences.

That was true for Laurence Harvey, whose roles in *Room at the Top* (1959) and *Life at the Top* (1965) epitomised this compelling, fatalistic strand of British drama. In the first of these adaptations of John Braine novels, Harvey's character, Joe Lampton, seduces Susan, the daughter of an industrialist. He is more intrigued and besotted by an older married woman, Alice. As the cards turn against them all, Susan becomes pregnant and Joe is forced to marry her – thereby winning a more prestigious job. When he breaks the news to Alice, she drives drunkenly away, and is killed, her fate as inescapable as his.

Six years later, it is Susan who wields the power, and carries on an affair with Joe's best friend. He turns for consolation to Norah, a self-assured London journalist, but when he escapes from his Northern hometown to follow her south, the incongruity of their relationship is revealed. Susan, Joe, Norah: all of them have tasted pleasure, and felt it decay into ashes. 'Have you been unfaithful to him?', Susan's father asks her, 'Are you all like that now, you young couples?' 'I suppose we are', Susan admits.

Variations on the same theme ran through the decade. In *Bitter Harvest* (1963), Janet Munro's Jennie pursues the illusion of passion from a Welsh mining town to Soho, and ends up used, abandoned and ruined by her rapid descent into the sordid life of an escort. Unable to face what she has become, she commits suicide. Anthony Newley's title character in *The Small World of Sammy Lee* (1963; a manic, vivid portrait of Soho life) determines his own tragic fate, in the Shakespearian mould, through his reckless financial manoeuvrings and callous treatment of a shopgirl. She slips into a career as a strip-tease artiste, the camera focusing on the sweaty, tense, lurid faces of her audience as she removes her clothes. After she returns home in disgrace and despair, Sammy is left to confront his debtors and his barren soul. But as he falls into the pit, he leaves his club punters with an all too stark reflection of their pathetic souls: 'Shall I tell you something? These birds back here, they hate you, right. They hate you. You make them sick ... There's not even any sex here.'

The L-Shaped Room, Up the Junction, Poor Cow ... British film could scarcely consider sex in the 1960s without the threat of disaster or disgust looming over every embrace. And so it proves for Michael Caine's *Alfie*, the pleasure-seeking missile who seems, at first, to bounce painlessly off the bodies of the women he leaves in his wake. As usual, though, there is a cost. Gilda (played by Julia Foster, a perennial victim in these movies) has a child, and Alfie finds himself with the burden of a family when responsibility was never part of his game. Exhausted and sick, he winds up in hospital, where he meets and seduces the wife of another patient. This affair leads to an illegal abortion, and his sometime lover screaming with agony until he slaps her to be quiet. 'My understanding of women only goes as far as the pleasure,' he tells the audience. 'When it comes to the pain, I'm like every other bloke – I don't wanna know.' To illustrate the point, he leaves her to suffer, but returns later to find the foetus in a bucket; at last he can muster tears of his own. For himself, for the lost child, for the women he has touched and scarred, or for the entire human race? He scarcely knows.

8 The Most Talked About Woman in the World

It was a hubbub of flashing lights, honking horns, reckless motor scooters, and an atonal orchestra of voices, as those desperate for a taste of the Roman high life tumbled out of clubs and cars. It was at the heart of Fellini's epic 1960 film, *La Dolce Vita*, which introduced the world to the unholy marriage of celebrities and paparazzi photographers. And, according to the London newspaper *The People* in 1961, it was also the 'Wickedest Street in the World'.

'You never dare take things at face value on the Via Veneto,' feature writer Ronald Handyside explained. His claim sat alongside a blurred, almost impenetrably grey snapshot of an ageing, balding man as he stooped to kiss the hand of a fashionably androgynous young woman. A second figure was poised discreetly behind her in Attilio Porcari's snatched portrait. But, as Handyside declared, 'The "girls" that this rich industrialist thought he was getting along so well with both turned out to be MALE BALLET DANCERS ... one of them British.' It was a typically British exposé, mildly titillating for those easily amused, but of no wider interest to the general public. To one of those in that scene on the Via Veneto, however, this casual revelation was life-changing; and it would also alter the profile of a sexual minority who had been widely regarded with disdain and distaste.

As the same paper exclaimed three months later, '"Her" Secret is Out'. This was a classic piece of exploitation from the cheaper end of the Sunday press: a blackmail operation, whereby someone believed to be concealing an embarrassing secret would be offered a stark choice. Either the paper would splash their private life across its pages, without restraint, or the victim could co-operate with the story and be treated more kindly (though the voyeuristic intent was unrelenting). The subject of this intimidation was a young model, newly signed to one of London's fashion agencies. Her name was April Ashley, and by November 1961 she had already notched up a string of catwalk roles, plus some anonymous appearances in TV advertising.

According to *The People*, one of its readers had contacted the paper after its earlier focus on Rome's notoriety, to say that it must have made a mistake: he had recently seen one of the 'male ballet dancers' in a line-up of models at the Dorchester Hotel in London, and *he* was very definitely a *she*. The reader in question obviously boasted hawk-like powers of observation, as the subjects' mothers would have been hard pressed to recognise their offspring in the printed picture of age smooching the hand of youth. More likely the paper had been tipped off by a jealous rival. Either way, April Ashley was approached by another reporter, Roy East, and offered that choice between Scylla and Charybdis: talk to *The People*, or be damned in its pages.

April Ashley confirmed what East already knew: 'until five years ago she was a man', George Jamieson by name. 'At school, I was a real boy,' she explained, 'and after I left school, I was still a boy at heart. But long before I was 21, there had been a great change in me. Not at that time so much a physical change. But there was a very great mental change. All my ideas and thoughts were a woman's. That's why, when I reached 21, I decided to live as a woman, dress as a woman and be known to my friends as a woman.'

This account glossed over years of anguish, which began (in one of her many autobiographical accounts) when she was abused by an adult family friend before she had reached her teens. By the age of fifteen, 'I was constantly taunted for being like a girl and, yes, I wanted to be one'; her peers regarded her as she saw herself, 'a misfit'. Unable to imagine how she would fit into adult life, she ran away to sea, where her fellow sailors called her 'ducks' or 'girlie'. Back on land, she told a doctor that she wanted to be a woman, and was given sleeping pills, which she utilised in a forlorn attempt at suicide. This led to her being detained in a psychiatric hospital, where the medics assumed that she was a male homosexual. When she denied this diagnosis, they fed her a mammoth dose of male hormone tablets and subjected her to electro-shock treatment to reinforce their verdict: you are a man, and you will always be a man.

Released from captivity, 'I started wearing the sort of clothes that are now called unisex. Unfortunately, about this time I met a boy who believed me to be a girl. We fell in love. He was a normal, healthy boy with nothing strange or homosexual about him, and I felt as any girl would feel. It upsets me to think about him now,' she conceded in 1970, 'because I had to tell him that I was not really a girl.'

There was one forum in which appearance outranked flesh: Paris night life. Around 1958, when she was twenty-three, George Jamieson reinvented herself as Toni April, and lined up alongside such legendary period figures of sexual ambivalence and disguise as Coccinelle (born Jacques Dufresnoy) and Peki d'Oslo. Clad in a flamboyant wig and glamorous gowns, tastefully embellished with rouge and jewels, she slid easily into the line-up of Le Carrousel in Rue du Colisée, whose clientele expected nothing less than the most lavishly feminine of entertainment. Having abandoned the male hormones when she left England, she experimented instead with injections of oestrogen, which helped to boost the development of her breasts. In her new identity, she began to associate with a rich and decadent clientele far removed from her own humble roots.

But Toni April – or April Ashley as she decided to rebrand herself, the 'Ashley' a tribute to Leslie Howard's role in *Gone with the Wind* – still felt at odds with her own body. 'My male genitals were quite alien to me,' she explained later. 'I would never let anyone touch them, not even when we slept together. The elimination of these organs became essential to my finding life tolerable.' Her only option was to undergo what was still, in 1960, a risky and controversial surgical procedure: what was known at the time as a 'sex change'. She first approached a surgeon in London, who amused her by assuming that she was a girl who wished to become a boy. 'He said I was the most fantastic specimen he had ever seen', she bragged.

Influenced by her Parisian friends, however, Ashley decided to head for Casablanca, where Dr Georges Burou ran a world-renowned clinic for those who wished to alter their identity. A seven-hour operation in May 1960 saw Ashley's penis and testes removed, and the construction of a vagina in their place. Her most sensitive nerve tissue was preserved and replaced on her reconstructed body to ensure that she would still be able to experience an orgasm. There followed a lengthy period of healing and recuperation, after which Ashley was able to return home, confident at last in the identity she knew as her own. Her friend Sarah Churchill, daughter of the former prime minister, schooled her in the etiquette required in polite society.

April said that whenever she embarked on a new sexual relationship with a man, 'I felt that I had to tell them about my background. Most of them accepted me purely as a woman, and I did make love with several and enjoyed it enormously.' But one of those with whom – or so subsequent events would suggest – she did not engage in intercourse was the Honourable Arthur Cameron Corbett. Eton-educated, a married father of four, destined to become the 3rd Baron Rowallan on the death of his father, Corbett first met Ashley six months after the operation in Casablanca. He described himself later as 'sexually unhappy and abnormal' in his marriage, which ended in divorce the following year. 'From a comparatively early age,' a subsequent court hearing would confirm, 'he had experienced a desire to dress up in female clothes', and Corbett claimed (rather mysteriously) that his interest in Ashley was 'essentially transvestite in character'.

April and Corbett took up residence on the Costa del Sol, where they lived separately, but were to be found every evening in the Jacaranda, the Fuengirola nightclub he managed. Perhaps inevitably, their burgeoning relationship became the subject of press intrusion. The *Sunday Pictorial* revealed that 'A Peer's Son Loves a Sex Change Girl', whereupon Ashley decided that she might as well capitalise on her fame by selling her life story – over six weeks, no less – to yet another Sunday newspaper, the *News of the World*.

This was the trigger for Ashley to approach her ultimate fantasy: show business stardom. She informed Corbett that he must sell his Spanish club and return with her to London. 'He will do what I say,' she insisted. 'He is in love with me.' Corbett hired her a personal manager, Ken Johnstone, who capitalised on his client's notoriety by booking her into a London society haunt, the Astor club. She attracted sell-out crowds throughout her stay, although the critics were not so generous. 'About the much-publicised April Ashley,' said the anonymous reviewer in *The Stage*, 'it is perhaps better to remain silent. Suffice it to say that although Miss Ashley, much to my relief, did not refer to the matter which got her in the news, her talents are so modest as to be almost non-existent.' She was better received in the provinces, where it was noted that she would 'revive memories of Eddie Cantor for many of the older generation. She sings "Makin' Whoopee", the song he sang so memorably. She also dances and invites members of the audience to dance the Twist with her.' Away from London, she was billed dramatically as 'the sensation of the year', even 'the most talked about woman in the world' – or, at least, in Weston-super-Mare, where tickets were sold under that promise. She continued to stimulate press coverage, through dramatic tales of car crashes, romantic break-ups and joyous reunions, before she and Corbett were married without fuss at the register office in the British territory of Gibraltar in September 1963. To demonstrate that Ashley really was all woman, the *Daily Mirror* illustrated its account of their nuptials with a photograph in which she sported a skimpy bikini, her 34-24-36 curves to the fore.

Ashley's premier rival as a showbiz novelty was her old friend Coccinelle, whose surgical path to a female identity was completed in 1961. Four years earlier, she had turned down the offer of a night club residency in England, explaining: 'I refuse to wear male clothing in the street. In London, I could be arrested for dressing like a woman.' Her French act, so the *Sunday Pictorial* alleged, climaxed with 'a revolting half-strip'. But by 1962 the renamed Jacqueline Dufresnoy was ready to marry Francis Bonnet in Paris. Onlookers lined the streets to see the show, some yelling insults and accusations of sacrilege at the couple. Both civil and sacred authorities sanctioned their union – though this vision of paradise quickly dissolved, amid accusations that Coccinelle was being beaten by her husband.

To escape the small-town mentality of Paris, the dancer fled to the Americas, where she worked up a nightclub act full of finesse and pizzazz. In May 1964, she arrived at London's Stork Room, where *The Stage* was this time prepared to admit that 'Coccinelle has rather more talent than one might expect', besides 'looking extremely glamorous in a Bardot-ish kind of way'.

An unwelcome side-effect of the attention paid to Ashley and Coccinelle was that the press competed to unearth other transgender cases; and no opportunities were lost to portray these individuals as outcasts or worse. Kim, a twenty-five-year-old raised as 'Jim', vowed in 1962 that 'I will never, never marry. It would not be right to deceive a boy. I cannot have children. All I want is to be a career girl', preferably as a typist. Instead, Kim reappeared three months later under an accusatory headline: 'Just How Low Can You Get? Sex-Change Kim is a Stripper'. She was due to appear at the White Monkey in Soho, several steps down the social ladder from the Astor or the Stork. 'I feel that this way I will be able to prove to the world that I really am a woman', she is supposed to have said. 'I am not at all ashamed of taking my clothes off. I know I have a body I can be proud of, and one that men will admire.' The club manager, who called himself Johnny De Maine, added proudly: 'This will be the greatest thing the strip clubs ever saw – just the thing to bring in the crowds. And don't get the wrong idea. Kim's act is artistic. There is nothing smutty about it.' Meanwhile, Kim rushed through an abortive series of engagements, before finally marrying a shy young man in 1965. 'At last I'm a wife,' she declared. 'I've longed for this ever since I became a girl.'

The treatment of Kim was mild alongside that meted out to the woman sometimes known as Robin Ashton-Rose. The papers were prepared to overlook the fact that when 'he' was involved in a February 1962 car crash, she passed herself off as Countess Rowena de Silva of Greece, before claiming that was actually her mother's name. But this non-event stimulated *The People* into investigating further, and two weeks later, their journalist Patrick Kent chose to bully Ashton-Rose as 'The Vilest Creature in Town', who was 'running a monstrous establishment of depravity and vice in the heart of London'. The exact nature of this 'depravity and vice' had to wait for another three years, when *The People* returned to reveal the 'vile trade' being enacted by the person who now declared herself to be Lady Barbara Ashton (although the honour appeared to be entirely self-appointed).

Now it could be told: under her original male identity, Ashton had been convicted of masquerading as a female prostitute in 1962, and fined £385. A psychiatrist testified: 'He is the nearest approach to a neuter I have come across'. A 'sex-change' operation later, Ashton – so *The People* alleged – 'has thought fit to continue with this vile trade'. Yet another *People* reporter (they clearly had dozens on their books, each eager to venture into the dark heart of Soho clubland), Trevor Kempson, phoned to enquire what services were available, and was promised that 'the most perverted sex practices' would be on offer.

Kempson duly made an appointment, arrived at the residence in the same Belgravia mews where the Beatles' drummer and manager both lived, and was greeted by Ashton, who offered an 'immoral suggestion'. In time-honoured Fleet Street style, Kempson 'made an excuse and left'. He returned later, declared his trade, and confronted his hostess with a challenge: 'You are Ashton-Rose'. She replied irately: 'Don't you dare write anything about me. I am Lady Barbara Ashton – and a respectable person.' Kempson retorted that there was no such person in the ranks of the British peerage, 'and that a service offering torture and bondage was hardly the mark of respectability'. This time Ashton was traduced as 'the most loathsome vice creature in London', with Kempson promising to keep a close eye on her future activities.

Stories such as these helped to establish an unbreakable connection between transition and crime. For every tale of a 'former pipe-smoking Navy dentist', born with both female and male genitalia, who after a corrective operation was happily married to a man in 1962, there were half a dozen in which the accused claimed in court that their 'change of sex' was either an excuse for their wrongdoing, or would make it impossible for them to be sent to a male prison. Someone described as a man was found innocent on charges of possessing illegal drugs, and appeared in court in 'a black-spotted orange dress, high-heeled shoes, a string of orange pearls and a black bow in pink-tinted blond hair'. The same person was convicted on charges relating to keeping 'a disorderly house' (or a brothel) and recruiting clients for prostitution a few months later – whilst being described as 'in a transitional state, neither man nor woman'.

The cases rolled in. There was the man who stole from his Notting Hill landlady, and pleaded: 'All the crimes I've done in the past is because I've always wanted to become a woman'. Others were charged with masquerading as a woman for the purposes of prostitution, although when one such individual was arrested officers 'noticed she was a well-developed woman'; with propositioning clients in West London whilst being in the middle of a series of surgical procedures; of possessing cannabis, while working as a club 'hostess' with a male identity in the eyes of the law; of importuning men in Soho while wearing women's clothing; of stealing cheques to avoid being black-mailed about a 'sex change'. All of these cases, and more of their kind, involved people who had been born male, in the eyes of doctors, and now either wished to become or had succeeded in transitioning into women. It was as if this was a journey that could only be undertaken in one direction, from male to female, and inevitably led towards a flirtation with crime.

Although sexology and sexuality became increasingly legitimate and familiar avenues of investigation for scientists, psychologists and sociologists during the early 1960s, questions about the nature of gender identity were rarely considered. Attention was focused instead on what appeared to be a more burning issue: the problem (as it was seen at the time) of those who were sexually oriented towards individuals of their own gender. On the rare occasions in which transition was treated as anything more than a novelty, it tended to be regarded as an adjunct to the study of homosexuality – an aberration, almost, rather than a search for identity. Even such a liberal (again, for the times) sexual commentator as Alex Comfort was disdainful about 'the outcrop of cases in which adults "change their sex"', crediting its increasing prevalence to 'the advance of plastic surgery'. He divided these patients into those who were 'intersexual in their genital characters' (or 'hermaphrodite', in 1960s terms); those who were 'genetic females with markedly over-developed male characters due to adrenal virilism'; or 'perhaps most commonly, genetically and physically normal males who are homosexual travesties'. It was probably just as well that he did not take that definition any further, although he was disparaging enough in the way he explained how they 'succeeded in talking a surgeon into sharing their conviction that they are "females imprisoned in a male body". The possibility of radical alteration of the genitals by simple joiners' work is something new to man' – and, it was clear, something distasteful to Comfort.

In recent years, transgender issues have become a battleground over terminology and definitions, and the ways in which those verbal choices expand into wider social categorisation and discrimination. It is not surprising to learn that the entire transgender landscape had been a melée of verbal confusion from the start. Approximately 150 years ago, doctors first began to acknowledge the existence of individuals who crossed – or 'transgressed', as it was more often seen – traditional gender boundaries and roles. In an attempt to understand and 'cure' these patients, the medical community grasped blindly for a form of words that would both describe and confine them, each regarded as a variation on the same basic disorder.

Most of these terms have vanished into medical history: few today would recognise, yet alone employ, language such as 'psychic hermaphroditism', 'sexo-aesthetic inversion', 'contrary sexual feeling' or 'eonism'. The eminent German psychiatrist Richard von Krafft-Ebing may have introduced the concepts of sadism and masochism to global language, but his categorisation of transgender individuals as suffering from 'metamorphosis sexualis paranoica' did not catch on in the same way. As late as World War Two, there was a blurring of definition between those who wished to change or correct their sexual identity, and those who simply wished to adopt the outward appearance of the opposite sex, as if the two categories were identical. As a result, the term 'transvestite' was widely used, in both popular and medical literature, to encompass all these cases. Even in the 1960s, commentators routinely had to inform the public that a man's desire to wear a woman's dress did not entail that he also sought surgical intervention.

It was 'transvestites' who were the subjects of the first surgical operations designed to alter a patient's sexual organs. These were carried out during the 1920s and 1930s in Germany, at the Institute for Sexual Science headed by Magnus Hirschfeld. Tales of these apparently bizarre individuals, and the new identities they adopted, began to appear in the more daring magazines and newspapers around the world. In English-speaking territories, their operations were described as a 'sex change' or 'sex reversal'; occasionally a 'sexual metamorphosis'. The most famous of these patients was Lili Elbe, whose life was celebrated in the 2015 film, *The Danish Girl*. In her touching memoir, *Conundrum*, Jan Morris remembered how, as a young man, she discovered a copy of Elbe's autobiography, only published after her death. It was Morris's first realisation that she was not alone in her sense of gender displacement.

In 1949, the American psychiatrist Dr David Cauldwell coined the term 'transsexual' to describe those who 'are physically of one sex and apparently psychologically of the opposite sex' and who, as a result, 'desire surgery to alter their physical characteristics to resemble those of the opposite sex'. This term came to dominate serious discussion of these matters over the next decade and was widely used throughout the 1960s. Two centres of medical expertise in this area emerged: Scandinavia, with doctors operating in both Stockholm and Copenhagen; and Casablanca, in Morocco. It was only in 1965 that clinics in London (Charing Cross Hospital) and Baltimore (Johns Hopkins Hospital) opened to dispense regular 'sex change' operations: previously patients in both the UK and US had only been treated on an occasional and exceptional basis.

For the general public, a blend of education and shocked amusement was provided by two prominent cases in the early 1950s. 'Ex-GI Becomes Blonde Beauty', announced the *New York Daily News* in December 1952, as 'Operations Transform Bronx Youth'. The former soldier in question was Christine Jorgensen, a twenty-six-year-old who had served with the US Army in the immediate aftermath of the war. She did not originally seek publicity for her transition from man to woman, over the course of several pioneering operations. But once news of her case broke, she discovered that the only means open to her of forging a career was to capitalise on her notoriety by launching a career as a nightclub act. It was a template that many others – April Ashley among them – had little choice but to follow.

Jorgensen's closest British equivalent was Roberta Cowell. She had been a wartime Spitfire pilot, a POW, and a grand prix racing driver – the very definition of a British male hero. As with Jorgensen, however, life inside her male body had become unbearable, and she was able to secure a series of operations at private London clinics so she could assume her core identity. It was a further three years before, in March 1954, she underwent a similar baptism in the acidic waters of notoriety. Intense publicity surrounded her efforts to maintain her sporting career, and she was unable to find secure employment.

The barbed experiences of Jorgensen and Cowell, and their enforced fame, laid an uneasy path for their successors to follow. As late as 1967, an anonymous doctor described only as 'a UK specialist' warned: 'There are too many complications. Some people who make the sex-switch find afterwards that they want to change back again.' (Evidence for this belief was minimal, it should be stated.) The flippant article in which these views were shared reinforced the view that transition was nothing but a passing fancy: 'The main problem that faces doctors is weeding out the thrill-seekers – those who are anxious to try any-thing for kicks.' To which one could only add the testimony of April Ashley, looking back at her old identity: 'The horror of a life of ambiguity, and disguise, the constant fear of being exposed – I could not live with it and remain sane.' While onlookers regarded the process as rooted in nothing deeper than whim, transgender individuals believed that their crisis was both urgent, and existential.

Their cause was not aided by the exploitative nature of the media and arts. Comedians relished the transition scenario. Bob Hope (always on the wrong side of a social issue) focused on Christine Jorgensen: 'He's the only GI who went abroad and came back a broad.' Woody Allen was scarcely more subtle: 'My first wife had that change of sex operation six times. They couldn't come up with anything she liked.' She responded with a defamation suit.

In 1959, two leading playwrights employed a transgender storyline, in contrasting styles, but with equally dire results. In John Osborne's portrait of a gossip columnist, *The World of Paul Slickey*, the eponymous hero is subjecting a rich young couple, Lesley and Michael, to the scrutiny of the popular press. After a frantic series of affairs, the pair decide that they might resolve their marital impasse by undergoing dual operations to change their sex. This scene – 'allegedly comic', as one reviewer put it – was just one unpopular element of a production that evoked boos and derisive whistles around the country.

An equally stern reception awaited *Aunt Edwina* a few months later. This was the creation of William Douglas-Home, younger brother of the future Prime Minister. It is set in the Home Counties residence of a much-decorated colonel, where his son and daughter are awaiting the return of their parents from America. 'Mummy, there's a woman by the goldfish pond', says David. 'Yes, I know, dear,' his mother replies. 'That's what I was going to tell you. That's your father.' David is stunned: 'I thought it only happened in the *Daily Sketch*'.

Having established his scenario with his opening gambit, Douglas-Home sought to pursue the theme for comic effect. What follows is in the time-honoured tradition of the Whitehall farces, with the family seeking to convince visitors that the colonel is actually their long-lost aunt. There is nothing about motivation or consequence; no torment or ambivalence; merely a succession of misunderstandings, as the characters skip through the (admittedly slick) dialogue. In what is undoubtedly intended to provide a hilarious climax, the colonel's wife decides to switch her own identity, from Cecilia to Cecil, so that her marriage can continue.

Aunt Edwina survived its initial run in the provinces, before opening in the West End on 3 November 1959. After just six performances, it was threatened with closure, although the author managed to plead that the public was demanding a longer run. The review in *The Stage* epitomised the critical response and highlighted a central flaw in the production: 'If you must try to get fun out of these rare surgical phenomena, you must give some convincing explanation at the start. Otherwise you won't suspend disbelief. If a man has really become a woman, then the part should be played by a woman. The difficulty here is that no-one will believe she has ever been a man.'

This notion of appearance, of disguise, of one sex masquerading as the other, was never far away from transgender coverage in the 1960s. No profile of a woman who had once been known as a man was complete without its lavish description of her femininity and charm. Even the 'vile' and 'monstrous' Robin Ashton-Rose had her compensations: 'her platinum blonde hair was always beautifully coiffured'. Equally essential was the gulf between past and present identities: journalists particularly relished the opportunity to reveal that one of these deceptively alluring creatures had once been a 'tough, hairy-armed Commando'. In their new guise, the subjects always seemed to yearn for the most conformist of futures. 'I want to be free to put on my junior-miss shoes, my silk undies and my colourful dresses', one person in the midst of transition supposedly told the press. Another, one of the few publicised cases who were transitioning from female to male gender identity, boasted that he was now '90% a man'. He anticipated the day when 'I shall meet the perfect woman. My "Miss Right" will be a homely type who can make my children happy and keep our home spick-and-span', while he pursued paid work for the first time as a lorry driver or a labourer.

Then as now, the status of transgender individuals in the sporting world aroused intense controversy. Attempts by transgender women to appear at the Olympic Games were quashed as soon as their former male identity was revealed. At one Games, all female athletes were required to parade naked in front of a team of women judges, to ensure that they were not men in disguise. By the 1968 Olympics, a primitive form of chromosome testing was introduced, though it was soon found to be unreliable.

Before then, there was only innuendo. The small British women's team that attended the Rome Olympics in 1960 was horrified when, in a flurry of accusations and counter-accusations, it was alleged that one of their number was actually a man. The athletes protested their collective innocence and threatened to sue for libel. 'Ever since this story started,' one of them complained, 'people have been staring at us and laughing. Some of the foreign women competitors put on gruff mannish voices when we pass and pretend that they're men. It's terribly embarrassing.'

Rome passed off without any disqualifications on grounds of gender, but in 1967 a chromosome test led to the medal-winning Polish sprinter, Ewa Klobukowska, being stripped of her gold and bronze from the 1964 Games. In this instance, there was no suggestion that she had set out to deceive: it was simply determined that she carried 'one chromosome too many' to be classed as a woman. The fact that she gave birth to a child the following year did not offer a reprieve for her career – though the revised testing procedure introduced in 1968 would have done exactly that. One of the first casualties of the new regime was the 1966 world downhill skiing champion, Erika Schinegger. She failed a test for the Winter Olympics, after which it was revealed that her body concealed internal male sexual organs. Schinegger underwent a series of operations and was able to father a child several years later. Twenty years after his initial test, he returned his 1966 gold medal to the skiing authorities.

While most so-called 'sex change' cases were described as a mismatch between physical and psychological identities, or an unfortunate genetic or hormonal dysfunction, some doctors refused to believe that there could be a purely medical explanation. One, who wisely refused to allow his name to be printed, wrote to *The People* in 1963 to highlight 'a more disturbing side to the practice of giving boys girls' names'. His suggestion chimed with the frequent belief that encouraging the feminine side of a young boy would automatically turn him into a homosexual. 'The records of one London hospital show that a high proportion of young men who sought sex-change treatment had girlish Christian names,' the doctor claimed. The offending monikers? They included Pat, Evelyn and Tony. The argument didn't end there: 'A study of the childhood photographs of these patients showed that they had been kept in long hair and frock-style dresses much longer than is normal with boys. These, it seems, could be cases of mothers who longed for girl babies, both naming and treating their sons in early life in a way which had disastrous consequences later.' Naturally, the mother was always to blame.

Fortunately, more enlightened doctors held sway as the decade unfolded. In 1966, the *British Medical Journal* published a sober but influential article on the 'Treatment of Wrongly Corrected Sex', by Mr Charles N. Armstrong. He was keen to downplay the idea that transition might constitute 'an extreme psychological hazard'; and he explained that both hormonal and environmental (or psychological) influences might contribute to the certainty that an individual 'has been assigned to the wrong sex'. That same week, the BBC's TV science programme *Horizon* offered an equally unsensational portrait of what the producer, Anthony Isaacs, called 'one of the most agonising of human experiences'. A surgeon from Johns Hopkins Hospital in Baltimore added some raw flesh to the agony: those who arrived at his clinic were 'a truly miserable group of people who have a burning, overwhelming desire to change their sex. They feel that nature has somehow gone awry ... many had mutilated themselves to persuade doctors to perform sex-change surgery.'

Those mutilations, those anguished attempts to remove the sexual organs they despised, littered the transgender stories of the 1960s. Many of them also recounted efforts to commit suicide – anything to escape the bondage of being imprisoned within the cage of their own body. Not that surgery or other forms of gender reassignment necessarily brought the deliverance which they craved. The human truth was that society was prepared to gaze voyeuristically at tales of their misery in the Sunday papers, but much less willing to accept them in everyday life. Few were as fortunate as Jan (formerly James) Morris, whose wife remained a constant presence in his life, almost half a century after Jan's own visit to Casablanca. Much more common were tales of being snubbed by families and friends, barred from their existing careers, mocked or bullied in the street. In such circumstances, anyone might be forgiven for seeking out a form of survival in a milieu where their 'difference' from the norm was either irrelevant, or might (as in the case of a Soho strip joint) prove a positive asset. Men who would have thrown a transgender individual out of their local pub might easily pay for the exotic thrill of watching the same person remove their clothes in the back streets off Shaftesbury Avenue.

Occasionally those strip clubs could become the platform for a slightly more elevated form of show business. One such beneficiary was Brigitte Bond, who briefly escaped from Soho in 1964 to pursue a musical career as 'The controversial Sex Change girl with the velvet singing voice', according to her agent. (Unfortunately, the only evidence of her velvet qualities, a 1964 single entitled 'Blue Beat Baby', is one of the least convincing vocal performances of that halcyon era.) Bond was also billed as a 'shapely French rock singer', although that ethnic origin was also open to question (other sources suggest she was Maltese). She enjoyed three flirtations with fame that year. In February, she was photographed at London Airport, as the self-styled Queen of Bluebeat, ready to greet a genuine recording star from Jamaica, Prince Buster. In June it was revealed that her engagement to forty-six-year-old Sir John Waller (who desperately needed a wife to provide him with a son, so that his inheritance would be valid) had been called off, after he learned that she would not be able to have children. And in November she was mentioned in a court case about a notorious Soho bar, in which she was said to have danced naked in front of seventy salivating men. After that, she vanished from the nation's popular history.

Alone among Britain's celebrity transition cases of the 1960s, April Ashley retained her news-worthy status – as she has done to this day. There were occasional brushes with the law, as when she was briefly arrested in Rome on the charge of insulting a policeman. In 1965, she was even reported to have been detained in connection with a robbery in Savannah, Georgia, before it was revealed that the person employing her name was a local twenty-two-year-old man wearing women's clothing.

But it was her marriage to the Honourable Arthur Cameron Corbett that sealed her fame, and ultimately led her to an unwelcome collision with British law. Wed in September 1963, she and Corbett were reported to be living apart a year later. In fact, their married bliss had barely survived the exchange of vows. They drove back from the register office in Gibraltar to Corbett's home near Marbella, and that evening he made what was described as 'some sexual approach' to his wife. But Ashley convinced him that she was afflicted with some mysterious abscesses, and in Corbett's telling, their relationship was never consummated. (Ashley insisted that they did have intercourse on several occasions.) Barely ten days after the wedding, Ashley flew back to London to attend drama school, and she only ever returned for two or three days. In total, a court was told in 1969, they had only lived together for a fortnight.

This gossip filled the London papers when Corbett filed for the marriage to be stricken from the records in 1969, on the grounds that his wife was legally still a man. He did not attempt to claim that he had been unaware of Ashley's background; their relationship had, after all, been splashed across the press when it began. He even admitted that it was he, not she, who had been most adamant that they should marry. None of that, he believed, removed the basic legal obstacle to their union: they could not be husband and wife, because April Ashley – George Jamieson – had been born a man, and the gender identification made at birth could not be altered. There was much embarrassing testimony to be endured: talk of 'wilful refusal' or 'incapacity' as the cause of their non-consummation, the excavation of ancient doctor's reports from Corbett's youth describing him as 'a constitutional homosexual', and vivid accounts of his lifelong desire to wear women's clothing.

The judge announced his decision on 2 February 1970 (in Corbett's absence, as he had slipped and fallen the previous day on the stone floor of his Spanish villa and was lying in a coma when the verdict was revealed). As one report put it, 'Medical witnesses agreed, the judge said, that an individual's biological sexual constitution was fixed at the latest at birth and could not be changed. Miss Ashley's operation could not affect her true sex.' The judge added that the only legal exception to this rule would be if doctors had mistakenly identified a child's gender at birth, in which case the birth certificate could be corrected.

There was a hint of sympathy in the judge's recognition that it had been Ashley who first recognised that the marriage would not work: 'Reality had broken in on her, and she, quite understandably, could not face the intolerably false position in which they had got them-selves.' But his account of her demeanour in court was quite brutal: 'Socially she is living as and passing as a woman. Her outward appearance, at first sight, was convincingly feminine, but on closer and longer examination in the witness box it was much less so. The voice, manner, gestures and attitudes became increasingly reminiscent of the accomplished female impersonator.' That 'accomplished' offered no balm: the judge had, at a stroke, removed the identity that Ashley knew as her own.

No wonder that she blurted out after the verdict that 'I'm absolutely shattered'. More composed a little later, she spelled out what the judge's words meant: 'I feel in a state of limbo. I hoped one day to adopt children. Now, until the law is changed, I won't be able to. You can only be what you function as – and I can't function as a man.'

In 1961, it had been a newspaper that forced April Ashley to 'confess' her past. Now the *Sunday Mirror* offered her the opportunity to counter the judge's declaration and insist on her reality as a woman. The words in the paper may not have been strictly hers – indeed, they read as if a lawyer had sculpted them – but they undoubtedly conveyed her feelings. 'Medicine and science simply completed what nature had started,' she argued. 'At the time of the operation I was more female than male. The operation brought a small part of my body into line with the rest of it, and with my mind. I did not have to readjust, because I was always a woman mentally.' There was a brief nod to the prurience of the *Mirror*'s audience: 'If I stood naked, it is a woman you would see, not a man'. She professed her determination to marry again, abroad if necessary; but she concluded wryly that she was almost tempted to commit a crime worthy of a prison sentence, to see where the British legal system would send her.

Her plight – the fact that legally she belonged to a gender that she did not recognise as her own – evoked much concern. Leo Abse MP, who had spearheaded the campaign in parliament to legalise homosexuality, pondered whether the Homosexual Reform Society should widen its horizon, and change its name to the Sexual Reform Society. Then it could champion the rights of women such as Ashley and rescue them from 'legal limbo'. The issue was debated in the House of Commons in April 1971, after which it was determined that marriage still required both a man and a woman. But an individual who had transitioned, and was living under a different gender identification from that listed on their birth certificate, could now marry in their current guise – a decision that effectively overruled the court judgement of February 1970. It was not until 2005, however, that April Ashley was finally issued with a new birth certificate that recognised her right to be considered a woman by every branch of the state. Seven years later, the *London Gazette* documented the fact that 'Miss April Ashley' had been recognised as a Member of the British Empire, awarded 'For services to Transgender Equality'. It was exactly half a century since she had been a figure of notoriety and fun on the British stage: 'the most talked about woman in the world'.

Interlude: The Sexual Avengers

Myron Breckinridge was a wimp and a pushover; but one operation later, Myra Breckinridge emerges to take Hollywood by storm. The eponymous heroine of Gore Vidal's 1968 comic novel has returned to reclaim what is rightfully hers, whether it is an inheritance or the naked body of a naïve cowboy stud named Rusty. (The original UK edition was butchered by the censors, Vidal preferring to display their savagery by leaving many sentences hanging without a conclusion, rather than collude by preparing a more timid version of the text.)

'The roof has fallen in on the male,' Myra exclaims early in her narrative, 'and we now live at the dawn of the age of Woman Triumphant, of Myra Breckinridge!' One hundred pages later, she has Rusty bound to a table, a giant dildo strapped to her groin, and she is ready to possess the treasure that, as Myron, she had been forced to yield to stronger men. 'I had avenged Myron,' she writes. 'Now, in the person of Rusty, I was able, as Woman Triumphant, to destroy the adored destroyer. Oh, it was a holy moment! (...) I was the eternal feminine made flesh, the source of life and its destroyer, dealing with man as incidental toy, whose blood as well as semen is needed to make me whole!'

Hers was not the only sexual vengeance imagined during the decade. In 1965, the essayist and imprisoned rapist Eldridge Cleaver – soon to become a black power leader – explained how he had repaid the racism of American society by seeking out white women for his 'prey'. After his release, he conceptualised this act into a philosophy, in which the Ultrafeminine is 'allured and tortured' by the knowledge that only the Supermasculine Menial 'can blaze through the wall of her ice, plumb her psychic depths, test the oil of her soul, melt the iceberg in her brain, touch her inner sanctum, detonate the bomb of her orgasm, and bring her sweet release.'

In 1969, the Nigerian author and activist Obi Egbuna, then a member of the British arm of the Black Panthers, carried Cleaver's vengeful rhetoric still further. 'No black man ever makes "love" to a white woman he does not despise,' he wrote. 'When a black man is in bed with a white woman, he is not looking for pleasure. He is seeking revenge. (...) He sees the white woman, not as a woman, but as a piece of England or any other white nation that has rampaged his fatherland.' Once the white woman had lost her humanity, 'This makes her the target of black vengeance. From a black man's point of view, she, as a symbol of European motherhood, deserves to be raped ... That is why the black man in bed with a white woman behaves like a destroyer. (...) The celebrated black man's flesh-craziness for white woman is, after all, a declaration of war ... the black man's genitals have become the weapon of the unarmed.'

For the most unrestrained manifesto of sexual destruction as political liberation and revenge, however, one had to turn to the pages of *S.C.U.M. Manifesto* by Valerie Solanas. She was the founder and possibly sole member of the Society for Cutting Up Men; and was imprisoned in 1968 after she shot Andy Warhol. She entrusted her wild, funny, vicious and frequently mad credo of female liberation to (ironically) Maurice Girodias and the Olympia Press. It was the bastion of male-oriented pornography that distributed her screed demanding the mass murder of all men except for a few, who could be preserved to repeat the mantra that 'a woman's primary goal in life should be to squash the male sex'. Ultimately the male would be removed from the planet, once artificial forms of conception had been perfected. Until then, 'the male should be of use to the female, wait on her, cater to her slightest whim, obey her every command, be totally subservient to her, exist in perfect obedience to her will' – exactly what was demanded, in fact, by millions of men, in the 1960s and beyond, from the women they claimed to adore.

9 The Man of the Decade

He had barely slept on the night train up to London, or the return journey the following night. So Kenneth Harvey, a company director, was understandably short-tempered and impatient when he returned to his West Country office that morning. The focus of his anger was a sixteen-year-old junior typist, who had failed not once or even twice but three times to follow the simplest of instructions and bring some papers to his desk.

What happened next was reported around the world. The Associated Press news agency was sympathetic: their syndicated account appeared under a choice of headlines – either 'Office Problem Solved by Boss' or 'He Just Tried to Save Her Job'. His solution, as a court prosecutor would argue, was 'a unique option in employee-employer relationships'. Harvey offered the teenager a brutal choice: instant dismissal, or punishment on the spot. She elected to pay for her sins. Her boss ushered her into a side room, sat down, and told the girl to bend over his legs. Then he spanked her vigorously. Her debt repaid, Harvey sat the girl on his knee, gave her his handkerchief to dry her tears, and issued a warning: 'Don't go back making a fuss, and don't tell anyone else about it.' Finally she was allowed to continue her duties.

The typist broke her word and confessed to her parents what had happened. Harvey was summonsed to appear in court on a charge of common assault. After hearing the evidence, the Recorder found him guilty, and imposed a £20 fine, plus costs. But the Recorder was at pains to tell the court that he was convinced there was no possible sexual motive for the spanking; no hint of indecency in Harvey's mind as he inflicted the spanking. After all, he had not even raised the girl's skirt. 'I take the view that this assault was committed in a moment of exasperation,' the Recorder declared. The girl's reward was to lose her job (she took up a new role as a shop assistant), to be named in national newspapers, even though she wasn't identified in court, and to have her photograph printed in the *Daily Mirror*, while Harvey's picture was not shown.

In his defence, Harvey might have explained that he was simply indulging in what the French had long called *le vice anglais*. British schools had a centuries-old, defiantly proud tradition of corporal punishment for boys and young men, which flowed down from the nation's public schools to almost every secondary establishment in the country, and many primary schools as well. At home, of course, parents could reproduce the caning techniques they had endured during their own education, or invent their own variants with a slipper, a clothes brush, or simply a hand. A specialist shop in Bognor Regis even published a sales leaflet explaining the most effective techniques when handling a cane and detailing which size of swishing stick would be appropriate for a particular child. So established and natural was this brand of discipline that it was central to a BBC comedy programme, which commanded huge audiences on radio and later television: *Whacko!*, starring 'Professor' Jimmy Edwards. There was even a film spin-off, unashamedly entitled *Bottoms Up*, in which Edwards wielded a gargantuan cane which would enable him to punish an entire line of boys with a single flex of his wrist.

Errant pupils in comic strips aimed at children aged seven and upwards were routinely subjected to beatings with a cane or a slipper; their pain was all part of the amusement. One English grammar school employed a gym master who would regularly beat the entire class if one boy stepped out of line; he called each thwack of the plimsoll against flimsy shorts or bare skin 'a love tap'. Especially within the immured world of a boarding school, corporal punishment could assume savage proportions, as reflected (to choose just two examples from many) in David Benedictus's fictional creation of his time at Eton, *The Fourth of June* (1962), or Lindsay Anderson's demolition of the public school ethos in his film *if* .... (1968). The British predilection for the culture of a sound beating was so established and accepted that it was mentioned in A.G. Macdonell's 1933 satirical depiction of *England, Their England*: 'It is a well-known fact that a really good piece of flogging in the early chapters of a novel sells between four and five hundred extra copies.' That was probably a gross under-estimate.

In one of the most controversial passages of his 1967 study of humanity, *The Naked Ape*, the zoologist Desmond Morris linked corporal punishment – the body bent over, to present the youthful posterior uppermost to the adult – to the animal trait of a weaker mammal adopting a similar position, to demonstrate its passivity. 'It is largely confined now to a form of schoolboy punishment, with rhythmic whipping replacing the rhythmic pelvic thrusts of the dominant male,' Morris argued, with a degree of relish. 'It is doubtful whether schoolmasters would persist in this practice if they fully appreciated the fact that, in reality, they were performing an ancient primate form of ritual copulation with their pupils. [Of course, it might encourage some of them.] They could just as well inflict pain on their victims without forcing them to adopt the bent-over submissive female posture.'

Morris concluded that it was rare for schoolgirls to suffer punishment in the same way, as 'the sexual origins of the act would then become too obvious'. Pornography, written and visual, has long filled this gap, of course. Occasionally, however, the papers could report salaciously on instances when this apparent taboo was ignored. One of the most notorious cases arose in Cornwall in May 1964, when two eighteen-year-old girls were punished viciously and with a clear sexual motive by a headmaster and a senior mistress (who pleaded that she was only following orders). The story made the national papers and was reported by the weekly journal *The Cornishman* with the kind of forensic detail usually reserved for a royal wedding or a football match. The girls had been enjoying a 'kiss and cuddle' with two boys their own age. The head teacher asked them to write him a letter saying that they preferred to be beaten rather than expelled, and then ensured that countless blows with a foot-long hairbrush were administered to their bare backsides by both teachers. The account in *The Cornishman* could have been sold at ten times the price as pornographic literature; suffice to say that the teachers (aged sixty and fifty-eight respectively) were found guilty of common assault and were fined £50 (him) and £30 (her). Charges of inflicting actual bodily harm – one of the girls had wounds that were still visible several days later – were dropped in return for their guilty plea. The magistrate asked that the girls' names should not be repeated outside the courtroom, but when the hearing was reported overseas, this instruction was not followed. And the two male pupils involved in the original incident, you may be wondering? They escaped punishment entirely.

A year later, the first issue of *Penthouse* magazine brought a patina of sophistication to the previously grubby world of British 'glamour' magazines (what would now be categorised as 'soft porn'). Like the rather more respectable journals aimed at women, *Penthouse* introduced a readers' forum, where they could exchange anecdotes and pick the minds of the magazine's resident experts in all aspects of sexual behaviour. Someone named J. Hudson wrote to enquire about the best methods of disciplining his teenage daughter: 'Should the cane be used, or strap, or whip? What, if any, clothing should be worn by the girl – pyjamas? Slacks? How should she be placed – over an armchair? The side of a bed? Should she be whipped in private or in front of the rest of the family? How should a reluctant teenager be persuaded to submit to a caning? How many strokes?' Every question, every phrase, might trigger a masturbatory fantasy.

Unsurprisingly, the correspondence on this subject continued, and continued, until every conceivable facet of fantasy and imagination had been stimulated, satisfied and dulled. 'I would not hesitate to allow my father to cane me,' a female reader obligingly explained, 'even though I am now 23.' A learned student of human physiology offered encouraging advice to the would-be flagellator: 'Almost the whole of a woman's body is an erogenous zone, thus beating a woman's buttocks soon causes sexual orgasm.' (He didn't specify *whose* orgasm.) Another ostensibly female reader offered a tingling account of her experience: 'As a young wife of 23, I am regularly spanked on my bare bottom by my husband, who uses my hairbrush or a very thin whipping cane, but if I can keep his love and affection, I will put up with it, and quite honestly I now look forward to my weekly spanking.' Of course she did. The debate was still running a year later – it is probably running to this day. Inevitably, the letters included testimonials from schoolgirls, expressing the pleasure they had experienced from being beaten in front of their classmates. The fact that the vast majority of these reminiscences and suggestions, including all of those with a female author, were fictional did nothing to lessen the interest of *Penthouse* readers; or the onanistic delight with which they devoured each month's instalment.

If *Penthouse* (or *The Cornishman*, for that matter) was not lurid enough, thousands of newsagents across Britain sold freshly imported copies of American men's monthly magazines. For at least the first half of the 1960s, dozens of these interchangeable titles bore lavish cartoon illustrations on their front covers. Almost without fail, they illustrated unfeasibly brutal episodes of torture, usually located in Nazi Germany, in which scantily clad young women either received, or in some cases dished out, agonies via a diabolical array of instruments. The titles spoke for themselves: 'Nazi Horror Tortures of the Resistance Girls'; 'Torturing Tarts of Frankfurt' ('The sight of pain made her shriek with pleasure'); 'Nude Tortures of 1,000 Cuts'; 'A Crypt of Agony for the Screaming Beauties of Belgium'; 'Writhe, My Lovely, in the Tent of Torture!'; 'Nude Death Orgy of the Woman Crazy Cossacks' (some relief from the Germans there); 'The People Who Worship Pain' ('I could only stand in horror watching as my wife became a victim'); 'Torture Trap of the Nympho Schoolgirls' (covering two perversions at once); and, as variation, 'The Facts About Sex and Pain'. Three consecutive issues of *All Man* magazine in 1964 featured covers showing women being burned alive, or threatened with the same. To be 'all man', it seemed, it was necessary to destroy 'all woman', especially if they were naked and exaggeratedly proportioned.

Besides those who were titillated by women in pain, these articles also appealed to those who had a searing interest in World War Two, and its attendant atrocities. Something never stated by these magazines was that many of those who bought them would have been veterans of that conflict and had seen – or perhaps even participated in – real-life atrocities that had none of the stylised glamour of the magazine illustrations. (On a more local scale, those excited by accounts of children being punished were likely to have received similar treatment themselves.) By attributing all such evils to a foreign regime, safely relegated to history, readers could distance themselves from any collusion or associated guilt. Memoirs of the wars in Korea and Vietnam confirmed that American soldiers were just as capable of abominable acts, as protagonists, spectators or accessories after the fact. Nor were other countries free from this taint: *Britain's Gulag*, Caroline Elkins' horrifying history of the nation's actions in post-war Kenya, is filled with details of tortures and massacres carried out in the name of the monarchy, with the same callous indifference displayed by Hitler's SS.

The war crimes of Germany and Japan, from torture to genocide, were delineated in excruciating detail by Lord Russell of Liverpool, via two best-selling books of the mid-1950s: *The Scourge of the Swastika* and *The Knights of Bushido*. Written with a historian's zeal for exposing the evils of totalitarianism, Russell's books also attracted a subsidiary market amongst those who experienced a vicarious thrill, sexual or otherwise, from reading lurid accounts of punishments and executions. (No publisher ever went bankrupt by issuing histories of man's inhumanity to man – and especially woman.)

The first of those titles was discovered in the library of a twenty-seven-year-old man who was arrested in a Manchester suburb in August 1965: Ian Brady. Several weeks later his girlfriend, Myra Hindley, was also picked up by police. Brady was charged with a single count of murder; Hindley as his accessory. Over subsequent weeks, it became apparent that the pair – each blamed the other – had been responsible for the deaths of several young children around Manchester over the previous two years. Brady and Hindley became known as the most infamous British killers of the twentieth century, remembered popularly as the Moors Murderers.

Few crimes have been chronicled in such exhaustive, voyeuristic detail. The first full-length account of the children's deaths, and the subsequent trial, was John Deane Potter's *The Monsters of the Moors*, published in 1966. It mixed detailed research with lurid speculation about the exact circumstances of the children's deaths, especially ten-year-old Lesley Ann Downey, whose abuse and murder was documented by Brady and/or Hindley in both photographs and sound recordings. Potter was especially fixated on what happened to Downey in her final minutes, and some readers might feel that his guesswork drifted into its own form of psychopathology, as he wondered: 'Is it not conceivable that [Hindley] may have obtained a high degree of perverted pleasure from watching her lover force his penis into the whimpering girl's mouth?' (There was no forensic or scientific evidence to prove this ever happened.)

Potter recounted how Brady had groomed Hindley into a passion for violent crime, by lending her books on the crimes of the Nazis, followed by chronicles of torture and sexual deviation. 'She proved a willing disciple,' he writes. 'Soon she was sitting at his desk every lunchtime, reading aloud the more salacious passages from these books.' The exact contents of his library were made public at the trial. Brady's shelves were apparently filled with works of scholarly prurience, such as *The History of Corporal Punishment*, *The Pleasures of the Torture Chamber* and *Sex Crimes and Sex Criminals*, and a selection of back-room magazines and paperbacks from merchants in Soho (or its Mancunian equivalent), from *Cradle of Erotica* to *Kiss of the Whip*, via *Satin Heels and Stilettos* and *High Heels and Stockings*.

Amongst this voracious scholarship and cheap tat were several volumes that would feature prominently in the judicial proceedings of the trial, and in subsequent commentary on the Moors Murders themselves. They included at least two accounts of the life, times and eccentric philosophy of a French nobleman who perished in an asylum in 1814; and the only edition of one of the aristocrat's novels to have been allowed unfettered publication in Britain. The writer was Donatien Alphonse François de Sade, who passed into infamy as the Marquis de Sade; the novel was *Justine, or the Misfortunes of Virtue*.

As Brady and Hindley's trial progressed, it occasionally sounded as if the 150-years-dead Marquis was standing alongside them in the dock. He was certainly described as an accessory to the crimes, albeit an undeniably posthumous one. Brady was said to have advised a young male friend to read *Justine* and the Sade biographies, because 'Sade had the right outlook on life'. Hindley, however, according to John Deane Potter, was more intrigued by the Nazis than by Sade: despite reading one of his books (*Justine*, presumably), she 'was not an admirer of him, and did not approve of his views about sadism'.

Much interest during and after the trial was focused upon Brady's cross-examination by the Attorney-General, Sir Elwyn Jones. The prosecutor was determined to prove that Brady's library comprised 'squalid pornographic books'. 'They can't be, if they can be bought at any bookstall', Brady replied. 'They are dirty books, are they not?', Sir Elwyn countered. Brady took a philosophical position: 'It depends on the dirty mind.' 'This was the atmosphere of your mind – a sink of pornography,' Sir Elwyn pressed, with an air of desperation. 'No, some of them were written by doctors,' was the response. 'Was your interest on a high, moral plane?' Here Brady admitted, 'No, erotic reasons.' But before Sir Elwyn could build upon this apparent victory,

Brady added resentfully: 'There are better collections than that in lords' manors all over the country.' His, he explained, 'was a very poor collection'.

This was undoubtedly true, given the expansive nature of Sade's oeuvre, and the voluminous literature devoted to exploring his legacy. In the work of Geoffrey Gorer, a reprint of whose 1953 study of Sade was owned by Brady, anyone searching for erotic excitement would have been sorely disappointed. Gorer recounted the bare events of Sade's life, including the crimes of violence against women which led to his imprisonment in the Bastille. The biographer was careful to distance his readers from the threat of sexual titillation and to avoid providing an incitement to act out Sade's fantasies. Yet amidst Gorer's high-minded scholarship was an occasional line that could be twisted and perverted into a rationale for appalling crimes – as when he detailed how Sade described the inclinations of children, in his definitive work, *The 120 Days of Sodom*: 'According to de Sade, very young children are shameless, sexually inquisitive and endowed with strong sexual feelings. Children are naturally polymorphous perverts.' This was Sade's view, not Gorer's; but quite possibly it provided the impetus for Ian Brady to put the Frenchman's theories to an appallingly practical test.

A set of diverse circumstances coincided, perhaps inevitably, after the Second World War to usher Sade from ignominious literary exile into the centre of contemporary culture. Theorists in many disciplines, from psychoanalysis to existentialism, began to recognise what Sade's few audible champions had been claiming for decades: that, while being very much a creature of the eighteenth century and aristocratic privilege, he had also uncovered insights that would only be fully appreciated long after his death. As Sade scholar David Coward explained, 'Existentialists like Camus recognised him as a rebel against the absurd, and by the 1960s the Tel Quel group of radical Paris intellectuals saw him as the universal subversive. Roland Barthes saluted him not for his ideas but for creating a revolutionary language capable of communicating them.'

Yet for all the intellectual ferment sparked by Sade in the work of Barthes, Foucault and many others of their ilk, this was not the predominant reason why the Marquis' writings began to circulate in English translations from the early 1950s onwards. The publisher

Jean-Jacques Pauvert completed a scholarly edition of Sade's collected works (in his native French) in the mid-1950s and was convicted of obscenity for his pains. Maurice Girodias escaped similar legal penalty when his Olympia Press published all of Sade's most notorious fictional work – for the simple reason that his volumes were in English, and the French authorities were sublimely unconcerned about the moral harm that might befall English or American expats and tourists. Girodias wasn't blind to the merits of literature, but aesthetic prowess was overpowered in his business model by commercial potential. The Olympia Press's initial batch of English-language titles in summer 1953 featured the first English edition of *The Bedroom Philosophers*, a Sade book better known today as *Philosophy in the Bedroom*.

The translator was an American named Austryn Wainhouse, who proceeded over the next few years to assemble English renderings of most of Sade's major works. Academics were often critical of his accuracy, and Wainhouse revised his translations before they were published in America during the 1960s. But their appearance in any form was both a coup for literary freedom, and a vital source of funds for Girodias's publishing house.

Some buyers of Olympia's Sade books must have obtained them for scholarly reasons; but most were attracted by Sade's reputation as a chronicler of man's sexual deviations at their most unhinged. *The 120 Days of Sodom*, the manuscript of which was believed lost at the time of Sade's death, and was in any case never completed to his satisfaction, surpassed any pornographic title that could be imagined with the depth of its depravity and violence. The almost 1,000-page edition of *Juliette*, eventually divided by Girodias into seven separate volumes for commercial reasons, was equally soaked in blood, semen and contempt. By comparison, *Justine*, with its occasional whippings and frenzied assaults upon the honour of virginal young women, seemed almost tame – although it still surpassed the boundaries of what could be legally published at the time in Britain or America.

That did not prevent intellectuals from citing, or pontificating about, the Marquis de Sade. The year 1960 began, for example, with no less respectable an institution than the BBC allowing the literary historian A.G. Lehmann to discuss 'Surrealism, Love and the Marquis de Sade' on radio's Third Programme. A transcript was subsequently published in the BBC's high-brow weekly magazine, *The Listener*. The broadcast informed the British audience about 'a special surrealist ceremony' witnessed recently in Paris, during which a young Canadian artist branded the initials of Sade's name into his chest. This, so Lehmann argued, reaffirmed a primary theme of the surrealist movement: 'its passionate, anxious questionings about Eros, about Love in the context of Art'. This was as close as Lehmann dared to come to exploring the true nature of Sade's philosophy, let alone the contents of his most notorious books.

The publication in late 1961 of an abridged English translation of the Sade biography by the French scholar Gilbert Lely served to chip away at the wall that had protected the British public from the Marquis for generations. In a perceptive review, Elizabeth Harvey admitted that 'Horrors pile on horror in de Sade's books, but they often seem like painted monsters to a generation which has supped as full of horrors as we have'. She drew parallels between Sade's writing and the 'element of dark, disturbing lyricism' found in the works of a contemporary French novelist, Jean Genet. And she offered a sardonic comment on the fact that whereas the Marquis had been kept under lock and key for much of his life, 'Now the books are locked up. At least they are in England, where you almost need a doctor's certificate or some such passport to respectability to get access to them. Puzzling are the ethics of punishments. Has society gained or lost?'

When Norman Gear wrote a magnificently flamboyant study of Sade, *The Divine Demon* (1963), he lamented that although all of Sade's work was now available in France, 'the civilised British people are not allowed to read it because their masters will not allow them to. Nor is the author of this book permitted to summarise [*The 120 Days of Sodom*] in any details: he would be sent to prison if he did so.' This was supposition rather than fact; and one British publisher set out to test the waters. Was the Marquis de Sade inherently obscene? Or could the indecency or otherwise of his work be judged on its individual merits, rather than the scurrilous reputation of its author?

Born in pre-war Germany to Jewish parents (one German, one English), Peter Owen was all too familiar with the consequences of literary censorship. From the 1950s onwards, he published a magnificent array of experimental and recherché literary translations, besides texts by authors such as Anaïs Nin, whose work was considered too shocking to be handled by more conservative houses. He entrusted the French quarter of his list to the translator and editor Margaret Crosland, and it was she who prepared Owen's first Sade volume, *Quartet* (1963). Crosland echoed the prevailing view that Sade's major works could not be published in England, but argued that 'the pornographic passages in de Sade's works need to be considered within their context as a proof that he was deeply concerned with ethical, philosophical and psychological problems'. Not that pornography was an issue with *Quartet*, comprising four of Sade's *Contes et Fabliaux*, which were no more than bawdy or suggestive in the classic French tradition. The 1965 anthology *Eugenie de Franval and Other Stories* was equally inoffensive, and (so Crosland said) 'intended mainly for entertainment'.

A third Sade volume from Peter Owen, *Selected Letters* (1965), tiptoed close to the edge of decency, as when the Marquis advised a former mistress: 'Adieu, my angel, think of me sometimes when you are between two sheets, your thighs open and your right hand busy ... feeling for your fleas. Remember that in that case the other should be busy too; otherwise you have only half the pleasure.' In her introduction, Margaret Crosland was more explicit about Sade's crimes than most previous chroniclers in this language: 'He made her [a servant] undress, tied her down on a bed and beat her, using alternately a rod and a "martinet", a whip with knotted cords, occasionally putting wax on her wounds, until he had an orgasm.'

By that time, however, Peter Owen's crusading literary courage had been surpassed, and the first of Sade's longer works had been published in Britain. The publisher on this occasion was Neville Spearman, in conjunction with The Holland Press, although it was the Corgi paperback edition of 1965 that opened Sade up to a mainstream audience. *Justine* was, in the words of its translator Alan Hull Walton, 'one of the most shocking books ever written'. But, he insisted, it was not pornographic: 'The hungry smuthound will not find therein anything for which he hopes ... Sade is lacking in all the elementary qualifications of the erotic novelist ... so closely does he associate pain, violence and cruelty with sex – whether inflicted or experienced – that his scenes in this genre are either repulsive or terrifying.' But, as Walton must have known very well, Sade's philosophy entailed exactly that barbed marriage between sex and violence, and anyone who shared his views or his tastes, to the slightest degree, might find erotic excitement from the scenes of flagellation or deflowering which undoubtedly thrilled their author too.

Walton opted to translate the earliest known text of *Justine*, from 1785. It was revised in more extreme form in 1791 but, as Walton noted, 'The obscenities of the second volume make it such that publication in England today would be inadvisable'. There was also a third, infinitely longer manuscript from the late 1790s, which Sade titled *La Nouvelle Justine*; but that has still evaded any English translation. Nonetheless, Walton admitted that both later texts contained matter of philosophical and literary interest; while the differences in tone and content between the various manuscripts was instructive in itself. To avoid publishing material that might prove 'inadvisable', Walton chose to fill his introduction and footnotes with quotations in the original French. He followed the same course with a passage from the earliest *Justine* in which two characters fellate each other, the only censorship of the text in this edition. But Walton was prepared to describe, in English, an episode from *La Nouvelle Justine* in which one of the cruellest characters rapes a pregnant woman while simultaneously carrying out a Caesarean section on her body. His purpose? To prove that Sade's most pornographic work could not possibly provide erotic stimulation. 'Such insane and terrifying fantasies', he argued, 'more than guarantee the anaphrodisiac qualities of this narrative. It is simply the horror-novel gone mad.' Once again, Walton was perhaps underestimating the full extremes of his readers' erotic imaginations.

The truth about Sade – and Ian Brady – is that sexual thrills as transgressive and potentially stimulating as those in *Justine* were available from countless legal sources, without the would-be sybarite (or pervert, as you might prefer) ever needing to venture inside the premises of a pornographer's bookstore or cinema. As the psychiatrist Eustace Chesser noted of Brady and his partner, 'They were "corrupted" before they read de Sade. In their case the pornographic books which embodied their fantasies were not a satisfactory substitute. When we think of the wealth of sadistic material with which the market is flooded – not to mention the saturation of violence on television – the Moors murders would not be such a rarity if reading about cruelty led to its enactment.'

In 1964, a year before anyone outside his immediate milieu had ever heard of Ian Brady, the translator of *Justine* was able to detect unmistakeable strands of Sadeian philosophy, and its lurid depiction, in books as far ranging as the James Bond thrillers, Hank Janson's cowboy novels, Jean Genet's decadent explorations of homosexuality, and John Rechy's chronicle of the hustler adrift in the *City of Night*. He might as easily have added to his list the violent thrillers of Micky Spillane; the black magic travesties of Dennis Wheatley; or the chronicles of Sergeanne Golon's endlessly raped and abused heroine, Angélique, who suffered through a series of novels set in seventeenth-century France, and two somewhat milder film adaptations. Walton mentioned the sexual torture inflicted on Ian Fleming's secret agent in *Casino Royale*; he glossed over a book actually owned by Brady, Harold Robbins' pathetic epic of male fantasy, *The Carpetbaggers*, which the author John Fowles once denounced as 'possibly the nastiest book ever written'. (A sample line: 'The hymen ruptured, and she staggered as a wave of pain washed over her.') Even such veteran crime-fighters as The Saint and Sexton Blake found themselves drawn into ever more perverse sado-masochistic scenarios. The faintly saucy weekly magazine *Tit-Bits* published a Blake story entitled 'Hurricane Warning' in June 1965. It began with a man being fatally impaled by spikes of sharpened bamboo: 'He was spread-eagled, defenceless and writhing.' Teenagers in 1967 were entertained by *Rave* magazine's serialisation of Adam Diment's spy story, 'The Red Guard Girl' – its cast including a naked woman strapped to a table so she could be tortured with electric shocks.

On screen, Walton admitted to recognising Sadeian impulses in the British television serial, *The Avengers*. Besides the episodes of violence and physical endurance, he was also struck by the heroine, Cathy Gale, played by Honor Blackman: 'The leather jacket and trousers of Cathy, too, were symbolic of an infinite number of sadistic (and masochistic) fantasies'. He was writing before Blackman gave way to Diana Rigg, in the role of Emma Peel (or M[an] Appeal, a quality that transcended generations). Rigg may have protested that she was 'wholesome', not sexy, and dubbed herself 'the Doris Day of Boreham Wood'; claimed, too, that she was 'a sort of pre-puberty sex symbol' and 'terribly inhibited when it comes to projecting sex overtly'. But that was not how she was viewed by her enduring male audience, who relished her character's cool demeanour and wry humour. In many episodes, Emma Peel found herself tied up or down, awaiting agony or death with amused resignation. She might be bound to railway tracks like a silent movie heroine; locked into mediaeval stocks for her feet to be branded by a fiend who loved to cause women pain, 'especially the pretty ones'; or fixed to a ducking stool, for a lengthy exercise in torture by drowning. ('Kinky', my grandmother said to me when this programme, entitled *Murdersville*, was first broadcast, though I was too young to know what she meant.) Throughout most of these ordeals, Mrs Peel was zipped into a skin-tight catsuit to reinforce the show's fetishist allure. If the pain was quickly abated or interrupted, her life always preserved, her constant imperilment – when combined with her innate sex appeal – lent the fundamentals of sadism a gently erotic frisson. The camerawork did its best to emphasise her sexuality, rolling languorously and lasciviously across her body and making voyeurs of us all.

The same techniques were employed in the James Bond films, which became increasingly kinky (to borrow my grandmother's word) as the 1960s progressed. *Goldfinger* (1964) may have played bondage and torture for laughs ('I expect you to die, Mr Bond'), but *Thunderball* (1965) exploited the infliction of pain for the viewer's sexual delight. When the villain Largo discovers that his seductive mistress Domino has been plotting against him with Bond, he traps her in his cabin. 'You've given me much pleasure, Domino', he purrs. 'But in return, unless you tell me how much James Bond knows, I'll be forced to cause you great pain – this [he waves his cigar] for heat, this [he indicates some ice] for cold. Applied scientifically and slowly – very, very, slowly.' And he rips at her clothes, to leave her shoulders bare. At this point, the director cuts away from the room, and the soundtrack is filled with Domino's appalling cries of pain and anguish, leaving us to fill our imaginings with her agonies.

The Marquis would never have been such a tease; he would have described, with disarming lack of emotion, every sizzle of flame against skin, every scarring and tearing of the flesh, until the victim's body was reduced to a lifeless pile of meat, and she could be dismissed from the narrative as if she had never existed. That extremity, that destruction of morality and humanity, was not to be found in *Justine*, at least as it was published in 1965. But there was one way in which the text translated by Walton, and published in Britain whilst Brady was committing his heinous crimes, might conceivably have provided encouragement to someone searching for legitimacy to commit evil. It came not from the passages of sexual assault or other physical tortures, but in a bitter moral digression.

Sade's words were placed in the mouth of Mme la Dubois, a libertine who has earlier exploited Justine's innocence. Reunited with the benighted and besmirched young woman, Dubois tells her: 'It is not the choice which a man makes between vice and virtue which ultimately opens his door to happiness, my dear; for virtue, like vice, is just a way of conducting oneself in the world. It is not a case of following either the one or the other, but, rather, a question of following the common route. The man who strays from it is always wrong and liable to injure himself. In a world which was entirely virtuous I would advise you to be virtuous, because such conduct would then bring its natural recompense, happiness dancing infallible attendance upon it. But in a world totally corrupted I can never advise anything but vice. The man who doesn't follow in the same world as others, inevitably perishes. Everything he meets will bump into him, contrariwise, and he will necessarily be broken.' It was not Sade's obscenity or perversion in this edition of *Justine* that shattered our sense of a shared moral code, but his cynicism. And cynicism is impossible to legislate against.

Those reviewers who deigned to note the publication of the hardback *Justine* in late 1964 did not accuse the publisher or translator of obscenity, or warn that they might be licensing rape or murder. *The Illustrated London News* said mildly that the book was 'Coy by today's standards [in other words, perhaps, not pornographic enough], but essential in any collection of erotica'. The literary historian Martin Seymour-Smith engaged with the text more carefully, but concluded that Sade was 'not much good' as a pornographer and 'a total failure' as a novelist. 'The Marquis de Sade was not a particularly evil man,' he claimed. 'He is regarded as a monster of depravity mostly by those who have not read him but who have heard he wrote books describing orgies that are uncomfortably close to their own fantasies.'

Readers in the United States – at least, those who had access to the editions published by the Grove Press in San Francisco – had the opportunity during the 1960s to judge those orgies, and those fantasies, for themselves. Across three weighty volumes, and more than 2,750 pages, Grove fearlessly presented texts that would be unavailable (legally) in Britain for another two decades. (In 1966, Colin Wilson reckoned that *Sodom* 'could never be legally printed or sold in England or America', but it was eventually issued by a commercial UK publisher in 1989.) In 1965, Grove offered the 1791 version of *Justine* that was judged to be 'inadvisable' for publication in the UK, alongside a wealth of other material designed to reinforce Sade's stature as a philosopher as well as a pornographer. Alex Szogyi in the *New York Times* welcomed the anthology, speculating: 'Perhaps the day is not far when [Sade] will be seen as a much maligned and miserable man who allowed his imagination to revenge itself on society in the form of a literature of documented neurosis – a pleasure-oriented revolutionary who put the full measure of his madness into his work.' He also offered an intriguing vision of Sade in (then) contemporary society: 'Today, a writer of the power and persuasions of the Marquis de Sade would more easily find protection from the powers that be. Instead of being condemned to years of imprisonment, he might very well have ended up in Hollywood as consultant for Vincent Price horror films, the secret collaborator of James Bond novels.' The underground paper, the *East Village Other*, went much further: 'Burn the Bible, discard Dante, dispatch Shakespeare to a footnote, study Plato in your old age. But read de Sade. He is the Beginning.'

The stage was set in 1966 for Grove's most daring publication: the first American edition of the book that Sade regarded as his masterpiece, *The 120 Days of Sodom*, or at least all that survived of its manuscript. (Its editor, apparently with no pun intended, introduced the text as 'the seminal book in all de Sade's writing'.) This cataclysmic tapestry of human deviance was described by the same *New York Times* reviewer as Sade's 'sexual Bible, the *Kama Sutra* of the coprophilic cognoscenti, before Freud, Krafft-Ebing and Kinsey, his last word on human perversion'. But there was a sting: 'It is also a relentlessly dull book, of chiefly clinical interest'. *Sodom* was followed by the mind-bogglingly relentless *Juliette* in 1968. This time the *New York Times* handed its commission to the experimental fiction writer William Gass, who judged *Juliette* as literary experience rather than philosophical or sexual landmark: 'De Sade said he wished to go beyond what one may imagine. He desired to be gripped by desires whose satisfaction defied description. He failed utterly in this. There is scarcely an imaginative word in *Juliette*.' But there was, in its 1,200 pages, a limitless supply of naked virgins to be despoiled and defiled and ultimately despatched, each debauch followed by the next and the next and the next until only Sade's protagonists could possibly have preserved the faintest of appetites.

After the first version of *Justine* appeared in Britain, and survived without its publisher being sued or ruined by the association with the Marquis, plans were laid for editions of *Sodom* and *Juliette* to appear. Undoubtedly, given the state of the censorship laws at that time, the Grove Press editions would have been banned; but it might have been possible to produce judiciously edited texts, perhaps following Alan Hull Walton's technique of lapsing into French when the action became too hot. Certainly, the public appetite was there – at least until the first week of December 1965.

That was when an early magistrate's hearing in the case of the Moors Murderers revealed the presence in Ian Brady's possession of volumes by and about the Marquis. Indeed, his books were recovered in the same suitcase, abandoned at a railway left-luggage counter, as the tapes and photos documenting the death of Lesley Ann Downey.

Instantly the Marquis de Sade came to the attention of an appalled nation, as if he had been personally responsible for the killings. The publisher Peter Owen, who had issued his collection of Sade's letters the previous week, announced: 'I don't think I shall do any more de Sade material, particularly his so-called fiction. I don't regret having published any of them ... but now I have published everything I want to publish about him. I think he was a genuine researcher into human behaviour, but he was not the sort of man you would have invited to tea with the family.' (One can imagine the outrage and Twitter storm that this last, ill-judged comment would arouse today.) The publishers of *Justine* also stepped back from the fray, although Corgi Books did not think it appropriate to withdraw their paperback edition, which was reprinted on an almost annual basis for the remainder of the decade. Even nations far removed from Brady and Hindley's crimes, such as Japan, Italy and Spain, were quick during the 1960s to confiscate any copies of Sade's books that were offered for sale. Only in France and the United States was his work freely available. Even there, Sade's name could still attract moral and legal opposition. One of the more bizarre court hearings of the 1960s took place in Chicago in February 1967, when a local state attorney's office attempted to have two volumes of *The Complete Marquis de Sade* declared obscene. (These anthologies offered much less than they claimed, including only brief extracts from his novels, in translations so loose as to be fanciful.) As the author of his own work, the Marquis de Sade was summoned to appear as a defendant – despite the fact that he had died 153 years earlier. A court reporter captured the scene: '"The Marquis de Sade," called out Henry Woodmaster, clerk of the Circuit Court, Friday. There was no response. "The Marquis de Sade," Woodmaster repeated. Still no answer. "The case of the Marquis de Sade", the clerk intoned for a third time. "If he shows up, I'll quit the bench", Magistrate Maurice V. Lee whispered.'

In his absence, and in the wake of his belated appearance on the bookshelves, the Marquis bestrode the 1960s as not so much an author, more a commercial brand, signifying sex, violence and steamy notoriety. His name undoubtedly boosted the commercial profile of Peter Weiss's 1963 play, commonly known as *Marat/Sade* (its full title was *The Persecution and Assassination of Jean-Paul Marat as Performed by the Inmates of the Asylum of Charenton under the Direction of the Marquis de Sade*). This was both an experiment with Brechtian theatrical principles and an exploration of political and moral philosophy, with only the barest hints of Sade's alternative identity as a fiction-maker (or pornographer). But it was a dazzling stage success in Berlin, London and New York, and it spawned a compelling and faithful cinematic adaptation in 1967. When the play reached the city of Coventry for an amateur production in 1968, however, there was 'outrage'. A local mother read Weiss's script and declared, 'I have never felt so sick in my life'. Mary Whitehouse was asked to comment and was reliably condemnatory. The most appalled figure, however, was the theatre critic of the *Coventry Evening Telegraph*, who offered a master-class in taking offence: 'In my opinion this play is sick, it is unspeakably perverted, it is evil. Never have I read anything of such depravity. Parts of it made me feel sick in my stomach. I want to see this play banned.' It was just as well that this critic was not a subscriber to the Grove Press. For good measure, he offered a sweeping political denunciation: 'To me the entire theme is red Marxist claptrap – a hymn of hate to every middle-class citizen who ever lived.' The group staging the play responded politely that 'the critics have a right to express their honest opinion of the play, once they have seen it'.

Marat/Sade was, in terms of possible obscenity, the tamest of the Marquis' cultural appearances in this decade. The French director Roger Vadim was the first to attempt a cinematic rendering of a Sade fiction, with *Vice and Virtue* (1963). It translates the action of *Justine* to World War Two, when one hundred nubile young women are summoned in turn for sex or punishment by SS men who have taken over a chateau. 'The sight of suffering inflames the nerves more powerfully than pleasure', one of the officers says lasciviously. But neither extreme is witnessed to any shocking degree, and Vadim lacked the seriousness to be able to conjure with Sade's philosophy.

The Marquis' next appearances on film were more oblique. In the middle of the crime drama *Bunny Lake is Missing* (1965), up popped Noel Coward as a creepy landlord, waxing lyrical to detectives about nuns who used to 'lash each other into a positive frenzy of self-mortification'. Coward was the most louche of Sadeians: 'For myself, I confess I find the sensation rather more titillating, if you'd care to have a bash,' he tells the inspector, reaching for his whip. 'It's my particular pet. It's reputed to have belonged to the great one himself.' Cue a look of puzzlement from the CID men. 'The Marquis de Sade', Coward continues, as if talking to simpletons. 'I have his skull here – at least, that's what they told me in the Caledonian market. There's nothing like having his very own whip. It's so lovely, so very, very lovely.'

This was fine literature when compared to *The Skull* (1965 again), an amusingly ridiculous horror film in which ownership of Sade's bony head heralds inexorable doom. The picture was billed as 'A New Height in Fright', which was rather an exaggeration. So appalled was a supposed relative of the Marquis, Count Xavier de Sade, that he served an injunction upon the French distributors of the film, who wished to retitle it *The Atrocities of Marquis de Sade*. The court (perhaps comprised of film critics) declared this was 'an unnecessary insult to the family', and the movie was released in Paris as *Le crâne maléfique* (or *The Harmful Skull*).

There were countless less prominent renderings of Sade and his work on offer during the 1960s: some realised, some thwarted. Among the latter was Michael White's intention of staging a 1966 production of *The Bedroom Philosophers* in London's West End. Instead, Sade's own life was used as the bedrock of Howard Sackler's *The Pastime of Monsieur Robert* that spring. It was, opined *The Stage*, 'a really rollicking sex play', with a finale that 'must have delighted any sadists in the audience, as well as titillating any Lesbians'. 'There was no copulation on stage,' the paper explained, 'but very nearly.' Despite this recommendation, the play did not become a theatrical standard – being so obscure, in fact, that a Californian revival in 1969 was actually promoted as being a world premiere. Also forgotten by history was *Satan's Saint*, a novelisation of Sade's life by the horror writer Guy Endore. Its British paperback publisher employed the same Gothic lettering on the cover as Corgi's edition of *Justine*, in a vain attempt to claim some of that book's notoriety (and sales).

These projects were proof that the name of the Marquis was not sufficient to guarantee commercial success. So obscure was Richard Hilliard's 1967 film, *I, Marquis de Sade*, that for many years it was believed lost; in fact, one print is known to have survived. Rather than exploring Sade's work, this movie featured a modern writer determined to live out his fantasies. According to the poster, it promised 'a woman for every taste' in a picture that was 'More than just a film about sex – much more!' Shot in a style that is both a homage to the French *nouvelle vague* and extraordinarily low-budget, the film is effectively an extended dream sequence, which hints at more perversion than it delivers – never more so than in the scene in which a topless young woman is whipped with what appears to be a flimsy twig.

The apex of mischievous interference with the legacy of the Marquis de Sade was yet to come. By 1968, the combination of his notoriety, and the gradual loosening of the censor's bonds around the cinema in Europe and America, sparked a torrent of semi-pornographic movies, each claiming to represent Sade or his books. Publicity was focused on Cy Enfield's monumentally dull biopic, *De Sade* (1969), with its poster's proud boast: 'Once perhaps in a thousand years does such a man exist. Once perhaps in a hundred years is such a motion picture made' – for which one could be duly grateful. Its blurred, sometimes off-camera whippings and orgies comprised a caricature of Sade's life, rather than any form of representation. Equally tawdry was *Juliette de Sade* (1969), in which a convent girl travelled to Rome and met a devotee of the Marquis. 'Juliette, she did everything', proclaimed the film poster, 'and vice versa', but the movie suggested otherwise.

The prolific exploitation director Jess Franco crammed three Sade adaptations into a few months: *Marquis de Sade: Justine* (1969), with its jumbled but undeniably nude body parts and palpably fake blood; *Eugenie*, alias *De Sade 70*, with its star Christopher Lee apparently not having been told that he was starring in a soft porn film; and *Juliette* (1970), which had to be abandoned midway through the production when its leading actor, Soledad Miranda, was killed in a car crash. But the only film of this era even to approximate the spirit of Sade was Jacques Scandelari's *Beyond Love and Evil* (1969). This adaptation of *Philosophy in the Bedroom* offered all the Marquis' trademark diversions, sexual or violent, filmed with a delirious abandon that suggested the entire cast and crew had been dosed on LSD throughout. Salacious and visually compelling, it was also undeniably silly, like much of the decade from which it came. Whether they were being tortured or raped, Scandelari's victims writhed in spasms of ecstasy. In 1969, that was as far as one could edge towards a truly Sadeian piece of cinema. Total immersion in the Marquis' bleak soul had to wait for Pier Paolo Pasolini's *Salo, or the 120 Days of Sodom* (1975), which followed Vadim's earlier venture in being set amidst mid-century fascism. But where Vadim skimmed the surface of Sade's oeuvre, Pasolini allowed himself to wallow in the gargantuan horror of the writer's landscapes. His film trapped its viewers in *Sodom*'s nightmare, making them feel culpable for every torment unleashed upon the innocents assembled for their vile abuse.

Without admitting those extremities, translating the work of the Marquis de Sade into other media was impossible, and ultimately pointless. The most authentic response to Sade – his philosophy as well as his pornography – could be identified in three novels and one satire, all of which were written during the 1950s but endured to become *causes célèbres* of literary and artistic freedom in the subsequent decade.

When novelist Mary McCarthy reviewed William Burroughs' novel *Naked Lunch* (published in Britain, to the annoyance of the author, as *The Naked Lunch*), she might have been writing about the impact of reading *The 120 Days of Sodom*: 'The phenomenon of repetition, of course, gives rise to boredom; many readers complain that they cannot get through *The Naked Lunch*. And/or that they find it disgusting. The prominence of the anus, of faeces, and of all sorts of "horrible" discharges, as the characters would say, from the body's orifices, becomes too much of a bad thing, like the sado-masochistic sex performances.' And sex in Burroughs' work, she concluded, was translated into 'a kind of mechanical man-trap baited with fresh meat. The sexual climax, the jet of sperm, accompanied by a whistling scream, is often a death spasm, and the "perfect" orgasm would seem to be the posthumous orgasm of the hanged man, shooting his jissom into pure space.' *Naked Lunch* (with its unnecessary substantive) was published first by the Olympia Press in Paris, and entered the new decade three years later, with its 1962 publication by the Grove Press. John Calder dared to publish the book in Britain in 1964, but legal pressure ensured that it did not become available in a cheap paperback edition until 1968.

The combination of Grove and Calder also brought Hubert Selby's *Last Exit to Brooklyn* to press. The US edition of this profoundly disturbing, sexually ambiguous collection in 1964 survived intact, but Calder's initial attempt to publish in 1966 foundered when a Member of Parliament brought a private prosecution. Anxious not to grant Selby's panorama of urban horror the balm of publicity, politicians initially sought to block the publication without naming the book in question. 'In my view,' said Philip Noel-Baker, 'passages of the book which I read could be of no interest to anybody who was not a sadistic sexual maniac.' The Attorney-General declined to ban the book, for fear of creating an instant best-seller. Instead, a Scottish Labour MP intervened to impede 'a book which quite simply wallows in filth'. Bow Street Court ordered police to seize a copy from a London bookstore, so that its obscenity or otherwise could be investigated; but officers were unable to locate one. It took them two weeks to realise that they could raid the premises of Calder & Boyars instead.

Last Exit to Brooklyn remained available to the public, and apparently sold around 14,000 copies in hardback. Then the Conservative MP for Wimbledon, Sir Cyril Black, issued a private summons against the publisher. The resultant court case judged the book to be obscene, and the three copies seized by police were ritually destroyed. But Calder & Boyars insisted that the verdict only applied to the physical copies in the police's possession and continued to offer the book for sale. Criminal prosecution finally ensued, and in November 1967 a notorious court case unfolded at the Old Bailey. As was customary on these occasions, the defence assembled various expert witnesses, who testified to the literary magnitude and social importance of Selby's book. In return, the prosecution put up a former test cricketer who was now a priest; and the publisher Sir Basil Blackwell, who said that 'I felt I was seriously hurt by the book and wanted to go away and cleanse my mind'. The all-male jury shared his disgust, and Calder & Boyars were ordered to withdraw the book from sale. Eight months later, the Appeal Court found serious errors in the judge's summing-up, and the ban was overturned – after which *Last Exit to Brooklyn* joined *Naked Lunch* as one of the most celebrated, most bought but (perhaps) least read books of its era.

If those books resembled fresh perspectives on the orgies of Sade's *Sodom*, Pauline Réage's *Story of O* was a genuine response to the Sadeian vision of *Justine*. Whereas Sade's plaintive heroine is delivered from one abuser to another in relentless succession, O chooses to allow her lover to pass her over to an aristocratic sadist, in whose home she joins a small harem of other submissives. Justine is repulsed by her fate; O learns to relish hers, and her tale is all the more subversive for it. Réage (a pseudonym for Anne Desclos) saw her work brought to fruition in 1954 by Jean-Jacques Pauvert, the man who was also collating Sade's complete works. An English translation of dubious merit surfaced in 1965 via the usual conduits, The Olympia Press in Paris and Grove Press in San Francisco. Eliot Fremont-Smith in the *New York Times* saw the book as marking the end of any distinction being possible between 'literary' pornography and 'hard-core' porn, as Réage's book was clearly intended to be both. The British novelist Brian Aldiss went further, and suggested that she had transmuted pornography into art. But that would not have been sufficient to allow publication in sedate Britain during the 1960s. Instead, the book remained notorious but unseen in the UK until 1972, when its mass-market paperback edition appeared unimpeded.

The dangers of confronting the censors too soon were demonstrated by *Candy*, the satire of pornography that appeared in 1958 under the name of Maxwell Kenton; unsurprisingly, its publisher was the Olympia Press. Kenton disguised the identities of Terry Southern, later the co-author of the remarkable film *Dr. Strangelove*, and Olympia novelist Mason Hoffenberg. As Southern complained, Olympia boss Maurice Girodias wasn't impressed by the book's literary élan: 'He'd sort of count the blow-jobs, the sexual incidents and evaluate them;

a blow-job wasn't as important as a buck-in-the-ass.' Immediately, the vice squad of Paris intervened and forced the book to be withdrawn: it was ostensibly, after all, the unashamed memoir of a young innocent who had experienced a Sadeian narrative of sexual exploitation, albeit without the Marquis' customary lashings of blood.

British publication was equally turbulent. The publishers of *Candy* were convinced that the book would be banned, so they pre-empted the police investigation by cutting material from the text until it was merely a parody of a parody. There were howls of outrage: not from moralists, but from intellectuals who deplored such cowardice and barbarism. When the complete text was issued in paperback in April 1970, however, there was no police raid, no court case, no attempt at bowdlerisation. And perhaps there was no need: attention had been distracted by the woeful film adaptation of the book, which undoubtedly diminished the prestige of this exercise in social irony. Southern's subsequent exercise in mock-pornography, *Blue Movie* (1970), was arguably more entertaining than *Candy*, but proved to be less controversial.

In their various ways, those four controversial explorations of Sade's territory robbed his own books of their literary notoriety, without ever (even in the orgies of violence concocted by Selby and Burroughs) approaching his nihilistic extremes. But there remains one medium that delivers the world of *Sodom*, and *Salo*, into every home. In 1968, William Gass pondered: '[Sade] begins with desires we normally feel, then makes them monstrous; and we who read of them are robbed of emotion, deprived of our persons. (...) Isn't the Marquis warning us that if we will not recognize the humanity in man, and respond to our human outcries, *Juliette* is our future? It is a future near at hand.' Indeed. For total revelation of the Sadeian universe, one need look no further than the internet, where – in two or three clicks, depending on one's degree of discrimination – one can find horrors among which he would feel entirely at home. Somewhere, in one of the circles of Dante's inferno, the Marquis de Sade must surely regret having been born two hundred years too soon.

Interlude: The Naked and the Dead

It is a truth universally overlooked that many of the most notoriously sexual films of the 1960s are studies not of voluptuary satisfaction but of dysfunction – where any hint that there might be pleasure in congress is abandoned in a desert of impotence, frigidity and alienation.

A year before Michael Powell's *Peeping Tom* (1960) delivered a masterclass in cold, calculating sadism, the British B-movie *Cover Girl Killer* explored similar territory. The killer of the title – played by future TV comedian Harry H. Corbett, in pebble glasses and toupée – is morbidly disgusted by sex, and by those who exploit it. In the name of virtue, he murders the young women who expose themselves in cheap magazines. 'Surely sex and horror are the new gods in this polluted world of so-called entertainment', he complains. To the woman intended as his final victim, he lays out the premise of his self-pitying philosophy: 'If wanting to give man back his dignity, to free him from the prison of lustful images which foul his mind and his sanity, is madness ...'

Five years later, in *Rattle of a Simple Man* (1964), the same actor exemplified the same moral from the opposite end of the emotional spectrum. Here Corbett plays a thirty-nine-year-old virgin from Manchester, down for the Cup Final in London, and soon adrift in clubland. He charms a prostitute with his unworldliness but is unable – or unwilling – to take advantage of her offer of sex without cash. Her 'front', aristocratic and glamorous, is revealed to be just as much a myth as the masculinity that he would love to claim as his own. Their only possible union is one stripped of eroticism; one that already reeks, in his traditionally male eyes, of his failure.

Alfred Hitchcock's *Marnie* (1964) is a battle of wills between Sean Connery's macho psychiatrist, and Tippi Hedren's beautiful but utterly anti-sexual young woman. 'I am not like other people,' she tells him. 'I *know* what I am', and she is closed to the very notion of the erotic, let alone any performance in that realm. Still Connery marries her, and on her wedding night she hides in the bathroom for almost an hour, before emerging like a cornered mouse, frozen, resentful and terrified. There is an endless scene in which she screams out her self-knowledge, over and over: 'I can't bear to be handled by you – men!' Connery promises not to touch her, then tears off her gown and (effectively) rapes her, while she stares blankly over his shoulder. Only by reading a book entitled *Sexual Aberration of the Criminal Female* does Connery unlock her traumatic childhood, and lead Hedren to break through her almost psychotic self-restraint. But the film ends with a group of children freezing on the spot as the couple walk away, as if to dramatise the fact that Marnie's shattered psyche can never be healed.

Roman Polanski's 1965 film *Repulsion* starred Catherine Deneuve in the chilling role of another beautiful young woman unable to exist in a world of human communication. Her sexual dysfunction is played out in her disgust as she hears her sister make love; and then in the horrific way in which her personality merges with the walls of her South Kensington flat, which dissolve into a sea of arms, grabbing and pawing at her like every man. The critic Kenneth Tynan wrote that she was 'a psychotic young virgin, [who] wants sex, hates herself for wanting it, and hates the opposite sex for making her want it'. Deneuve reappeared two years later in Luis Buñuel's *Belle de Jour*, as a rich but frigid housewife who can only unlock her body and her soul through prostitution and fantasies of sado-masochism. Ultimately her husband pays for her pleasure, ending the film blind and wheelchair-bound after being shot by one of her lovers.

The much-vaunted promiscuity and sexual liberation of the decade was close to the enigmatic surface of Michelangelo Antonioni's 1966 thriller, *Blow-Up*. No cinematic scene had sizzled with erotic delight like that involving David Hemmings' photographer with two young women, played by Gillian Hills (the teenage heroine of *Beat Girl*) and Jane Birkin (three years before 'Je T'aime'). But Hemmings abandons the orgy midway through and walks away unmoved: as unmoved as when he acts out all the motifs of sexual power with his models, but only when they are in front of his lens; or when Vanessa Redgrave's curiously culpable character offers her body to him in return for the roll of film that proves whatever it proves. The entire film is suffused with sex, but only those two young women imagine that it has anything to do with fun; and they are left naked in a heap of props while their lover rejects them in pursuit of a more satisfying, less carnal quest.

All of which leads us inexorably to Roger Vadim's *Barbarella* (1968), with its cartoon science-fiction landscape in which sex only exists on two planes: violent sadism, and pure functionality. Jane Fonda's innocent visitor reintroduces the people of a distant planet to the notion that sex might involve sensuality, seduction and orgasmic excitement. So deep is her own erotic reservoir that she breaks Milo O'Shea's torture machine, designed to pleasure her to death. Throughout, Vadim treats the body of Fonda (then his wife) as a sexual and symbolic playground. As he admitted in his memoirs almost a decade later, 'she disliked the central character for her lack of principle, her shameless exploitation of her sexuality, and her irrelevance to contemporary social and political realities' – all undoubtedly true. But Fonda declared with hindsight that *Barbarella* 'just barely misses being a feminist movie'. Her character is, almost despite Vadim's best intentions, a feminist prototype: strong, sexually self-aware, heroic, self-supporting and ultimately triumphant. She might exist on screen for the male gaze, but somehow she survives and surpasses that objectification, and breaks the mould of a decade of films in which being a woman seems to lead nowhere but to captivity, disillusionment or mortal despair.

10 Vagina Rex and the Female Eunuch

It was the final session of the International Drama Conference at the Edinburgh Festival in September 1963. An audience of theatrical luminaries, students, academics and local dignitaries – among them the cousin of The Queen, Lord Harewood – was patiently absorbing a discussion on 'The Theatre of the Future'. They were trying, with good grace, to assimilate a particularly oblique argument by the American drama producer, Charles Marowitz. His thesis, so it appeared, was that Samuel Beckett's *Waiting for Godot*, the paragon of absurdist drama, was in fact an allegory of the American slave trade.

So tendentious did Marowitz's reasoning become that a heckler rose from the stalls of McEwan Hall to challenge him. It was the pre-arranged signal for a series of events that revealed Marowitz's true purpose: introducing the staid gathering to that 1960s archetype, a 'happening'. Electronic music began to emerge from loudspeakers, there was a flurry of confused movement amongst the crowd, and then a shout from the organ gallery drew the audience's gaze upwards. There, to collective astonishment, they watched as a nineteen-year-old model named Anna Kesselaar removed all her clothes, before she was ferried across the balcony on a trolley. Her ride complete, she donned a red raincoat and was ushered out of view. Tumult and confusion were erupting across the hall – a piper parading down the stalls, another young woman scrambling across people's seats, skeletons of animals being lowered in front of the conference banner – but it was Kesselaar's nudity that caught people's attention. 'Uproar as Girl Strips at Big Conference', read the page one headline in the *Sunday Mirror*, the sense of outrage heightened by the presence of a Royal personage.

Police charged Kesselaar with acting 'in a shameless and indecent manner, in that during the course of a drama conference she did, in full view of those present, allow herself to be wheeled across the organ gallery in a state of nudity'. She was found not guilty, the magistrate effectively ruling – for the first time – that nudity in the cause of a theatrical event was not automatically 'shameless' or 'indecent'. Having been paid four guineas for her participation, Kesselaar declared herself only too happy to do it all again, provided the same money was on offer.

Outrage was easy to confect in the Britain of 1963. After the Profumo scandal, the *Guardian* dared to suggest – in a leading article, no less – that adultery could be condoned, so long as it occurred in 'a serious, responsible extramarital relationship' (and therefore did not involve anyone who was shamefully promiscuous). The upshot of this 'liberated' sex life, warned columnist Audrey Whiting, was that children as young as eleven were attending venereal disease clinics. As an anonymous doctor declared, 'It is the result of seeking sexual experience before marriage – a sad commentary on the times in which we live. In 1963 we are faced with a change in moral values, which has caused too many young people to regard sexual experience as a legitimate pastime.' The nineteen-year-old novelist Shena Mackay epitomised this philosophy, when she explained: 'Sex is taken for granted, isn't it? When a couple are going steady, you assume they have sex and it's entirely their own business.' There was concern that Britain was on course to follow the 'free love' ethos of Copenhagen, where the number of unmarried teenage mothers had quadrupled in recent years.

The strict censorship that controlled what could legally be seen on stage, screen and television helped to protect the public from visual evidence of this drive towards promiscuity. Magazines could titillate their readers with gossip about the so-called 'Swingers', or 'Modern Marrieds' of American society, where wives were swapped as if they were mere commodities. At these surreptitious suburban gatherings, 'Undressing is always a protracted ritual ... The climax is always nude, native-style dancing.' But, as *Tit-Bits* reported ruefully, 'when disease spreads, when women become pregnant and alcohol and drugs become a life transfusion, then, when it is too late, they realize the party is over.'

The closest that Britain came to visualising such shenanigans was in the mildly audacious form of movies such as *The System* (1964) and *The Party's Over* (1965) – in each of which Oliver Reed discovers that the attractions of free love are balanced by responsibilities. But as Carnaby Street became established as the bastion of global fashion, and British youth culture conquered the world, visitors from overseas could be forgiven for imagining that the entire nation was awash in guilt-free hedonism.

In the autumn of 1964, an Australian postgraduate student named Germaine Greer arrived in Cambridge, where she was due to study for a PhD in English Literature. (Her thesis concerned 'The Ethic of Love and Marriage in Shakespeare's Early Comedies'.) Academic research was not her sole concern. Cambridge, she wrote in 1967, 'seems an ideal spot for the dedicated practitioner of the arts of love, for nearly all the men are in the full flower of their potency, being between the ages of 18 and 22. When I arrived I was elated at the vastness of the opportunity for proselytising.'

Greer had already attended university in Melbourne and Sydney (where she found communion among the city's anarchists and bohemians). 'I was always leaping into bed with guys I liked the first time I saw them,' she recalled, 'because I knew exactly what I wanted to do with them.' But such freelance pleasure proved more elusive in Cambridge: 'For six months after I arrived there, the only sex I experienced directly, apart from endlessly repeated discussions in which I found it necessary to explain that there had been improvements upon *coitus interruptus* as a contraceptive method ... was the sight, one by one, of three grubby, scrawny men in their 40s, who derived some wan satisfaction from exposing to me their genitals, pallid and bluish in the frosty air.'

Imposing of height, imperious of air, Greer invaded London in the summer of 1965. Alongside Eric Idle, she starred in the Cambridge Footlights show *My Girl Herbert* at the Lyric in Hammersmith. 'Germaine Greer is no gentleman', her programme biography explained helpfully. Reviewers lighted upon her as 'quite the brightest spot' of a mediocre revue: 'a blessing she is there,' the *Guardian* decided, as this 'tall, lanky girl with a voice that can echo back from the back of the gallery has the attack and finesse that eludes her male companions'.

Through repeated visits to the capital, Greer infiltrated 'the wilds of Bohemia', where the sexual menu was 'much more promising, after I had ferreted out the fuckers from the drunks who can't and the drugged who don't want to and, of course, your classic pederasts'. Among those she encountered was a fellow Australian, Richard Neville, who in late 1966 was about to revive the underground magazine he had originally published in Sydney: *Oz*. After Greer entranced him with her savage analysis of the failings of the men she had met since 1964, Neville suggested that she should turn her experiences into an article. 'In Bed with the English' appeared in the inaugural London edition of *Oz*, published in February 1967. The pseudonymous 'Polly Peachum' (Greer again?) provided a sequel, 'In Bed with the Americans', which focused upon that nation's almost obsessively forensic need for hygiene: 'mere seconds after the final blinding moment of ecstasy, Mister and Miss Clean race each other to the bathroom with a ferocity and cleanliness unmatched anywhere in or out of the animal kingdom'.

By then, Miss Germaine Greer, of Girton College, Cambridge had been awarded an assistant lectureship in English at the University of Warwick, where she began to teach in the autumn of 1967. Simultaneously she won a role on the madcap early-evening TV show *Nice Time*, which she hosted in a cut-glass accent alongside Kenny Everett and Jonathan Rouse. Critics variously described her as 'the tallest girl on TV' and 'a natural clown'. Academic, entertainer, Greer was also an enthusiastic admirer of the rock music community. Repelled by professors and self-styled 'studs', she was drawn to the creative sensitivity of musical performers. 'I've considered myself a musician's woman ever since I was eighteen,' she recalled in 1971. Or, as she was labelled in a 1969 issue of *Oz*, 'a celebrated (and over educated) international groupie'.

Whether or not *Oz* intended to be insulting, Greer bore the 'groupie' badge with pride. 'What happened when the groupie cult started [in 1968] was that the musicians moved in straightaway to put groupies down,' she explained. 'They called them "slags", which is an English term to say they are rubbish, phlegm, nothing, spittoons. So I moved in to say that a groupie is a musician's woman, and a musician's woman is just like he is. She's an artist in her own right – the really good ones. What I tried to do was to redress the balance by labelling myself a groupie. I will not accept any of the disparaging words that are used for women. Sometimes I even call myself an intellectual super-whore, because I'm sick of being treated differently because I have more intellectual credentials than the girl who sleeps around without the credentials. My feeling is if there is a whore in the world, then call *me* a whore.'

But that was in 1971. Two years earlier, Greer's academic position demanded a degree of subtlety when it came to self-exposure. *Oz* went to press early in 1969 with an article in which 'Germaine' interviewed the mysterious 'Dr G' about her life as a groupie. *Oz* did its best to demolish her flimsy disguise, by selling the issue with her unmistakeable image. On the front cover she was reaching into the open flies of Bonzo Dog Band singer Vivian Stanshall; on the back she exposed her breasts as she embraced him. Anybody who had attended her classes – or, for that matter, seen her on television – would have recognised her. Her writing was equally confrontational, as she hymned the groupies, 'the women who really understand what the bass guitar is saying when it thumps against their skin, a velvet hard glans of soundwaves nuzzling'. Then 'Germaine' passed the microphone to 'Dr G', who admitted: 'I guess I'm a starfucker, really. You know it's a name I dig, because all the men who get inside me are stars' – and, as she no longer needed to explain, she was a star herself.

The *Coventry Evening Telegraph* had recently profiled its local media sensation as 'The "pop" professor who loves buffoonery', whose 'hairstyle has been likened to a Jimi Hendrix freak-out'. But that was before anyone saw the cover of *Oz*. The paper was quick to inform its readers – parents, perhaps, of the innocent Warwick students – that the learned professor was also a libertine. Greer was unapologetic, insisting that her pictures with Stanshall were intended as a 'send-up' of the groupie phenomenon. Was she the 'Dr G' who slept with musicians? 'It is impossible to write about things one doesn't know', she replied. The paper added sternly that 'She condoned free love'. The University of Warwick, to its credit, issued a bald statement to the effect that whatever Dr Greer did in her spare time, it did not impact on her academic status.

In retrospect, the most surprising element of her exposés in the Coventry evening rag was her commentary on the female sex. 'Women!', she exclaimed with a snort. 'I don't like them. What I mean is that they're basically likeable, but that their situation makes them less likeable.' And then she moved in for the kill: 'I'm writing a book about women which promises to be utterly out-RAGEOUS. I shall call it *Why I Despair of Women*' – or, as she told another journalist, *The Clitoris Strikes Back.*

Three years earlier, Michael Caine had issued a laconic verdict on the position of women in the supposed era of free love. 'Look at all these promiscuous young girls of 17 and 18,' he said. 'OK, at that age it seems a lot of fun. At 25 they're all putting their heads in gas ovens in Earl's Court.' It was the philosophy behind his starring role in *Alfie*, and a rare admission from a male star that he might enjoy a sexual privilege unavailable to the women with whom he went to bed.

Caine was heralded in the mid-1960s media as one of the young lions of the British arts, alongside photographer David Bailey and the Beatles. But whereas Caine, Bailey and their fellow working-class heroes, in the photographic and thespian trades, gravitated naturally towards smart and eventually high society, the Beatles maintained a foothold among the bohemians. John Lennon had an art school background, while Paul McCartney (the last bachelor of the group) tumbled into the company of writers, gallery owners, composers and artists – the leading lights, in fact, of the underground.

In 1965–7, when McCartney was at the height of his explorations into the avant-garde, the British underground was undoubtedly serious, and often resolutely intellectual. Its most coherent manifesto was Jeff Nuttall's inspired but curiously sexless *Bomb Culture* (1968). He traced its roots back through surrealism and dada to William Blake and the Marquis de Sade, and then mapped its infatuations with jazz and the American beat poets. Nuttall's version of the underground hinged around the savage orgiastic fantasies of William Burroughs and the ravenous homosexual imagery of Allen Ginsberg; the emotional ambiguity of Andy Warhol's cinematic *oeuvre*; and the spontaneous eruptions of film-making collectives and poetry groups, radical newspapers and poetry magazines. Sex was intrinsic to the work of many artists who worked in this tradition, but – at least in Nuttall's interpretation – it was sex employed as a revolutionary tactic, rather than sex pursued strictly for pleasure.

The underground was where you might stumble across experimental films capturing sexual encounters with an exuberance not possible in 'straight' pornography, let alone in the commercial main-stream. Its roll of honour included Jack Smith's *Flaming Creatures* (1963), an almost indecipherable but unmistakeably explicit carnival of cocks and drag and gang rape; and the even more graphic *Christmas on Earth* (1963–4) made by seventeen-year-old Warhol associate Barbara Rubin – an erotic collage involving double-print images and extreme close-ups of genitals in every imaginable permutation. Warhol himself flirted with sexuality in many of his own films, although often with a languid air of disinterest that stripped them of any erotic thrill. Sometimes, as in his notorious 1963 film *Blow Job*, the sexual activity took place off screen; what the audience saw was the players' response to Eros, ensuring actors and viewers alike were distanced from the physicality of the sexual encounter.

Dozens of films such as these were featured at the Festival of Underground Movies staged at London's Jeanetta Cochrane Theatre in the autumn of 1966. It was the culmination of a month of diverse but somehow synchronous experiments in modern art, staged around the city. Joe Orton's satirical play *Loot* was revived ('If people had more sex,' Orton said as the show was launched, 'there might be less real vice in the world.'). An exhibition of images by the American artist Jim Dine at Robert Fraser's gallery was raided by the Metropolitan Police on the grounds that their depiction of sexual organs was obscene. ('This is a kick in the teeth for modern art', Fraser complained.) Artists, bohemians and anyone who felt the stirring of a psychedelic counterculture were invited to meet at a Happening to celebrate the launch of the underground newspaper, *International Times* (*IT*). The organisers called for 'Lovers of the World' to 'Unite' and promised a 'Surprise for the Shortest & Barest Costumes'. The prize in both categories was won by actress/singer Marianne Faithfull, wearing a shirt that left her nether regions exposed.

The heart of the city's artistic rebellion was the Destruction in Art Symposium, staged across four days that September. Unlike the Edinburgh event in 1963, this did not require a naked woman to transgress beyond cultural norms: each of the participating artists, among them Yoko Ono, Gustav Metzger and Juan Hidalgo, was deliberately subverting audience expectations. Besides the central conference in Covent Garden, the event involved happenings across central London, some requiring a crowd, others occurring spontaneously in front of passers-by. They included Ono performing her *Strip Tease for Three*. Spectators anticipated naked bodies, but instead were treated to a tableau of three chairs on a stage, which were removed one by one with the same whiff of taboo one might sense in a Soho strip club. The British public could also experience the *materialaktionen* films of the German artist Otto Mühl, in which naked bodies were slathered in fluids and foodstuffs of every imaginable consistency, before being joined in sexual union, until they sacrificed their humanity amidst the melée of slime and paint. Through the debris, reviewer Raymond Durgnat identified 'mayonnaise pouring over titties, champagne trickling round haunches, and delicate canapés of private parts trimmed with shrimps, cucumber slices or sausages'. Police left Mühl's work untouched, but swooped on a less inflammatory film that played behind Hermann Nitsch's performance piece involving the skinned body of a lamb and copious quantities of blood. The film was obscene, the police argued, but organisers managed to smuggle the offending reel out of the theatre before it could be seized.

'To a certain degree the Underground happened everywhere spontaneously,' Nuttall explained in *Bomb Culture*. 'It was simply what you did in the H-bomb world if you were, by nature, creative and concerned for humanity as a whole.' But his conception of the underground as an artistic movement, succeeding the surrealists, futurists and the rest, came to seem outmoded and almost irrelevant after 1966. If *IT* was very much a product of that vision, then Richard Neville's *Oz* inhabited an entirely different vision of (sur)reality. *IT* prioritised words and deeds; but *Oz* recognised the power of the image, employing psychedelic collage, state-of-the-art graphics and subversive cartoons to reinforce its iconoclastic rhetoric. Throughout its existence, *Oz* favoured gratuitous use of female nudes, whether they were drawing attention to subscription offers or merely decorating the page. Unlike more timid men's magazines, it made no attempt to hide women's supposedly offensive pubic hair. Strangely, however, there was little overt editorial coverage of sexual matters within the magazine, beyond the work of Germaine Greer, one of whose early contributions was a lament for the way in which the breast was being 'driven out' of contemporary British fashion designs. 'Basically it is to be seen and caressed,' she insisted (no nonsense about the mothering instinct here), 'and clothes must suggest that.'

Oz spoke for an alternative vision of an underground culture: one rooted in rock music and experimentation with exotic chemicals and plants, fired by political outrage about the war in Vietnam, but at the same time fixated on the prospect of self-realisation, whether that came via sexual ecstasy, spiritual visions or acid trips. Its answer to *Bomb Culture* was Richard Neville's book *Play Power* (1970). A simple comparison between their titles measured the shifts in perception from one generation to the next: post-war dread from Nuttall was answered in Neville's work by the hazy, dope-clouded but still optimistic hedonism of youth.

IT may have been visually more staid than *Oz*, but its fortnightly digest of Britain's increasingly anarchic bohemia frequently cast an uninhibited eye across the sexual landscape. In its pages during 1967, you could find the American poet Tuli Kupferberg defining the sexual revolution: 'Our bodies are opening. A thousand penises will bloom. Cunts too!' Raymond Durgnat reported on the intricacies of Soho prostitution: 'Personal service means intercourse, as opposed to specialities, and the standard rate runs from about £2 to £5 for a "short time"; kinks take a little longer and come from £3 to £8.' Richard Gardner offered a guide to 'Magical Love Making': 'Adoration is the key for both sexes ... if they concentrate on truly worshipping each other's genitals, their power will be brought to this point of transference. The genitals are like a plug and socket, and through this point of connection should pass the vital spiritual essences of M and F (Fire and Water).' And through it all, *IT*'s small ads showcased a parade of potential erotic unions: from 'Young Eastern Male wants to pollinate any young flower in need of pollination', to 'Slim impotent [Hell's] Angel wishes to express his disgust of the female sex on submissive busty chicks'.

The mere existence of the underground, psychedelic or otherwise, was not sufficient to keep the 'straight' world at bay. When members of the Rolling Stones were busted in 1967 for drug possession, Marianne Faithfull was in their company, her body covered only by a rug. Surely she must have been embarrassed to be in this state, Keith Richards was asked during their trial? Of course not, he replied: 'We are not old men. We are not worried about petty morals.' Such was the Stones' implicit erotic power, and the prurient depths of the public imagination, that increasingly exotic rumours surfaced to explain why

Faithfull had been naked when the police arrived. At first it was assumed she was involved in an orgy ('She has been presented by the prosecution as a drug-taking nymphomaniac', the Stones' barrister complained). Later it was traded as fact, by those who trusted their source of such arcane knowledge, that Mick Jagger had been eating a Mars chocolate bar out of her vagina. (In fact, she had just taken a bath.) Faithfull later appeared naked in Jack Cardiff's faux-psychedelic movie *The Girl on a Motorcycle* (1968), although her sex scenes were heavily cut by the censors. 'What I want is peace,' she admitted at the end of 1967, 'and that I get only through sex. I work because pleasure is sex and sex is my sin and my sin is the future.' Among those who perfectly encapsulated what she called 'my scene' was her sometime lover, Mick Jagger. His orgy scenes in *Performance* (1970), Donald Cammell and Nicolas Roeg's incendiary study of violence, lust and the disintegration of the psyche, were exactly what adults conjured up when they tried to envisage the sins of the sexual revolution.

If Marianne Faithfull and the Rolling Stones sometimes felt besieged by the authorities because of their anti-establishment morality, homosexuals had to tread even more carefully, both before and after the changing of the law in 1967. The media reinforced that reticence. In August that year, Joe Orton was murdered by his partner, Kenneth Halliwell. The London press stepped delicately around the subject of his sexual orientation, referring to Halliwell only as 'his best friend' with whom he shared 'a very strong emotional relationship'. Similar discretion was shown when Beatles manager Brian Epstein died from a drugs overdose later that month; nothing more explicit was said about his erotic tastes than that he was (in classic Fleet Street shorthand) 'a confirmed bachelor'. He had felt under increasing pressure from the outside world since being blackmailed by a former lover. When journalist Hunter Davies wrote an authorised biography of the Beatles in 1968, he was asked by Epstein's family to remove any suggestion that Brian had been a homosexual. Davies still described Epstein as 'good-looking, charming, popular and gay', but virtually nobody who read the book – in Britain, at least – realised that 'gay' might carry a double meaning.

The same degree of hesitation surrounded the formation of a British vehicle for homosexual rights. In America, a variety of local and regional organisations preceded the founding of the Campaign for Homosexual Freedom, which was soon superseded by the Gay Liberation Front (GLF). New York's so-called 'Stonewall riots' in June 1969 helped to create a sense of solidarity that stimulated the GLF's growth from a pressure group into an enduring movement. In Britain, gay men and women had to rely on sporadic recognition from other, more diverse forces. One of the most striking instances was the decision of *Oz* to publish a 'Homosexual Issue' in September 1969. Its front cover featured two naked men embracing on the front cover (an image given an extra frisson, in the context of the times, because one figure was white, the other black).

It was only in late 1970 that a UK version of the Gay Liberation Front emerged. But homosexuality was not entirely absent from late 1960s culture. When the Lord Chamberlain's censorship regime in the British theatre was relaxed, many different facets of sexuality could finally be reflected on the stage. Before then, dramatic attempts to pierce the wall of sexual repression had been doomed to failure. Very briefly at the start of 1968, the Edinburgh Experimental Group had succeeded in presenting *Mass in F* at the Traverse Theatre, with its improvised tableaux of naked bodies, entangled in representations of various sexual positions. But the show was quickly raided and cancelled.

Then, in the summer of 1968, as if a flood of experimentation had been choreographed, a multitude of directors and companies signalled their intention to shatter the theatrical taboos. Maggie Wright walked naked across the stage at Stratford as she played Helen of Troy in the RSC's production of *Dr Faustus*. Jenny Lees sported only a long blonde wig in a John Arden play. The stars of Michael McClure's *The Beard* at the Royal Court played out an entire seduction scene between two American archetypes, Billy The Kid and Jean Harlow. And in John Herbert's *Fortune and Men's Eyes*, a drama unashamedly centred around homosexuality, three young men stood together naked in one ground-breaking scene. (Naked, that is, except on the night when the mother of one of the actors visited him backstage before the curtain rose and instructed him to wear his underpants.) Suddenly gay themes were everywhere in the theatre, from Colin Spencer's *Spitting Image*, in which a young man gave birth, to Paddy Chayefsky's *The Latent Heterosexual*.

If gay men could experience a brief sense of liberation from these theatrical productions, many women remained unimpressed by the new tolerance of sexual expression on stage and screen. They felt that what was being sold as liberation was merely exploitation in progressive disguise. Their misgivings were supported by the writings of the polemicist Emmanuel Petrakis, self-appointed leader of the Sexual Emancipation Movement. He demanded nothing more of men than that they should 'try not to be selfish and aim to give the woman pleasure too. Remember that a woman is a human being with feelings, not just a cosy hole.' But a cosy hole was exactly what he expected the woman to offer, it seemed: 'WOMEN: learn to give of yourselves a bit more (with adequate contraception). Even if you don't enjoy it at first, why not give pleasure to others? Given time, you might learn to enjoy the experience.' And if they didn't? Well, at least their emancipated men would be satisfied.

The Petrakis philosophy – men are pre-eminent, women serve them – was prevalent throughout the 1960s underground. It was there in political meetings when men spoke and made the decisions, and women fetched drinks and took the minutes. It was there at demonstrations where (according to Germaine Greer) one could see the prominent Trotskyist Tariq Ali 'marching with his classy blonde chicks'. It was there in magazines and art shows and experimental films, where the woman was expected to pose nude every time a man demanded it. And, of course, it was there in interpersonal relations, when the door to the outside world was closed.

'Try and think how many chicks in the underground are doing anything using their heads and not their cunts,' was how the dramatist Jane Arden put it. 'Women in the underground think they're free and groovy, but in fact they've just got through a lot of the surface crap and exposed all the basic hang-ups, like the neurotic need for a strong dominating male presence to fill up their otherwise meaningless lives. We're supposedly free to sleep around and do all the things that men do, yet really we're totally trapped inside our own heads, submissive and dependent, unable to believe that we have the ability to control our lives.'

There was a school of radical psychiatry in the late 1960s arguing that the only rational response to modern capitalist society was madness. As the pressure group Campaign Against Psychiatric Atrocities declared, 'People who break down because they cannot find a way to live sanely in an insane society are shattered forces of change.' Jane Arden might easily have adopted this sentiment, although she would have changed the word 'people' to 'women'. As she explained in 1969, 'One in every nine women will spend some time in a mental hospital, where they'll be told they're mad because they're mad, and not because they're living in a fucked-up society where women are regarded as the sub-species and immature hysterics if they can't face the idea of rearing children.'

Arden, who had two sons from her broken marriage to playwright Philip Saville, knew something about the frustration of being treated as less than a man. A student at RADA, who appeared in her first film aged twenty, she emerged in 1954 as a writer-actor, with a double bill of plays at the New Lindsey in London. She penned a series of thrillers for ITV, before her commercial breakthrough with *The Party* in 1958. 'It's about the kind of people who have too much to give to the world,' she explained, 'and end up in psych wards' – the first threads of a dominant seam in her work. The initial production starred not only the young Albert Finney and Arden herself, but also Hollywood star Charles Laughton. He compared her to Tennessee Williams and pronounced *The Party* 'the sexiest play I've ever read'. Despite this endorsement, a combination of the pressures of family life and London theatre's disparagement of creative women ensured that she was unable to follow it up. 'In the early days I escaped out of the oppression into breakdowns', she recalled in 1969. 'All you can do is scream.' Instead, she made intermittent TV appearances as an actor, starring alongside Harold Pinter in a 1964 adaptation of a Sartre play that provoked the ire of Mary Whitehouse. She also co-wrote a surreal television drama with her husband, which examined the internal contradictions of wedded bliss (*The Logic Game* in 1965). 'Marriage defines women's oppression,' she explained later.

When her marriage collapsed – Saville had begun a lengthy affair with Diana Rigg – Arden collaborated with actor-director Jack Bond, whom she had met during the making of another dramatic analysis of marriage, *Exit 19* (1966). Two years later, she channelled her confusion and rage about the role of women, the nature of sanity and the hypocrisy of marriage into a film script, *Separation* (1968). She took the starring role, of a woman hemmed in by a landscape sculpted from paranoia and claustrophobia, while Swinging London, with its stylish men and naked young women, unfolded around her. Scarcely seen at the time (and heavily criticised when it was), *Separation* has been revisited in recent years as a pioneering piece of experimental filmmaking.

Arden increasingly felt that women may have been emancipated, in the sense that they could now participate more fully in male society, but that *liberation* was still a distant fantasy. She poured scorn on the emancipated women who dominated the media – women such as Edna O'Brien, who in Arden's opinion claimed a rhetoric of freedom while still living entirely in thrall to men. She saw them leading 'a divided life split between their heads, where they're trying to be men, and their beds, where, frightened of "losing their femininity", they feel they've got to be submissive'. Pursuing worthy but limited causes such as better childcare or equal wages was restricting women's possibilities and sidestepping the need for revolution. The result was a trajectory that led from passivity to dishonesty to disappointment – or, if women dared to challenge their destiny, madness.

Her philosophy was placed in the mouth of Woman, the leading character in Arden's remarkable play, *Vagina Rex and the Gas Oven*: 'At fifteen the alternatives presented themselves – fight – submit – or go mad. I made a compromise – a dance contracted between these three that would keep me occupied for the next twenty years – until history turned up a better card – or I was certified insane.'

Vagina Rex was presented at a bastion of experimental creativity, the Arts Lab in London's Drury Lane, for six weeks from February 1969. Alan Aldridge's poster depicted a pregnant, naked woman, clutching two babies, with her stomach cut open to reveal (literally) a bun in the oven. Tears streaked down her face as she gazed into a looking glass, to be confronted by a skull staring back at her. 'The central theme of the play, and my life, is the oppression of women', Arden explained. Savage, grim, violent, ultimately despairing, her play unfolded in front of a huge screen showing a close-up of the vagina of one of the cast. Besides the Woman, a role inhabited with defiant courage by Sheila Allen, the protagonists included a crowd of Furies, portrayed by the hippies who used the Arts Lab as a commune. 'Women enjoy being dominated sexually', they chanted sarcastically. 'We enjoy being humiliated ... The natural role for women is the submissive one.' The female players were interrupted and insulted in turns by Man, alias the actor Victor Spinetti, who emerged out of the audience to heckle the women on stage: 'Bloody lesbians! Bloody dykes! What they need is a good fuck.' Offstage, Spinetti was totally supportive of Arden's message: 'For centuries women have been treated as objects by the Church, the State and the Establishment. Mentally, men still live with the primitive image of dragging women to the caves by their hair.'

Arden herself was more brutal in her assessment of the balance between the sexes: 'Women are seen to be a slave-group,' she pronounced as the play was launched, 'appendages of men without identities of their own.' So profound was women's agony that it could only be relieved by a response equally violent. 'If it were possible at this moment for women to take their masochism and radicalise it, there would be the bloodiest revolution ever', she explained. 'The amount of resentment and pain within women is so enormous.' And these emotions were exactly what she planned to analyse in a periodical she wanted to call *The Gas Oven* (which was never brought to fruition). Of course, she noted acerbically, 'Many women use them for suicide'. Perhaps she could already imagine her own fate: ultimately Arden would take her own life in December 1982, her death passing without public notice.

Hers was a profoundly different view of women and their revolutionary power from some of those found elsewhere in the late 1960s feminist movement. As Germaine Greer commented in 1969, 'Women have been conned by men. Women must free themselves and rescue themselves from men.' For some feminists, such as Juliet Mitchell, author of the influential book *Women's Estate* (1971), rescue and revolution would only be possible via collaboration with other forces of liberation – the black power movement, for example, or radical Marxism. Mitchell did not want to divorce women's oppression from their economic situation. Even the new sexual morality was being exploited for profit, she argued persuasively: 'Having been offered all possibilities for self-glorification, having produced the sexually radiant you, the commercial dimension of capitalism can re-use you,' she explained. 'No city in the world boasts such a density of "sexual objectification" on its bill-boards and subway ads as does London.'

During 1969, while Germaine Greer was proudly declaring herself 'a musician's woman', planning to record a Frank Zappa song, and participating in the formation of the 'First European Sexpaper', *Suck*, she was also researching her 'out-RAGEOUS' book about women. 'My agent wanted me to write about the failure of emancipation,' she revealed, 'but I couldn't even get mildly enthusiastic about that.' Instead, a journalist reported, 'she intends exploring what she regards as the fundamental reason why women are still pretty mixed up and far from equal – the myth of the ultra-feminine woman, which both sexes are fed and which both end up believing.'

Nobody would accuse Greer of conforming to that stereotype. She was equally concerned to distance herself from what she called 'the self-appointed leaders of female revolution'. As far as she was concerned, they were simply 'A bunch of would-be administrators in frilly knickers, who bray about equality and then rush off to put the joint in the oven before *he* gets home'. Jane Arden herself could hardly have been more dismissive.

Greer channelled her distrust of contemporary feminism into an *Oz* manifesto entitled (self-mockingly) 'The Slag Heap Erupts'. Inexplicably, the article was illustrated with a picture of a nude Asian girl on the cusp of puberty – exactly the kind of gratuitous exploitation of a child that was already visible in the early issues of *Suck*, to which Greer was a contributor. Not that children strayed into Greer's rhetoric, which was a declaration of 'Cuntpower' rather than 'women's liberation'. She highlighted the shortcomings in the pioneering work of Betty Friedan, whose 1962 book *The Feminine Mystique* is still regarded as a feminist landmark – politically liberal rather than revolutionary, it was true, but still simmering with controlled rage. Greer's anger was more overt than Friedan's. 'Men are the enemy', Greer declared, and 'Men don't really like women' – but then she too had filled the press in recent months with dismissive comments about women and their muddled thinking. Now the other strands of the feminist movement were either too mild for her taste, and therefore powerless; or 'militant', which she interpreted as being associated with 'inefficiency', 'belligerence' and (a particularly cruel and misogynistic jab) 'obesity'. The solution was that women must 'liberate themselves … The cunt must take the steel out of the cock; female masochism must be eradicated if male sadism is to become ineffectual.' Ultimately, she said, 'A woman who cannot organise her sex life in her own best interest is hardly likely to transform society'.

This was brilliant rhetoric, no doubt, but in practical terms, what did it mean? The next issue of *Oz* contained a riposte from British feminist Michelene Wandor, which laid out the many facets of everyday life in which women could demand, and achieve, change. Most of all, they could unite to debate, argue and ultimately agree on a joint platform. There had been a Women's Weekend at Ruskin College in Oxford, from which Greer's absence was both noted and lamented. But Greer was determined to pursue a single furrow, at the opposite end of the field from her peers. Its first manifestation was a special 'Cuntpower' edition of *Oz*, which proudly declared that it 'does not reflect the official Women's Liberation party line'. (There wasn't one.) 'Everyone digs the idea of the new female militancy so long as all it does is demand things from men. Rejecting that workshop mentality, *Oz* argues that if anything will free women, it will be their own peculiar force.'

Greer offered an ambiguous explanation of that 'peculiar force' in an interview with the *Guardian* in September 1970. 'If we are to escape from the treadmill of sexual fantasy, voracious need of love and obsessiveness in all its forms, we will have to reinstate our libido in its rightful function. Only then will women be capable of loving. Eternal Eros is imprisoned now in the toils of the sado-masochistic symbiosis, and if we are to rescue him and save the world, we must break the chain.' Again, this was rhetoric, not enlightenment. And it was offered in a climate where – in an otherwise sympathetic profile of Greer – Quentin Crewe of the *Sunday Mirror* could describe feminists as 'particularly repulsive', either 'hideous bags' or possessing 'a desiccated, humourless intelligence', 'unhappy crabs steeped in useless envy' – all of them except Germaine Greer. Perhaps Crewe was mollified when Greer told him: 'What I most envy is the kind of love men have for each other'; or when he read her promise in *Suck* that 'If I had a cock for a day, I would get myself pregnant'. Why couldn't all feminists be so entertaining?

Greer's foray into public relations was triggered by the publication in October 1970 of *The Female Eunuch*, her learned, compelling, sometimes infuriating and anything but desiccated account of woman's place in the world. It would find its place in bookstores alongside

Mitchell's *Women's Estate*, Kate Millett's *Sexual Politics*, Robyn Morgan's anthology *Sisterhood is Powerful* and many less fêted titles; a tidal wave of analysis, reportage and political instruction, which seemed certain to rebalance the relationship between the sexes, inspired millions of women worldwide, young and old, and yet was soon assimilated to ensure that any change was slow and agonising. Perhaps because it stood outside any organisation or movement, Greer's text has survived, like her – capable of refashioning people's thinking in a way that books more centred around contemporary political and social issues could not.

While her academic career continued, Greer was now a celebrity, above and below ground. She found herself on talk shows and in public debates – most notably in a 1971 verbal battle with novelist Norman Mailer, documented in the film *Town Bloody Hall*. She was endlessly quotable, reliably controversial, fiercely intelligent and incapable of being cowed by the arguments of anything as weak as a man. Even her least likely supporters found her enchanting. Donald Zec, veteran showbiz columnist of the *Daily Mirror*, was more accustomed to fawning over film starlets than arguing about feminism. But Greer entertained him nobly with her opinion of bras: 'The most stupid, thoughtless garment ever invented. Two-thirds of the women in this country suffer from obesity – if they didn't, they wouldn't need to carry all this spare flesh around in bags. Set them free.' She talked in headlines as easily as in perfectly constructed, philosophically logical paragraphs, and her book was now proclaimed 'the Bible of Women's Lib', even if she felt no kinship with anything as confining as a feminist movement (or a bra).

Something of an intellectual anarchist, Greer was perhaps more at home in the company of her colleagues from *Oz* and *Suck*, with their wilful refusal to recognise limits to their self-expression or consequences to their actions. In the brief pause between British and American publication of *The Female Eunuch*, she joined *Oz* founder Richard Neville and other counter-culture luminaries in Amsterdam, on the panel of judges at the Wet Dream Film Festival. Organised by *Suck*, this event was both a parody of the Oscars and a celebration of pornographic and/or sexual filmmaking. During the screening of a documentary about artist Otto Mühl, Greer frolicked naked with fellow *Suck* contributor Heathcote Williams, before intervening to

Yoko Ono (with her then-husband Tony Cox behind the camera) during the making of her *Bottoms* film in 1967. Three years later, the Metropolitan Police raided the London Arts Gallery and seized lithographs by John Lennon on the grounds that they were obscene.

Two singular women of the 1960s: Valerie Solanas, founder of the Society
for Cutting Up Men, in 1967; and Jane Arden, creator of the confrontational play
Vagina Rex and the Gas Oven, during a 1966 film shoot in Portobello Road.

The scholar, author and provocateuse Germaine Greer posing with Bonzo Dog Band
vocalist Vivian Stanshall during a 1969 cover shoot for *Oz* magazine.

Two of the most sexually frank and morally ambiguous films of the 1960s:
Alfie (with Michael Caine and Shirley Anne Field); and
Blow-Up (David Hemmings with Tsai Chin, Jane Birkin and Gillian Hills).

Jane Fonda as the naïve but sexually unashamed star of her husband
Roger Vadim's science-fiction comedy film, *Barbarella*.

The Killing of Sister George, starring Susannah York and Coral Browne,
was one of commercial cinema's first serious studies of a lesbian relationship.
By contrast, *What's Good for the Goose*, starring Norman Wisdom and Sally Geeson,
insulted and exploited both its actors and its audience.

Fifteen-year-old Linda Hayden, star of the 1969 film *Baby Love*, with her onscreen mother (and British glamour queen of the 1950s), Diana Dors.

The decade's most formidable moralist, Mrs Mary Whitehouse, encounters Mick Jagger on David Frost's TV show in 1968. Whitehouse was a founder of the Nationwide Festival of Light, a Christian pressure group which picketed a screening of Dr Martin Cole's film *Growing Up* in 1971.

prevent Mühl from sacrificing a goose in the name of art. (Mühl subsequently formed a notorious political/artistic commune near Vienna and was imprisoned for sexual offences against several of the children there.) Later the judges watched off-cuts from *Performance*, in which more of Mick Jagger's revered manhood was revealed than could be exhibited on the commercial screen. Greer's writings in *Suck* were equally explicit ('Ladies Get on Top for Better Orgasms' was a very sensible example), and the magazine's ultra-liberal attitude to sex equally freewheeling. She eventually removed her name from the *Suck* masthead because she felt exploited by the way in which the other editors had published pictures of her naked body. *Suck* disappeared after a final issue in 1974, in which Heathcote Williams claimed that he had lost his virginity with the Queen's cousin, Prince William of Gloucester, when they were at prep school in Kent.

While the morally and socially compliant citizens of Britain were perfectly capable of living through this era without noticing *Suck*, *Oz* became notorious in 1971 when it was the subject of an Old Bailey trial. Between Germaine Greer's rant about feminism in February 1970, and the 'Cuntpower' special she inspired that summer, *Oz* invited teenagers to gather at its West London office and plan what became known as the 'School Kids Issue'. Boys and girls between fourteen and eighteen contributed uncensored articles: their subjects ranged from the state of contemporary rock to the idiocy of pupils being forced to take part in army cadet training. One young woman dared to explain how she and her young contemporaries had gradually discovered the facts of life: 'We first became aware of sex during one biology lesson at the age of 11 or 12. From then on we were all dying to see a prick, but we all swore that we would keep our virginity until we got married (some have – others not!).'

The only sexually explicit material in the 'School Kids Issue' came not from the teenagers, but from the adults who supervised their efforts. A full-page pin-up of a fifteen-year-old contributor in her school uniform was presented as 'Jail Bait of the Month'. An American comic strip was refashioned so that the popular *Daily Express* cartoon character Rupert the Bear was seen to deflower 'Gipsy Granny' in graphic close-up.

Mysterious 'complaints' were made to the Metropolitan Police after 40,000 copies of this issue were distributed around the country, and the Obscene Publications Squad gathered evidence for an arrest. Three *Oz* editors, among them Richard Neville and future poet and entrepreneur Felix Dennis, faced a series of criminal charges. These were based upon the police view that the 'School Kids Issue' was not only obscene but had the power to 'debauch the morals of children and young persons'. Worse still, the magazine was intended – so the police alleged – 'to arouse and implant in the minds of these young people lustful and perverted desires'.

The Old Bailey trial in June 1971 effectively put a generation and its culture on trial. All three defendants were found guilty on some charges, not guilty on others, but were awarded the strongest possible punishment for each offence – prison sentences of between nine and fifteen months in total. On appeal, it was ruled that the judge had exceeded his authority and misdirected the jury, and the convictions were overturned. *Oz* was never the same, however, and the trial hammered the final nail in the coffin of Britain's counter-culture idealism. (Several Obscene Publications Squad officers subsequently went to jail themselves on corruption charges.)

Arguably the most famous of all the *Oz* contributors had cleverly managed to sidestep the 'School Kids Issue' and the resulting furore. As the obscenity trial was playing out in London, Germaine Greer was still promoting *The Female Eunuch* around the world and cementing her notoriety and/or fame. She was almost alone amongst her peers in being allowed to market her dissent from male-dominated society in such a lucrative manner. For example, no international stage was available to Jane Arden; her anger had to be internalised, and then released in small but savage outbursts of creative energy.

In 1970, Arden had appeared alongside Juliet Mitchell in a BBC documentary entitled *A Woman's Place*. Both were dismissed by the press as 'extremists', although there were substantial differences between Arden's existential rage and Mitchell's blend of psychoanalysis and sociology. January 1971 saw a group of what the *Daily Mirror* called 'nine angry women' forming a collective entitled Holocaust. Arden was the primary contributor to the group's manifesto, a prose-poem filled with scabrous imagery and bitter anguish: 'WE / the domestics and the baby-minders / WE / the load of chaos strapped upon us / FUNCTION is on the back of our despair / WE / are the oxen of the irrational / RANDOM MADNESS is the burden of the feminine.'

By April, Holocaust had prepared *A New Communion for Freaks, Prophets and Witches*, a confrontational piece of performance art that featured an entirely female cast (often naked) and was, so Arden insisted, only to be reviewed by women. Nicholas de Jongh of the *Guardian* broke the embargo on male journalists and returned to report 'an act of faith transformed into rambling silliness … a therapy session run wild and stupid, an ego-trip turned into a full-scale expedition'. He detected 'an emphasis on sexual guilt and a disgust with the body' in the 'hectoring hysteria, exaggerated caricature and incoherence' of the show, but left with 'bewilderment and anger'. These were exactly the same emotions that, in starkly contrasting ways, Jane Arden and Germaine Greer had experienced when they confronted the state of women and men in the contemporary world. Greer glimpsed a means of escape, via 'female tactics for survival in a world destined for the typically masculine end of suicide'. Arden's vision was more nihilistic and claimed suicide as a woman's right. That left Greer with the final word. As she wrote in *The Female Eunuch*, 'the greatest service a woman can do her community is to be happy; the degree of revolt and irresponsibility which she must manifest to acquire happiness is the only sure indication of the way things must change if there is to be any point in continuing to be a woman at all.'

Interlude: Flogging a Dead Horse

In the pornographic novels published by Maurice Girodias in Paris, which daring British tourists could smuggle back through customs, every conceivable scenario conjured up by the onanistic male at his most unhinged was brought to flamboyant fruition. Here the lonely bachelor could transport himself from his barren bedsit to a Parisian pleasure garden, in which: 'One after another, or simultaneously, ten penises splashed ten darting loads of semen over bellies, down throats, into cunts, between sticky, wet fingers and into the palms of masturbatory hands. One after another, ten cunts twitched and angered into communal orgasms, and seemed to explode in the swollen intensity of their vaginal orgasms.' (Nobody ever claimed that *Wayward* by Peter Jason was literature.)

Or they could imagine themselves as the lover of Louise in the same author's *Unfaithful*, as she is fucked so ferociously that she can only exclaim (the full quote occupies several hundred words): 'Rip my cunt in two with that enormous thing! Christ but it's big! It's the biggest penis in the world! Let this be the fuck to end all fucking! Let me die on the damned thing, impale me on it!' On and on until she shrieks: 'Give it to my clitoris, my twat, my hairy cunt, my aching, aching cunt'. (In the interests of historical accuracy, it should be noted that Louise is being vigorously serviced by a woman named Claudine, who is wearing a gargantuan dildo.)

Nowhere, even in the darkest corners of New York or Copenhagen, could anyone in the 1960s find the pictures, still or moving, to accompany such fantasies – though they would arrive soon enough. Indeed, before 1964, men who demanded even the softest of pornography had to seek out an imported issue of *Playboy*, or some shabbily produced collections of remarkably unerotic nude or topless photographs. Hugh Hefner's *Playboy* set the template for the racy but otherwise respectable men's magazine. Its nudes were carefully positioned or airbrushed to avoid revealing their genitals, and the pictorial content was outweighed by the pages devoted to serious essays and interviews.

Now it was time for Britain to offer its own version of *Playboy*, though it took an American publisher to bring it to life (thirty-four-year-old Bob Guccione). The launch of *Penthouse* was preceded by a carefully concocted scandal, as a brochure announcing the magazine's imminent arrival was delivered unsolicited to hundreds of thousands of addresses. But Guccione's thunder was stolen by London club-owner Paul Raymond, who rushed the Winter 1964 issue of his own *King* magazine into the shops. 'We like sex,' Raymond said in his first editorial. 'A bold statement, maybe, but it needs saying today as much as ever. New social conditions bring new attitudes, and it is now admitted, even by the phoney moralists who try to fetter the entertainment business, that sex can be fun.'

An essential part of Raymond's business was scantily clad women, of course: 'Our girls are laughing-and-sunshine girls, not grimacing plastic-mac-and-whiplash girls'. Among them in this debut issue was none other than a topless Christine Keeler, looking every bit the guileless girl next door. At the other extreme of the glamour scale, moralist Malcolm Muggeridge was, as ever, anxious: 'One feels that in a sane society, pornography wouldn't be necessary. This obsession with it must be due to some flagging of normal appetites or an excessive stimulation of them.' Raymond didn't care which it was, as long as it kept the magazine in print. Likewise the male readership, which luxuriated in the opportunity to see such modest showbiz stars as Susan Hampshire and Anita Harris without their clothes.

The first issue of *Penthouse* bore a March 1965 date and billed itself simply as 'The magazine for men'. Inevitably it sported a glamorous cover model, holding down a sweater just far enough to conceal her naked groin. Guccione boasted in his sex-free editorial that this was 'the noisiest debut in publishing history' thanks to his postal stunt. His initial wares included a surprisingly forthright symposium about the nature of British sexuality, in which the young novelist Laura Del-Rivo complained that magazines such as *Penthouse* were 'just as bad' as the weekly women's magazines in the way they portrayed the female sex.

Like *Playboy* and *King*, *Penthouse* depended on its erotic portfolios. A nineteen-year-old model with the unlikely name of Bambi Lynn-Davies revealed not only most of her body, but also a bent for philosophy: 'Sex should be fun, and the sooner we begin to see it for what it is, something natural and wonderful and God-given, the sooner we'll get over the sickness and the kinkiness that distorts our thinking.'

Besides its indulgent 'Forum' on the subject of caning teenage girls, the magazine also pored over the increasingly daring cinematic output of Europe, unearthing stills from sequences cut at the UK censor's request. Its monthly interviews became more prestigious – Dirk Bogarde, for example, was moved to comment in 1968 that 'The cinema is just a form of masturbation ... a sexual relief for disappointed people'. His views on soft-porn magazines were unfortunately not recorded.

One of the ironies – or strengths – of these men's magazines was their ability to encompass opinions that totally undercut their own *raison d'être*. *King*, for example, allowed the American writer Clancy Sigal to puncture the fantasy of the *Playboy* lifestyle – and thereby the rationale for *King* and *Penthouse* too. 'Social anxiety, and the age-old difficulties of sexual initiation, lie at the root of the *Playboy* concept,' Sigal declared in 1966, stereotyping his readers as callow, nervous teenagers. That year, novelist Edna O'Brien contributed a similarly outspoken piece: 'A woman should have the right to as many husbands or lovers as a man has mistresses ... Women have got to accept the fact now that one man is not able to make us happy anymore.'

The latter article appeared in the premier issue of a new title, *Mayfair*. Its editor announced chirpily: '*Mayfair* is National and Classless. It is designed for a select group of men. Tomorrow's Men.' These courageous few exhibited certain qualities: 'Intelligence. Sophistication. Toughness.' Once admitted to the magazine's inner sanctum, they could linger over the semi-naked models, or enjoy the columns on such subjects as bridge, chess and the theatre. *Mayfair* was the first of these publications to venture anywhere near feminism, with a 1967 piece entitled 'Equality in Love' (written by a man).

By spring 1968, *King* was no longer financially viable, and so it was swallowed by *Mayfair*. The subsequent circulation battle with *Penthouse* endured for decades, though their contents were virtually indistinguishable from each other. Both edged ever closer to the day when they could finally reveal the mysterious luxuriance of female pubic hair. Until then, they vied with each other to lure in the uncommitted reader: *Penthouse* offered ever more explicit pictorial spreads from European films; *Mayfair* countered with a late 1968 profile entitled 'Jenny Stays Dry – youngest yet nymphet in the rain' (she was seventeen). Readers remained loyal to the concept, if not the individual titles, and continued to fill the letters columns with impassioned tales of spanking their wives and daughters, or paeans for individual models. 'The pictures of Christina are breath-taking,' gushed a reader from Watford, speaking for the entire soft-porn audience of 1968. 'I have never seen a girl's breasts so tanned.' Or a readership so satisfied, it seemed.

11 The Return of Lolita

The middle-aged male cuts an unappealing figure in the history of British sex comedies. Gawky, clumsy, grotesque and dull, he is either plunged into crimson embarrassment by the merest presence of an attractive woman or convinced that his lack of redeeming physical features makes him irresistible to the opposite sex. Usually, such routines are played strictly for laughs, and it is obvious that the buffoon is the butt of the joke. But the 1969 film *What's Good for the Goose* shattered these stereotypes, by the simple method of letting the unappealing middle-aged man write the script.

That was how, in a film one contemporary reviewer lambasted as 'offensive, distasteful, often repellent', fifty-four-year-old Norman Wisdom offered himself as the most unlikely sex object of the 1960s. Its scenario may be ridiculous, its politics appalling, but *What's Good for the Goose* should be watched by any man of a certain age or beyond who still secretly believes himself to be an icon of erotic fascination to women decades younger than himself.

It is also a crash course in the exploitation of a young actor, in this case Sally Geeson, who celebrated her eighteenth birthday towards the end of the shoot in summer 1968. She was the younger sister of Judy Geeson, who had been the same age when she was required to perform several nude scenes in the highly successful *Here We Go Round the Mulberry Bush* (1968). 'I was very unhappy at that side of it,' Judy admitted when the film was released. 'I had no idea it was going so far.' Her co-star, Barry Evans, was also resentful about the situations into which they had been forced during the production. Several of the scenes that upset them most were cut from the print screened in Britain, but the experience remained a painful one.

A year later, Sally Geeson underwent the same ordeal. It was her first major film role, and the chance of appearing alongside Wisdom, one of the country's most beloved comic actors, presumably trumped any misgivings she may have felt. She has only ever spoken warmly about Wisdom, and it is possible that both players were ultimately pushed into sex scenes with which they felt uncomfortable by director Menachem Golan.

The set-up and plot were sufficiently embarrassing by themselves. Wisdom – the veteran of countless roles as 'the little man', bullied and overlooked by all around him but rescued by his natural heart of gold – played businessman Timothy Bartlett. Timothy is bored with his equally middle-aged wife, and easily tempted when two teenage hitchhikers, clad as skimpily as the English climate will allow, thumb him down as he drives to a seaside conference. One of them is Geeson, in the role of Nikki, who for some unaccountable reason finds Timothy impossibly endearing. She expresses her affection by fiddling with his clothes while he is driving. 'I can't control it', Timothy burbles, and we are supposed to laugh.

That evening, he eludes his business colleagues and wanders, in full evening dress, into a basement discotheque. Of course, Nikki and her psychedelic chums are there, and she drags him over to their table, and pets him like an eager puppy. Timothy sheds his wedding ring and dances like an elephant at the Royal Ballet. Later, he offers to walk her home and discovers that she is planning to sleep under the pier. 'Can I come back to your place?' she asks Timothy, who looks baffled (as well he might). 'Well, you want it, don't you?' she says. 'What?' asks Timothy. 'Sex,' she laughs, and rushes giggling into the night. 'Yes,' he drools, and as she reaches out to stroke him, it begins to pour with rain.

Is Nikki's passion dampened? Not at all – not even when, in a long sequence designed to capitalise on Wisdom's comedic reputation, various capers ensure that she is marooned outside his hotel room in the downpour. She's freezing, bedraggled, but is she downhearted? Of course not. 'You look gorgeous,' says Timothy helpfully. Any normal woman would have thumped him, but Nikki beams with pleasure and heads off for a bath. She emerges in a towel, which she throws aside to reveal a see-through bra. Then – for no reason other than to see her adolescent breasts jiggle – she bounces up and down on his bed, before kissing him teasingly. Cue another slapstick sequence, during which we are privileged to see Norman Wisdom, the fifty-plus stud, revealing his pubic hair in the bath.

'Hey, you're not in bad shape,' Nikki gushes as she caresses his body. 'I love you,' Timothy responds, utterly out of his depth. 'Oh, don't be silly,' the seventeen-year-old girl says. 'You don't have to love me, let's just have fun.' There's more slapstick, and then we cut to the following morning, when the pair are in afterglow.

The next day, he skips his conference, so they can frolic on the beach. 'Silly, isn't it,' Nikki says, in one of the few realistic lines in the film. 'I'm enjoying this, yet you're old enough to be my father.' Or grandfather, if her mother had started as early as her, but Nikki ignores her qualms and the pair run naked into the sea (a shot we fortunately see only from behind).

There is more, much more of the same, but Timothy is appalled when he discovers the feckless Nikki in bed with one of her psyche-delic friends. 'I can't understand it,' he tells a sensible hippie girl. 'She behaved like a whore.' 'Oh, grow up', the sensible girl replies, and explains the new morality – make love where you find it, and move on with no regrets.

Whereupon Timothy, perhaps realising that he is unlikely to score with two teenagers in the same weekend, invites his wife to join him at the conference, and attempts to relive the heady rush of his affair, taking her through the same routine of sight-seeing and boutique-raiding. Back at his hotel, he prepares for his second erotic thrill of the trip, but is horrified to see his wife emerge from the bathroom slathered in cold cream and sporting a full set of curlers. Somehow they conjure bliss out of this unpromising situation, and on the way back to London, they ignore Nikki hitch-hiking her own way home. The girl is picked up by one of Timothy's bosses, Timothy's wife strokes him sensuously as he drives, and every middle-aged fantasy is satisfied. Not only can you have your wife and a lover too, but teenage girls will throw themselves at you simply because you happen to be male and alive. Nikki will obviously sleep with Timothy's boss, and there will be no unfortunate consequences – no pregnancy, no venereal disease, no divorce, no sense that in five or ten or twenty years' time, Nikki will wake up one morning and realise that men have been using her body all her adult (and pubescent) life.

This was the delightful concoction offered to British cinemagoers in March 1969. But there was more. Wisdom and Geeson were required to film two versions of their 'romantic' bedroom scenes. For the UK market, Geeson kept her breasts under wraps, to ensure that *What's Good for the Goose* would gain an 'A' certificate, allowing it to be seen by children under parental supervision. For European audiences, Geeson was filmed topless, whether she was bouncing on the bed, awaiting Wisdom's erotic charms, or embracing him with coital intent. These scenes were stretched out for several minutes, to make the most of Geeson's youthful nudity. There were even two different versions of a scene cut by the censors from the British print: Geeson puts her hand inside Wisdom's shirt, works her way downwards, and (it is implied) discovers his erection – cue startled looks on both sides. 'It was very embarrassing,' Geeson admitted even before the film was released. 'But I think Norman was more embarrassed than me!'

British reviewers knew nothing of the more explicit European cut, but the film's tawdry atmosphere was unmistakeable, even to those reviewers who relished Wisdom's comic persona. An unfortunate reporter had the task of phoning the comedian, who was working in Australia as the film was released, and informing him about the media's 'distasteful' verdict. Wisdom was silent for a few seconds, and then burst out defensively: 'Why shouldn't I appear in a sexy film? Anybody would think I had invented sex. Don't little men with flat hats and bum-freezer jackets ever take their clothes off and have sex? And if they do, must it always be something to be laughed at? I think little men are probably much more concerned with serious sex than most of the six-foot glamour boys.' He failed to grasp what made his film 'often repellent', Geeson's exploitation aside: the fact that it reinforced every stereotype that made men of all ages and shapes feel as if they had a divine right to sample every female body.

As Wisdom's sex fiasco crawled its way around the nation's cinemas, a more serious view of the same subject was being completed. Olivia Hussey had already won acclaim for her leading role in Franco Zeffirelli's 1968 screen version of *Romeo and Juliet*. Here at least the brief nude scene was tasteful and featured lovers of virtually the same age (seventeen and sixteen). 'I just can't understand all this morbid interest in her bare bosom and my bare bottom,' said her co-star,

Leonard Whiting. Hussey admitted that the prospect loomed over her as the day approached: 'I could hardly sleep for nights before we did that. I'd never taken my clothes off in front of anybody. But in the end it all seemed so easy and natural, and I almost forgot what I was doing.'

In *All the Right Noises* (shot in 1968–9, but not released until 1971), Hussey was seventeen when the filming began and, according to *Penthouse* magazine, 'innocent to the point of naïveté'. This suited her role, as a gauche teenager in a stage musical. With her Alice band controlling her long straight hair, she looks every bit the child. Tom Bell operates the stage lights; he was thirty-five during the shoot. Soon the pair are holding hands on the tube, and he tricks her into a late-night tryst in a London park. At their next meeting, she is in her school uniform, and Bell discovers that she is a month short of her sixteenth birthday. 'I should have told you', she apologises. Bell repeats a familiar refrain: 'I'm old enough to be your father'. He is also, as ever in these scenarios, already married.

Their affair continues when the musical goes on tour. 'Don't treat me like a kid,' she complains to him. 'Don't get stroppy,' he replies, 'or I might tan your backside.' 'What if I liked it?' she says coquettishly. Eventually they both begin to realise that their relationship has run its course. 'Why didn't I meet you before?' Bell asks plaintively. 'Because I was in the infants' class at the time,' is Hussey's tart reply.

Similar scenarios have been staged in every decade of the cinema; Woody Allen built his career around the so-called May-to-December romance (which became January-to-December by the end). But in no other era than the late 1960s has this motif, of teenage, perhaps under-age girl engaging with adult male, been so prevalent, and so symbolic. Variations on this theme were everywhere: young Helen Mirren (playing a teenager at the age of twenty-four) frolicking with *Lolita* veteran James Mason in *Age of Consent*; Susan George in *Twinky* alongside Charles Bronson; Romina Power in the mid-1960s Italian sex comedies she made when she was thirteen and fourteen. *Twinky* was a particularly unpleasant example: it was issued under a variety of different titles, one of which was *Lola* (the *Lolita* comparison could hardly have been more blatant). 'She's almost 16,' the poster boasted, 'he's almost 40.' (In fact, George was eighteen or nineteen during filming; Bronson in his late forties.) 'It may be love,' the poster continued, 'but it's definitely exhausting' – not to mention illegal, then and now.

Meanwhile, European cinema was awash with 'coming of age' movies, the most notable of them *Claire's Knee*, one of six 'Moral Tales' directed by Éric Rohmer. Here a man in his late thirties enjoys a delicious holiday flirtation with two young girls: the elder (around seventeen years old) has a crush on him, while he yearns in a purely romantic way, of course, for the younger (who was fifteen when the film was made). In the tumultuous climax, he is able to touch junior's bare knee. The film is exquisitely shot and made with great tenderness and restraint; but it still legitimises the allure of the under-age girl, as if nobody had ever heard of *Lolita*.

Why did a young woman's 'coming of age' become so central a theme to this particular era of filmmaking? There were a variety of factors at work, which coincided to make adult male desire for the pubescent female appear to be the most natural, the most joyous, of liaisons. The first was the international adoration of youth in a decade in which the baby-boomer generation began to set the terms of global culture. In music, film, marketing and especially fashion, everything was about the young: clothes were designed to fit them, and young bodies displayed those designs to optimum effect. Forget the hippie maxim about never trusting anyone over thirty; even twenty could seem ancient if you walked down Carnaby Street or the King's Road, Sunset Strip or 5th Avenue, the Champs-Élysées or Via del Corso.

This was also the time when the iron clasp of the censor over what could and could not be decently depicted on the big screen was being loosened to the point of slackness. Mainstream cinema was still some years from being able to depict unsimulated intercourse, but the naked body – the young body – became a standard selling point, and the 'coming of age' scenario allowed cameras to be focused on those limbs and torsos at their least tarnished by the rigours of age and experience. Riding above everything was the sense that this was an age of liberation, of freedom, of being released from the petty morality of the past; and who better to express the joy of this moment than the generation who were coming upon it almost as their birthright?

What is most striking when one compares the world into which the literary and cinematic versions of *Lolita* were born, and its late

1960s equivalent, is that any vestige of guilt, of corruption, of exploit-ation, let alone of abuse, had disappeared. No longer did auteurs in any medium have to rely upon their insistence that (*pace* Rohmer) they were delivering moral tales, exposing the cynicism of adulthood, revealing the corrosive power that the old held over the young. Now it was as if youth commanded all the power and dictated all the moves; young women could not only attract older men, as they had always done, but they could manipulate them to their will – and their will was always carnal. Except, of course, these situations and encounters were almost always created and arranged by middle-aged men: not the icons of late 1960s liberation, but their fathers or grandfathers.

There was one glaring exception to this rule; or a partial exception, at least. The film that did most to reinforce the suggestion that there was nothing in the world more powerful than a girl under the age of consent, who uses her sexuality as a weapon, was based upon a novel written by a young woman. The film, and the book, were entitled *Baby Love* – an innocuous pet name for a lover in the Supremes' 1964 hit single, but here something much darker.

The film producer Michael Klinger bought the screen rights to the novel before it was published in 1968. Its author was Tina Chad Christian, a pseudonym for Christine Chadwick, a Liverpudlian woman in her early twenties. In 1964, after suffering serious illness during her adolescence, she enjoyed a brief moment of recognition as 'Chad Christian', a songwriter. She then worked as a journalist for women's magazines, before the advances for *Baby Love* enabled her to move to London and embark on a full-time career as a novelist – though this appears to have been her only published book.

Its 'baby' is fourteen-year-old Luci, who is transplanted from poverty to the home of a wealthy London doctor after her mother's suicide. The family comprises Robert Quayle, his wife Amy and their 'awkward, ugly' thirteen-year-old son, Nicky. Tormented by her mother's death, but vaguely aware of her burgeoning sexual power, Luci sets out to seduce – or perhaps conquer would be a more accurate word – the entire household. Her first prey is Nicky, who is allowed to fondle her naked body while his parents are out. 'Holding, it's enough, isn't it?' he says naively. 'I don't care about doing it properly. I don't know why old people are so frightened we will. I bet it isn't as good. It can't be. Nothing can be as beautiful as this.'

So far, so innocent; but soon Luci is setting Nicky's parents at odds. Amy insists that if the girl is being flirtatious, she's doing it unawares. But her husband sees through the act: 'Look at those lips. What are they parted for – a lollipop or a kiss? (...) Does she arch her back like a sensual little cat or a sadly disturbed unfortunate child?'

Amy seeks to widen Luci's education, assuring her that 'sex isn't all it's made out to be. It's just a means to an end, really. A gesture we go through for the sake of having beautiful children like you!' Soon she is sharing Luci's bed, and seeking to satisfy her own well-camouflaged lesbian urgings. With Robert, Luci tries to replicate the motions of seduction, but breaks down: 'I don't want sex. I don't even like it. It's a filthy game.' Robert responds acidly: 'It's never a game. It's total war.' Only with Nicky, after she has nearly been raped by ruffians while walking with him in the countryside, does she achieve any kind of satisfaction, as his hand 'settled where no hand had ever settled before'. To the last, the author is ambiguous about whether Luci is victim or corruptor; precocious or emotionally damaged.

The setting and characters were transferred to the 1969 movie, although Nicky is now more mature (played by an actor of nineteen). But Luci's character is far less ambiguous: after school, she snogs an older boy in front of her friends, who gawp and cheer as if she is staging an orgy for their amusement. In London (or Hampton Court, to be exact), she is forced to share a bathroom with Nicky, and leaves the door conveniently open when she is undressing, luring him into her erotic web. Throughout the film, she is tortured by flashbacks to her mother's death, and perhaps we are meant to view her sexual compulsion as a symptom of trauma rather than an immoral crusade. But she is utterly careless about flaunting herself – stripping down to her underwear in a boutique and entering the window display to collect a dress; letting the archetypal dirty old man (his face covered in sweat, features contorted in lust) rub his hand up her bare thigh in the cinema; teasing Nicky to the point where he bursts into her room and sees her standing naked. She wears no bra beneath her skimpy T-shirt at the breakfast table; picks up an older man at a disco; sunbathes topless next to Nicky in the garden. When comedian Dick Emery, playing a rare straight role, enters the action as a family friend, she lets him purr all over her bikini-clad body.

Eventually she seduces Amy, and encourages Robert to massage her bare back, before sitting up so that he can see her breasts. There is a brief scene of almost Gothic horror, when she walks into the shower with Nicky, and he is knocked unconscious, but that is only a distraction. In one of the final scenes, she taunts Nicky's mother in front of Robert: 'Don't you want to play with your little doll, Amy?' And the film ends with Luci painted like a fashion model, ready for a visit to Dick Emery's home, and another seduction. In her sensual way, she is as destructive as Damien in *The Omen*: a homewrecker who cannot help employing her natural pubescent sexuality to wreak emotional carnage on those who have opened their lives to her.

Without drawing an exact parallel between author and character, Tina Chad Christian once explained: 'Like Luci, I was for years obsessed with destruction. When you feel you are physically doomed, as I did then [as a teenager], everything goes bad inside you. I was destructive in many ways, I know.' The film locates the birth of Luci's destruction in the erratic, near-abusive parenting she received from her mother. For this key but silent role, Michael Klinger made the intriguing choice of Diana Dors – the glamour girl of British cinema in the 1950s, the country's closest equivalent to Marilyn Monroe. A hint of her appeal can be gathered from her incredibly bland, and undoubtedly ghost-written, memoir, *Swingin' Dors* (1960). 'I've Been a Naughty Girl!', the front cover proclaims, while the back confirms, 'Never before has a life been so revealed'. But the book is careful to say absolutely nothing about sex, at least when it involves Dors. Instead, she breezes through a series of episodes in which men lust after her voluptuous body, including this wartime reminiscence: 'At thirteen, when I had quit school and was taking acting lessons in London, I posed for the Camera Club in lingerie and brief swimsuits. I got a guinea an hour and goose-pimples.' So she probably understood Luci's life very well. In *Baby Love*, her brief appearance could barely have been less glamorous. As one reviewer noted, the film 'opens quite stunningly with a monstrous close-up of a monstrous Diana Dors, staring at her bloated, worn-out whore's face in the mirror.'

The same piece praised the performance of the actor who plays Luci as 'quite remarkable', and so it is. Like her character, Linda Hayden was fourteen or fifteen when she auditioned for the role, a process which involved her (and presumably some of the several hundred other young girls anxious to claim the part) posing topless for the producers. As Hayden recalled, 'It was all quite near the knuckle'. It was clear from the start that both the role and, perhaps more urgently, the times required that she would appear in various degrees of undress throughout the film. Hayden was apparently unconcerned, unlike her parents: 'Mummy and Daddy were a bit worried about it at first, but when I pointed out that if some of the most respected actresses of the day played such parts, there was no reason why I shouldn't, they agreed.' Klinger entered the audition process with an ideal in mind: 'the fifteen-year-old girl must look like an innocent girl who underneath is a woman, as every man who looks at her will realise'. Hayden satisfied all his requirements, her performance conveying an emotional complexity that suggested her future would deliver leading roles in Shakespeare, rather than the sensational horror films and exploitative sex comedies into which she drifted next.

Unlike the Geeson sisters, or Sue Lyon at the other end of the decade, Linda Hayden has never expressed regret at what she was asked to do in *Baby Love*, or hinted at having felt used or abused. 'It's not a dirty movie', she had insisted when it was released. 'The nudity showed her character.' Michael Klinger hit the same note: 'Yes, the film has sex, not for exploitation purposes or for shock effect. It's a natural thing for two young people who become aware of their sexual desires.' Or, as Hayden explained, 'It was her way to get at the boy.' Both accounts focused on only one facet of her triple seduction, however. What made *Baby Love* so shocking at the time, and notorious in hindsight, was Luci's dedication towards corrupting son, mother and father in rapid succession.

No wonder that Hayden, still just fifteen as the shooting ended, was immediately seized upon by the American press as 'Second Lolita' (or even 'Psycho Lolita'), their stories accompanied by shots of the under-age girl posing in her bikini. American columnists leered over her: she was a 'precocious femme fatale', 'a teenage sexpot', a 'sex goddess', 'the year's No. 1 sex babe'. 'Saw Linda Hayden in *Baby Love*,' one mature adult male wrote. 'I love my wife, but oh, you baby!'

Not that Britain could feel superior. In *Tit-Bits* magazine, Roger Woodcock salivated over the idea that 'The sweet blonde schoolgirl has become a sex-mad nymph'. Hayden was, of course, 'the new

Lolita', Woodcock declared, before he coaxed her into admitting, 'I am Lolita, in a way'. Asked about the nude scenes she had been asked to shoot, Hayden replied with a sigh of resignation: 'Actresses have to put up with this kind of thing'. They also had to put up with being displayed in a mass-circulation periodical in a bikini, or a jumpsuit unzipped down below the navel. In case anyone was uncertain of her appeal, the headline told the entire story: 'Her friends know her as schoolgirl Linda. But at the drop of a film contract – SHAZAM! She sheds her gymslip and becomes ... SUPERDOLLY!' They might as well have offered her body as a competition prize.

When the premature lust ebbed briefly away, and the film arrived, the reviewers were no more tasteful. *The People* declared that *Baby Love* included 'All the perversions you can think of in one big film. It's got incest, lesbianism, rape and a suicide for Diana Dors.' (The 'incest' reference suggested that the critic had been too busy drooling over Hayden to follow the plot.) Having done their best to reduce its star to a sex object, the *New York Daily News* decided that the film was 'trashy' and 'absurd', and full of 'tawdry sex' – to which it added by suggesting that it was 'a showcase for young Linda Hayden's squirming voluptuous body' (a line designed to appear on a poster). Another US response was that the film was doomed by Hayden's 'over-ripe physical maturity'. It took Michael Billington, later Britain's most distinguished theatre critic, to rise above the lechery and describe *Baby Love* as 'a faintly repulsive exploitation of the cinema's new permissiveness'. Yet even Billington did not raise an eyebrow at the way in which Hayden had been depicted on screen. A syndicated columnist neatly summarised the way in which adolescent girls were viewed in 1969: 'Teenage starlets are the ones who bare all to the eye of the motion picture camera in the cause of the new cinematic "art". What *Lolita* only intimated, today's actresses display without care or cover. To them, the celluloid return to nature is neither traumatic nor titillating; neither dirty nor daring. It is as natural as the tempestuous times in which they live.'

Or as natural as the front cover of the only album by rock supergroup, Blind Faith, which was released a few months after *Baby Love*. Photographer Bob Seidemann decided that the spirit of the 'tempestuous times' could best be captured by photographing someone, as he put it, 'at the beginning of the transition from girl to woman'. He identified a suitable candidate on a London tube train. But when he arrived at her parents' house to seal the deal, he was disappointed to discover that the fourteen-year-old girl 'had just passed the point of complete innocence and could not pose'. Instead he recruited her eleven-year-old sister, who duly appeared topless on a chart-topping, million-selling album, while clutching a model spaceship with a strangely phallic design. The cover design was substituted in America, where the moral objection was that she was showing her nipples, not that she was years below the legal age of consent. *Time Out* magazine criticised the 'gutter press' for 'taking its usual high moral tone' when the album was released and offered this justification: 'If we scratch around a little more deeply in our National Heritage, we will find that the taking of photographs of pre-pubescent girls is a tradition as old and honourable as photography itself.' The reference was to Lewis Carroll's penchant for photographing his inspiration for Alice. But *Time Out* complained that the innocence of the Blind Faith cover had been spoiled, because the girl was clearly wearing something beneath her waist. 'At least Alice wasn't a cop-out', the magazine said grumpily. A year later, Seidemann's fellow designer, Storm Thorgerson, came clean about what the Blind Faith cover was intended to achieve: 'It was very sexy for a male because of its socially taboo implications. Just the thing you want.'

Indeed it was. There was a long, though not perhaps honourable, tradition of R&B songs hymning the praises of very young women: 'Good Morning Little Schoolgirl', which became a rock standard in 1964, was only the most obvious example. In the initial burst of rock'n'roll, countless hits signalled the imminent arrival of a girl's all-important sixteenth birthday, when the men could legally move in for the kill. But in the late 1960s, all subterfuge was abandoned, and rock stars lusted openly after under-age girls, from the fifteen-year-old groupie who was the subject of the Rolling Stones' 'Stray Cat Blues' (on stage, Jagger sang that she was actually thirteen), to Donovan's blessed Fourteen (on 'Mellow Yellow'). Ten Years After revived the 'Little Schoolgirl' song and made their intentions plain: 'Baby, I wanna ball you / I wanna ball you all night long / Tell your mama and your papa / Baby, baby, doing nothing wrong, child'. Meanwhile, P.J. Proby boasted openly about the harem of twelve- and thirteen-year-old girls he maintained at his home. Groupies of the same age, such as Sable

Starr, would soon achieve a sad brand of notoriety by offering their pubescent charms to some of the world's leading rock stars.

Only twice did pop figures fall foul of the law for their tastes during this period; and neither was one of the notorious bad boys of rock who wore the stains of their lust on their jeans. The first was the British tenor singer David Whitfield, a major star during the pre-rock era, who was reduced to seaside concert parties by 1966. He was fined £25 for indecent exposure to an eleven-year-old Girl Guide who had visited his cottage for an autograph, though the court chose not to believe her evidence that he had also tried to put his hand down her dress. Three years later, Peter Yarrow, from the mellifluous, liberal-minded folk trio, Peter, Paul and Mary, opened his hotel room door naked to a pair of teenage girls. He proceeded to 'take liberties' with the fourteen-year-old in front of her older sister and was arrested when their mother complained to police. He was given a three-month prison sentence, though he was subsequently pardoned by President Jimmy Carter. His defence was that the girls were 'groupies', and therefore fair game, regardless of their age. Multiple stars of the era could have faced the same charge, and mounted a similar excuse.

Those not qualified to attract groupies had to search for their pubescent prey via more traditional methods. London's burgeoning underground press began to attract the unwelcome attention of the law when it published small ads from men, well beyond the age of consent, seeking male partners. Yet other, much more dubious fare was allowed to pass untouched. There was the 'Successful Business Gent (44)' who advertised in 1967 for an 'Erotic Female, age unimportant. Young child would be appreciated.' Or, from 1968, the 'Slim attractive boy', in search of 'beautiful and sophisticated instructress, 14–30' – though exactly how sophisticated the fourteen-year-old might be was open to question.

Marjorie Proops believed she knew the answer. In the same week that the slim attractive boy asked for help with his erotic education, the doughty columnist had another shot at describing the sexuality of very young women. 'Girls are born flirtatious and knowing,' she began confidently. French infants look 'precocious' in their bikinis. 'American girls are not far behind the French for precocity. Pre-teen dating is commonplace. Girls who haven't found a steady by the time they're 12 feel faded. In this country, sexual awakening has traditionally come later. But it looks as if our girls are starting to catch up.' She quoted a surgeon who believed that 'sex is out of control in secondary schools' and 'soon hospitals would be unable to cope with the number of schoolgirls going for abortions'. Proops concluded that before long, 'our girls will start learning to wear provocative bikinis at a younger and younger age'.

There was plenty of encouragement in the air. In 1966, a London publisher offered a photographic collection entitled *Six Nymphets*. Its subjects, according to the publicity release, were 'a kaleidoscope of lovely girls', all 'caught in transition from the tender buds of adolescence to the rich fulfilment of womanhood'. Its foreword and captions were contributed by Norman Thaddeus Vane, a screenwriter who would soon pen the script of *Twinky*, the film starring Susan George and Charles Bronson. Nearing forty, he had just married a sixteen-year-old actress. 'I had a small flat on King's Road in Chelsea,' he recalled just before his death, 'and she used to come over secretly on the way back from school, and we used to fuck.'

He was therefore in the perfect place to hymn the multiple attractions of those girls just escaping from 'the tender buds of adolescence'. Though 'nymphet' was in the book's title (to entice the admirers of *Lolita*), Vane preferred to dub this creature 'the Sex Child'. 'What man does not quiver,' he wrote, 'at the picture-image of a tuft of long blonde hair dishevelled in the wind, a pair of impudent blue eyes across the room, gay and promising eyes.' Having warmed to his theme, he attempted a definition: 'The Sex Child is that curious co-mingling of innocent and temptress ... The true Sex Child [is] more waif than woman ... She is a Sex Child only once, briefly and tremulously, and never again ... probing, full of discovery, self-analysis, deep longings, sexual stirrings, and the roots of something her child-like mind can only just conceive in dim outline' – although Vane was able to picture it only too clearly. He must have been disappointed with the visual element of *Six Nymphets*, which featured soft-focus 'art' photographs of females who were definitely women rather than girls.

Other cameramen were more than ready to go where *Six Nymphets* refused. In 1966, the naturist magazine *Sun and Health* published *The Boy*, 'the joys of boyhood crystallised in a magnificent book of over 400 photographs'. The unchallenged master of photographing children in the nude was Hajo Ortil. He was an equal-opportunity exploiter, publishing anthologies of naked boys and girls, but his speciality was the adolescent or pre-pubescent male. 'I've had sexual encounters with maybe 800 boys – only boys,' he boasted to an interviewer, 'and only five, six or seven boys said no.' His rationale and self-defence were brutal: 'All these boys are heterosexual. I am only their helper while they are twelve to seventeen, in adolescence, and they need help.' His photo albums were available by mail order through a wide variety of underground newspapers in the late 1960s, alongside other 'forbidden' works, such as the Grove Press editions of the Marquis de Sade and books of 'marital' instruction too candid for publication in the UK. Potential purchasers were asked to swear that the books 'will not be passed to other than *bona fide* Naturists, or those sympathetic to the movement'.

Another avenue for exploitation that flourished in the late 1960s was sex tourism, which was chronicled quite openly by travellers of the period. Sean O'Callaghan devoted a series of books to trafficking of various kinds, among them *The White Slave Trade* and *The Yellow Slave Trade*. Girls as young as ten were on offer in Macao, he discovered, 'some of them almost pure white'. Allen V. Ross concentrated on *Vice in Bombay*, 'an erotic tour of this whispered-about city … in all its shocking excess'. There was an entire chapter on 'boy brothels', where young males were 'used for sex by fetishists and perverts', while he also delighted in recounting the tale of the seven-year-old girl who supposedly approached him by saying, 'I am a virgin and you will be the first man to touch me'.

By comparison, other literary successors to the flame of *Lolita* seemed tame. There had been a brief furore in 1962 about *The Passion Flower Hotel*, a novel allegedly written by a seventeen-year-old schoolgirl – who turned out to be thirty-three-year-old Roger Longrigg. It concerned an inventive group of young boarding-school girls who set up 'personal services' for the pupils of a nearby boys' school. Most of the actual encounters, which extend to intercourse for boys with deep pockets, take place away from the narrator's eye; the enticement of the novel is the risk of naughtiness and the thrill of anticipation.

Having become a best seller, Longrigg's book was snapped up for (of all things) a stage musical. A number of significant talents were attached to and then detached from the project, which by the time of its premiere in 1965 could boast a score by the era's foremost soundtrack composer, John Barry. The cast included several future stars, such as Jane Birkin and Francesca Annis, plus impresario-to-be, Bill Kenwright. But nobody could find anything remotely obscene in the songs or script, which included such sub-Wildean dialogue as: 'I'm over sixteen and terribly nubile.' 'Sixteen is the age of consent in Scotland – and I consented years ago.'

If *The Passion Flower Hotel* reduced the *Lolita* theme to farce, other novels of the era regarded it more seriously. In Glendon Swarthout's Faulknerian drama of a small American town, *Welcome to Thebes* (1962), half the local population appears to have been having sex with fourteen-year-old Carlie. Rosalyn Drexler's *I Am the Beautiful Stranger* (1965) is ostensibly the diary of thirteen-year-old Selma Silver, who goes on a date with 'a dirty businessman' named Larry: 'He just kept on repeating in a very breathy way, "Let me fuck you, baby, let me fuck you, please let me fuck you".' (Spoiler alert: she doesn't.) Another thirteen-year-old, Mercia, is the *fille fatale* of *Frost*, a 1966 spy novel by Andrew Hall. His civil servant hero is actually innocent of any illicit intentions, but is blackmailed after Mercia bumps into him in a park, and immediately removes her clothes so that the pair can be photographed together. Several other men are less reticent about sampling Mercia's charms, including her supposed father, who says the girl is 'Mature for her age, but still a minor. What a classic row that'd be. I mean, you can go to prison for years for offences against a girl of that age. The Sunday papers would go berserk.' And so it went on: the naked thirteen-year-old girl in Robbins' *The Carpetbaggers*, the eleven-year-old introduced to masturbation by a Swedish governess in Patrick Skene Carling's *The Experiment*, plus of course the groupies already chronicled in *All Night Stand*. Even when women were over legal age, they still had to be compared to children, such as seventeen-year-old Allison in Lionel White's *Obsession* ('She had looked like a little girl ... She is a child and she is also a woman') and the andro-gynous Simon of Kingsley Amis's *I Want It Now*, who in her bikini resembles 'an overgrown and underdeveloped thirteen-year-old. One who would give rise to a great number of sexual felonies, though.' Amis's vacuous TV personality hero, Ronnie Appleyard, finds her on-off acquiescence so confusing that he ponders whether 'it might be the best thing simply to plunge ahead, bash on regardless, rape her'. The reader was supposed to sympathise with him, not her. By 1971, the man/child theme had become so common that it was milked for comedy, each of the first two episodes of the TV drama series *Budgie* adding an under-age sub-plot for laughs.

Perhaps inevitably, nobody returned to the scenario of *Lolita* more often, or more assiduously, than the originator of the entire genre, Vladimir Nabokov. For almost a decade after the belated UK publication of his scandalous novel, he seemed to have abandoned the subject entirely, alluding to it in interviews with a tone of amusement as if to suggest that, really, everybody should have recovered from *Lolita* by now. Then, in the final years of his writing life, it was as if he had built up an irrepressible torrent of frustration, which had to declare itself in his pages, regardless of the ostensible subject of his novels.

His compulsion erupted into *Ada, or Ardor* (1969), an exquisitely written but frankly interminable conceit of a novel that hinges around Van Veen, and his lifelong obsession with his two young cousins. For once, male and females are of similar age in this account of adolescent sexuality, but Nabokov devotes so much time to detailing the girls' erotic charms that his prose begins to assume a pathological nature. His next book, *Transparent Things* (1972), was an act of wicked self-parody, in which an author, Mister R, admits: 'I have been accused of trifling with minors, but my minor characters are untouchable, if you permit me a pun.' R's editor is Hugh Person, who pursues a young woman to her mountain-top home and is left alone by her mother with albums filled with photos showing Armande naked at the age of ten, all of which Nabokov describes in relentless detail. (At one point, he typically employs an obscure adjective, 'impuberal', to disguise his compulsive focus on the pre-pubescent girl.)

Nabokov completed only one more novel, *Look at the Harlequins!* (1974), which of course includes a novelist begging to be identified with the author, and a succession of girls aged between ten and thirteen, all ripe for indecencies of various kinds. One of them is even described as 'what in a later era amateurs were to call a "nymphet"', and offers the narrator 'a sweet lewd smile'. At the time of his death, Nabokov had revisited this barren well one more time, leaving behind an unfinished manuscript entitled *The Original of 'Laura'* (or *Lolita*, of course). Humbert S. Humbert is reimagined as Hubert H. Hubert, who attempts to seduce Laura when she is twelve. She escapes his predation, maintaining her virginity for another two years, after which she frolics playfully with her female friends – every one of them naked, naturally. Staunch Nabokovians, of whom there are many in the upper echelons of the literary world, continue to insist that the author's endless galaxy of seductive nymphets is evidence of a literary obsession rather than anything more carnal.

One manifestation of the eternal twelve-year-old girl for which Nabokov could not be blamed, or at most only obliquely, was another stage musical, *Lolita, My Love*. Coincidentally, this involved a score co-written by the composer of *The Passion Flower Hotel*, John Barry, and the librettist of *My Fair Lady*, Alan Jay Lerner. The show was premiered in Philadelphia in early 1971, prior to a Broadway run that never materialised. The reviews were negative (one critic accused the show of 'pernicious anaemia') and the lack of blatant sexuality in the production kept the prurient and voyeuristic at bay. The producer, Norman Twain, did his best to talk up the piece: 'There are certain types of girls – little girls – nymphets that, all else being equal, would turn me on. If you met them in a motel by chance . . .' But Nabokov, who never saw the show, seemed to disapprove of the fact that the leading role was played by a fifteen-year-old. 'Both girls – the one they fired and the one who replaced her – were awful, little bosomy girls,' he complained, 'the wrong type altogether.'

There was only one direction in which this attention upon the pubescent and pre-pubescent child could go. Sexual abuse became confused, deliberately or otherwise, with the contemporary spirit of liberation. Former youth worker Roger Moody, an open 'boy-lover' who wrote a book called *Indecent Assault* to defend the rights of children to have consensual sexual relations with adults, chronicled elsewhere the 'pederastic element in utopian-left thinking'. This, he claimed, was revived between 1958 and 1968, 'primarily because of the reaction of students in the affluent West (some as young as eleven or twelve) to adult repression of both their social aspirations and their sexuality'. (To put Moody's testimony in context, he complained that feminism incorporated 'the concept of child protection', thereby keeping kids at arm's length from well-intentioned men such as himself.)

The American sex newspaper *Screw* encapsulated this self-serving attitude towards the 'liberation' of child sexuality in a series of articles in 1969, which were devoted to describing every imaginable avenue of sexual congress. The author, disguising himself as 'JD', insisted: 'Those who enjoy sexual acts with children are not necessarily "child-molestors", because in many cases the juveniles know exactly what is going on, and are perfectly willing. And there is a very good rationale for being partial to youngsters as sexual partners: teens and even younger children tend to be much more attractive, physically, than persons twice their age' – which was obviously justification enough for JD. 'An even more unusual class of the category child-lover contains persons who like their partners really young: pre-pubescent, or even far younger. Some are attracted to the innocence of children, while others enjoy the idea that what they are doing is deliciously perverse. However, unless both child and parent consent to the affair, this practice is definitely not encouraged.' In JD's world, parental disapproval was clearly the only restraint on the urges of the paedophile.

Screw was quite happy for its libertarian readers to enjoy child pornography in verbal form, whether it was the famous 'cunnilinguist', Great Ray, deciding that girls in their early teens 'make the best suck' in 1969; or Dean Latimer recalling an 'Orgy at Riverdale High', opening his account with a declaration: 'Let's face it, gang – everybody wants to ball his daughter, right? Even guys who don't have daughters want to ball them.' By 1973, this strand of underground literature had reached its nadir, with the magazine *Los Angeles Star/Finger*, which leavened its orthodox diet of drugs, rock'n'roll and revolution with adverts and fictional readers' letters that would have made the Marquis de Sade nauseous (and would risk immediate prosecution if they were reprinted here).

The European answer to *Screw* was *Suck*, early issues of which scattered naked photos of pre-pubescent girls across its pages for decoration. Small ads included a photographer willing to offer accommodation to a 'well-proportioned' girl from thirteen upwards, or a doctor wanting a family to lend him their children for sex. There were fictional accounts of 'fuck-happy children' to sustain the readers' crusade for erotic liberation. By its final issue in 1974, *Suck* was printing photographs of unambiguous child abuse in a portfolio entitled 'Still a Virgin', alongside which Pasolini's *Salo* seemed unadventurous. This, apparently, was one possible destination for the sexual revolution: predators of both sexes despoiling the body of a young child, in the name of liberation. One of the *Suck* team recalled many years later that their editorial director, Bill Levy, loved to shock his audience But did the desire to *épater les bourgeois* really justify the abuse of children? It was surely the most hollow of victories, and from this vantage point it seems utterly indefensible.

Elsewhere the daughters and sons of Lolita were subject to a more direct form of exploitation: child pornography. The complete legalisation of all forms of porn in Denmark between 1969 and 1979 allowed a small group of publishers and filmmakers to identify and then supply a market for the abuse of young children. Inevitably, perhaps, the name of Vladimir Nabokov's adolescent heroine became their calling card. *Lolita* was the brand that linked the output of the Color Climax Corporation, whose series of short films included such self-explanatory titles as *Fucking Children* and *Little Girl Sex*. Made in Denmark, these films were widely exported overseas by mail order. In Holland, meanwhile, *Lolita* was a magazine, which widened the field of abuse to include toddlers as well as those on the cusp of puberty. It even included a contact service allowing abusers to solicit children directly.

That strand of 'liberation' led inexorably towards the formation of organisations designed to promote the sexual interaction of adults and children. The Paedophile Information Exchange (PIE) was founded in 1974 and was regarded by some British civil liberty activists as the standard-bearer for the sexual rights of children. As a PIE discussion paper put it, 'We believe it is inhuman to children to outlaw their sexuality, and we support moves to lower the "age of consent". We are against the rape and physical assault of anyone, but we want to see the removal from the statute books of the unjust laws which define mutual and loving relationships with children as assaults.' For five years or so, this viewpoint edged its way into the mainstream of political discussion about sexuality, as a subject of fringe debate at party conferences or in the proceedings of the National Council for Civil Liberties. It began to seem possible that some liberalisation of the law would sanction the acts described in Nabokov's novel and its successors. Instead, during the 1980s, PIE and its activists were targeted by the police and the press; and by the 1990s, the paedophile was ranked among the most despised individuals in this and every other civilised society.

But Lolita could not be forgotten so easily. The artist Graham Ovenden assembled a well-received print portfolio entitled *Aspects of Lolita* in 1976, and his work in this field was bought by the Tate Gallery, among other institutions. (The Tate withdrew Ovenden's pictures from its online collection when he was convicted of historical child sex abuse in 2013.) Edward Albee adapted Nabokov's novel into a Broadway play in 1981, with twenty-four-year-old Blanche Baker playing the girl half her age. In 1997, Adrian Lyne directed a film remake of *Lolita*, for which such celebrated playwrights as Harold Pinter and David Mamet wrote screenplays that were ultimately rejected. Dominique Swain was cast in the title role at the age of fifteen, but she escaped the voyeuristic attention that had ruined the life of her cinematic predecessor. It was, according to the *Austin Chronicle*, 'a *Lolita* for the English Lit crowd rather than the raincoat crowd'. The film's reception demonstrated how easily history could be twisted and changed. Another reviewer claimed that 'Nabokov's novel [had] helped open society's eyes to the evils of paedophilia in the 1950s'. Somewhere in their collective afterlife, Vladimir Nabokov and Humbert Humbert were smiling.

Interlude: Oh! Quel cul t'as!

It was a theatrical summit meeting: London's premier critic, Kenneth Tynan, now the literary manager of the National Theatre; and William Donaldson, the co-producer of *Beyond the Fringe*, and future author of *The Henry Root Letters*. They communed at Tynan's house in June 1966 and emerged with a plot to hatch a theatrical coup: An International Erotic Revue. 'The idea is to use artistic means to achieve erotic stimulation', Tynan wrote to Donaldson afterwards. 'Nothing that is <u>merely</u> funny or <u>merely</u> beautiful should be admitted: it must also be sexy.' As a title, Tynan suggested *Oh! Calcutta!*, borrowed from 'a painting by the French surrealist Clovis Trouille of a reclining girl displaying her bottom ... this is a pun [from] "Quel cul t'as" meaning "What an arse you have!" ... Those who get the joke will get it, and those who don't will be intrigued. Anyway, it's unforgettable.'

Tynan's original recipe would have resulted in an artistic stew, involving ballet, film sequences directed by one of the European masters and theatrical vignettes, each contribution representing a different nationality. To depict Britain, Tynan suggested 'a *St Trinian's* sixth-former being birched by John Gordon', the ultra-conservative editor of the *Sunday Express*.

By Christmas 1966, Tynan had switched collaborators from Donaldson to playwright Harold Pinter. This partnership was short-lived, though it survived long enough for Pinter to demonstrate 'what he thought an erotic show should be like', as Tynan recalled. 'He put a table napkin over a glass and slowly drew it off, very, very slowly, and he said that even if there was just a tiny whisper of scotch in the glass, the slow revelation of that scotch could be enormously exciting to him.' Whoever was in charge, the project was limited by the need for every theatrical performance in the country to be passed as acceptable for public viewing by the Lord Chamberlain. (The passing of the Theatres Act 1968 finally removed this obstacle.) Among the recent interventions by this ogre of censorship was the removal of a masturbation scene from the Royal Court's 1965 staging of Frank Wedekind's 1891 play, *Spring Awakening*. 'Genital exposure and four-letter words are out', Tynan told author Mary McCarthy; while male homosexuality was also excluded, to avoid a dependence on 'the rather boring area of theatrical camp'. Throughout 1967, he began to solicit contributions from leading authors and intellectuals, among them Samuel Beckett, Tennessee Williams, Edna O'Brien and cartoonist Jules Feiffer. More surprisingly, Tynan also recruited John Lennon.

In 1969, the musician told the US magazine *Screw* about his early experiences of masturbation. 'There was a little club, a gang, formed, and I caught them having the wank, out in the barn, and I said, "What's this?" I didn't like gangs that I wasn't running. So they said, you have to be able to wank, you see, and I said, "How's that?", and they showed me, and so I wanked and was the leader of the wanks. I was always beating the meat.' Repeating the tale to Tynan, Lennon added that sometimes, when the gang was nearing its collective climax, spurring each other on with the names of glamorous film stars, he would shout out the least sexy name he could think of – 'Winston Churchill', perhaps.

Tynan recognised the makings of an *Oh! Calcutta!* contribution. Lennon suggested that it should be entitled 'Liverpool Wank', although it was eventually staged under the more reserved name of 'Four in Hand'. 'You know that idea of yours for my erotic revue, the masturbation contest?', Tynan wrote to Lennon after the Beatles returned from India in spring 1968. 'Could you possibly be bothered to jot it down on paper?' This proved to be too much like work for Lennon, who told Tynan: 'You know the idea, four fellows wanking – giving each other images – descriptions – it should be ad-libbed anyway – they should even really wank, which would be great.'

Some of Tynan's theatrical thunder was stolen by the arrival in 1967 of the 'tribal rock musical' *Hair*, which reached Broadway in April the following year and London in September 1968. (The British opening was timed to coincide with the demise of the Lord Chamberlain's reign of terror.) Though it was intended as a celebration (or exploitation, depending on your view) of the hippie movement, *Hair* did feature a climactic moment when members of the cast stripped off on stage. Tynan's production began with the unveiling, which he named 'Taking Off the Robe'. Subsequent sketches sampled and satirised a variety of sexual topics, from swingers to rape, employing comedy, drama, dancing and song.

Oh! Calcutta! opened in New York off-Broadway in June 1969. Reviews from the theatrical establishment were lukewarm: Clive Barnes in the *New York Times* settled on 'failure' and 'disappointment' to encapsulate his response. 'The critics all went along with their wives,' Tynan recalled, 'and as soon as one saw these very nice men – my former colleagues, in fact – sitting with their wives, one thought of their children at home and said to oneself: "My God, I'm inviting them to say publicly, in their columns, that the sight of the girls' breasts and bottoms gave them an erection." Because, after all, that is one of the criteria by which the show is to be assessed. And it was unthinkable that they should respond like that, it's still impossible in this society for that kind of enjoyment to be publicly admitted.' He was probably more pleased by the response in *Screw*, which called the show 'a masturbator's masterpiece, a *Magical Mystery Tour* for the horny and underprivileged'. A year later, *Oh! Calcutta!* could be seen in revised form at the Roundhouse in London. The *Guardian* opined that there were 'stretches which seemed more like a long dirty schoolboy joke than "elegant erotica"', as Tynan had promised. But the show ran in both cities, and was revived, and filmed, and generally proved its creator's point that there was room on the stage for a franker and more celebratory view of sex than had ever been possible in the past.

Of course, there was opposition, not least from the reliable Charles Keating. He mounted a campaign to ban a performance that was to be beamed live, by closed-circuit, to cities across America. 'Never has such utter filth been projected to all parts of the nation,' he protested in vain. 'If there is or ever was such a thing as public decency, these actions offend it.' Plans for an Australian production were stymied by a concerted protest movement, and two charity performances in Sydney ended with the entire cast being arrested for offensive behaviour and obscene language in public. In Paris, meanwhile, the local producers took it upon themselves to substitute French sketches for much of Tynan's script. He confided to his diary: 'All hints of heterosexual deviations are ruthlessly cut; and it seems that even the most liberal French audience would walk out if it heard on stage the vernacular words for prick and cunt. Instead, we have pseudo-poetic sketches about men in love with goats and trees, and women in love with haute cuisine.' He was more amused by Andy Warhol's response to his revue: the artist staged a mixed-media event entitled *Oh! Bombay!* on Long Island, which invited unrestrained audience participation as Warhol's films ran behind them.

Tynan admitted in 1970 that he saw *Oh! Calcutta!* as 'little more than a first sketch, or, let's say, a series of trailers for a possible erotic show that someone might be able to do in ten years' time'. What form might this show take? 'The future of erotic art ... lies in full-length animated cartoons that show human beings in sexually provocative situations.' Two years later, Ralph Bakshi's film of the Robert Crumb cartoon strip, *Fritz the Cat*, began that journey into the future. But by then the notion of a single sexual revolution that could be packaged into a stage production had passed, as pornography and feminism pulled the nature of the erotic in polar opposite directions.

12 Growing Up With Dr Sex

It was, he was assured, 'without doubt the most audaciously daring book that has ever been privately published' – the definitive account of 'sex and savagery'. And so a factory worker from Wales sent £3 to the advertiser in *Exchange and Mart*. By return, he was sent a school exercise book worth only pennies. On the cover was written '*Prenda Il Mio Concilio*' – or 'Take My Advice', in Italian. Inside there were no photographs, no descriptions of sex or savagery, merely three words: 'Leave it alone'.

Advice about sex, if not savagery, was everywhere during the 1960s, most of it more informative than the book sent to Wales. Regardless of one's experience and expertise, there was a widespread acceptance that the level of knowledge about all matters sexual amongst the British public was distressingly low, and woefully inadequate. That much was evident when a teenage girl wrote to *Boyfriend* magazine in 1962 and begged for enlightenment: 'We've been told you can have a child without having intercourse, but just by your boyfriend kissing you passionately, especially if it's your first love.' Four years later, when London was supposedly enjoying an orgy of ecstatic hedonism, a young woman could write to the *Daily Mirror*'s agony aunt: 'If a girl has intercourse, and then has nothing more to do with boys for a year, can she have become a virgin again?' Marje Proops' reply was noticeably short-tempered: 'Afraid not. She's had *that*.'

Both questions could have been answered had the enquirers dipped into one of the guides to sexual and marital morals and techniques that littered the decade's bookshelves. Their attitudes and opinions varied, depending on whether their authors were clerics, medics, teachers, puritans or pleasure-seekers. But their collective success, and notoriety, justified and explained their existence. At issue were not only the public's sexual satisfaction, but its ethics, happiness, health and future. The experts offered their erudition on subjects as diverse as how babies were made, the true nature of the female orgasm, the dangers of pre-marital petting and the prevalence of venereal disease. The desire for counsel and insight was shared by all ages and stages of life, from supposedly innocent children to those whose marriages had descended into erotic lethargy. The handbooks and essays might be confusing or contradictory, permissive or puritanical; but together they both created and supplied a need – a need that became increasingly urgent as sexual delight emerged as one of the decade's loudest demands.

An exchange in the pages of the *Birmingham Daily Post* in August 1965 highlighted the two extremes of the argument. Dr Martin Cole, a geneticist who taught at the city's College of Advanced Technology (later Aston University), was a prophet of honesty and freedom when it came to all areas of sexuality. He headed the local branch of the Abortion Law Reform Association and was a prominent member of the Family Planning Association. He believed that contraception should be available to all, regardless of age and marital status; and was an early champion of the rights of women to control their own bodies. In 1965, despite the vigorous opposition of the British Medical Association, he was planning to launch a clinic that would offer advice about contraception and sex to the young and unmarried – precisely those who were unable to seek help from their doctors.

He offered the *Daily Post* an article on 'Sexual Responsibility in the Young'. His views proved to be explosively controversial and cemented his growing local reputation as a sexual troublemaker. What was so offensive? His insistence that sex outside the bounds of marriage was 'part of the culture of many young people today' and should not be regarded as an outrage. Indeed, the country's youth had 'established their own moral values in spite of society'. His conclusion was simple: 'Whether we like it or not, sexual experimentation is commonplace, and it is an obligation to make certain that it becomes informed experimentation. We must do away with the taboo on sex, dispense with the titillation of substitutes [pornography] and lose some of our fear of the real thing.' He warned the young of the perils of unrestrained sexual indulgence: venereal disease, unwanted pregnancy and people using other individuals as erotic objects rather than fellow human beings. But if those dangers were avoided, 'I suspect that sexual relationships will become acceptable as a necessary means of expression of love'.

A hint of what Cole, and those who shared his beliefs, were facing came from an anonymous 'Christian', who expressed horror at his incitement to promiscuity: 'The virtue of chastity is so important that God Himself has implanted in human nature a strong sense of shyness and delicacy concerning sex matters, and shame in sins against virtue. This sense is one of the strongest preservations against depravity.' Or, as the leading Methodist minister (and committed socialist) Lord Soper had put it: 'Sex is part of the raw material of the Kingdom of God. If it is dedicated to that high purpose, it is both beautiful and good. If it is dissociated from that purpose, it is both ugly and bad.'

The 1960s was not the first decade in which people chose to ignore that ethical and aesthetic judgement, and the God from whom it was supposed to have come. There had always been sin, and sex, inside and outside marriage. But this was indeed the first era of British history in which a substantial minority of the population was prepared to say aloud, like Cole, that the traditional Christian virtues of chastity and fidelity within marriage were not just misguided, but utterly irrelevant. The extent of the shift in opinion and conduct was reflected in the gulf between two programmes intended to educate children, which bookended the decade. Both were entitled *Growing Up*. The first, a BBC radio series from 1960, taught that 'things' tended to mature and reproduce, but left humans entirely out of the equation. The second, an independent film made in 1969 by none other than Dr Martin Cole, not only allowed people into the viewfinder, but demonstrated them masturbating and having intercourse. Of all the comparisons and contrasts that can be drawn from the changing culture of the 1960s, none is so stark, or so revelatory.

The original *Growing Up* emerged in an age when a clip from an X-rated Danish film, *The Young Have No Time*, could be withdrawn from a television discussion programme involving a vicar and a bunch of teenagers. The reason? The film dealt with 'immorality' and showed 'a wild sex party', in which some of the offensive young Danes could be seen kissing and cuddling. That was in 1959, when the British Medical Association issued an updated version of its pamphlet, *Getting*

Married – and then hurriedly withdrew it from circulation. The problem was that its otherwise tame contents included two provocative essays by medical men: 'Marrying with a Baby on the Way', which was a scandalous notion in itself; and 'Is Chastity Outmoded?', to which Dr Eustace Chesser had the temerity to suggest that the answer might be 'maybe, yes'. Chesser even stated that 'pre-marital sexual intercourse ... can be more than ordinarily pleasant', and that individuals should be able to make their own decisions about sexual morality. As a result, 250,000 copies of the brochure were pulped. Even without *Getting Married*, modern kids – according to a female Labour MP – 'just know too much too soon. Sex knowledge, though important at the right time, fills their minds to the exclusion of everything else.'

But when was the right time – and what constituted sex knowledge? These questions were subject to feverish debate throughout the decade. Government guidelines, as the 1960s began, made it compulsory for children of fourteen and fifteen to be given a modicum of sex education, unless their parents asked for them to be removed from these lessons. But in the absence of a national curriculum, each school was left to interpret that directive as they chose. Central to the ethos that the government wished to promote was the simple idea that 'chastity is essential, both morally and socially'.

The most pressing issue of the day was venereal disease. On 30 October 1959, the *Daily Herald* gave over its front page to an editorial on the subject, which was being published at the request of the Ministry of Health. 'Not since wartime has such a public warning been necessary,' the paper said. 'Particularly alarming is the number of cases among girls, some under 15. Promiscuous sex habits are the cause of the increase. The growth of promiscuity can be put down – as the Ministry stresses – to a false sense of security about modern penicillin treatment of the disease.' Was this the moment to acknowledge that young people wanted to assert their sexuality, and needed easier access to contraception? Not at all. 'To teenagers and alike the warning is this', the *Herald* concluded. 'Clean living is the only safeguard.' This message was reinforced by a television documentary supported by the Ministry, and broadcast on ITV the following March. *Shadow of Ignorance* was praised for its open and non-judgemental tone. But in trying not to alienate youngsters by hectoring or lecturing them, it faced criticism for leaving the impression that perhaps VD wasn't that frightening after all.

The same cloud of ambivalence confused the debate about when and how children should be informed about the facts of life. The choice was simple; the aftermath was trickier to predict. If children were left in blissful ignorance, they might stumble into sexual involvement without realising the possible consequences. But if they were instructed before they were old enough to make adult decisions, then they might be encouraged to experiment, with similar results. Every year, there were educationalists and commentators who pressed the case for teaching children the essentials of conception and pregnancy while they were aged ten or eleven, and those who argued just as forcefully that knowledge should be withheld until they were well into their teens.

Meanwhile the prevalence of venereal disease continued to rise: figures for teen infections were higher in 1959 than all but one year since the end of the war. The British Medical Association steadfastly preached that sex education should be based firmly on Christian morals and include stern advice not to indulge before marriage. Canon Bryan Green encapsulated the shared credo of the Church and the BMA: 'To have intercourse before marriage is deceitful in the eyes of society ... There is NO need for engaged couples to experiment to see if they are satisfactorily adjusted. True inner love will lead to satisfactory physical love in nearly every case ... Very intimate fondling and sexual intercourse should wait until marriage. Some of the preceding love acts should wait for engagement.' The Canon's advice depended upon young people demonstrating a remarkable degree of foresight and restraint.

In 1961, the BMA channelled its understanding of the crisis of youth into a report, *The Adolescent*. 'There has been a revolution, in one generation, in the general attitude towards sex', it explained. Doctors in London complained that they were being faced with 'a staggering rise in sexual immorality'. There were obvious cultural factors at work: 'Films, posters, plays, advertisements and the open sale of near-dirty books have all made it virtually impossible for a youngster to grow up unaware of the lure of sex.' But there was another innovation that was fuelling the new promiscuity, the BMA believed: 'Helping to give the youngster of today a new outlook towards sex is the motor scooter.

It has freed the adolescent from having to do his courting in the front lounge. With their scooters, motor cycles, even cars, their well-filled pay packets, today's young people are able to enjoy their youth for a few brief years, before they are submitted to the more mature disciplines of marriage.'

With the government unwilling to strip young people of their modes of transport, the BMA was left to bewail the sins of the recent past, like an Old Testament prophet. By 1964, a further report, *Venereal Disease and Young People*, suggested that the problem had expanded beyond any hope of control. The only possible solution was a return to chastity – or if that was a restriction too far, then at least fidelity within a single relationship. As the science editor of the *Daily Mirror* noted when the report was published, 'Sleeping around HAS become fashionable, as part of the modern craze of "living for kicks".'

Ego was another contributing factor, the BMA declared: 'Many young men look upon sexual performance as an achievement in itself, almost like a sport', while young women liked to marry a man with experience, as it was 'proof of his virility and also gives the girl confidence that he will be able to initiate her satisfactorily into the sexual relationship'. The *Mirror* interjected: 'Girls now consider that they too should enjoy the same sexual freedom as boys. Intercourse is often regarded as nothing more than a polite pay-off for an evening out.' As far as the BMA was concerned, it was the girl's responsibility to control any sexual encounters: boys would inevitably try to go too far, and girls needed to stop them. The problem was, as a pamphlet for teenagers included in an issue of *Family Doctor* explained, that girls had sexual desires of their own. 'In spite of the fact that she is not easily roused,' it stated, '[she] can be extremely provocative and sexually demanding.'

So awash was teenage Britain in sexual indulgence that it had become 'a frightening, filthy thing, endangering the life of the whole nation' – or so BMA official Dr Ernest Claxton announced in 1963. He cited some sobering examples: fourteen-year-old girls heading for the VD clinic on their way home from school, or raising their hand in class so they could rush to the lavatory and deliver their own babies. Soon he was speaking at a meeting of the pressure group Moral Re-Armament, and adding 'mixed liaisons, mixed marriages and children of mixed blood' to his litany of contemporary evils. He called for 'a return to absolute moral standards': no promiscuity, no sex outside marriage, no consorting with people of different races, and definitely not even a hint of homosexuality. 'Chastity is a weapon we can grasp and use', he concluded, in a phrase that might have amused Professor Freud.

The BMA's stark moral tone was not reflected among those commentators who appointed themselves experts in teenage sexuality. Among them was Dr Alex Comfort, better known to subsequent generations as the creator of the illustrated manual, *The Joy of Sex* (1972). In 1963 he joined a BBC discussion on sex and family life to suggest that sex education for teenagers should include advice about how to use condoms safely. 'We might as well make up our minds that chastity is no more a virtue than malnutrition,' he argued; and to prove the point, he suggested that there was no reason why a man couldn't be faithful simultaneously to a wife and a lover. In place of the Mosaic commandments, he proposed two basic instructions for teenagers: 'Thou shalt not under any circumstances produce an unwanted baby', and 'Thou shalt not exploit another's feelings'. His views were described as 'startling' in the popular press.

There was further disquiet the following year, when Comfort updated his 1950 tome, *Sexual Behaviour in Society*, as a mass-market Penguin paperback, *Sex in Society*. Here, for the first time in the history of British publishing, was a comprehensive account of what Ernest Claxton had denounced as 'The New Morality'. Homosexuality was 'possibly a phase in normal development', although Comfort was not yet prepared to concede that it could be a valid sexual choice – despite the fact that he hoped it would soon be legalised. Masturbation was natural and inevitable, except in those societies that allowed children to have sex as soon as they reached puberty. 'Sadism and masochism are widespread elements in our make-up' and were perfectly acceptable so long as no serious injury resulted. Comfort concluded with a call for sex to be rebranded as a leisure pursuit rather than a moral danger: 'There is a strong case for a literature of sexual enjoyment which treats the elaboration of sexuality as Indian and Arabic works have treated it – at the level of ballroom dancing.' Improved sexual technique 'can provide reassurance and pleasure, and heighten the element of play which is perhaps the marker of good sexual adjustment'.

Several of those exotic works of sexual instruction from far-flung lands and distant civilisations were now being published in affordable editions for the first time. Among them was *The Perfumed Garden*, a fifteenth-century Arabic text which examined the full gamut of relations between the sexes. The Labour MP Dingle Foot bought a copy at the Heathrow Airport bookstall in December 1963 – and then had it confiscated as an obscene publication when he arrived back in Britain. (His copy was eventually returned, and he received a personal apology from the Government.)

1963 was also the year when *The Kama Sutra of Vatsyayana* escaped from the discreet shelves of the aristocracy into the public domain. Two editions, based on different translations, were issued simultaneously: one sumptuously illustrated, and priced beyond the reach of all but the wealthiest members of society; the other available at two guineas (the equivalent of more than £40 today). 'It is a book which will shock, outrage and offend many people,' wrote Audrey Whiting on its day of publication. 'Its observations and advice on courtship, seduction, love-making and sexual techniques leave nothing to the imagination.' At which point her readers would have expected her to recommend an immediate ban. Instead, she defended *The Kama Sutra* as 'a major literary work' and insisted that 'There is a lot of wisdom in the book mingled with quaint superstition. In its curious poetic style, it gives common-sense advice on men-women relationships which remains apposite after sixteen centuries.'

Others were less welcoming. William Foyle, chairman of the famous London bookshop, allowed *The Kama Sutra* to be sold, but denounced it (and *Lady Chatterley's Lover*, also freely available in his store) for its immorality. When police raided a Manchester shop in February 1964, this book of Indian wisdom was among those seized as being obscene. By 1967, *The Kama Sutra* had reached the divorce court, after a wife objected to her husband of twenty years' standing trying to incorporate the book's lessons into their waning love life. She remained adamant that only the missionary position was right and proper. Months of bickering led to the husband assaulting and threatening to murder her, before a judge granted them a divorce.

The precise nature of the perfect relationship between husband and wife preoccupied many authors during the 1960s. Marie Robinson, a doctor, devoted an entire book to *The Power of Sexual Surrender*

(1960). It will not be a surprise to discover that surrender was a female, not male, responsibility. A woman's surrender entailed being ready to 'yield to her biological and psychological destiny' – which was, of course, to please her husband. Robinson conceded that more than 40 per cent of married women suffered from some form of frigidity; and 'It is highly unlikely that the husband of a frigid wife is responsible for her frigidity problem', which was quite a relief. Instead, the frigid woman must surrender to her husband's wishes, and by this means she would discover herself as ... well, a woman. ('Surrender is no defeat – for a woman', Diana Rigg purrs flirtatiously as she is seduced by Oliver Reed in 1969's *The Assassination Bureau*.)

Logic was not Robinson's forte. She admitted that 'Caressing or manipulating the genitalia or secondary erotic zones of certain types of frigid women would only result in exacerbated nerves or in a condition of inwardly screaming protest.' But despite that, the frigid woman's primary instinct must be to bend to her husband's desire, even if she has no reciprocal feelings. That way, a form of magic would occur: 'She knows that 99 times out of 100 even negative sexual feelings in herself will soon turn to eagerness, and eagerness to desire. And even in that one in one hundred times, she will still get a profound satisfaction from the pleasure she is able to give her husband.' Although her goal would always remain 'the miracle of childbirth', she might be fortunate enough to stumble across another pleasure: an orgasm. 'The excitement comes from the act of surrender', Robinson insists, underlining the phrase to make sure it could not be ignored. 'There is a tremendous surging physical ecstasy in the yielding itself, in the feeling of being the passive instrument of another person, of being stretched supinely beneath him, taken up will-lessly by his passion as leaves are swept up before a wind.' It was the stuff of romantic fiction, a total abrogation of power and personality in the face of the mighty phallus.

Where Robinson was modern was in her declaration that, by 1960, 'We have been through a sexual revolution of major proportions ... we know now that woman has the same need for passion, the same capacity for sexual response that man has' – even if it was irrelevant whether it was aroused or not. But whereas men could only achieve one form of orgasm, women had a choice: the 'normal', or vaginal, orgasm; and the 'masculine' or clitoridal orgasm. Those women who only experienced excitement from their clitoris were to be pitied: 'Though, owing to her lack of experience with the mature form of orgasm, she may defend her orgasm as perfectly normal and adequate, it is not.' By contrast, 'It is within the vagina that orgasm of the truly mature woman takes place. Upon it and within it, she receives the greatest sensual pleasure that it is possible for a woman to experience.' A woman must choose wisely: if she opted for the 'immature' gratification available from the clitoris, she would inevitably be steering her course towards neurosis.

This distinction, between the lesser orgasm of the clitoris and the full satisfaction afforded by the vagina, originated with Sigmund Freud and his *Three Essays on the Theory of Sexuality* (1905). Credit for disproving Freud's theory is usually allotted to Bill Masters and Gini Johnson, whose 1966 book *Human Sexual Response* was based around detailed and dispassionate scientific study of women and men during sexual acts (as illustrated in the TV drama series, *Masters of Sex*). But two of the most progressive (for the times) sexologists of the decade, Albert Ellis and Edward Sagarin, located the site of the female orgasm in the clitoris two years earlier, in the first edition of their unpromisingly titled book, *Nymphomania: A Study of the Oversexed Woman*. Less exploitative than it sounded, their text contained a stirring call (again, for the times) on behalf of the sexually active female: 'A few women suffer from nymphomania or compulsive promiscuity. But many more suffer from lack of sexual freedom, from condemnation of their free lives, and from pressures to survive and retain a healthy self-image in an unegalitarian atmosphere. When sexually alive women are fully accepted and are not considered oversexed trollops, much of the anguish will be relieved.' Ellis and Sagarin weren't the first to question the existence of the vaginal orgasm, either: the same issue was one of many covered with remarkable frankness in *The Housewife's Handbook on Selective Promiscuity* (1961), by the pseudonymous Rey Anthony. She described asking one of her lovers to rub her clitoris, to which he is said to have replied: 'It is not normal. It makes me feel like I'm not a *real* man if I can't use my peter [penis].' And suddenly the origin of Freud's belief became clear ...

Much else in the field of sex remained at odds. Opening the right – or wrong – book at an impressionable moment might shape a teenager's sexuality for years ahead. Rose Hacker's guide to young people,

The Opposite Sex (1963), was adamant: 'Boys are more likely than girls to be drawn by bodily desire to seek intercourse.' Women's sense of sexuality was always directed inward, towards her goal of creating a baby; 'A boy's sex is directed outwards and his nature impels him to explore the world'. Amongst Hacker's other pearls: a frigid woman might drive her man to become an exhibitionist or a child abuser and she deserved much of the blame if she did; while prostitutes were lazy or 'mentally subnormal', and preferred to lie about all day. But beware: 'there are some women who are not prostitutes ... but who become slaves to their own sensations and give themselves to men indiscriminately and without payment. Such girls are called nymphomaniacs.' And those girls who depended on *The Opposite Sex* for their introduction to adult life would hardly have known how to find the narrow spot between frigidity and nymphomania (let alone the clitoris).

In time, the reader of Hacker might have graduated to Jerome and Julia Rainer's *Sexual Adventure in Marriage* (1965), built on the premise that 'The only genuine sexual adventurers are the well married'. The Rainers offered a complex, almost technical guide to marital coupling which covered everything from female gymnastics ('A sensual refinement of the pelvic tilt is the pelvic roll') to the challenges of the overweight lover ('When both spouses are corpulent, the most satisfactory are the posterior postures'). Liberal about everything apart from the homosexual ('a deviant'), the Rainers assumed that the male would automatically lead – maestro upon his wife's pliant instrument. Or as Jerome and Julia put it: 'In his lovemaking, the experienced husband is a voyeur-aesthete who can evoke sequences of pleasurable chords as he plays upon his wife's gradually eroticizing body. And indeed his wife's responses will, in time, quicken and match or even exceed his own.' Indeed, the Rainers offered a heavenly portrait of the sexually enlightened woman: 'There are a few wives so ready in their response that they can experience orgasm merely by orally fondling the spouse's penis' – thereby avoiding the troublesome clitoris and vagina altogether.

An alternative view of the woman's role was on offer from Helen Gurley Brown, whose 1962 book *Sex and the Single Girl* inaugurated a series of guides with strangely similar titles. Gurley Brown was not only rewarded with a best-seller, to which she rapidly sold the film rights, but was recognised by becoming the inaugural editor of *Cosmopolitan* magazine in New York – a post she held for more than three decades. She was forty years old when her book appeared and newly married. But her writing was aimed at the unattached career woman who, 'far from being a creature to be pitied and patronized, is emerging as the newest glamour girl of our times'. The single woman was independent, lively, vivacious, financially solvent, sexually attractive (of course) and endlessly tempting to the poor married men alongside whom she worked. As a result, 'She has a better sex life than most of her married friends ... Her choice of partners is endless, and they seek *her.*'

The sole preoccupation of the Single Girl should be the man, who would woo her, wine her, dine her, and then lead her through the delicious menu of adultery. Obviously, there was a price to be paid: 'You have to work like a son of a bitch', 'Your figure can't harbour an ounce of baby fat. It never looked good on anybody but babies', 'Clean hair is sexy. Lots of hair is sexy too. Skimpy little hair styles and hair under your arms, on your legs and around your nipples isn't.' Gurley Brown offered detailed lessons in flirting, all in aid of the ultimate goal: snaring your men. 'You must spend time plotting how to make him happier,' she wrote, before remembering herself: 'Not just him ... *them!*' But the true cynicism of her project sometimes slipped through the curvaceous cracks in her smile: 'Granted, it *is* harder to like men generously and selflessly when you're single. They are, after all, the enemy!'

To prove this point, Albert Ellis – the same man who identified the clitoral orgasm in *Nymphomania* – penned a response, entitled *Sex and the Single Man* (1965). Ellis was now fronting an organisation entitled The Institute for Rational Living, but one man's rationality was another woman's madness. Ellis divided his time between teaching his male readers 'How to Avoid Becoming a Sex Pervert' (such as a homosexual) and offering them tips in such subjects as 'Bedmanship'. All too often, he sounded like a twenty-first-century pickup artist: 'Even girls who don't want to be talked into having sex relations with a male can frequently be persuaded. For most girls have exceptionally poor reasons for not indulging, and those reasons can often be logically undermined.' After which the besieged female would presumably be ready for Libby Jones' 1967 book *Striptease*, which sold more than 50,000 copies in its first few weeks of publication. It was filled with drawings to teach the uncertain young woman how to remove her clothes for her husband. 'Are you a secret stripper?', asked the back cover blurb. 'Have you ever stood before a mirror and silently wished that you could do all those subtle little shimmies that have intoxicated men ever since Salome dropped that seventh veil?' Jones annotated the equipment that the aspiring stripper would require – gloves, dress, chemise, stockings, garter belt, bra and panties – and demonstrated the sensual moves that the man would love, from tassel twirling and the breast bounce to the lunge and the stomp.

If these depressingly male-oriented publications were not to a young woman's taste, she might try to steer a course through the varied and sometimes alarming advice offered by the British press. The *Daily Mirror* began in 1965 by warning unmarried couples not to experiment with any kind of sexual foreplay: they would either slide into trouble (i.e. pregnancy), or peak too soon and lose their zeal before they had reached the church. Married women were no more fortunate. One wrote to the agony uncle in *Tit-Bits*, distressed that her husband was 'now asking me to allow him to take part in unusual sexual practices'. The doctor replied: 'You must try to lose your inhibitions and concentrate on making you and your husband happy.' No wonder that, as Alma Birk noted in an early issue of the women's magazine, *Nova*, 'A society like ours which is riddled with repressions is fertile soil for the kind of guilt feelings that result in impotence and frigidity.'

Indeed, if women's own sexual responses were not problematic enough, they also had to deal with their partners' demands and shortcomings. A woman of fifty-two, who complained that her husband was constantly insisting upon sex, was advised to ask their doctor for a sedative, which she could slip into his bedtime cocoa. A man's premature ejaculation had to be loyally endured and forgiven, until in 1967 the underground press began to advertise a cure: 'Prolong the pleasure of intercourse with Suifan's "Kwang Tze" Solution. This Chinese preparation is specially beneficial to men who suffer from premature ejaculation, and is Guaranteed to end mutual frustration and bring satisfaction to both partners.' Magazines such as *Oz* and *International Times* were also where young lovers would find discreet, indeed oblique advertisements for 'marital aids': condoms that were either so thick that the man would be in no danger of becoming over-stimulated (such as the Secura Longtime), or were ribbed for female pleasure; or, by 1968, an invitation to 'A course of Intense Vibration Treatment' (a vibrator, in other words), which would 'soon revitalise you and make you realise your real capabilities'. But not all innovation was an assurance of satisfaction: the birth control pill, widely available from sympathetic doctors in 1967, brought warnings that it was a direct cause of male impotence. 'An alarmingly high proportion of men have found their ardour decreasing in relation to their wives' increasing desire,' according to Marjorie Proops. (The link between the pill and an increased risk of breast cancer would not be recognised until the following decade.)

Those not yet old enough for the ribbed condom or the pill faced a desert of information compared to their more sophisticated elders. Magazines for the teenage girl were still, at the height of Swinging London in 1966, advising caution rather than hedonism. 'You can have a lot of fun trying to find out if you are in love without going all the way,' suggested *Petticoat*. 'Never be in a hurry to drop the seventh veil.' *Rave* divided its readership between 'Girls Who Don't' (and were all the happier for it), 'Girls Who Do' (might be happy, might be permanently miserable without knowing why) and 'Girls Who Might'. These were probably the majority among British teens at the end of 1966, and so the magazine reserved its harshest lecture for them: 'These are the girls who have only the haziest idea of what sex is all about. Oh, they know it can be fun – they are surrounded by advertisements, films, TV shows, novels, all shrieking Sex is the Best ... What they don't know is that after a short while of enjoyable kissing and caressing (which is designed by nature to be pleasurable, so that intercourse will follow naturally and, with it, the conception of a baby), their own bodies will make them urge the boy along, make them demand complete intercourse.'

Even in that world of constant sexual exposure, of pop stars and film idols basking in an erotic nirvana, Britain's children still had to master, and employ, the basics – without frightening their parents. When the BBC launched a new schools radio series, *Starting a Family*, in 1966, they warned parents and teachers alike that it was 'the frankest sex talk ever broadcast'. 'We have done similar programmes before, but never in such detail,' the producer explained. Dr James Tanner, from Great Ormond Street Hospital, was hired to present 'a detailed talk on love-making'. His incendiary narrative went so far as to refer to 'the process of human mating, or sexual intercourse, as it is usually called'; and informed its youthful audience that sexual desire could sometimes be stimulated 'by the husband seeing his wife taking her clothes off'. There was no mention of how the wife's erotic juices might be encouraged to flow.

In late 1968, there was a brief media scare when the BBC announced its intention to use illustrated slides showing (very discreetly) the birth of a baby and the anatomical differences between male and female, within a TV sex education series aimed at primary school children. A psychiatrist called it 'wicked'; while Mary Whitehouse reliably admitted, 'This sounds rather unhealthy to me'. Compounding the drama was the producers' decision to omit any talk of 'love' and 'marriage' from the series. It was felt these terms might confuse some youthful viewers and upset others who were 'illegitimate'. The series was subsequently screened without any apparent harm to the children of Britain.

Since 1951, sex-education expert Robert Kind had been acting as a one-man polling organisation, to gauge the opinion of eighteen-year-olds about the instruction they had received, at school and home. He was able around 1970 to confirm the findings of a Harris Poll, which calculated that more than half of British men, and 40 per cent of women, had never received any formal sex-ed at all. Around 20 per cent of the sample said that their mothers had provided some guidance; less than 10 per cent reported any involvement from their fathers. As parents tended to talk only to children of their gender, this meant that young men were missing out on what Kind believed to be a vital part of their learning.

It was in this context – titillation at large, but only the bare minimum of appropriate education – that Dr Martin Cole, the controversial Birmingham commentator of 1965, re-emerged as perhaps the most despised man in Britain. He had maintained his high profile in the country's second city, with his frequent comments on abortion and birth control. He was the natural choice for chairman when the Birmingham clinic of the Pregnancy Advisory Service (PAS) opened in April 1968, to coincide with the Abortion Act 1967 coming into effect. This legislation allowed abortions to be carried out by registered practitioners so long as the pregnant women met a very specific set of conditions: two qualified doctors had to certify that there was risk to the life of the woman, or to her long-term mental or physical health; or there was a 'substantial' risk that the foetus would 'suffer from such physical or mental abnormalities as to be seriously handi-capped'. Doctors and nurses were free to state a conscientious objection to the practice of abortion, in which case they would not be required to lend their services. It was scarcely the abortion on demand for which many had campaigned for so long; but it did at least offer the chance for many women to escape the perilous back-street trade that had previously been their only recourse.

Martin Cole remained with the PAS until September 1969, when he announced that he was now the director and secretary of the Institute for Sex Education and Research Ltd. By the start of December, that organisation was running a non-profit abortion clinic in Birmingham; in June 1970 its remit was widened to offer vasectomy operations. Throughout this period, Cole was a reliable source of controversial views for the press. He suggested that the birth control pill should be available from vending machines, like cigarettes, and should also be handed out to all eleven-year-old girls, thereby ending teenage pregnancy at a stroke. He revealed that – purely in the interests of sex education, of course – he had been screening 'blue' films to university students. And he recommended that in future, sex clinics such as his should offer what he termed 'a free brothel for therapeutic sex' – a system of sex surrogates, in other words, to deal with such disorders as impotence and premature ejaculation. (Cole stopped short of suggestions that male sex workers might deliver a similar service to women; or that the needs of homosexual clients might also be taken into account.)

Though he was an irrepressible self-publicist, who enjoyed the exhilarating sting of media attention, Dr Cole remained silent throughout 1969 and 1970 about the project that would transform him into a household name around the country. Yet his instinct for arousing scandal was unerring. On 9 September 1970, to the horror of many and the curiosity of many more, Britain's first 'sex super-market' opened on London's Edgware Road, a stone's throw from Oxford Street. It was intended, according to its owner, to 'take sex off the back streets'; to widen the public's knowledge of all matters sexual; and to offer easy access to contraceptives and other so-called 'marital aids'. It carried the name of its female founder, Ann Summers; and at the head of an independent panel, set up to advise this neophyte business, was none other than Dr Martin Cole.

The curious and the voyeuristic buzzed outside the Ann Summers store, attempting to peek through windows masked by psychedelic designs. Bouncers had to limit access, to prevent the tills being swamped and the shelves stripped. Those who jostled their way through the crowds were rewarded by a mixture of the tantalising and the soporific. Gently erotic background music calmed the nerves while buyers surveyed the mix of contraceptives, nightwear described as 'wildly sexy', 'quick acting tonics to increase the sexual urge', 'pills to slow down the excitement', arty collections of nude photographs, and various artificial aids to love-making, from primitive dildos and vibrators to handcuffs and restraints. Piled high were copies of *Variations on a Sexual Theme*, an illustrated guide to intercourse by Terence Hendrickson – alias Michael Caborn-Waterfield, Summers' sometime boyfriend.

Annice Summers herself was a former secretary, single, twenty-nine years old and perfectly styled to catch the attention of male editors and photographers. She assured reporters of her serious intent ('There are no under-the-counter sales here') and progressive outlook ('We want to make sex education easily available to all'). But she was also quite willing to provide some saucy copy for the papers, as when she explained to the British public the purpose of a vibrator: 'It is phallic-shaped and is used to produce an orgasm in a woman or to bring her to the point of climax before love-making begins. I know some people don't approve of it, but it's nothing to be afraid of.'

While she claimed to be the firm's only director, her gargantuan plans (100 more shops around the country within eighteen months) suggested that she either had major financial support or was fantastically naïve about business affairs. In Martin Cole, she certainly had the most vocal of advisers, who did his best to incite the populace of Birmingham long before there was a concrete plan to open an Ann Summers shop in the city. The local *Daily Post* printed a petition form on its front page, so that opinion could be rallied against what Judith Cook called 'a porn shop on the corner'. Cook had visited the London store, and was ready with a counter-blast to Cole's PR campaign: 'It is virtually catering for men. It does not just sell contraceptives, but a whole range of nasty looking and most peculiar gadgets: it would have to be a strange woman who would want her husband to possess this unusual array of spiked rings, rubber brushes and so forth. Some of the goods are a straight con. There is no such thing as an aphrodisiac cream, even if you do put something in a jar, call it Intimate and charge two guineas [£2.10] a go.' On this last point, Cook was right, and Ann Summers had to withdraw some of the more dubious potions and creams from sale.

Cole, by contrast, saw the shop as 'the most effective way of disseminating both serious sex education literature and approved contraceptives [condoms, in other words] to a large section of the general public. The provision of tastefully designed, anxiety lowering shops, catering openly and specifically for their needs, will help many to overcome their embarrassment.' And he pinpointed a social trend which applied just as accurately in 1970 as it had in 1960: 'The reaction to anything that involves sex seems to be beyond belief'.

So, it transpired, was the origin story of Ann Summers and her store. She was real enough, but her lack of control over the business that bore her name was revealed when she resigned from the company in June 1971, unhappy with 'certain circumstances' in the way it was being run. By October, she was threatening to sue, insisting her name should be removed from the shops in London and Bristol, but instead the entire company went into liquidation. Only then did she reveal that she had merely been fronting the business for Michael Caborn-Waterfield – who besides penning a sex instruction book had also been Diana Dors' boyfriend as a teenager, had run guns for the anti-Castro forces in Cuba, worked his way into the Mayfair social set and spent some time in prison for fraud.

Now, Summers revealed, she and her boyfriend-publicist were planning to reopen the business on her terms. In March 1972, she went into business with brothers David and Ralph Gold, owners of a lucrative adult publishing house. There was even talk of an *Ann Summers Magazine*, to be launched that summer. Once again, Summers herself was in the PR game, selling the notion of 'sex without shame'. But the hints of feminism that could be detected in the original launch – that talk of avoiding abortions and unwanted pregnancies – was now absent from her rhetoric. Asked about the women's liberation movement, Summers replied: 'I think most of those women should put their bras back on very quickly. They're missing out on such a lot. I like being fussed over. I want to be a man's plaything until the day I die.' Perhaps she should have listened more carefully to the feminists: early in 1973, she had to concede that she had been sacked from the business and dumped by her fiancé. The Ann Summers chain survived and prospered; Summers herself left the country and avoided media attention to such an extent that her death in 2012 passed almost without notice.

Meanwhile Dr Martin Cole no longer required a link to the Summers brand to attract notoriety. While his new Institute for Sex Education and Research was being established in 1969, Cole had been hard at work scripting and then overseeing the production of the most explicit film ever intended for children's sexual education. He had been able to keep his cinematic mission a secret because he had relied entirely on personal friends, as both technicians and stars. For *Growing Up* did not rely, like its predecessors, on words, diagrams and discreet illustrations. Cole's 'new approach to sex education' involved real-life models, demonstrating not only what the naked human body looked like, at a variety of ages, but also how adults engaged in masturbation and intercourse.

Growing Up was not the first film to attempt this 'new approach'. But its predecessors all heralded from continental Europe, and were only screened in Britain for adults, having been carefully snipped and softened by the British Board of Film Censors. The Swedish film *Language of Love* (1969) typified the genre. It featured earnest sofa discussions between four experts in the field, interspersed with clips of consenting adults demonstrating sexual empathy or dysfunction. On occasion the screen split, to offer a range of camera angles – none more graphic than when a close-up of a woman's groin during masturbation was shot in such unsympathetic lighting that it was more reminiscent of the meat counter than the bedroom.

Cole's film was equally determined to be unstimulating ('most unerotic' was how he put it), its naked models photographed in dreary, pallid tones. But for anyone raised on sex-ed programmes that coyly evaded any depiction of genitalia, let alone how they could be used, its contents were shocking. *Language of Love* avoided showing an erect penis, that being the final pornographic taboo (as it remains today on terrestrial TV). Where penetration was shown, the lighting was so dim that the actual moment of entry was impossible to distinguish. Cole had no such scruples. He not only exposed the genitals of children, adolescents and adults, but even captured a penis seeking out true north, apparently under its own steam. The brief film of a couple enjoying intercourse merely showed the conjunction of moving bodies, from a discreet distance, and restricted itself to the standard missionary position. But what really alarmed many viewers was the filming of man and woman, each seen separately as they manipulated their genitals with obvious pleasure. True, there was no orgasm seen on screen; no cascade of semen or contractions of the vagina. The participants had the focused look of scientists participating in a solemn experiment. But such scenes had never been passed for adult viewing in British cinemas, and now Cole was intending that they should be shown to children well under the age of consent.

The existence of *Growing Up* was revealed by the *Birmingham Daily Post* on 12 January 1971, and immediately condemned by local councillors who hadn't seen it. The following day, the national press swooped upon the story: 'Sex Act Film Show', trumpeted the *Daily Mirror*. Cole was offered the chance to defend his work, which he did by comparing it to the existing canon of educational films. 'They all lack an essential level of honesty and truth,' he said, 'in that they revert to drawings to explain the sex organs and intercourse. I thought this should be rectified by showing a photographic sequence. We aim to show it in the right context and prove that it is not dirty or sinful – but something that is good, wholesome and enjoyable.'

The film emphasised that sex was a pleasure, rather than merely a biological function, though Cole didn't stint on advice about preventing pregnancy. But the orientation of his 'New Approach to Sex Education' was entirely heterosexual. 'Men find women sexually attractive to look at', his commentary insisted, and vice versa: there was no hint that anyone might be more intrigued by people who shared their gender. He was equally anachronistic when he defined male and female roles. Women were designed to give birth and raise children, he stated, while men 'are made to follow a more energetic existence, to leave the home to go to work'. Worse still, women's responsibility for bearing children was not just biologically determined but psychologically limiting. Cole explained that men 'are often better at giving birth to new ideas. They are in fact usually more inventive and creative' than women. No matter how progressive his educational agenda, his sexual politics left much to be desired.

Even without criticism from feminists and homosexuals, Cole faced violent opposition. He was denounced at a Birmingham council meeting as a 'pedlar of sex'. It did not help his cause that, as the furore aroused by *Growing Up* raged on, he and his wife were divorced. Within a matter of weeks, he married a twenty-three-year-old undergraduate from his university. Newspaper pundits began to dub him 'Dr Sex', or 'Sex King Cole'.

The doctor was still adamant that his film would soon be seen by many thousands of children; indeed, he predicted that by 1976, every school in the country would be screening it. What age did he imagine his ideal audience to be? Cole reckoned that it could be shown to those between ten and fifteen – and when quizzed about whether it was right for pre-teens to be taught so much about sex, he declared that children as young as eleven should be allowed to have intercourse. He explained that he wasn't trying to encourage this: 'I don't even know if many boys of eleven could even manage it. But if they wanted to do it – if they felt the need to do it – they shouldn't be punished or stopped by their parents. Young children go in for all sorts of sex play which shouldn't be stopped. If it is stopped, it can cause a lot of harm in repressing the children later.' And inevitably, his own prejudice resurfaced: 'It can, for instance, turn them away from women and into homosexuals.' Even for Dr Sex, liberation only went so far.

The early stages of the *Growing Up* scandal were entirely based on reputation: none of those attacking the film had viewed a single frame. But on 16 April 1971, there was a screening in London for an invited audience of politicians, teachers, social workers and other concerned parties (among them the leaders of the Festival of Light, a Christian pressure group). The event coincided with the BBC's decision to screen an edition of the TV comedy *Monty Python's Flying Circus* at 8 pm, despite its nudity and sexual innuendo. Here was more evidence of the disgraceful decline of British morality. No surprise, then, that *Growing Up* prompted howls of outrage from Lord Longford, then leading an enquiry into pornography ('I am utterly shocked') and Mary Whitehouse ('This is quite simply public sex. It is a violation of the most basic of human rights – privacy.'). But the Labour MP Joan

Lester said she would recommend that head teachers should allow their children to view the film.

In the great tradition of campaigning British journalism, the press managed to unearth the identity of the young woman seen masturbating in the film (though her male counterpart was left undisturbed). She was a twenty-three-year-old teacher of liberal studies (irony was not yet dead) at a technical college in Birmingham, who was suspended on full pay. 'I feel quite strongly about getting rid of the hypocrisy and guilt surrounding sex', she explained. But the press, and the majority of Birmingham councillors, felt equally strongly that she should not be allowed to continue teaching the city's innocent fifteen-year-old boys. Gerald Nabarro MP, a well-known self-publicist, launched a parallel campaign for Cole to lose his own teaching job. 'You are the epitome of a man of licence and corruption', Nabarro told him. The Birmingham council leader continued the attack: 'This was a deplorable spectacle coming out of the mind of a man who must be totally obsessed with sex.' Unabashed, Cole dashed off an article entitled 'Why I Made That Film', in which he contended that 'teenagers should be promiscuous' and, quite correctly, that 'masturbation plays the prominent sex role in the age group between, say, nine and seventeen – so why not talk about it?'

While Nabarro conspired to persuade the Attorney General or the Director of Public Prosecutions to have Cole charged, convicted and perhaps also horsewhipped, one of his fellow Tory MPs, Elaine Kellett, went a stage further: 'I'd shoot that man. [*Growing Up*] is the most offensive thing I have ever had the misfortune to see.' Fortunately, after the prospect of capital punishment had been raised, the temperature of the scandal slowly subsided. The female teacher kept her job, and so did Cole – although the BBC dropped him from an existing series of sex-ed programmes. Meanwhile, *Growing Up* gathered dust: aside from a handful of teenagers who sneaked into the London screening, and responded positively to its message, it was not shown to any children at all. There was just one more attempt to have Cole arrested, led this time by psychologist Louise Eickhoff, who claimed that he had ruined several children's lives by proselytising sexual promiscuity. 'One, a 15-year-old, became involved in a masturbation club and later attempted suicide,' she alleged. 'Another, a 15-year-old girl, indulged with sexual practices at home as others played cards.' Gambling and sexual indulgence: it was a dastardly combination.

Even though its denouement slipped into the subsequent decade, there was much of the true 1960s spirit about the *Growing Up* controversy. It pitted progressives against conservatives, promiscuity against chastity, freedom against censorship; it equated sexuality with progress, or with the imminent death of civilisation; it promoted liberation, but more for men than women (or indeed homosexuals); it chimed with the creation of a stream of sex shops that sold themselves as freeing the public from guilt and fear, but instead merely trivialised sex; it even featured a cameo appearance by Britain's most lampooned champion of moral integrity. Most of all, it was centred around the nation's young people – and all the decisions about what was right for them to experience, or endure, or watch, or learn, were being made by adults who had grown up long before any aspect of British life could have been described as 'swinging'.

The 1960s was a decade when Britain grew up, but whether it was also the age in which the nation matured; whether its new-found relish for all things sexual signified an escape from repression or a fresh dawn of exploitation – or both: well, that is still moot. One thing was certain. As Martin Cole had argued in 1965, the young of the day had 'established their own moral values in spite of society'. The culture that they had ingested as they grew up had been designed by their elders, some of whom cynically set out to exploit the attractions and desires of youth. Now the responsibility was changing hands. It would be up to the young people of the 1960s to create a culture in their own image and submit it to the ultimate test of experience. All the while, the influences on which they had been raised would continue to leave their mark, echoing down the decades with a resonance that could peal like bells, or toll like thunder.

Acknowledgements

This book has evolved over a period of six years, during which it was set aside twice to allow me to work on other projects. Lockdown blocked some potential avenues of research, but also enabled me to concentrate on writing without the distractions of the outside world.

Before then, I was indebted as ever to libraries and their staff – notably the University of London Library at Senate House and the British Library. Those behind the desks in the Humanities and Rare Books rooms at the latter institution handled my increasingly unusual and sometimes alarming requests for material with professional aplomb and efficiency.

As ever, friends, family and fellow writers have provided support and entertainment during the long gestation of this book. Thanks, to name but a few, to Lou Ann Bardash, Stuart Batsford, Ivor Bundell, Debbie Cassell, Imogen and Damian Clarke, Paul Doggett, Julia Driver, Clinton Heylin, Sarah Hodgson, Brian Hogg, Mark Lewisohn, Nikki Lloyd, Tom Ovans, Caroline Ross, Andrew Sclanders (*beatbooks.com*), Rob Sheldon, Kieron Tyler and Carey Wallace. Special thanks also to Ema Corciu for donating the right book at the right time; and to the extended Doggett and Baylis families.

At the end of a sad year, I would also like to remember those we lost most recently: my dear sister-in-law, RoseAnne Doggett, and two long-time friends: my fellow frustrated socialist, Tony Wadling, and Johnny Rogan, one of the first people with whom I discussed this project.

The finished book owes its existence to the enthusiasm of my very supportive agent, Matthew Hamilton, and my editors, Stuart Williams and Jörg Hensgen. My working relationship with Jörg now stretches over thirteen years and has been a constant source of pleasure and enlightenment. Thanks also to copy editor Fiona Brown and proof-reader John Garrett for their assistance with this book, and to Matt Broughton for designing the jacket.

One person has been forced to live with this project from start to finish: my wife Rachel Baylis. Her contributions to this book included being the first person to read and critique the manuscript; offering a tireless sounding-board for ideas (and doubts); and suffering as a fellow passenger on my journey through a decade of obscure and occasionally obscene cinema and TV, in search of an authentic portrait of sex in the 1960s. I promise never to make her watch *The Avengers* again. Her love, positivity and creativity as a painter and filmmaker have survived it all, and I couldn't have done any of this without her. Much love to her, and to Becca & Max and Catrin & James, whom we have missed so much during our enforced Covid-era separation. Some compensation for their absence from our lives has been provided by Gilbert and George, artists of feline grace and madness.

Peter Doggett, March 2021

Bibliography

Besides the books listed below, I accessed articles from hundreds of magazines and newspapers during my research.

The following publications proved most valuable: *Birmingham Daily Post, Boyfriend, Daily Herald, Daily Mirror, Encounter, The Guardian, Idiot International, International Times, Jeremy, King, The Ladies Directory, The Listener, Los Angeles Free Press, Los Angeles Times, Mayfair, New Musical Express, New Society, New York Times, News of the World, Nova, The Observer, Oz, Penthouse, The People, Petticoat, Radio Times, Rave, Screw, The Spectator, The Stage, Suck, Sunday Mirror, Sunday Pictorial, Time, Time Out, TIMM, Tit-Bits, Village Voice, Women's Mirror.*

Ableman, Paul: *Vac* (London: Gollancz, 1968)

Ableman, Paul: *The Mouth and Oral Sex* (London: Christopher Kypreos/ Running Man Press, 1969)

Aldiss, Brian W.: *The Hand-Reared Boy* (London: Souvenir Press, 1999 [1970])

Alilunas, Peter: *Smutty Little Movies: The Creation & Regulation of Adult Video* (Oakland: University of California Press, 2016)

Amis, Kingsley: *I Want It Now* (London: Jonathan Cape, 1968)

Arcand, Bernard: *The Jaguar & the Anteater: Pornography Degree Zero* (London: Verso, 1993)

Arden, Jane: *Vagina Rex and the Gas Oven* (London: Calder & Boyars, 1971)

Ashley, April, with Douglas Thompson: *The First Lady* (London: John Blake Publishing, 2006)

Bainbridge, Beryl: *Harriet Said* (London: Virago, 2012 [1972])

Barcan, Ruth: *Nudity: A Cultural Anatomy* (Oxford: Berg, 2004)

Barthes, Roland: *Sade Fourier Loyola* (Berkeley: University of California Press, 1989)

Benedictus, David: *The Fourth of June* (London: Corgi, 1964 [1962])

Bering, Jesse: *Perv: The Sexual Deviant in All of Us* (London: Doubleday, 2013)

Berne, Eric: *Games People Play* (Harmondsworth: Penguin Books, 1968 [1964])

Bingham, Clara: *Witness to the Revolution* (New York: Random House, 2016)

Bishop, Claire: *Artificial Hells: Participatory Art and the Politics of Spectatorship* (London: Verso, 2012)

Bogarde, Dirk: *A Particular Friendship* (London: Viking, 1989)

Bogarde, Dirk: *Snakes and Ladders* (London: Chatto & Windus, 1989)

Bourdon, David: *Warhol* (New York: Harry N. Abrams Inc., 1989)

Braun, Walter: *The Cruel and the Meek: Aspects of Sadism & Masochism* (New York: Lyle Stuart Inc., 1967)

Bray, Christopher: *1965: The Year Modern Britain Was Born* (London: Simon & Schuster, 2014)

Brooker, Will: *Batman Unmasked: Analysing a Cultural Icon* (London: Continuum, 2000)

Brown, Helen Gurley: *Sex and the Single Girl* (London: Frederick Muller, 1963 [1962])

Brownmiller, Susan: *In Our Time: Memoir of a Revolution* (London: Aurum Press, 2000)

Burger, Jeff: *Lennon on Lennon: Conversations with John Lennon* (London: Omnibus, 2017)

Burroughs, William: *The Naked Lunch* (London: Corgi Books, 1968)

Caprio, Frank S.: *Variations in Sexual Behaviour* (London: John Calder, 1966 [1957])

Caputi, Jane: *The Age of Sex Crime* (London: Women's Press, 1988)

Carlson, Allen: *England's Sex Explosion* (Woodside NY: Social Behaviour, 1967)

Cartland, Barbara: *Husbands & Wives* (London: Arthur Barker, 1961)

Cartland, Barbara: *Love and Marriage* (London: Thorsons, 1971)

Castle, Alison (ed.): *The Stanley Kubrick Archives* (Cologne: Taschen, 2016)

Catling, Patrick Skene: *The Experiment* (London: Anthony Blond, 1967)

Chesser, Dr. Eugene: *Women: A Popular Edition of The Chesser Report* (London: Jarrolds, 1958)

Chesser, Dr. Eugene: *Odd Man Out: Homosexuality in Men and Women* (London: Victor Gollancz, 1959)

Chesser, Dr. Eugene: *The Human Aspects of Sexual Deviation* (London: Jarrolds, 1971)

Chesser, Dr. Eugene et al: *Teenage Morals* (London: Councils & Education Press, 1961)

Christian, Tina Chad: *Baby Love* (London: Jonathan Cape, 1968)

Cleaver, Eldridge: *Soul on Ice* (London: Panther Modern Society, 1971 [1970])

Clegg, Christine (ed.): *Vladimir Nabokov: Lolita: A Reader's Guide to Essential Criticism* (Cambridge: Icon Books, 2000)

Comfort, Alex: *Sex in Society* (Harmondsworth: Penguin Books, 1964)

Comfort, Alex: *The Anxiety Makers: Some Curious Preoccupations of the Medical Profession* (London: Thomas Nelson & Sons, 1967)

Cremer, Jan: *I, Jan Cremer* (London: Calder & Boyars, 1965)

Davenport-Hines, Richard: *An English Affair: Sex, Class and Power in the Age of Profumo* (London: HarperPress, 2013)

Davies, Dan: *In Plain Sight: The Life and Lies of Jimmy Savile* (London: Quercus, 2014)

Davies, Hunter: *The Beatles: The Authorised Biography* (London: Heinemann, 1968)

Davis, Maxine: *Sex and the Adolescent* (London: Four Square, 1960 [1959])

Davis, Maxine: *The Sexual Responsibility of Woman* (London: May Fair Books, 1961 [1957])

Dean, Tim, Steven Ruszczycky & David Squires (eds.): *Porn Archives* (Durham NC: Duke University Press, 2014)

DeCurtis, Anthony: *Lou Reed: A Life* (London: John Murray, 2017)

De Grazia, Edward, and Roger K. Newman: *Banned Films: Movies, Censors and the First Amendment* (New York: R.R. Bowker Company, 1982)

D'Emilio, John: *Sexual Politics, Sexual Communities: The Making of a Homosexual Minority in the United States 1940–1970* (Chicago: The University of Chicago Press, 1983)

Deschin, Celia S.: *The Teenager & VD: A Social Symptom of Our Times* (New York: Richards Rosen Press, 1969)

Diski, Jenny: *The Sixties* (London: Profile Books, 2009)

Doggett, Peter: *There's a Riot Going On: Revolutionaries, Rock Stars, and the Rise and Fall of '60s Counter-culture* (Edinburgh: Canongate, 2007)

Doggett, Peter: *Electric Shock: From the Gramophone to the iPhone – 125 Years of Pop Music* (London: The Bodley Head, 2015)

Doggett, Peter: 'Introduction' in *X-Rated: Adult Movie Posters of the 60s and 70s* by Tony Nourmand & Graham Marsh (London: Reel Art Press, 2017)

Dors, Diana: *Swingin' Dors* (London: World Distributors, 1960)

Douglas-Home, William: *Aunt Edwina: A Comedy* (London: Samuel French, 1960)

Drexler, Rosalyn: *I Am the Beautiful Stranger* (London: Weidenfeld & Nicolson, 1967 [1965])

Duffy, Maureen: *The Microcosm* (London: Hutchinson, 1966)

Durgnat, Raymond: *Sexual Alienation in the Cinema* (London: Studio Vista, 1972)

Dyhouse, Carol: *Girl Trouble: Panic and Progress in the History of Young Women* (London: Zed Books, 2013)

Ellis, Albert: *Sex and the Single Man* (London: Luxor Press, 1965)

Ellis, Albert, and Edward Sagarin: *Nymphomania: A Study of the Oversexed Woman* (St Albans: Mayflower, 1968 [1964])

Erskine, Rosalind: *The Passion Flower Hotel* (London: Jonathan Cape, 1962)

Fabian, Jenny, and Johnny Byrne: *Groupie* (St Albans: Mayflower, 1970 [1969])

Faderman, Lillian: *Odd Girls and Twilight Lovers: A History of Lesbian Life in Twentieth-Century America* (New York: Penguin Books, 1992)

Fallowell, Duncan, and April Ashley: *April Ashley's Odyssey* (London: Arena, 1983 [1982])

Farber, Leslie H.: *The Ways of the Will: Essays Towards a Psychology and Psychopathology of Will* (London: Constable, 1966)

Field, Andrew: *The Life and Art of Vladimir Nabokov* (London: Queen Anne Press, 1987)

Fleming, Ian: *Goldfinger* (London: Penguin Classics, 2004 [1959])

Fleming, Ian: *On Her Majesty's Secret Service* (London: Penguin Classics, 2004 [1963])

Forshaw, Barry: *Sex & Film: The Erotic in British, American and World Cinema* (Basingstoke: Palgrave Macmillan, 2015)

Foucault, Michel: *The History of Sexuality Volume 1: An Introduction* (London: Allen Lane, 1979)

Foucault, Michel: *The History of Sexuality Volume 2: The Use of Pleasure* (London: Penguin Books, 1992 [1984])

Fountain, Nigel: *Underground: The London Alternative Press 1966–74* (London: Comedia, 1988)

Fowles, John: *The Collector* (London: Jonathan Cape, 1963)

Fowles, John: *The Journals Volume 1* (London: Vintage, 2004)

Freeman, Gillian: *The Undergrowth of Literature* (London: Panther Modern Society, 1969 [1967])

Fryer, Peter: *Private Case – Public Scandal* (London: Secker & Warburg, 1965)

Fuchs, Daniel: *The Limits of Ferocity: Sexual Aggression and Modern Literary Rebellion* (Durham NC: Duke University Press, 2011)

Gear, Norman: *The Divine Demon: A Portrait of the Marquis de Sade* (London: Frederick Muller, 1963)

Goldstein, Al, and Jim Buckley (eds): *The Screw Reader* (New York: Lyle Stuart Inc., 1971)

Gorer, Geoffrey: *The Life and Ideas of the Marquis de Sade* (London: Peter Owen, 1953)

Gorer, Geoffrey: *Sex and Marriage in England Today* (London: Thomas Nelson & Sons, 1971)

Grant, Thomas: *Jeremy Hutchinson's Case Histories* (London: John Murray, 2015)

Green, Jonathon: *Days in the Life: Voices from the English Underground 1961–1971* (London: Minerva, 1989)

Greene, Gael: *Sex and the College Girl* (London: Mayflower-Dell, 1964)

Greer, Germaine: *The Female Eunuch* (London: Paladin, 1971 [1970])

Gregory, Stephan: *How to Achieve Sexual Ecstasy* (London: Christopher Kypreos/Running Man Press, 1969)

Hacker, Rose: *The Opposite Sex* (London: Pan Books, 1963)

Hall, Andrew: *Frost* (London: Cassell, 1966)

Hamblett, Charles, and Jane Deverson: *Generation X* (London: Anthony Gibbs & Phillips, 1964)

Haste, Cate: *Rules of Desire: Sex in Britain, World War I to the Present* (London: Pimlico, 1992)

Heidenry, John: *What Wild Ecstasy: The Rise and Fall of the Sexual Revolution* (New York: Simon & Schuster, 1997)

Herzog, Dagmar: *Sexuality in Europe: A Twentieth-Century History* (Cambridge: Cambridge University Press, 2011)

Hill, John: *Sex, Class and Realism: British Cinema 1956–1963* (London: BFI Publishing, 1986)

Hill, Lee: *A Grand Guy: The Art and Life of Terry Southern* (London: Bloomsbury, 2001)

Hoffman, Brian: *Naked: A Cultural History of American Nudism* (New York: New York University Press, 2015)

Ingham, Mary: *Now We Are Thirty: Women of the Breakthrough Generation* (London: Eyre Methuen, 1981)

Itzin, Catherine (ed.): *Pornography: Women, Violence and Civil Liberties: A Radical New View* (Oxford: Oxford University Press, 1993 [1992])

Jason, Peter: *Unfaithful* (Paris: Olympia Press, 1960)

Jason, Peter: *Wayward* (Paris: Olympia Press, 1961)

Jeffreys, Sheila: *Anticlimax: A Feminist Perspective on the Sexual Revolution* (London: Women's Press, 1990)

Jenkins, Philip: *Intimate Enemies: Moral Panics in Contemporary Great Britain* (New York: Aldine de Gruyter, 1992)

Jennings, Rebecca: *Tomboys and Bachelor Girls: A Lesbian History of Post-War Britain 1945–71* (Manchester: Manchester University Press, 2007)

Johnson, Jill: *Lesbian Nation: The Feminist Solution* (New York: Touchstone, 1973)

Johnson, Pamela Hansford: *On Iniquity* (London: Macmillan, 1967)

Jordan, Roger: *Hollywood's Sexual Underground* (Los Angeles: Medco Books, 1966)

Kandel, Lenore: *The Love Book* (San Francisco: Stolen Paper Editions, 1966)

Karlinsky, Simon (ed.): *The Nabokov–Wilson Letters: Correspondence Between Vladimir Nabokov and Edmund Wilson 1940–1971* (New York: Harper & Row, 1979)

Kaufman, Stanley: *The Philanderer* (London: Secker & Warburg, 1953)

Kearney, Patrick: *The Paris Olympia Press* (Liverpool: Liverpool University Press, 2007)

Kelly, Robert: *The Scorpions* (Garden City NJ: Doubleday, 1967)

Kerr, Darren, and Donna Peberdy (eds): *Tainted Love: Screening Sexual Perversion* (London: I.B. Tauris, 2017)

Keyes, Thom: *All Night Stand* (London: W.H. Allen, 1966)

Kingsley, Charles W.: *Insex Mania* (Denmark: Nordisk Bladcentrals, 1970)

Kranz, Seymour (ed.): *The H Persuasion: How Persons Have Permanently Changed from Homosexuality through the Study of Aesthetic Realism with Eli Siegel* (New York: Definition Press, 1971)

Krzywinska, Tanya: *Sex and the Cinema* (London: Wallflower Press, 2006)

Lahr, John (ed.): *The Diaries of Kenneth Tynan* (London: Bloomsbury, 2001)

Lamb, Larry: *Sunrise* (London: Papermac, 1989)

Lambert, Royston: *The Hothouse Society* (London: Weidenfeld & Nicolson, 1968)

Leech, Kenneth: *Youthquake: The Growth of a Counter-Culture through Two Decades* (London: Sheldon Press, 1973)

Leslie, Peter: *Fab: The Anatomy of a Phenomenon* (London: Macgibbon & Kee, 1965)

Lesse, Ruth: *Lash* (Paris: Olympia Press, 1962)

Lloyd, Robin: *Playland: A Study of Boy Prostitution* (London: Blond & Briggs, 1977)

Macdonell, A.G.: *England, Their England* (London: St Martin's Library, 1957 [1933])

Magee, Bryan: *One in Twenty: A Study of Homosexuality in Men and Women* (London: Secker & Warburg, 1966)

Mailer, Norman: *An American Dream* (London: André Deutsch, 1965)

Major, Clarence: *All-Night Visitors* (New York: Olympia Press, 1969)

Marr, Andrew: *A History of Modern Britain* (London: Macmillan, 2007)

Martin, Andy: *Waiting for Bardot* (London: Faber & Faber, 1996)

McCaffrey, Joseph A. (ed.): *The Homosexual Dialectic* (Englewood Cliffs NJ: Prentice-Hall Inc., 1972)

McCarthy, Mary: *The Group* (London: Weidenfeld & Nicolson, 1963)

McGraw, Hugh: *The Man in Control* (London: Arthur Barker, 1953)

Meyerowitz, Joanne: *How Sex Changed: A History of Transsexuality in the United States* (Cambridge MA: Harvard University Press, 2002)

Michael, Colette Verger: *The Marquis de Sade: The Man, His Works and His Critics: An Annotated Bibliography* (New York: Garland Publishing, 1986)

Miller, Henry: *Black Spring* (London: John Calder, 1965)

Miller, Henry: *The World of Sex & Max and the White Phagocytes* (London: Calder & Boyars, 1970)

Miller, Henry, Lawrence Durrell & Alfred Perlis: *Art and Outrage: A Correspondence* (London: Village Press, 1973 [1959])

Miller, Neil: *Out of the Past: Gay and Lesbian History from 1869 to the Present* (London: Vintage, 1995)

Mitchell, Juliet: *Women's Estate* (Harmondsworth: Penguin Books, 1971)

Moody, Roger: *Indecent Assault* (London: Word Is Out/Peace News, 1980)

Morgan, Robyn (ed.): *Sisterhood is Powerful* (New York: Random House, 1970)

Morris, Desmond: *The Naked Ape: A Zoologist's Study of the Human Animal* (London: Vintage, 1994 [1967])

Munroe, Alexandra, and Jon Hendricks (eds): *Yes Yoko Ono* (New York: Japan Society and Harry N. Abrams Inc., 2000)

Nabokov, Dmitri, and Matthew J. Bruccoli (eds): *Vladimir Nabokov: Selected Letters 1940–1977* (London: Weidenfeld & Nicolson, 1990)

Nabokov, Vladimir, *Invitation to a Beheading* (London: Weidenfeld & Nicolson, 1960)

Nabokov, Vladimir, *The Gift* (London: Weidenfeld & Nicolson, 1963)

Nabokov, Vladimir: *Ada or Ardor* (London: Weidenfeld & Nicolson, 1969)

Nabokov, Vladimir: *Strong Opinions* (New York: McGraw Hill, 1973)

Nabokov, Vladimir: *Transparent Things* (London: Weidenfeld & Nicolson, 1973)

Nabokov, Vladimir: *Look at the Harlequins!* (London: Weidenfeld & Nicolson, 1975)

Nabokov, Vladimir: *The Enchanter* (London: Pan, 1986)

Nabokov, Vladimir: *The Original of 'Laura'* (London: Penguin Classics, 2009)

Nabokov, Vladimir: *Collected Poems* (London: Penguin Classics, 2012)

Nabokov, Vladimir: 'Lolita: A Screenplay', in *Plays* (London: Penguin Classics, 2012)

Nabokov, Vladimir and Alfred Appel Jr: *The Annotated Lolita* (London: Penguin Classics, 2000)

Neville, Richard: *Play Power* (London: Paladin, 1971 [1970])

Neville, Richard: *Hippie Hippie Shake* (London: Bloomsbury, 1995)

Nowell-Smith, Geoffrey: *Making Waves: New Cinema of the 1960s* (London: Bloomsbury, 2013)

Nuttall, Jeff: *Bomb Culture* (London: Paladin, 1970 [1968])

O'Neill, Nena and George: *Open Marriage: A New Life Style for Couples* (London: Peter Owen, 1973 [1972])

Ono, Yoko: *Grapefruit* (London: Sphere Books, 1971 [1970])

Osborne, John: *Plays for England* (London: Evans Brothers, 1963)

Osborne, John: *Inadmissible Evidence* (London: Faber & Faber, 1965)

Osterweil, Ara: *Flesh Cinema: The Corporeal Turn in American Avant-Garde Film* (Manchester: Manchester University Press, 2014)

Palmer, Tony: *The Trials of Oz* (London: Blond & Briggs, 1971)

Paslé-Green, Jeanne, and Jim Haynes: *Hello, I Love You! Voices from Within the Sexual Revolution* (New York: Times Change Press, 1977 [1974])

Peale, Norman Vincent: *Sin, Sex and Self-Control* (Tadworth: The World's Work [1913] Ltd, 1966)

Pennington, Jody W.: *The History of Sex in American Film* (Westport CT: Praeger, 2007)

Pifer, Ellen (ed.): *Vladimir Nabokov's Lolita: A Casebook* (Oxford: Oxford University Press, 2003)

Pilinska, Anna: *Lolita Between Adaptation and Interpretation: From Nabokov's Novel and Screenplay to Kubrick's Film* (Newcastle-upon-Tyne: Cambridge Scholars Publishing, 2015)

Plath, Sylvia: *The Bell Jar* (London: Faber & Faber, 2005 [1963])

Plummer, Kenneth (ed.): *The Making of the Modern Homosexual* (London: Hutchinson, 1981)

Potter, John Deane: *The Monsters of the Moors* (London: Elek, 1966)

Queneau, Raymond: *Zazie in the Metro* (London: The Bodley Head, 1960)

Rainer, Jerome and Julia: *Sexual Adventure in Marriage* (London: Anthony Blond, 1966 [1965])

Réage, Pauline: *Story of O* (London: Corgi Books, 1972)

The Report of the Commission on Obscenity and Pornography (New York: Bantam Books, 1970)

Rhodes, Lisa L.: *Electric Ladyland: Women and Rock Culture* (Philadelphia: University of Pennsylvania Press, 2005)

Robbins, Harold: *The Carpetbaggers* (London: New English Library, 1982 [1963])

Robins, Patricia: *Lady Chatterley's Daughter* (London: Consul, 1961)

Robinson, Jeffrey: *Brigitte Bardot: Two Lives* (London: Simon & Schuster, 1994)

Robinson, Marie: *The Power of Sexual Surrender* (London: W.H. Allen, 1960)

Rolph, C.H. (ed.): *Women of the Streets: A Sociological Study of the Common Prostitute* (London: Secker & Warburg, 1955)

Rolph, C.H. (ed.): *Does Pornography Matter?* (London: Routledge & Kegan Paul, 1961)

Roper, Roland: *Nabokov in America: On the Road to Lolita* (London: Bloomsbury, 2015)

Ross, Allen V.: *Vice in Bombay* (London: Tallis Press, 1969)

Rosset, Barney (ed.): *Evergreen Review Reader 1957–1966* (New York: North Star Line/Blue Moon Books, 1993)

Sade, Marquis de: *Quartet* (London: Peter Owen, 1963)

Sade, Marquis de: *Justine, or the Misfortunes of Virtue* (London: Neville Spearman/The Holland Press, 1964; reprinted by Corgi Books in 1965)

Sade, Marquis de: *Eugenie de Franval and Other Stories* (London: Neville Spearman, 1965)

Sade, Marquis de: *Justine, Philosophy in the Bedroom, and Other Writings* (San Francisco: Grove Press, 1965)

Sade, Marquis de: *Selected Letters* (London: Peter Owen, 1965)

Sade, Marquis de: *The One Hundred & Twenty Days of Sodom* (San Francisco: Grove Press, 1966)

Sade, Marquis de: *Juliette* (San Francisco: Grove Press, 1968)

Sade, Marquis de: *The Crimes of Love* (Oxford: Oxford University Press, 2005)

Sagan, Françoise, and Ghislain Dussart: *Brigitte Bardot: A Close-Up* (New York: Dell Publishing, 1976)

Sauerteig, Lutz D.H., and Roger Davidson: *Shaping Sexual Knowledge: A Cultural History of Sex Education in Twentieth Century Europe* (Oxford: Routledge, 2009)

Savage, Jon: *1966: The Year the Decade Exploded* (London: Faber & Faber, 2015)

Schaefer, Eric (ed.): *Sex Scene: Media and the Sexual Revolution* (Durham NC: Duke University Press, 2014)

Schiff, Stacy: *Vera (Mrs Vladimir Nabokov)* (London: Picador, 2000 [1999])

Schneck, Stephen: *The Night Clerk* (London: Weidenfeld & Nicolson, 1966 [1965])

Schofield, Michael: *The Sexual Behaviour of Young People* (Harmondsworth: Penguin Books, 1968)

Selby, Hubert Jr.: *Last Exit to Brooklyn* (London: Corgi Books, 1970)

Sheraton, Mimi: *The Seducer's Cookbook* (London: André Deutsch, 1964)

Shilton, Lance R. (ed.): *No No Calcutta* (Melindie S. Aust.: Brolga Books, undated [1971])

Sinclair, John: *Guitar Army* (New York: Douglas, 1972)

Singer, Barrett: *Brigitte Bardot: A Biography* (Jefferson NC: McFarland & Co., 2006)

Skinner, James M.: *The Cross and the Cinema: The Legion of Decency and the National Catholic Office for Motion Pictures, 1933–1970* (Westport CT: Praeger, 1993)

Smith, Pauline, and Brian Blake: *Portrait of a Young Girl* (London: Hutchinson, 1965)

Solanas, Valerie: *S.C.U.M. Manifesto* (New York: Olympia Press, 1968)

Southern, Terry: *Blue Movie* (St Albans: Panther, 1975 [1970])

Southern, Terry, and Mason Hoffenberg: *Candy* (London: New English Library, 1970)

Spicer, Andrew and A.T. McKenna: *The Man Who Got Carter* (London: I.B. Tauris, 2013)

Spillane, Mickey: *The Body Lovers* (London: Arthur Barker, 1967)

Stearn, Jess: *The Sixth Man* (London: W.H. Allen, 1962)

St Jorre, John de: *The Good Ship Venus: The Erotic Voyage of the Olympia Press* (London: Pimlico Books, 1995)

Storr, Anthony: *Sexual Deviation* (Harmondsworth: Pelican Books, 1964)

Straker, Jean: *Nudes of Jean Straker* (London: Charles Skilton, 1958)

Straker, Jean: *Jean Straker* (London: self-published, 1963)

Straker, Jean: *Freedom of Vision* (London: Academy of Visual Arts broadside, 1967)

Straker, Jean: *On Pubic Hair* (London: Academy of Visual Arts broadside, 1969)

Strub, Whitney: *Perversion for Profit: The Politics of Pornography and the Rise of the New Right* (New York: Columbia University Press, 2011)

Sutherland, John: *Offensive Literature: Decensorship in Britain 1960–1982* (London: Junction Books, 1982)

Swarthout, Glendon: *Welcome to Thebes* (London: Heinemann, 1963)

Tavel, Ronald: *Street of Stairs* (New York: Olympia Press, 1968)

Thomas, Donald: *The Marquis de Sade* (London: Allison & Busby, 1992)

Thomas, Harford (ed.): *The Permissive Society* (London: Panther Modern Society, 1969)

Thomas, Leslie: *The Virgin Soldiers* (London: Arrow, 2005 [1966])

Thompson, Ben (ed.): *Ban This Filth! Letters from the Mary Whitehouse Archive* (London: Faber & Faber, 2012)

Travis, Alan: *Bound and Gagged: A Secret History of Obscenity in Britain* (London: Profile Books, 2000)

Tsang, Daniel (ed.): *The Age Taboo: Gay Male Sexuality, Power and Consent* (London: Gay Men's Press, 1980)

Tyler, Parker: *Sex Psyche Etcetera in the Film* (New York: Horizon Press, 1969)

Tynan, Kathleen: *The Life of Kenneth Tynan* (London: Weidenfeld & Nicolson, 1987)

Tynan, Kathleen (ed.): *Kenneth Tynan Letters* (London: Weidenfeld & Nicolson, 1994)

Tynan, Kenneth: *Tynan Right & Left* (London: Longmans Green, 1967)

Tynan, Kenneth: *The Sound of Two Hands Clapping* (London: Jonathan Cape, 1975)

Ullerstam, Lars: *The Erotic Minorities: A Swedish View* (London: Calder & Boyars, 1967 [1964])
Updike, John: *Couples* (London: André Deutsch, 1968)

Vadim, Roger: *Memoirs of the Devil* (London: Arrow Books, 1978 [1976])
Vadim, Roger: *Bardot, Deneuve & Fonda: The Memoirs of Roger Vadim* (London: Weidenfeld & Nicolson, 1986)
Vane, Norman Thaddeus (ed.): *Six Nymphets* (London: Kings Road Publishing, 1966)
Vickers, Graham: *Chasing Lolita: How Popular Culture Corrupted Nabokov's Little Girl All Over Again* (Chicago: Chicago Review Press, 2008)
Vidal, Gore: *Myra Breckinridge* (London: Panther, 1969 [1968])
Vincendeau, Ginette: *Brigitte Bardot* (London: BFI/Palgrave Macmillan, 2013)

Weeks, Jeffrey: *Coming Out: Homosexual Politics in Britain from the Nineteenth Century to the Present* (London: Quartet Books, 1990)
White, Lionel: *Obsession* (London: T.V. Boardman, 1963)
Whitehouse, Mary: *Cleaning-Up TV: From Protest to Participation* (London: Blandford Press, 1967)
Whitehouse, Mary: *Who Does She Think She Is?* (London: New English Library, 1971)
Whitehouse, Mary: *Whatever Happened to Sex?* (Hove: Wayland Publishers, 1977)
Wildeblood, Peter: *Against the Law* (London: Weidenfeld & Nicolson, 1999 [1955])
Williams, Linda (ed.): *Porn Studies* (Durham NC: Duke University Press, 2004)
Wilson, Colin: *Sex and the Intelligent Teenager* (London: Arrow Books, 1966)
Wolff, Charlotte: *Love Between Women* (London: Gerald Duckworth, 1971)

Zimmerman, Jonathan: *Too Hot to Handle: A Global History of Sex Education* (Princeton: Princeton University Press, 2015)

Sources for Quotes

Abbreviations: AP: Associated Press syndication; BDP: *Birmingham Daily Post*; DH: *Daily Herald*; DM: *Daily Mirror*; IT: *International Times*; SM: *Sunday Mirror*; UPI: United Press International syndication

Introduction

1 'Sex – and nothing but sex': *Tatler*, 17/4/57
  'A woman's promise': Vadim, 1978, p. 83
  'She is half-man and half-girl': SM 3/9/67
  'without hypocrisy a woman's right': Vadim, 1986, p. 95
  'so feline with her wide': *DM* 16/12/57
  'You know I have a temper': ibid.
2 'had effectively created a heroine': Vincendeau, p. 70
  'I love living far too much': *DM* 10/2/58
3 'My life is becoming impossible': Robinson, *Brigitte Bardot*, p. 1
  'I don't care what you do': *New York Daily News* 1/10/60
  'She is on the razor's edge': ibid.
  'She is in danger': ibid.
  'the Sex Kitten': *Sunday Pictorial* 9/10/60
4 'I am independent, different': *DM* 10/3/65
5 'third-rate minds': *Independent* 24/2/90

1. Mad About the Girl

9 'Titled family shortly motoring': quoted *DM* 5/10/61
  'the daughter of a': AP report 1/12/61
10 'pretty, fair-haired girl': *DM* 1/12/61
11 'because Uncle interfered with me': *Coventry Evening Telegraph*
   3/11/58

'He is a sick man': *DM* 4/10/58
'Young children have got to be protected': *DH* 4/10/58
'Naked, except for one sock': Nabokov/Appel, *Annotated Lolita*, p. 125
12 'By six she was wide awake': ibid., p. 132
'There are two equally serious': *New York Times* 18/8/58
'She was Lo, plain Lo': *Annotated Lolita*, p. 9
'In a tone which is calculatedly': *Encounter* October 1958
13 'How magically his singing violin': *Annotated Lolita*, p. 5
14 'I had torn something': ibid., p. 141
'Between the age limits': ibid., p. 16
'the slightly feline outline': ibid., p. 17
15 'submitted to the imagination': ibid., p. xxiii
'*Lolita* is the last book': ibid.
'then the trap has been sprung': ibid., p. lix
'He did like young girls': Schiff, p. 140
16 'Lilith': Nabokov, *Collected Poems*, pp. 83–4
'Intelligent readers will abstain': Nabokov, *Poems and Problems*, p. 55
'the first throb of *Lolita*': *Annotated Lolita*, p. 311
'the temptation, the eternal torment': Nabokov, *The Gift*, p. 186
'short story some thirty pages long': *Annotated Lolita*, p. 311
'the sleek little foxlike': Nabokov, *The Enchanter*, p. 27
17 'small cleft': ibid., p. 27
'the indistinct tenderness': ibid., p. 89
'wild-eyed ... rearing nudity': ibid., p. 92
'What if the way to true bliss': ibid., p. 22
'a short novel about a man': Karlinsky, p. 188
18 'a Russian sex masterpiece': ibid., p. 201
'As a boy': ibid., p. 202
'a very moral middle-aged gentleman': D. Nabokov/Bruccoli, p. 128
'that Vladimir, as a college teacher': ibid., p. 142
'a timebomb': ibid., p. 144
'I shudder retrospectively': *Playboy*, January 1964
'I was on my way': *Vogue*, December 1966
19 'They say it will strike readers': Karlinsky, p. 285
20 'smuggled them back to England': Kearney, p. 2
'It depresses me to think': Karlinsky, p. 296
21 'Her admirers, middle-aged men': *Night and Day* 28/10/37
'sheer unrestrained pornography': *Sunday Express* 29/1/56

'My poor Lolita': Nabokov/Bruccoli, p. 197

'In England one may go': ibid., p. 198

22 'a tall, pretty, ex-Latin Quarter showgirl': *Esquire* 8/60

'The case has always been anomalous': *Guardian* 23/1/58

'one of half a dozen': *Dayton Daily News* 3/8/58

23 'The book is far too literary': *Tucson Daily Citizen* 16/8/58

'Any librarian will surely': *New York Daily Post* 17/8/58

'a major literary event': quoted *Miami News* 24/8/58

'a pleasant feeling': Canadian Broadcasting Company TV interview,
26/11/58

'just a story': *New York Daily Post* 17/8/58

'a detached intellectual exercise': *Cornell Daily Sun* 25/9/58

'a poor girl ... a maniac': *Elmira Telegram* 14/12/58

'Gina's Dreams Come True': *Miami News* 24/8/58

24 'Dammit, what's the matter': *Playboy* 7/59

'The people who live in this town': AP report 29/1/59

'it has been renamed': Nabokov, *Ada, or Ardor*, p. 464

'thoroughly obscene': AP report 17/12/58

25 'Here we have the archetype': *Guardian* 23/1/59

'There May Be a "Lolita" in Your Street!': *Women's Mirror* 6/2/59

'One solution might be': ibid.

'Boys and girls today': *Women's Mirror* 13/3/59

'Sex is put before them': *DH* 1/5/59

'We live in a society': ibid.

'shivering schoolgirls': *DH* 10/1/59

'they decorate our street corners': *DH* 14/5/59

'These cases show that the standard': *DH* 10/7/59

26 'mass indecency': *DM* 28/11/59

'acts of gross indecency': *DM* 17/2/60

'In the eyes of your teacher': *Boyfriend* 7/11/59

'I was shocked': *DH* 2/11/59

'We have considered this book': UPI report 4/5/59

27 'a discreet but grown-up': UPI report 27/7/59

'Both were more girlish': ibid.

'This is the day to think': *Los Angeles Times* 27/6/59

'In our 55 years': *DH* 7/11/59

'I buy everything in the controversial line': ibid.

28 'I may be Victorian': *Daily Express* 1/12/59

'Few books published in this country': *The Spectator* 6/11/59
'boring rather than shocking': *The Sphere* 21/11/59
'probably the nastiest child': *BDP* 10/11/59
'is through the taste barrier': *Guardian* 6/11/59
'Those whom it could influence': *Aberdeen Evening Express* 7/11/59

Interlude: Sex by Numbers

29 Statistics from Schofield: *The Sexual Behaviour of Young People*; and
Gorer: *Sex & Marriage in England Today*.
'England still seems to be': Gorer, ibid., p. 30
30 'The double standard of sexual morality': ibid., p. 36

2. The Nymphet Leaves Home

31 'seven ages of sex appeal': *DM* 15/1/63
'You can wear bikinis': *DM* 11/4/63
'Pre-marital sex is impracticable': *DM* 6/4/62
'Between the ages of 9 and 14': *DM* 15/1/63
32 'I feel that a child of eight': *DM* 28/9/60
'had formed specific mechanisms': Foucault, *History Vol. 1*, p. 103
'double assertion': ibid., p. 104
'Perhaps no aspect of childhood': Jenkins, p. 72
'Celebrated pornographic works': ibid.
33 'When he smiled, I decided': *DH* 2/12/58
'She's very nice': *DM* 11/12/58
34 'a girl of fifteen': *DH* 14/2/59
'Sexy roles are not at all right': *DH* 23/12/58
'smoothed her long blonde hair': *DH* 28/1/59
'Gilly is all innocence': ibid.
'I realise now that she is far too young': *DH* 14/2/59
35 'ten-year-old Janina Faye': ibid.
'I don't think it's really sexy': *DH* 20/2/59
37 'Hedda Hopper is waging': Nabokov/Bruccoli, p. 265
'is unfit for the motion picture screen': syndicated column 20/10/58
'I suppose they could make her older': syndicated column 15/9/58
38 'We have an idea': *Minneapolis Star Tribune* 15/3/59
'I wish Elizabeth Taylor': ibid.

'expects to conduct': ibid.

'We've had fifty or sixty letters': ibid.

39 'A letter came into the office': *Hollywood Five-O* Fall 2002

'several pictures which are being prepared': Nabokov/Bruccoli,
    p. 305

'nymphettes with the faces of angels': UK film poster, 1961

40 'She's the only 16-year-old around': AP report 15/8/60

'I didn't have to play Lolita': quoted *Los Angeles Times* 30/4/78

'a graceful ingénue': Nabokov, *Plays*, p. 7

41 'Portland is no longer': *DH* 17/10/59

'a younger version of Marilyn': ibid.

'I wouldn't even let her *see Lolita*': *Los Angeles Times* 30/12/60

'I wouldn't let my kids': ibid.

'I don't go madly': *New York Times* 9/9/62

42 'Like the average age of puberty': *Harper's Magazine* 6/63

'He said I'm no longer a child': US film poster, 1960

43 'They just sat there and asked': uncredited TV interview, 1987

'Sue Lyon got by us': *Hollywood Five-O* Fall 2002

44 'She was always a little dickens': *Davenport Daily Times* 28/9/60

'The well-developed girl': *Quad-City Times* 16/5/61

'the girl with the most perfect teeth': *Los Angeles Times* 9/2/60

45 'There was a certain amount of craftiness': *Hollywood Five-O* Fall
    2002

'We've always said that this was a bizarre': ibid.

'The craftiness was': ibid.

'we made sure when we cast': *filmcomment.com* interview by Nick
    Pinkerton

46 'demure nymphet': Nabokov, *Plays*, p. 10

'could easily be made to look': ibid.

'We feel that we are handling the subject': *Sydney Morning Herald*
    13/11/60

'This is a highly moral story': ibid.

'being hidden and guarded': *Indianapolis Star* 14/11/60

'We want audiences to identify': *Sydney Morning Herald* 13/11/60

'that grimy bore of a novel': *DM* 28/11/60

'Whether this is a suitable subject': ibid.

'Lolita, 14-year-old Sue Lyon': *Miami News* 8/11/60

47 'how that characterization': *Palm Beach Post* 4/10/60

'There is no question': *Palm Beach Post* 5/10/60
'Sex isn't a mere matter': *DM* 7/11/60
'Bodily self-pollution': *Concise Oxford Dictionary*, 6th edition (1964)
'The sex urge in a man': advert in *DM* 8/3/60
48 'The world won't come to an end': *DM* 22/11/60
'It is often the boy': *DM* 26/11/60
'For young people, love': advertisement in *DM* 6/1/61
'Films, posters, plays': quoted *DM* 24/3/61
'These are the children of our society': *Moral Welfare* 7/61
49 'seemed to have been designed': *DM* 28/7/61
'a nice little figure': *DH* 9/3/61
'I cannot help thinking': *DH* 24/3/61
50 'very, very young and terrified': *DM* 9/3/61
'He got undressed': *DH* 9/3/61
'Old enough': *DM* 9/3/61
'I suppose it is possible': *DM* 24/3/61
'in three short days': *Women's Mirror* 25/3/61
51 'the girls aware of the dangers': *DM* 14/11/63
'sick pictures will mean': quoted *Pasadena Independent* 28/9/60
52 'directed the whole thing': *Coventry Evening Telegraph* 31/7/61
'Sue Lyon is gorgeous': *Sydney Morning Herald* 18/12/60
53 'It's exciting to photograph desire': *Oakland Tribune* 2/6/68
'I knew all about the birds': UPI report 26/6/62
'Lollipops, too, are back': *DM* 17/5/62
54 'How did they ever make': US press ads published 6/5/62
'a moral love story': UPI report 28/5/62
'the perverse love': *New York Times* 28/5/62
'I was wearing an Oleg Cassini': *Philadelphia Daily News* 13/2/65
55 'just the right combination': AP report 15/6/62
'In life, Sue Lyon is said to be 16': *Observer* 17/6/62
'If you are to enjoy the movie': *Oakland Tribune* 10/7/62
56 'Sue Lyon makes you believe': *New York Daily News* 14/6/62
'can take up where Marilyn': syndicated column 21/6/62
'was just as dirty': syndicated column 26/6/62
'a long career': AP report 4/7/62
'I believe the public': *Asbury Park Press* 7/6/62
'Just because I played a nymphet': UPI report 26/6/62
'I felt sorry for Lolita': ibid.

'Believe me, my daughter': *San Francisco Examiner* 29/7/62
'sophisticated for her age': UPI report 26/6/62

57 'more than 200 chaps': syndicated column 24/7/62
'seems to love to buy': syndicated column 10/8/62
'her beau': syndicated column 27/8/62
'the most provocative teenager': DM 31/8/62
'If you had a daughter of 16': quoted *Sydney Morning Herald*
    9/9/62

58 'a tragic figure at the graveside': Louella Parsons syndicated
    column 27/10/64
'I got up and walked off': uncredited TV interview 1987

59 'She was in a horrible situation': *Los Angeles Times* 5/9/99
'I'd like to be a star': US syndication of *Daily Express* feature 22/10/63
'I've seen the hint that playing': *San Pedro News-Pilot* 30/7/64
'My destruction as a person': *Vancouver Sun* 9/8/96
'You have to learn to avoid': *Los Angeles Times* 6/8/67
'Is there something about living': *Harper's Magazine* 6/63

Interlude: Taking Advantage

61 'thought a spectacular change': Plath, p. 78
'weighed like a millstone': ibid., p. 218
'it hurt so that she flinched': McCarthy, p. 34
'velvet ... phallus sheer silver': Updike, p. 51
'ivory rod': ibid., p. 11
'his shaggy head sank': ibid., p. 194
'Soon her loins were jumping': Ableman, *Vac*, p. 81
'Her breasts were poised': Spillane, p. 12

62 'She held her body proudly': Fleming, *Goldfinger*, p. 148
'Jesus Christ, Sergeant': Thomas, *Virgin Soldiers*, pp. 137–8
'Take off those clothes': Fleming, *On Her Majesty's Secret Service*,
    p. 31
'You're a goddamn lousy lover': ibid., p. 32

63 'a thin high constipated smell': Mailer, p. 47
'the Devil reached to me': ibid., p. 49
'I do not know why you have trouble': ibid., p. 50
'That little tit in my hand': ibid., p. 57
'she was beginning as I was done': ibid.

3. The Woman Always Pays

65 'insisted on having intercourse': Osborne, *Inadmissible Evidence*, p. 79

'When are we going to have an orgy': ibid., p. 31

'I just talk about it': ibid., p. 23

'Pray God I am never so old': ibid., p. 34

'the wounds you inflict': ibid., p. 104

66 'the most important new play in years': quoted *San Francisco Examiner* 12/9/64

'a modern *Peer Gynt*': ibid.

'their nursery perversions': Osborne, *Plays for England*, p. 48

'Part of the trouble is that': *Nova* 9/65

'The sex war is a ragged term': ibid.

'The best relationship': *DM* 12/4/67

67 'the arrangement and equipment': Davis, *Sex & the Adolescent*, p. 91

'As a rule woman does not experience': Davis, *The Sexual Responsibility of Woman*, p. 85

'In order to create': ibid., p. 14

'the delight is mutual': ibid.

'the moment when a woman soars': ibid., p. 90

'her whole being': ibid., p. 91

'is likely to be the victim': *Women's Mirror* 22/10/60

68 'Many women rarely, if ever': ibid.

'the British woman finds sex difficult': ibid.

'Let's face the concrete fact': *Women's Mirror* 15/10/60

'HIS MOTHER': ibid.

'your weapon – or your wealth': *Women's Mirror* 22/10/60

69 'because they are oversexed': *Women's Mirror* 2/11/59

'I wonder how many wives': ibid.

'Sitting on a Fortune': *Encounter* 5/59

'the risk of being murdered': *DM* 1/5/64

70 'a habit of his when talking to people': *DM* 21/7/60

'vodka-and-jazz party': *DM* 18/2/61

'It may have been that they were seen': *DH* 21/1/61

71 'I guess I did that': ibid.

'Have you ever heard of a man': *DH* 18/2/61

'It just seems fantastic to me': *The People* 19/2/61

'a thoroughly decent man': *DM* 20/10/62

72 'Men may have their masculinity': *Boyfriend* 3/11/62
'a very well-developed girl': *Boyfriend* 7/4/62
'Things might have been quite different': *Boyfriend* 16/6/62
'We think that it is a good': *Boyfriend* 10/11/62
'The rights of man': *Boyfriend* 20/10/62
'You've hooked him': *Sunday Pictorial* 18/11/62
'a 300-horsepower Cadillac': quoted *Waterloo Courier* 8/11/62
'You have been dating a single man': *Sunday Pictorial* 18/11/62

73 'Men are natural hunters': *DM* 8/12/61
'Sex Cure for Frigid Wives': *All Man* 3/61
'Over-Passionate Women': *Bluebook For Men* 9/62

74 'Many a career woman': quoted *Women's Mirror* 29/7/61
'It's better than enduring hours': *Tit-Bits* 24/8/68
'It's far better to spend': ibid.
'One of the oldest lessons': *DM* 23/10/63
'Street of Shame': *DM* 2/5/61
'Nice girls in their ordinary': *DM* 5/5/61

75 'as a natural development': ITV broadcast 2/3/60
'Doctors say that sex before marriage': ibid.

76 'I saw myself as the King': *DM* 2/4/63
'Everything he did was big': *DM* 17/9/62
'a vain romantic': *DM* 30/3/63

77 'We stayed together as man and wife': *DM* 28/3/63
'She was like a young faun': *DM* 1/4/63
'A secret fear has followed me': *DM* 2/4/63

78 'Only one thing spoils our dream': *Sunday Pictorial* 24/7/60

79 'we both fervently pray': ibid.
'playboy and a bit of a bad lad': ibid.
'Christine had neither the maturity': *DM* 30/3/63

80 'They adored each other': *DH* 17/9/62

81 'We first went to Paris': *DM* 24/10/62
'Last night we met an American': *DM* 25/10/62
'Val and I are sitting': ibid.
'A woman receptionist': *BDP* 23/3/63

83 'Christine was playing Mr Holford': *DM* 23/3/63
'I told her she would be nothing': *Liverpool Echo* 26/3/63
'I told her that they were two women': ibid.
'When she came back from France': *DM* 23/10/62

'I still have not decided': *DM* 26/3/63

84 'I am glad you did that': *Liverpool Echo* 26/3/63
'For God's sake help her': *DM* 23/10/62
'I thought of him coming in': *Liverpool Echo* 26/3/63
'I knew I might lose her': ibid.
'I have probably done': *Liverpool Echo* 24/10/62

85 'Christine nearly lost her life': *DM* 24/10/62
'When Christine arrived': ibid.
'she had both eyes blacked': *Newcastle Journal* 25/10/62
'Day after day it kept building': *DM* 23/10/62
'she still saw Holford': *DH* 17/9/62

86 'I will probably kill myself': *BDP* 25/10/62
'building a palace': *Liverpool Echo* 26/3/63
'She seemed to become cold': *DH* 27/3/63
'Christine's mistake was that she': *DM* 30/3/63
'My words were just going': *BDP* 25/10/62
'Dear Harvey': *DM* 24/10/62

87 'What were those tablets': *DM* 23/10/62

88 'Gun Riddle Death': *Aberdeen Evening Express* 15/9/62
'I'll be a mother': *DM* 17/9/62

89 'I think she was just trying': *DH* 17/9/62
'They didn't bloody work': Holford's 'confessions' assembled from
     DM and *Newcastle Journal* 25/10/62

91 'You can't fight a millionaire': *Guardian* 27/3/63
'I know he would not': ibid.

92 'Then I thought of': *DM* 27/3/63
'I felt something go': *DH* 27/3/63

93 'When he was ten or eleven': *DM* 23/3/63

94 'Here is a man suffering': *DH* 29/3/63
'On almost anybody': ibid.
'prolonged medical stress': ibid.
'This man was not an angel': ibid.

95 'Would something have broken': *DM* 29/3/63
'What happens when the wife': *DH* 30/3/63

96 'indescribable agony': *DM* 1/4/63
'We had the most wonderful': ibid.
'I cannot hide my past': *Guardian* 16/2/74

97 'Some females sicken me': *DM* 13/10/65

'Obviously I don't go round': *Women's Mirror* 19/3/66
98 'to prove my virility': *DM* 21/12/65

Interlude: The Sweet Life

99 Julie Molley coverage: *DM* 9/11/63, 11/11/63, 12/11/64, 13/11/64
'They are distributing their phone numbers': *DM* 15/5/62
'offers special services': prostitutes' details from *Ladies' Directory* #7
& #8 (1959)
100 'sexual deviation, make-up': *DM* 12/11/64
'For ten shillings': *DH* 3/11/59
'a lovely 23-year-old model': *Sunday Pictorial* 8/11/59
'I know it is a legal wrangle': *DM* 4/8/60
'I am not a prostitute': *DM* 23/7/63
'incredible catalogue of sexual enterprises': ibid.

4. Mrs Smallgood and Mr Clean

103 'determined ... doctrinaire ... completely': *Radio Times* 10/9/64
104 'the story of a young couple': *BDP* 6/5/64
'made a mockery': *DM* 7/5/64
'If you disguise life': ibid.
105 'unrealistic ... unfair ... it also showed': *BDP* 24/8/64
'good time ... polite prostitution': *DH* 12/5/59
'What was once family entertainment': *Women's Mirror* 26/2/60
106 'the word of Satan': *DM* 15/12/60
'We've had the Naughty Nineties': *Women's Mirror* 18/3/61
'an assault on Christian morals': *DM* 23/9/63
'A study of sex': *DM* 5/8/63
107 'do things they shouldn't': Whitehouse, *Who Does She Think*, p. 45
'Will you please stop the girls': ibid., p. 44
'undermined everything they had done': *DM* 30/8/63
'aggravated the problems': *BDP* 2/3/64
108 'it is no longer absolutely': quoted *BDP* 11/3/64
'Young people are being betrayed': *BDP* 23/3/64
'fight for the right': letter to *Cheshire Observer* 1/5/64
'Poison in Print': *Reader's Digest* 5/64
109 'invades schoolyards': *Brooklyn Tablet* 23/11/57

'criminals, Communists': *Brooklyn Tablet* 12/7/58
110 'So the youngster': *St Louis Globe-Democrat* 5/6/59
'The publishers of this material': *Daily Oklahoman* 10/1/61
'I like to think that': *Cincinnati Enquirer* 25/10/70
111 'A Crypt of Agony': *Man's Age* 12/62
'Blood for a Nympho's Flesh': *All Man* 11/62
'portrays, in a singularly dramatic': *Cincinnati Enquirer* 25/4/62
113 'dedicates her arid life': *Radio Times* 13/8/64
'My work has been ruined': *DM* 29/8/64
'My mother said I never should': TV broadcast of *International Cabaret*
'the telly protestors': *Tit-Bits* 18/7/64
114 'If there was ever a spiritual Dunkirk': *BDP* 30/8/64
'I think we've dulled': *Daily Mail* 6/11/64
'will not leave pornography': *BDP* 11/1/65
115 'it did not deal': *BDP* 26/1/65
'through a morass of filth': *BDP* 21/1/65
116 'bound the hallucinatory state': *Radio Times* 13/5/65
'Reference to sexual acts': quoted *DM* 22/6/65
'Mrs Whitehouse may care to know': *The Stage* 29/7/65
117 'The BBC are part': *DM* 29/11/65
'One feels that in a sane': *King* Winter 1964
118 'Women's legal and social': *Radio Times* 16/2/67
'For years I have "enjoyed"': letters in full Thompson (ed.), pp. 272–4
'People are waking up': *BDP* 25/6/69
119 'The obsession of sex': *DM* 11/4/67
'You would think that the way': quoted Whitehouse, *Who Do You
    Think*, p. 188
120 'It is the symptom': *DM* 28/6/67
'There are criminals running amuck': *Cincinnati Enquirer* 14/6/69
'The plot plods': *Cincinnati Enquirer* 3/10/69
'filthy and lascivious': *Pittston Sunday Dispatch* 30/11/69
121 'a personal intimately acquainted': *Tulare Advance-Register* 21/10/64
'educational value': *Tulare Advance-Register* 24/10/64
'It is easy to dish it out': *Los Angeles Times* 22/11/64
'had a drawing of a curvaceous': *Los Angeles Times* 24/10/65
122 'trendy, left, atheist': *BDP* 18/5/70
'They seemed to conform': ibid.
'long hair, dishevelled': UPI report 17/5/70

'give the smut peddlers': *Ames Daily Tribune* 30/9/70
123 'The exploitation of women': *Cincinnati Enquirer* 18/7/70
'Of course I'm not anti-sex': on *Personally Speaking*, ATV, 22/2/71
'Our encounter was civil': Neville, *Hippie Hippie Shake*, p. 191
'underground sexual morality': Neville, *Play Power*, p. 58
'moderately attractive, intelligent': ibid., p. 60

Interlude: The Martyr of Soho Square

125 'He had collected pictures': Straker, *Freedom of Vision*
'The prosecuting sergeant': Straker, *On Pubic Hair*
126 'It had to have pictures': ibid.
'a simple shot of a girl': Straker memo to Arts Council of Great
    Britain, 24/2/69
'I know you are a brilliant': *DM* 10/4/62
'Does it make sense to you?': Straker, *Freedom of Vision*
127 'not in tune at all': Straker, *On Pubic Hair*

5. A Fashion for Exposure

129 'Busty girls have been': *Boyfriend* 11/7/64
'to whom it's all happening': *DM* 5/3/64
130 'hysterization': Foucault, *History* Vol. 1, p. 104
131 'to show why they took': *The Stage* 27/8/64
'the most distasteful': ibid.
'It's up to women': *DM* 20/7/64
'Bosoms will be uncovered': *Women's Wear Daily* 9/62
'My heavens, the reaction!': *DM* 26/8/64
132 'Fashion is moving so fast': *Life* 10/7/64
'It was *my* prediction': ibid.
'Just a bikini bottom': ibid.
133 'It's an illogical thing': ibid.
'young, firm, small, adolescent': ibid.
'Society is ready for this': *DH* 19/6/64
'The first public showing': *DM* 6/6/64
'We did not want to turn': ibid.
'I am no prude': *DM* 18/6/64
134 'We are arguing that': *DM* 17/7/64

135 'Since I wore the one-piece': *DM* 30/6/64
'I never meant for it': *DM* 26/8/64
'a bare-topped party dress': *DM* 18/6/64
136 'We made the original dresses': *DM* 25/6/64
'I think that the trouble': *DM* 25/6/64
'barefaced effrontery': *DM* 23/6/64
'links certain manufacturers': *DM* 7/7/64
'Back to Barbarism': quoted *BDP* 22/6/64
'The worst thing possible': *DM* 1/7/64
'As the mother': *DH* 24/6/64
'Disgusting!': *Tit-Bits* 25/7/64
'The current eroticism': *DH* 24/6/64
'If a woman is so provocative': *DM* 25/7/64
137 'a severe cold': *DM* 8/7/64
138 'Inasmuch as the spectacle': *Time* 12/3/65
'I have a marvellous': *DM* 26/8/64
'freedom for the girls': *Minneapolis Star Tribune* 22/9/59
'It's too tight': *DM* 8/1/66
'These days, you can't tell': *DM* 29/3/67
139 'a glamorous new you': advert in *DM* 3/3/60
'feel exciting': advert in *DM* 21/9/60
'filmy and fragile': *DM* 21/1/61
'heavenly brassiere': advert in *DM* 17/3/61
'zizzy ... where the girls': *DM* 20/4/61
'In any one shop': *DM* 24/6/63
140 'the edge of her girdle': *DM* 17/10/64
'flimsy, see-through': *Tit-Bits* 7/11/64
'made in stretchy': advert in *DM* 21/11/64
141 'Previously foundation garments': *DM* 18/3/65
'caused a sensation': *DM* 24/5/65
'Sexy Lingerie is Here': quoted in *DM* 20/10/65
'Why, suddenly, in 1965': ibid.
142 'My skirt isn't indecent': *DM* 6/4/66
'It was the miniskirt': *Boyfriend* 23/4/66
'dedicated to the freedom': advert in *Nova* 4/66
'Mary Quant gives you': *Boyfriend* 25/6/66
'a compromise group': *Tit-Bits* 26/11/66
'Lie back and enjoy it': *IT* 30/1/67–12/2/67

143 'in the opinion of Miss': *DM* 17/2/67
'Some say they've given up': *DM* 3/6/69
'I reckon that none': ibid.

144 'Lighting a match': *New York Post* ??/9/68
'We are put in a position': ibid.
'They were alternating': Brownmiller, p. 39
'a little blonde': *The People* 2/6/68

145 'There's nothing like a dame': ibid.
'showed everything underneath': *DM* 26/6/68

146 'Will we go totally nude?': *DM* 28/12/67

Interlude: Normals and Cannibals

147 'assumes that its readers': Magee, p. 8
'Some researchers': Faderman, p. 136
'are emotionally unstable': Caprio, p. 164
'essentially sick individuals': ibid., p. 165

148 'Female homosexuality': ibid., p. 163
'I used to go out': *DM* 9/8/63
'enlightenment about': *Arena Three* #1 [1963]
'Bond liked the look of her': Fleming, *Goldfinger*, p. 197
'not in a gangster's voice': ibid., p. 263

149 'In all lesbian relationships': *Tit-Bits* 29/2/64
'Girls are occasionally mental': *IT* 14–27/11/66
'I, like most other': *DM* 1/4/69
'clung to each other': quoted Jennings, p. 115

150 'Trapped by your own body': Duffy, p. 34

6. The Cure With No Disease

151 'a thick-lipped Jew boy': *SM* 28/4/63
'How to Spot a Possible Homo': ibid.

152 'long overdue': *SM* 5/5/63
'Surely these unfortunate': ibid.
'a sobering picture': *Daily Worker* 2/9/61

153 'It is extraordinary': Bogarde, *Snakes and Ladders*, p. 201
'I took a chance': *Sunday Pictorial* 26/11/61
'only complaint was that': *Los Angeles Times* 2/2/69

'If that's what people': *Observer* 9/10/88
'You MUST realise': Bogarde, *A Particular Friendship*, p. 97
'hysterical women hiding': ibid., p. 28
'I had my flies ripped': ibid.
'of course, the Manhood question': ibid., p. 33
154 'We couldn't get any': *San Francisco Examiner* 16/8/70
'A subtle attempt to corrupt': *Tewkesbury Register* 9/11/62
'had done a great deal': Bogarde, *A Particular Friendship*, p. 139
'I have mixed freely': *Sunday Pictorial* 27/8/61
155 'Rapid results with migraine': *Marylebone Mercury* 16/11/62
'evil development of character': *Tewkesbury Register* 9/11/62
'This is perhaps the most': *Gloucester Journal*, 29/7/67
'I cannot stand homosexuals': *Hansard*, 16/6/66
156 'arrest and incarceration': AP report 13/5/35
'injecting a camphor solution': *Atlanta Constitution* 13/7/38
'Love is a matter of habits': *Green Bay Press-Gazette* 23/4/38
157 'an over-pampering mother': *Berkshire Eagle* 18/9/50
'All the blame': *Sunday Pictorial* 8/6/52
158 'must now resolutely date': syndicated column 9/11/50
'Girls are probably': *Charlotte News* 12/11/51
'healthy satisfaction': *Cincinnati Enquirer* 16/12/55
'It used to be that': syndicated column 26/12/50
159 'Homosexuality is an abnormality': *Charlotte Observer* 4/11/56
'Your husband has no excuse': syndicated column 10/1/60
'Homosexuals congregating blatantly': *Manchester Evening News*
    19/12/55
160 'The existence of practising homosexuals': *Aberdeen Evening Express*
    19/12/55
'the homosexual underground': *Indianapolis Star* 8/12/60
'warped nature': *Indianapolis Star* 24/8/60
'experimental treatment centre': *Berkshire Eagle* 28/1/58
161 'There are some who could be cured': *Sunday Pictorial* 5/2/61
'Though he was highly intelligent': *San Francisco Examiner* 22/3/62
162 'Since his treatment': ibid.
'A photograph of a male attractive': *Calgary Herald* 29/12/64
163 'With the drug': *The People* 22/6/66
'the most important thinker': *Library Review* 15/2/71
'Aesthetic Realism says': Kranz, p. 2

'All homosexuality arises': ibid., p. 4

164 'an ethic matter': ibid., pp. ix–x

'Get rid of your contempt': ibid., p. 19

165 'I believe that': *DM* 17/9/62

Interlude: The Adventures of Jeremy and TIMM

166 'Striptease by a man': *Tit-Bits* 15/4/67

'These people were touting': ibid.

'Active male, highly-sexed': *IT* 31/1/69–13/2/69

'they were getting both': *IT* 13–25/6/69

167 'The magazine has been designed': *TIMM* #1 [1967]

'My view is that': *TIMM* #4 [1968]

'the magazine for people': *Time Out* 19/7/69–3/8/69

168 'You only have to find': *Jeremy* #1/1 [1969]

7. Pop Go the Virgins

169 'permissive society ... sick': *Report of the Commission*, p. 593

170 'a mob mind': *DM* 25/1/47

'painfully clear': quoted Leslie, p. 149

171 'Elvis Presley, young bump': *Minneapolis Star Tribune* 14/5/56

'eight hours sleep': *DM* 16/2/57

'unidentified white teenage girl': *Jet* 10/9/59

'She'll be fourteen': *DM* 29/5/58

'The guitar is the sex symbol': *DH* 17/6/59

'Sex is screamed at you': *DH* 4/8/59

'That boy – he's got more sex': *Daily Express* 27/11/59

172 'dreamy, near six-footer': *Boyfriend* 20/1/62

'dreamboat': *Boyfriend* 10/2/62

'luscious hunk': *Boyfriend* 17/2/62

'These group boys': *DM* 1/2/64

'There is nothing hard': quoted *DM* 28/5/64

'Some guy came along': *Screw* 27/6/69

173 'I got it for the first time': Davies, *The Beatles*, p. 33

174 'molested and exposed': *DM* 21/9/64

'The groups are only young': *Rave* 12/65

175 'I'm about as sexy': *Melody Maker* 9/11/63

176 'I feel I've been betrayed': *Teen Magazine* 10/64
'I almost had my Mom': *Tiger Beat* 8/66
'too sexy for family viewing': DM 20/3/67 & 24/3/67

177 'Nothing obscene': DM 2/2/65
'We were playing in Stevenage': DM 8/9/66
'Why must our children': *Tit-Bits* 7/1/67

178 'When will the older': *Tit-Bits* 18/2/67
'Our teenagers should': ibid.

179 'These chicks are ready': quoted *IT* 14–27/2/69

180 'I knew I had the girl': Keyes, p. 15
'Christ, fourteen': ibid., pp. 18–19
'Then it happened': Fabian/Byrne, p. 13
'a sordid and commercial': *Idiot International* #2 [2/70]
'Just like a man': *Screw* 1/3/70
'At last! A film that does': ad in *Philadelphia Daily News* 28/1/66

181 'the picture you've been': *Allentown Morning Call* 17/8/66
'the one you've been waiting for': *Spokane Chronicle* 25/10/67

182 'I was so embarrassed': *Detroit Free Press* 24/11/68
'She settled upon the bottom': *King* 4/67
'We did not feel the film': DM 10/3/67
'It's an objective study': ibid.

183 'It is usually performed': Ono, *Grapefruit* [unpaginated]
'It was a frightening experience': author interview 1992
'some Hollywood producer': *Film Quarterly* #43/1 [1989]
'The film is of a family': Munroe/Hendricks, p. 298

184 'an abstract notion': *Guardian* 18/7/68
'There wasn't any point': *Observer* 21/7/68
'The idea came from John': *Detroit Free Press* 24/11/68
'When we got the pictures back': *Rochester Democrat & Chronicle* 8/6/69
'He really is completely naked': *The People* 6/10/68

185 'Has anyone ever taken offence': DM 12/10/68
'It isn't a trend': ibid.
'The lowest form of criminal life': *The People* 20/10/68
'We tried to show': *Cash Box* 24/11/73
'definitely going a bit too far': *The People* 20/10/68
'I'm very shy': *Detroit Free Press* 24/11/68

186 'an unexpurgated edition': DM 14/10/68
'I can't believe anybody': *Billboard* 16/11/68

187 'If we can make society': *DM* 26/10/68
    'There's such a lot of fighting': Burger, p. 62
    'foreign-made pornographic': *Billboard* 29/3/69
    'I expected some noise': *Rochester Democrat & Chronicle* 8/6/69
    'Who in the hell': *Rolling Stone* 15/3/69
188 'a certain primitiveness': *Miami Herald* 6/2/69
    'a theme of innocence': *Camden Courier-Post* 7/2/69
    'solely to promote the sale': *Tampa Tribune* 12/2/69
    'If they'd released': *Billboard* 1/11/69
189 'They are not ashamed': *DM* 25/3/69
    'I hope it's not a let-down': *DM* 26/3/69
    'what I take to be': *The Guardian* 31/10/69
190 'It wasn't an erection': *Film Quarterly* #43/1 [1989]
    'the undulations of his': *Melody Maker* 20/9/69
    '*Self Portrait* has vibrations': ibid.
    'after the initial shock': ibid.
    'lively anyway from the graphic': *Observer* 18/1/70
    'John is very serious': *SM* 11/1/70
    'Lennon's sex life': London Arts Gallery press release 1/70
    'Just what kind of kook': *SM* 11/1/70
191 'I think it is a piece': *Aberdeen Evening Express* 16/1/70
    'They should have sent': UPI report 17/1/70
    'Total assault on the culture': Sinclair, p. 72
    'How low can the pop': *DM* 14/6/69
    'Teenagers want to know': ibid.
192 'ought not to have been prey': *Guardian* 17/1/70
193 'The gentleman said': *Guardian* 2/4/70
    'I think John Lennon': *New York Daily News* 22/1/70

Interlude: A Game of Consequences

195 'a new kind of below-stairs hero': *DM* 17/1/66
    'I've a hell of a part': *Petticoat* 19/2/66

8. The Most Talked About Woman in the World

199 'Wickedest Street in the World': *The People* 27/8/61
    '"Her" Secret is Out': *The People* 19/11/61

200 'until five years ago': ibid.

'I was constantly taunted': Fallowell/Ashley, p. 10

201 'I started wearing': *SM* 8/2/70

'My male genitals': Fallowell/Ashley, p. 75

'He said I was the most': *SM* 8/2/70

202 'I felt that I had': ibid.

'sexually unhappy': *Liverpool Echo* 2/2/70

'From a comparatively': ibid.

'A Peer's Son': *Sunday Pictorial* 29/4/62

'He will do what I say': *DM* 12/5/62

'About the much-publicised': *The Stage* 24/5/62

'revive memories': *BDP* 19/6/62

203 'the sensation of': ibid.

'the most talked about': *Cheddar Valley Gazette* 29/6/62

'I refuse to wear': *Sunday Pictorial* 25/8/57

'Coccinelle has rather more talent': *The Stage* 14/5/64

'I will never, never marry': *DM* 8/6/62

204 'Just How Low': *The People* 30/9/62

'At last I'm a wife': *The People* 24/10/65

'the Vilest Creature': *The People* 18/2/62

'vile trade': *The People* 29/12/65

205 'former pipe-smoking': *DM* 18/9/62

'black-spotted orange dress': *SM* 17/3/63

'in a transitional state': *Marylebone Mercury* 25/10/63

'All the crimes I've done': *Kensington Post* 11/6/65

'noticed she was': *Kensington Post* 20/5/66

206 'the outcrop of cases': Comfort, *Sex in Society*, p. 136

207 'are physically of one sex': Meyerowitz, p. 5

208 'Ex-GI Becomes Blonde Beauty': *New York Daily News* 1/12/52

'There are too many complications': *Tit-Bits* 14/1/67

'The horror of a life': Fallowell/Ashley, p. 75

209 'He's the only GI': quoted *SM* 29/12/68

'My first wife': quoted *DM* 5/4/67

'allegedly comic': *BDP* 6/5/59

'Mummy, there's a woman': Douglas-Home, p. 7

210 'If you must try to get fun': *The Stage* 5/11/59

'her platinum blonde hair': *The People* 19/12/59

'tough, hairy-armed Commando': *The People* 15/5/66

'I want to be free': *DH* 4/6/58
'90% a man': *Sunday Pictorial* 7/8/60

211 'Ever since this story started': *Sunday Pictorial* 4/9/60
'one chromosome too many': *DM* 16/9/67
'a more disturbing side': *The People* 6/1/63

212 'Treatment of Wrongly': quoted *Newcastle Journal* 18/11/66
'one of the most agonising': *DM* 21/11/66
'a truly miserable group': *Boston Globe* 23/11/66

213 'The controversial Sex Change girl': ad in *The Stage* 13/8/64
'a shapely French rock singer': *Hammersmith & Shepherds Bush
        Gazette* 30/1/64
'some sexual approach': *Liverpool Echo* 2/2/70

214 'Medical witnesses agreed': *Coventry Evening Telegraph* 2/2/70
'Reality had broken in': *DM* 3/2/70

215 'I'm absolutely shattered': ibid.
'Medicine and science': *SM* 8/2/70

Interlude: The Sexual Avengers

217 'The roof has fallen in': Vidal, p. 58
'I had avenged Myron': ibid., p. 152
'allured and tortured': Cleaver, p. 168

218 'No black man ever makes': *IT* 9–22/5/69
'a woman's primary goal in life': Solanas, p. 75
'the male should be of use': ibid., p. 83

9. The Man of the Decade

219 'Office Problem Solved': AP report 5/5/61
'a unique option': *DM* 5/5/61

220 'It is a well-known fact': Macdonell, p. 65

221 'It is largely confined now': Morris, pp. 113–14
'kiss and cuddle': *The Cornishman* 9/7/64

222 'Should the cane be used': *Penthouse* 6–7/65
'I would not hesitate': *Penthouse* 8/65
'Almost the whole': *Penthouse* 8/65
'As a young wife of 23': *Penthouse* 12/65

223 'Nazi Horror Tortures': *Man's Daring* 2/61

'Torturing Tarts': *Big Adventure* 3/61
'Nude Tortures': *Man's Daring* 1/62
'A Crypt of Agony': *Man's Age* 12/62
'Writhe, My Lovely': *Man's Age* 1/63
'Nude Death Orgy': *Action Illustrated* 2/63
'The People Who Worship Pain': *Man's Adventure* 3/63
'Torture Trap': *Man's Action* 10/63
'The Facts About': *Man's Adventure* 5/63

224 'Is it not conceivable': Potter, p. 100
'She proved a willing disciple': ibid., p. 218

225 'Sade had the right outlook': ibid., p. 15
'was not an admirer': ibid., p. 159
'squalid pornographic books': ibid., pp. 128–9

226 'According to de Sade': Gorer, *Life and Ideas*, p. 174
'Existentials like Camus': Sade, *Justine, or the Misfortunes*, p. xxiii

228 'a special surrealist ceremony': *Listener* 4/2/60
'Horrors pile on horror': *BDP* 2/1/62
'the civilised British people': Gear, p. 189

229 'the pornographic passages': Sade, *Quartet*, p. 5
'intended mainly for entertainment': Sade, *Eugenie*, p. 10
'Adieu, my angel': Sade, *Selected Letters*, p. 109
'He made her undress': ibid., p. 13
'one of the most shocking': Sade, *Justine or the Misfortunes*, p. 9
'The hungry smuthound': ibid.

230 'The obscenities of the second volume': ibid., p. 50
'Such insane and terrifying': ibid., p. 173n
'They were "corrupted"': Chesser, *Human Aspects*, p. 37
'possibly the nastiest book': Fowles, *Journals*, p. 607

231 'The hymen ruptured': Robbins, p. 57
'He was spread-eagled': *Tit-Bits* 19/6/65
'The leather jacket': Sade, *Justine or the Misfortunes*, p. 72
'wholesome ... Boreham Wood': *Women's Mirror* 28/5/66
'a sort of pre-puberty': *DM* 9/3/66

233 'It is not the choice': Sade, *Justine or the Misfortunes*, pp. 250–51
'Coy by today's standards': *Illustrated London News* 26/12/64
'not much good': *BDP* 19/12/64

234 'could never be legally': Wilson, p. 80
'Perhaps the day is not far': *New York Times* 25/7/65

'Burn the Bible': *East Village Other* 1/66
'the seminal book': Sade, *120 Days*, p. 187
'sexual Bible': *New York Times* 27/11/66
'De Sade said he wished': *New York Times* 22/9/68
235 'I don't think I shall': *DM* 13/12/65
236 'The Marquis de Sade': AP report 25/2/67
'I have never felt': *Coventry Evening Telegraph* 12/9/68
'In my opinion': ibid.
'the critics have': ibid.
237 'an unnecessary insult': *New York Times* 6/5/66
'a really rollicking': *The Stage* 10/2/66
239 'The phenomenon of repetition': *Encounter* 4/63
240 'In my view': *DM* 29/6/66
'a book which quite simply': *DM* 30/7/66
241 'I felt I was seriously': *DM* 21/11/67
'He'd sort of count': St Jorre, pp. 165–6
242 '[Sade] begins with desires': *New York Times* 22/9/68

Interlude: The Naked and the Dead

244 'a psychotic young virgin,: Tynan, *Tynan Right & Left*, p. 231
245 'she disliked the central': Vadim, *Memoirs of the Devil*, p. 164
'just barely misses': Bingham, p. 338

10. Vagina Rex and the Female Eunuch

247 'Uproar as Girl Strips': *SM* 8/9/63
248 'in a shameless': *DM* 14/9/63
'a serious, responsible': *Guardian* 15/8/63
'It is the result': *DM* 3/9/63
'Sex is taken for granted': *DM* 5/3/64
'Undressing is always': *Tit-Bits* 19/3/66
249 'seems an ideal spot': *Oz* #1 [1967]
'I was always leaping': Paslé-Green/Haynes, p. 26
'For six months': *Oz* #1 [1967]
'quite the brightest spot': *The People* 18/7/65
'a blessing she is there': *Guardian* 13/7/65
250 'the wilds of Bohemia': *Oz* #1 [1967]

'mere seconds after': *Oz* #3 [1967]
'tallest girl on TV': *SM* 15/9/68
'a natural clown': *Guardian* 23/10/68
'I've considered myself': Paslé-Green/Haynes, p. 27
'a celebrated (and over-educated)': *Oz* #19 [1969]
'What happened when': Paslé-Green/Haynes, p. 27
251 'the women who really understand': *Oz* #19 [1969]
'The "pop" professor': *Coventry Evening Telegraph* 3/4/69
'It is impossible to write': *Coventry Evening Telegraph* 5/7/69
'Women! I don't like them': *Coventry Evening Telegraph* 3/4/69
'The Clitoris': *SM* 27/9/70
252 'Look at all these promiscuous': *Women's Mirror* 6/8/66
253 'If people had more sex': *IT* 14–27/10/66
'This is a kick in the teeth': *DM* 29/11/66
254 'mayonnaise pouring': *IT* 14–27/10/66
'To a certain degree': Nuttall, p. 160
'driven out': *Oz* #2 [1967]
255 'Our bodies are opening': *IT* 27/2/67–12/3/67
'Personal service means': *IT* 21–28/4/67
'Magical Love Making': *IT* 27/10/67–9/11/67
'Young Eastern Male': *IT* 17–30/11/67
'Slim impotent': *IT* 27/10/67–9/11/67
'We are not old men': *DM* 30/6/67
256 'She has been presented': *DM* 29/6/67
'What I want is peace': *Tit-Bits* 23/12/67
'his best friend': *DM* 10/8/67
'good-looking, charming': Davies, *The Beatles*, p. 228
258 'try not to be selfish': *IT* 14–27/2/69
'marching with his classy': *Oz* #26 [1970]
'Try and think how many chicks': *IT* 10–23/10/69
259 'People who break down': *IT* 4–17/7/69
'One in every nine women': *IT* 10–23/10/69
'It's about the kind of people': *DM* 7/2/58
'the sexiest play': ibid.
'In the early days I escaped': *Guardian* 26/11/69
'Marriage defines woman's oppression': ibid.
260 'a divided life': *IT* 10–23/10/69

'At fifteen the alternatives': Arden, p. 9
'The central theme': *Observer* 9/3/69
'Women enjoy being dominated': Arden, p. 16

261 'For centuries women': *SM* 23/2/69
'Women are seen to be': *Observer* 9/3/69
'If it were possible': *Guardian* 26/11/69
'Many women use them for suicide': UPI report 1/7/69
'Women have been conned': *Edmonton Journal* 27/8/69
'Having been offered': Mitchell, p. 141

262 'My agent wanted me': *Sydney Morning Herald* 31/7/69
'the self-appointed leaders': *Oz* #26 [1970]
'A bunch of would-be': *Observer* 19/4/70
'The Slag Heap Erupts': *Oz* #26 [1970]

263 'does not reflect': '*Cuntpower*' *Oz* #29 [1970]
'If we are to escape': *Guardian* 28/9/70
'particularly repulsive': *SM* 27/9/70

264 'The most stupid': *DM* 1/2/71

265 'Ladies Get on Top': *Suck* #3 [1970]
'We first became aware': *Oz* #28 [1970]

266 'debauch the morals': *Kensington Post* 2/7/71
'nine angry women': *DM* 25/3/71
'WE/the domestics': reprinted in *A New Communion* programme

267 'an act of faith': *Guardian* 6/5/71
'female tactics for survival': *Oz* #26 [1970]
'the greatest service a woman': Greer, p. 282

Interlude: Flogging a Dead Horse

268 'One after another': Jason, *Wayward*, p. 190
'Rip my cunt': Jason, *Unfaithful*, p. 143

263 'We like sex': *King* Winter 1964
'Our girls are laughing-and-sunshine': ibid.
'One feels that in a sane': ibid
'the noisiest debut': *Penthouse* 3/65

270 'Sex should be fun': *Penthouse* 6–7/65
'The cinema is just a form': *Penthouse* 3:8 [1968]
'Social anxiety': *King* 7/66

'A woman should have the right': *Mayfair* 8/66
'*Mayfair* is National': ibid.
'Equality in Love': *Mayfair* 1–2/67
271 'Jenny Stays Dry': *Mayfair* 12/68
'The pictures of Christina': *Mayfair* 9/68

11. The Return of Lolita

273 'offensive, distasteful': *SM* 23/3/69
'I was very unhappy': *Tit-Bits* 24/2/68
276 'It was very embarrassing': *Tit-Bits* 7/12/68
'Why shouldn't I appear': *SM* 30/3/69
'I just can't understand': *DM* 3/11/67
277 'I could hardly sleep': *Tit-Bits* 6/4/68
'innocent to the point': *Penthouse* 4:8 [1969]
279 'awkward, ugly': Christian, p. 13
'Holding, it's enough': ibid., p. 69
280 'Look at those lips': ibid., p. 95
'sex isn't all it's made': ibid., p. 105
'I don't want sex': ibid., p. 151
281 'Like Luci, I was': Spicer/McKenna unpaginated ebook
'At thirteen, when I had quit': Dors, p. 75
'opens quite stunningly': *Bridgwater Courier-News* 31/3/69
282 'It was all quite near': 2011 interview at uwe.ac.uk
'Mummy and Daddy': *SM* 9/5/68
'the fifteen-year-old girl': Spicer/McKenna unpaginated ebook
'It's not a dirty movie': AP report 29/5/69
'Yes, the film has sex': *New York Sunday News* 17/3/69
'It was her way': AP report 29/5/69
'Saw Linda Hayden': *New York Daily News* 3/1/69
'The sweet blonde': *Tit-Bits* 21/9/68
283 'All the perversions': *The People* 9/3/69
'a showcase for young': *New York Daily News* 20/3/69
'over-ripe physical maturity': *Hackensack Record* 20/3/69
'a faintly repulsive': *Illustrated London News* 15/3/69
'Teenage starlets': AP report 29/5/69
'at the beginning of the transition': quoted in Doggett, *Riot*, p. 281

284 'gutter press': *Time Out* 30/8/69–13/9/69
'It was very sexy for a male': *Melody Maker* 24/10/70

285 'Successful Business Gent': ad in *IT* 15–28/12/67
'Slim attractive boy': ad in *IT* 26/7/68–8/8/68
'Girls are born flirtatious': *DM* 29/7/68

286 'a kaleidoscope of lovely girls': ad in *Penthouse* 3:4 [1968]
'I had a small flat': 2012 interview at hidden-films.com
'the Sex Child': Vane, [unpaginated] Introduction
'the joys of boyhood': advertising blurb for *The Boy*

287 'I've had sexual encounters': 1981 interview at greek-love.com
'will not be passed': classified advert by UK distributor
'some of them almost pure white': quoted *Tit-Bits* 9/10/65
'an erotic tour': Ross, cover blurb
'used for sex': ibid., p. 158
'I am a virgin': ibid., pp. 21–22

288 'a dirty businessman': Drexler, p. 78
'Mature for her age': Hall, p. 75
'She had looked like a little girl': White, pp. 18, 48
'an overgrown and under-developed': Amis, p. 75
'it might be the best thing': Amis, p. 115

289 'I have been accused': Nabokov, *Transparent Things*, p. 69
'impuberal': ibid., p. 41
'what in a later era': Nabokov, *Harlequins!*, p. 29

290 'pernicious anaemia': *Philadelphia Inquirer* 17/2/71
'There are certain types': *Camden Courier-Post* 27/1/71
'Both girls – the one they fired': *New York Times* 31/10/71
'pederastic element': Tsang (ed.), p. 149

291 'the concept of child protection': ibid., p. 150
'Those who enjoy sexual acts': *Screw* 16/5/69
'make the best suck': *Screw* 7/3/69
'Orgy at Riverdale High': *Screw* 22/12/69
'well-proportioned': *Suck* #5 [*c.* 1971]
'fuck-happy children': *Suck* #3 [*c.* 1970]
'Still a virgin': *Suck* #8 [*c.* 1974]

292 'We believe it is inhuman': quoted by Lord Stamp, *Hansard* 14/6/77

293 'a *Lolita* for the English Lit': *Austin Chronicle* 19/10/98
'Nabokov's novel helped open': *Christian Science Monitor* 25/9/98

Interlude: Oh! Quel cul t'as!

294 'The idea is to use': Tynan, *Letters*, pp. 353–4

'a *St Trinian's* sixth-former': ibid., p. 355

'what he thought an erotic show': Tynan, *The Sound*, p. 146

295 'Genital exposure': Tynan, *Letters*, p. 371

'There was a little club': *Screw* 27/6/69

'You know that idea': Tynan, *Letters*, p. 420

296 'failure ... disappointment': *New York Times* 18/6/69

'The critics all went along': Tynan, *The Sound*, p. 143

'a masturbator's masterpiece': *Screw* 4/7/69

'stretches which seemed more': *Guardian* 28/7/70

'Never has such utter filth': Shilton (ed.), pp. 35–6

'All hints of heterosexual': Lahr (ed.), *Diaries of Kenneth Tynan*, pp. 40–41

297 'little more than a first sketch': Tynan, *The Sound*, p. 147

12. Growing Up With Dr Sex

299 'without doubt the most audaciously': *DM* 28/4/65

'We've been told you': *Boyfriend* 27/10/62

'If a girl has intercourse': *Women's Mirror* 16/7/66

300 'Sexual Responsibility': *BDP* 23/8/65

301 'The virtue of chastity': *BDP* 25/8/65

'Sex is part of the raw': Rolph (ed.), *Pornography*, p 42

302 'pre-marital sexual intercourse': quoted *DH* 6/3/59

'just know too much': Jean Mann MP in *Women's Mirror* 13/3/59

'chastity is essential': *Women's Mirror* 6/11/59

'Not since wartime': *DH* 30/10/59

303 'To have intercourse': *Women's Mirror* 1/4/60

'There has been a revolution': *DM* 24/3/61

'Sleeping around HAS': *DM* 6/3/61

304 'In spite of the fact': *DM* 26/1/61

'a frightening, filthy': *Up* magazine, quoted *DM* 31/5/63

'mixed liaisons': *DM* 6/3/63

305 'We might as well make up': *DM* 15/7/63

'possibly a phase': Comfort, *Sex in Society*, p. 27

'Sadism and masochism': ibid., p. 30

'There is a strong case': ibid., p. 155
'can provide reassurance': ibid.
306 'It is a book': *DM* 21/2/63
'yield to her biological': Robinson, *The Power*, p. 205
307 'It is highly unlikely': ibid., p. 14
'Caressing or manipulating': ibid., p. 17
'She knows that 99 times': ibid., p. 45
'the miracle of childbirth': ibid., p. 208
'The excitement comes': ibid., p. 213
'We have been through': ibid., p. 10
308 'Though, owing to her lack': ibid., p. 57
'It is within the vagina': ibid., p. 30
'A few women suffer': Ellis/Sagarin, pp. 178–9
'It's not normal': quoted Strub, p. 72
309 'Boys are more likely': Hacker, p. 48
'A boy's sex': ibid.
'mentally subnormal': ibid., p. 93
'The only genuine sexual': Rainer, p. 18
'A sensual refinement': ibid., p. 114
'When both spouses': ibid., p. 128
'In his lovemaking': ibid., p. 98
'There are a few wives': ibid., p. 106
310 'far from being a creature': Brown, p. 13
'She has a better sex life': ibid., p. 15
'You have to work': ibid., p. 16
'Your figure can't harbour': ibid., p. 18
'Clean hair is sexy': ibid., p. 86
'You must spend time': ibid., p. 90
'Granted, it *is* harder': ibid.
'Even girls who don't want': Ellis, *Sex and the Single Man*, p. 65
311 'now asking me to allow him': *Tit-Bits* 1/5/65
'A society like ours': *Nova* 6/65
'Prolong the pleasure': ad in *IT* 2/6/67
312 'A course of Intense Vibration': ad in *IT* 5–19/1/68
'An alarmingly high proportion': *DM* 3/1/67
'You can have a lot of fun': *Petticoat* 12/3/66
'Girls Who Don't': *Rave* 12/66
'the frankest sex talk': *DM* 18/3/66

313 'This sounds rather unhealthy': UPI report 28/10/68

314 'suffer from such physical': 1967 Abortion Act
'free brothel': *BDP* 13/8/70
'take sex off the back streets': *Marylebone Mercury* 11/9/70

315 'wildly sexy': *BDP* 17/10/70
'There are no under-the-counter': *Aberdeen Evening Express* 9/9/70
'We want to make sex education': *BDP* 18/11/70
'It is phallic-shaped': *DM* 18/11/70
'a porn shop on the corner': *BDP* 17/10/70

316 'the most effective way': *BDP* 21/10/70
'The reaction to anything': *BDP* 17/10/70
'sex without shame': *Marylebone Mercury* 18/8/72
'I think most of these women': ibid.

317 'new approach to sex education': *BDP* 12/1/71
'Sex Act Film Show': *DM* 13/1/71

318 'They all lack an essential': ibid.

319 'pedlar of sex': *BDP* 2/2/71
'I don't even know if many': *DM* 11/10/71
'I am utterly shocked': *DM* 17/4/71
'This is quite simply public': ibid.

320 'I feel quite strongly': *SM* 18/4/71
'You are the epitome': *DM* 20/4/71
'This was a deplorable': *BDP* 24/4/71
'Why I Made That Film': *SM* 2/5/71
'I'd shoot that man': *BDP* 11/5/71
'One, a 15-year-old': *SM* 23/1/72

321 'established their own moral values': *BDP* 23/8/65

Picture Credits

Sue Lyon publicising the imminent release of Stanley Kubrick's film *Lolita*, June 1962 (Pail Slade/Paris Match/Getty Images).

Brigitte Bardot leaving the clinic where she was being treated after a suicide attempt in September 1960 (Bettmann/Getty Images).

Bookshop customers reading Vladimir Nabokov's *Lolita* on its UK publication day in November 1959 (Keystone/Getty Images).

Dirk Bogarde in *The Singer Not the Song*, 1960 (Silver Screen Collection/Getty Images).

Cliff Richard posing for his fans, 1960 (Day/Mirrorpix/Getty Images).

Woman wearing topless dress, August 1964 (Watford/Mirrorpix/Getty Images).

Publicity stunt at the Lady Jane boutique in Carnaby Street, May 1966 (John Downing/Express/Hulton Archive/Getty Images).

Helen Gurley Brown at the launch of her book *Sex and the Single Girl*, October 1964 (Daily Mirror/Mirrorpix/Getty Images).

April Ashley signing the register after her Gibraltar wedding to Arthur Cameron Corbett in September 1963 (Simpson/Daily Express/Hulton Archive/Getty Images).

'Professor' Jimmy Edwards administers corporal punishment to the pupils of the TV comedy *Whacko!* in 1959 (Reg Speller/Fox Photos/Getty Images).

Diana Rigg as Emma Peel in a 1965 edition of *The Avengers* (R. Viner/Daily Express/Hulton Archive/Getty Images).

Yoko Ono during the making of her *Bottoms* film in 1967 (Ron Case/Keystone/Getty Images).

Police officer patrolling the *Bag One* exhibition by John Lennon at the London Arts Gallery in January 1970, after Scotland Yard seized fourteen lithographs on the grounds that they were obscene (Evening Standard/Hulton Archive/Getty Images).

Valerie Solanas, founder of the Society for Cutting Up Men, in 1967 (Fred W. McDarrah/Getty Images).

Jane Arden, creator of the confrontational play *Vagina Rex and the Gas Oven*, during a 1966 film shoot in Portobello Road (Kaye/Daily Express/Hulton Archive/Getty Images).

Germaine Greer posing with Bonzo Dog Band vocalist Vivian Stanshall during a 1969 cover shoot for *Oz* magazine (Estate of Keith Morris/Redferns/Getty Images).

Michael Caine and Shirley Anne Field during the filming of *Alfie*, 1965 (Larry Ellis/Express/Getty Images).

David Hemmings with Tsai Chin, Jane Birkin and Gillian Hills in *Blow-Up*, 1966 (Archive Photos/Getty Images).

Jane Fonda during the shooting of *Barbarella*, 1967 (Jean-Claude Sauer/Paris Match/Getty Images).

Susannah York and Coral Browne on the set of *The Killing of Sister George*, 1968 (Harry Benson/Daily Express/Hulton Archive/Getty Images).

Norman Wisdom looks at Sally Geeson in a scene of *What's Good for the Goose*, 1969 (Hulton Archive/Getty Images).

Linda Hayden, star of the 1969 film *Baby Love*, with her onscreen mother, Diana Dors (Central Press/Hulton Archive/Getty Images).

Mick Jagger and Mary Whitehouse on David Frost's TV show in 1968 (Reg Burkett/Daily Express/Getty Images).

Members of the Nationwide Festival of Light, a Christian pressure group, picket a screening of Dr Martin Cole's film *Growing Up*, 1971 (Arthur Sidey/Mirrorpix/Getty Images).

Index